ANALYTICAL STUDIES IN THE PSALMS

Analytical Studies
in
The Psalms

Arthur G. Clarke

with Foreword by W. E. Vine

JOHN RITCHIE LTD
CHRISTIAN PUBLICATIONS

40 Beansburn, Kilmarnock, Scotland

ISBN-13: 978 1 907731 67 9

Copyright © 2012 by John Ritchie Ltd.
40 Beansburn, Kilmarnock, Scotland

www.ritchiechristianmedia.co.uk

Typeset by John Ritchie Ltd., Kilmarnock
Printed by Bell & Bain Ltd., Glasgow

Contents

BOOK FIVE

Foreword

THIS comprehensive and useful volume is the result of much painstaking labour, wrought very largely under the exceedingly trying conditions of Japanese internment and restrictions during the Great War. In this world of evil and adversity the best things are produced amidst and by reason of the greatest trials. The brightest and best steel comes through the hottest furnace. The beauty of the pearl is the result of the bitterness of pain. The most gorgeous butterflies gain their freedom by means of a struggle through the thickest cocoons.

The greatest triumphs, the highest joys, the most transcendent glory are the outcome of the unutterable woes and judgment of Christ's sufferings on the Cross.

The pleasure and profit which the reader who delights in the Word of God will derive from the following pages, accrue to him by reason of a determination amidst trying experiences to serve the Lord and His people, with the help of the Spirit of God.

The studies contained in this book are more than by way of mere analysis. This unfolding of the designs and the instructions revealed in the Psalms in the various aspects of their contents, makes a valuable contribution to the exegesis of this portion of the Sacred Volume. It therefore affords the writer of this Foreword a very great pleasure to commend the work to servants of God. May these pages be abundantly owned by Him to the blessing of many.

W. E. VINE.

BATH.

Preface

To account for the appearance of yet another book on the Psalms, when so much critical and devotional literature on the subject is already available, some explanation seems needful. The following brief history of its preparation, therefore, is now given.

Upon the very first day of Japan's entry into the recent world war the writer was arrested by Japanese gendarmerie in Weihaiwei, North China, where he had been privileged to serve the Lord for many years, and after severe interrogation was placed in solitary confinement for about three months under conditions of great hardship. At first the only reading matter permitted was his own long-used Bible, a very precious possession in the circumstances. The daily strength and comfort derived from the Scriptures, especially the Psalms, during those trying days, cannot be adequately expressed. The sense of the Lord's unseen presence and sustaining grace was a real and blessed experience.

Many lone hours were profitably occupied in fulfilling a long-standing desire to make an analytical study of the Book of Psalms, and the notes were recorded on any scraps of paper obtainable. When released later under a condition of "house arrest," the study was continued with the advantage of access to material gathered over many years from various sources. Sent to Shanghai by the Japanese in the autumn of 1942 and expecting immediate repatriation, the family was billeted with many other allied nationals on the premises of a former American country club. Here the notes intended for personal use only were finally copied into memorandum books.

Following the Japanese order for general internment of all enemy nationals, we were sent to a large internment camp for civilians a few miles from Shanghai. Here we remained with about eighteen hundred others from April 1943 to October 1945, when some of us were repatriated by hospital ship to Britain. During the internment, whenever time could be spared from a busy life as camp quarter-master, the typescript of these "Studies" was prepared. In order to meet the wishes of several missionary friends, the English notes were expanded and revised to make them suitable for circulation among those interested in studying the Book of Psalms while in camp. Home-made covers containing each group of "Studies" as completed were passed round for private use. Notwithstanding many difficulties and interruptions the work was finally finished soon after peace was declared in the middle of August 1945.

For many years the analytical approach to the study of the sacred Scriptures has proved of deep interest and most helpful to a clearer understanding of the Divine Word. This seems particularly true of the Book of Psalms. The structure or literary form especially of poetic compositions determines the scope, and so furnishes a valuable clue to correct interpretation. Study of the structure of any given portion of Scripture, far from being neglected as is too often the case, should be taken up by every earnest student of the Word.

The "Studies" are intended to be merely suggestive and should be considered only as aids to personal meditation upon the Word of God itself. All sources available at the time in the work of others, have been drawn upon for helpful thoughts, but one regrets the present impossibility of tracing the origin of certain quotations found in old Bible notes. Books by such well-known writers as J. N. Darby, F. W. Grant and Drs. Kirkpatrick[1] and Graham Scroggie, also the "Companion Bible" have yielded considerable help. The analyses and synthetic studies, however, especially in their alliteration, are almost entirely the result of one's own attempt at a mnemonic presentation.

Thanks are due to many for aid generously given, and particularly to the late Mr. F. J. Hopkins of Nanchang and Shanghai, for certain suggestions and much encouragement offered during the long internment. In the knowledge of much kindly interest on the part of former fellow-internees and others, the writer ventures to pass on some of the fruits of research and reflection gathered during a long and trying, yet spiritually profitable experience. The "Studies" are prayerfully committed to the Lord in the hope that they may bring a little further spiritual enlightenment and soul comfort to fellow-believers during these dark and difficult days. To Him alone be all the praise, now and for ever.

ARTHUR G. CLARKE.

II. Cor. i. 3-4.

[1] Especially in the Verse Notes.

Preface to Second Edition

LITTLE need be said to introduce this new edition of the analytical studies. Apart from emendation in some of the analyses, slight additions and the correction of a few typographical errors the text remains substantially the same. Many synthetic outlines may be traced by the intentional use of capital letters and alliterative forms.

The book is once more sent forth in hope that it may be used to the glory of God and to the edification of His people.

A.G.C.

Preface to Third Edition

THAT another edition of these "Studies" is called for seems to indicate the book's continued usefulness. The author renders humble thanks to God for this. When the notes were first prepared for the use of a group of believers including missionaries in a Japanese civilian internment camp over thirty years ago, he little thought they would eventually be published in book form.

The "Studies" have found a use in certain Bible schools and study classes in North America and elsewhere, but it is in private devotions perhaps that they have found most acceptance. Many Christian friends have written and spoken of help received therefrom.

No other book of the Old Testament touches more closely the daily life of God's people today though, strictly speaking, the Book of Psalms does not record church truth. There can be hardly one who does not find in the Psalms echoes of his experience during his earthly pilgrimage, often proving the truth of Rom. 15: 4 and II Tim. 3: 16–17. Moreover, the Spirit-taught believer finds joy in discovering in this portion of God's word many precious references to the sufferings and the glories of his beloved Redeemer. See Luke 24: 25–32.

This edition remains virtually unchanged. There is one added note at the end of Psalm 72.

A.G.C. Dec. 1975

Abbreviations and Contractions found in these "Studies."

A.V.	Authorised Version
A.R.V.	American Revised Version
App.	Appendix
assoc.	associated (with)
Bk.	Book
br.	better
bec.	because
cf.	compare
ctr.	contrast
e.g.	for example
esp.	especially
emph.	emphatic, emphasis
et. al.	and other places
freq. ..	frequent(ly)
fig. ..	figure, figurative
ff.	and following
Heb.	in Hebrew
i.e.	that is
illus. ..	illustration
impf. ..	imperfect tense
indic.	indicates

LXX. ..	Septuagint (Greek version of Old Testament).
lit.	literally
m. or marg.	margin
N.B.	note well
pf. or perf.	perfect tense
pres.	present tense
prep.	preposition
plur.	plural number
qtd.	quoted
R.V.	Revised Version
ref.	refers, reference
repr. ..	represents
Scrip.	the Scriptures
sim.	similar
sing. ..	singular number
syn. ..	synonymous
s.H.w.	same Hebrew word
trans. ..	translate(d)
v., vv.	verse, verses
viz.	namely
wd.	word

The Revised Version is used throughout these "Studies" as the basis for notes. Where other readings or versions are to be preferred, the fact will be mentioned.

The lines in each verse are referred to in the Analyses where necessary as *a, b, c, d*, following verse number. In "Verse Notes" the letters are placed in brackets thus, (*a*).

INTRODUCTORY NOTES

I. GENERAL.—From very early times the Jews arranged the canonical books of the Old Testament into three great groups, known as "The Law, the Prophets, and the Writings." The Psalms belonged to the last division and often gave to it its name (Luke xxiv. 44). There is strong evidence that in the original order of the third group, the Psalms stood first, and not as in our present bible. The Hebrew title "Tehillim" means "Praises", and the book is probably so designated because of its use as the hymn book for the religious services of the second temple. In Greek translations of the Old Testament the title is simply "The Psalms" or "The Psalter," derived from "*psallo*," to play an instrument. From this and other indications it appears then that the Psalms are songs intended to be accompanied by instrumental music: cf. 1 Chron. xvi. 4 ff; xxv. 1; 2 Chron. v. 12–13.

That Israel possessed lyric poetry apart from that included in the Psalter is proved by the absence, for instance, of David's lament over Saul and Jonathan (2 Sam. i.), which is not suitable for public service in the Sanctuary. Hezekiah's prayer (Isa. xxxviii.) also is excluded perhaps as being too personal. In the Psalms, David sings in his typical and representative character.

On the question of inspiration we do not dwell. For the true child of God the matter is settled by the clear testimony of our Lord and His apostles. Christ not only classes the psalms with "the law and the prophets" (Luke xxiv. 44), He declares that David spake "in the Spirit" (Matt. xxii. 43). Peter's inspired testimony is given in 2 Pet. i. 21; Paul's in 2 Tim. iii. 16–17. If the very musicians who founded the sacred music came under the inspiration of God (1 Chron. xxv. 1), much more the psalmists themselves when they wrote.

Here then is a collection of Israel's sacred songs, the "inspired response of the human heart to God's revelation of Himself in law, history and prophecy."

In general character the Psalms may be classed under one or other of the following:—

(*a*) A *Calling* upon God in the direct address of petition or praise.

13

(b) A *Communion* of the soul with God in which its emotions and experiences are expressed.

(c) A *Celebration* of the works of God in nature and in history.

(d) A *Cogitation* upon the perplexing problems of life in relation to divine government in the world.

The Psalter rightly holds the middle place of the Bible as the heart of both Old and New Testaments. It commences with God blessing man (i. 1) and ends with man blessing God (cl), while in between, every degree of human experience is to be found. As one writer has so beautifully expressed it, "Man's heart is the harp from which the divine hand produces the richest music." Change and movement are but the rhythm of a central life, hence adversity as well as prosperity, sorrow no less than joy, may bring forth strains in minor and major keys respectively. We find a combination of poetry and music wherein God brings all the seeming discords of life into a perfect harmony. Penitence, prayer and perplexity finally merge into perpetual praise. This consummation is a burst of universal song that "sweeps out of time into eternity in an unending anthem of immortal acclamation," a scene of unparalleled glory in which God for ever dwells and reigns as Supreme Head of a redeemed and restored creation.

II. ORDER.—The present arrangement of the Psalms is the same as in the days of our Lord (Acts xiii. 33). They are not in a chronological order either historical or prophetical, though David's own book of psalms is the first of the five and the post-captivity book last. Nevertheless, each psalm is found in its suited place and in organic relation with the whole. To the devout student it is evident that God's superintending providence guided the compilers of the Psalter, as well as the various composers of the individual psalms, thus producing "a divine harmony of moral order and spiritual affinity."

III. DIVISIONS.—The Book of Psalms falls into five natural divisions indicated by the doxologies which end the first four with Psalm cl. itself as the closing and glorious doxology to the whole. Such a division forms a pentateuch in harmony with the Five Books of Moses and the Five Megiloth (Scrolls), namely Canticles, Ruth, Lamentations, Ecclesiastes and Esther.

(a) *Psalms i–xli* form the Genesis book in which we see the counsels of God concerning man and his ways.

(b) *Psalms xlii.–lxxii.* form the Exodus book in which we see the

counsels of God concerning Israel as a nation—their ruin and
redemption. 73 - 89

(c) *Psalms lxxiii.–lxxxix.* form the Leviticus book in which we see
the counsels of God concerning His sanctuary and His assembly.

(d) *Psalms xc.–cvi.* form the Numbers book in which we see the
counsels of God concerning Israel and the nations.

(e) *Psalms cvii.–cl.* form the Deuteronomy book in which we see
the counsels of God concerning Himself and His Word.

The prophetic significance of these divisions will be noted later.

IV. DATE AND AUTHORSHIP.—The Psalms originated in the
religious revival under David and Solomon. Additions were made
during times of revival under Kings Jehoshaphat, Hezekiah, and
Josiah, and the final addition during the last revival immediately
following the Captivity. The long periods of growing declension
proved quite unproductive of such writings. The era before David
furnishes but one or possibly two psalms, namely xc. and xci, by
Moses. Germs of song, however, existed from the beginning of
Israel's national history (see Ex. xv.; Num. vi. 22–25; x. 35; Jdg. v.;
1 Sam. ii.). The titles establish David's authorship of the first book,
and there is trace of no other author. The other psalms, though
not all composed by David, are all pervaded by a Davidic spirit. In
David "the sweet singer of Israel" (2 Sam. xxiii. 1–2) were combined creative genius as a poet and inspirational gift as a prophet
(Acts ii. 30). As to other composers we shall have occasion to refer
to them as we proceed. Hezekiah seems to have restored David's
Psalms to their liturgical use in the temple (2 Chron. xxix. 30). There
is a notable absence of authors' names from the fourth and fifth
books, which implies that these compositions have not the same
individual and personal character as the Davidic psalms. The anonymous psalmists write as representatives of the community.

A point to be remembered is that the Hebrew preposition generally rendered "of" in the titles of psalms, may be rendered "to"
(indicating dedication), "for" (indicating appropriation), "of" (indicating theme) and "by" (indicating authorship), so that the actual
significance in each case must be decided upon other grounds.

The writer of these "Studies" is entirely out of sympathy with
the arguments of destructive critics who would refer almost all the
psalms to a date as late as Ezra and even to the period of the Maccabees. The present book is not intended for these so-called "advanced

scholars" therefore space and time are not wasted in refuting their many different and often wild assertions. Abler pens than mine have dealt with such critical aspects.

V. TITLES.—The evidence for the genuineness of the psalm titles seems overwhelming, though the writer does not propose to enter upon a detailed discussion here, see Appendix VI. Many reverent scholars and destructive critics alike have been sore puzzled by their exact significance, especially those connected with the musical setting. Dr. Thirtle's suggested solution adopted in the "Companion" and "Scofield" Bibles seems satisfactory and removes most of the difficulties. His arguments, based mainly upon the arrangement of the Prayer of Habakkuk iii. with its superscript and subscript, appear conclusive. In this view the dedicatory words found at the head of so many psalms in our present Bibles really belong to the preceding psalm as a subscript, the true division between the psalms having been lost at quite an early date.

Some titles descriptive of the character of the psalm are:—

(a) A Psalm.—Both Hebrew and Greek terms denote a song with musical accompaniment. Occurs fifty-seven times.

(b) A Song.—Hebrew term is a general one for song, denoting a vocal piece. It is applied also to secular songs in the Old Testament, e.g. Amos vi. 5 (R.V.). Fragments of songs are preserved in Gen. iv. 23-24; I Sam. xviii. 7 and elsewhere. Occurs thirty times.

(c) A Prayer.—In the titles occurs five times and once in the subscript to Ps. lxxii. closing Book II.

(d) A Praise.—In a title found only at the head of Ps. cxlv.

(e) Maschil.—Occurs thirteen times. The word means "instruction," and psalms so designated are intended to convey special teaching for the times, particularly for "the wise" (Heb. maschilim) in the last days. See fuller note under Ps. xxxii.

(f) Michtam.—Occurs six times with a somewhat doubtful meaning, but most probably denotes an epigrammatic composition giving maxims of faith worthy to be "engraved" on the memory.

(g) A Song of Degrees, i.e. more literally "of the goings-up" (or ascents).—This group is thought to be of songs sung by the pilgrims on their way up to the important festivals at Jerusalem. Dr. Thirtle's suggestion is worthy of note. He connects them with the "degrees" on the sun-dial of Ahaz and Hezekiah's "songs" (Isa. xxxviii. 8, 20). See notes under Book Five IV. (Analysis).

"For the chief musician," is a phrase that commonly appears in the superscript, but as already pointed out it belongs most probably to the subscript of the preceding psalm in every case. The chief musician was the precentor or conductor of the temple choir, one who trained it, and himself led the music in the sanctuary services (cf. 1 Chron. xv. 21). The phrase may indicate that the particular psalm to which it is appended originally belonged to a "Preceptor's Collection." It occurs fifty-five times and only in the psalms of David and his singers. These compositions may have originated in some special circumstances, but were formally handed over later to the choir leader for use in the Temple worship as suited to a more general application. With regard to the typical bearing we surely see in "the Chief Musician" our Lord Jesus Christ, who is both Leader of the heavenly praises (Ps. xxii. 22) and at the same time the blessed Object and End of all true worship.

Occasional Hebrew words used will be discussed in the psalms where they occur, but mention may be made here of:—

"*Selah*," which appears some seventy-one times, though not in the titles. It is characteristic of the psalms of David and his singers, Asaph, Heman and Jeduthun (cf. Hab. iii.). The word is derived from "salah", to pause, or "salal," to lift up, and may bear both meanings. In use it is closely bound up with the structure and appears to call attention to some important connection between what precedes and what follows, an emphasis by way of contrast or of amplification. It has to do with the meaning rather than the music, the matter rather than the melody, thus affording instruction to the hearers rather than direction to the singers. "Selah" often but not invariably divides a composition into strophes. See further note at Ps. iii.

"*Hallelujah*," generally translated, "Praise ye the Lord" (Jah = Jehovah), is strictly a two-word phrase originally intended as a general invitation to the assembled worshippers to join in the public responses. It is never found in the psalms of David and his singers.

VI. FORM OF HEBREW POETRY.—English poetry frequently uses a recurrence of sound, *i.e.* rhyme, but Hebrew poetry does not. Its main characteristics are a recurrence of thought and rhythm — rhythmical cadences of each separate clause and a rhythmical balance of clauses combined in a series. This is known as "parallelism," the law of which often determines the construction or connection of words, and decides a doubtful meaning. This last is important from the standpoint of interpretation for a valuable clue to a difficult passage or an ambiguous word may be given by the corresponding word in the parallel clause.

The simplest form of parallelism is the couplet, but this is sometimes expanded into a triplet or quatrain, e.g. Ps. xciii. 3. Introversions and alternations of member clauses constantly appear, and are combined in various ways and in more or less complex forms. *Such forms very often influence the structure of the whole psalm.* This is brought out in the analyses found in the present book, the writer himself having proved this principle of construction a most valuable aid to a proper understanding of these Scriptures. The A.V. arrangement into verses tends sometimes to mask the parallelism of thought, hence the R.V. is to be preferred.

The earliest instance of parallelism is found in Enoch's prophecy (Jude 14). Lamech's boast of impunity in his manslaughter and bigamy (Gen. iv. 23-24) was a parody of Enoch's poetical prophecy. Enoch warned his lawless and unbelieving age of God's coming judgment. Lamech mocks at the warning, making God's very forbearance in the case of Cain the ground of presumptuous confidence of impunity in his double crime, surely a solemn lesson for to-day.

Three kinds of parallelism may be noted:—

(a) *Synonymous Parallelism* in which form the same fundamental thought is repeated in different words in the second line of a couplet, e.g. Ps. cxiv. 1.

(b) *Antithetic Parallelism* where the thought in the first line of a couplet is corroborated or elucidated by the affirmation of its opposite in the second line, e.g. Ps. i. 6.

(c) *Synthetic Parallelism* in which two lines of a couplet stand in the relation of cause and consequence, or some other constructional relationship.

Poetic lines are frequently grouped by the psalmists in a series known as stanzas or strophes. Again, many psalms are in an alphabetic acrostic form, an arrangement first used by David, doubtless as a useful aid to memory. This affords a hint as to the importance of committing to heart portions of God's Word. The dramatic form of certain psalms must not be overlooked, e.g. Ps. ii. Different voices are heard in these and must be carefully distinguished, not only to understand the psalm, but that fitting expression may be given in public reading. Finally, numerous psalms are regulated by numbers, especially seven divided into four and three, but this subject is too large in scope for this book. Students will delight to discover for themselves such divine arrangements.

VII. INTERPRETATION.—For a true understanding of the Psalms, it is necessary to study them from three distinct view-points: (a) the Primary Association, or Historical Aspect; (b) the Prophetic Anticipation, or Typical Aspect; and (c) the Personal Application, or Devotional Aspect. If we neglect any one of these we shall miss important elements in divine instruction. Many critics have created difficulties where none really exist by seeking to assign to every portion of the Psalms definite events in the sacred and profane records of Israel's history. They too readily forget that David was not only a gifted poet but also a great prophet, who, like other writers of the Old Testament writing under inspiration of the Holy Spirit, often reached beyond what he knew (1 Peter i. 10-11; Acts i. 16; ii. 25-31; iv. 25-26; 2 Sam. xxiii. 1-2). Yet it is equally a mistake to underrate the spiritual apprehension of the Old Testament saints, which may well have been more profound than is generally supposed.

(1) PRIMARY ASSOCIATION—HISTORICAL ASPECT

From indications in the titles as well as from internal evidence and comparison with the records in the historical books, it is often possible to fix the date of particular psalms with more or less certainty. An insight into the circumstances giving rise to the production seldom fails to throw additional light upon the sentiments of the psalm. As already noticed, various periods up to the return of the remnant from the Babylonian captivity and immediately succeeding times are represented in the Psalter. Not a few scholars think that Ezra the Scribe was the last compiler of the Book of Psalms in its present form.

In David's psalms his inner life "is mirrored forth with a completeness of individuality not to be looked for in the historical books, which deal more with his outward life. At the same time incidental allusions occur which take for granted the facts narrated in the histories, and, in some cases, even curiously correspond in the very modes of expression."

(2) Prophetic Anticipation—Typical Aspect

The web of prophecy is mainly woven from the personal experiences of the psalmists. The controlling Spirit of God suddenly or gradually carried them away into realms of thought and feeling wholly beyond their actual circumstances.

A valuable clue to the correct interpretation of the whole Book of Psalms is afforded by Psalm i. which distinguishes the man who is godly according to the law from the rest of the nation. We continually find the Spirit of Christ (1 Peter i. 11) concerning Himself in the condition of the faithful remnant in Israel. Both in His life on earth and in His death, Christ is linked with the interests and destiny of this remnant. Such for instance is the significance of His baptism by John (Matt. iii. 15). While only a remnant their affections and hopes are those of the nation. Our Lord Himself was the only truly faithful One before God in Israel and became "the personal foundation of the whole remnant to be delivered, as well as the perfect finisher of that work, upon which their deliverance could be based." (J. N. D.).

We must not fail, then, to differentiate between God's dealings with Israel as a nation and with the godly remnant in it. In all periods of Israel's national departure from God, a remnant has remained faithful to Him. Even in the present "Church Age" there is a remnant according to the election of grace (Rom. xi. 5). They together with believing Gentiles form the one Body of which Christ Himself is the Head. These believing Jews share with us the heavenly calling, and all this blessed privilege implies. In the period immediately preceding and succeeding Christ's first advent, a devout remnant is seen, though the nation in heart, if not outwardly, had departed from God. Clear evidence of this is manifest in that the religious leaders failed to recognise the Messiah when He appeared. They even rejected and crucified Him. In the days preceding Christ's second advent also, a godly remnant will maintain the faith of their fathers, even though the great majority of the nation will follow Antichrist in his wickedness. It is to this remnant that many psalms point, especially in the later books. The divine blessings promised connect themselves chiefly with the future of Israel according to the terms of the new covenant, the nation becoming God's channel of grace to the Gentiles and the temple-throne of God in Jerusalem forming the centre from which His law goes forth and to which the kings of the earth will bring their willing tribute of praise and worship.

To reach the desired end, God in His governmental dealings with the nation brings the remnant to the sense of guilt in a broken law and a rejected Messiah, and the Psalms will be the means by which they will learn that God has fully met their spiritual need in the atoning work of the very One the nation had crucified. Before their actual deliverance comes with the glorious appearing of Christ, He, in virtue of the work wrought to effect it, sustains the souls of the faithful ones amid their many sore trials and leads them on to the long-hoped-for consummation. In the Psalms, the remnant is found pleading the divine loving-kindness as regards their state before a holy God, and the divine righteousness as their hope in their sufferings at the hand of opposing Gentiles. By the aid of the Psalms the true Israelite at any time since David could enter "into the living spirit of the law, and realising his need of the promised Saviour look for Him of whom the Psalms testify." Thus the book properly belongs to the circumstances of Judah and Israel and is altogether founded upon Israel's hopes and fears, especially in the last days which began with the rejection of Christ and will end in the glorious consummation of His personal reign in the millennial age. Prophetically the Psalms do not carry us beyond the millennial reign of Messiah.

Regarding the Messianic Psalms, it is necessary to utter a word of warning. The appropriation of a whole psalm to Christ because a portion of it is cited in the New Testament as referring to Him may lead one into serious error. It must be always borne in mind that no confession of personal sin ever came from His lips, see Appendix I.

(3) PERSONAL APPLICATION—DEVOTIONAL ASPECT

In studying the Psalms from this view-point it is of the utmost importance to recognise that the true scope of the book is earthly and that the people of God in it are earthly. This has been emphasized in the preceding paragraph. It is a very serious mistake to apply indiscriminately to Christians certain passages which belong only to the age of Law and to a future day when the suffering remnant of Israel will be moved by the Spirit of God to use language fully in accord with the character of the dispensation in which they live. The Christian who takes up the position described in the Psalms is reverting to experiences properly pertaining to one under discipline for failure in a legal state and to the hopes of God's earthly people. Many Christians through lack of knowledge do in fact pass through conditions of soul analogous to those in the Psalms before they come into the full assurance of liberty in Christ (cf. Rom. vii–viii.). Such, however, is not true Christian experience, for while the remnant pass through their trials before the knowledge of redemption and its application in power is reached, experiences proper to the Christian are the fruit of his union with Christ. His portion is quite different, for he belongs to a heavenly people. His hope, too, is different, for he will be delivered from his enemies by being taken up from their midst (1 Thess. iv. 16), whereas the Jew will be delivered only by the destruction of his enemies. The Ephesian epistle gives us the true position of those in union with Christ and that to the Philippians deals almost exclusively with Christian experience.

If the above be always borne in mind, the child of God will find in the Psalms a mine of wealth inexhaustible in its supply to meet his daily needs. The book provides "a treasury of devotion for the saints of every age." Here are sentiments which have discovered "an echo in the hearts of men of all nationalities." There is hardly a phase of human experience that does not strike a chord in this song book. Representing in his own person "the righteous principle assailed by the ungodly," or one suffering under the disciplinary hand of God, David teaches the faithful how to conduct themselves in trial. His faith is often seen addressing itself to, and triumphing over his fears. Many of the intensely personal details given in the Psalms find a peculiar suitability in private approach to God. The biographies of a host of departed saints of God and the testimonies of a multitude of living believers witness to this.

A brief outline of the five books viewed from the prophetic standpoint is now given. The first psalm or psalms in each book form a kind of preface. In general "some great truth or historical fact as to the Messiah or the remnant, or both, is introduced and then a series of psalms follows, expressing the feelings and sentiments of the remnant in connection therewith," (J.N.D.); in short, a *Revelation to the Remnant* followed by the *Response of the Remnant*, or *Facts presented* then *Feelings produced*. It should be remarked that in the unveiling of the prophetic programme the Book of Psalms, like other prophetic Scriptures, often retraces ground to fill in further details of events already outlined. Moreover, things to come are constantly spoken of as if they were present, as is always the case with the prophets. The theme of each psalm is generally to be found in the first few verses, but occasionally in the last. Note also that the predominant titles for God in each book are in beautiful accord with the character of its contents; see Appendix II.

Book I.—Israel's Redeemer and Remnant (Pss. i.-xli.). In its general character this is the Genesis book. It begins with the divine blessing upon man (i. 1, cf. Gen. i. 28). Note also reference to the tree in Ps. i., cf. Gen. ii. 9-10. The faithful Jewish remnant emerges, viewed as in the land under covenant relationship with God, hence the title "Jehovah" predominates. Christ Himself, Jehovah on earth, is connected with the remnant which is not yet driven out of Jerusalem. He is seen to be the source of all blessing for His people. There is more of the personal history of the Messiah in this book than in all the rest. Two periods seem to be covered, first, that corresponding to the Gospels and beginning of Acts, and second, that of the interval between the rapture of the Church and the glorious appearing of Messiah at His Second Advent. The title "Jehovah" occurs two hundred and seventy-nine times, "Elohim" forty-eight times (nine times joined with "Jehovah"). Ps. viii. is characteristic of the book

Book II.—Israel's Ruin and Redemption (Pss. xlii.-lxxii.). The Exodus book opens with a cry of distress and closes with the fruits of redemption, Israel brought out from among the nations. Christ is seen identifying Himself with the Jewish remnant cast out of Jerusalem, which city in the last days is given up to Antichrist and is full of wicked apostates. Christ restores these faithful ones to their position in relationship with Jehovah as a people, the book ending with the glorious appearing and reign of the Messiah. In Ps. li. the remnant own the national guilt in rejecting the Messiah. The title "Elohim" occurs two hundred and sixty-two times (twice joined with "Jehovah"); "El" appears fourteen times, "Jehovah" only thirty-seven times because His open relationship with Israel is viewed as broken and the nation cast off until the end time. The Spirit of the Messiah, however, still works in the hearts of the godly ones. The title "Jah" occurs for the first time in the Old Testament at Ex. xv. 3 and significantly, first in the Psalter at lxviii. 4 in this book. It is well to remember that eternal redemption, as taught for instance in the Hebrew epistle, is foreshadowed by the temporal deliverance of Israel from Egypt. It has two aspects, namely:

(*a*) as applied to the Church composed of all true believers in this dispensation, and

(*b*) as applied to Israel under the promised new covenant.

The glory, however, of the former (cf. Heb. x.) infinitely transcends that found for Israel in Ezk. xliii.–xlviii. The characteristic psalm of this book is Ps. lxviii.

Book III.—Israel's Return and Restoration (Pss. lxxiii.–lxxxix.) The Leviticus book brings into prominence the sanctuary and God's dealing in holinesss with His people. Books III. and IV. are more national and historical than I. and II. Here Israel is viewed as once more in the land, the nation at first in unbelief, a faithful remnant centering its hopes in the dwelling-place of the Lord of Hosts, the restored temple. The nation is prophetically shown towards the close of the latter half of Daniel's seventieth "week," suffering as a result of the opposition of the Assyrian and Idumæan confederacy of nations surrounding Palestine. The Messiah is still occupied with the remnant remaining faithful in days of great apostasy. The titles for God are mixed but "Elohim" predominates, occuring ninety-three times; "Jehovah" sixty-five times; "El" five times. The characteristic psalm is Ps. lxxxiv.

Book IV.—Israel's Relapse and Recovery (Pss. xc.–cvi.). The Numbers book opens with a wilderness prayer in view of Israel's sad failure. The Messiah's fidelity is contrasted with man's futility. The "first man" is replaced by the "second man" (1 Cor. xv. 45–47) under whose hand the world is re-established, and not only Israel but all the peoples are shown to be blest in Christ the coming King. Note the many references to wilderness-world types. The Abrahamic name "Almighty" and the millennial name "Most High" are prominent, significant of pilgrimage and rest respectively. Psalm xc. is characteristic.

Book V.—Israel's Regathering and Retrospect (Pss. cvii.–cl.). In this Deuteronomy book are found (*a*) a Review of God's Word, and (*b*) a Rehearsal of God's Ways. All blessing for Man (Book 1), for Israel (Book 2), for Zion (Book 3), and for the Gentiles (Book 4), is bound up with the Word of God even as its transgression is the source of (*a*) Distress of Man, (*b*) Dispersion of Israel, (*c*) Destruction of the Temple, and (*d*) Disorder in the World. The Recovery of Man, the Regathering of Israel, the Rebuilding of Zion and the Restoration of the World, are all connected with the

fulfilment of the divine word on the principles given in Jer. xxxi.
31–34; Ezk. xxxvi.24–38. This book fittingly closes with the results of
the Messiah's triumph and the universal response of praise to it. The
title "Jehovah" once more predominates (two hundred and ninety-
three times) for God has resumed covenant relationship with the
nation as such, with Israel back in the land ready to enjoy the abiding
fruits of the Messiah's atoning work and His glorious reign. "Jah"
occurs thirteen times, "Elohim" forty-one times (four times joined
with Jehovah"), "El" ten times and "Eloah" twice. Ps. cxix. is
characteristic.

Book I. Israel's Redeemer and Remnant. Pss. i.-xli.

This book contains several leading Messianic psalms in which the personal
history of Christ is recorded with accurate and graphic detail. It begins and ends
with our Lord as the fully devoted One, Ps. i. emphasising His devotion in life
and Pss. xl.-xli. emphasizing His devotion in death. For further notes see
Introduction.

ANALYSIS.

I. REVELATION OF THE DIVINE RULER, I-VIII.
    1. The Ruler, i.-ii. Son of God.
    2. The Remnant, iii.-vii. Exercise and Experience.
    3. The Ruler, viii. Son of Man.

N.B.—This section is an introduction not only to Book I, but to the whole
Book of Psalms. In it we see Messiah's Rectitude, i.; Rejection, ii.-vii.; and Reign,
viii. Kingship in Israel (ii.) widens into world empire as Son of Man, viii.

II. RESPONSE OF THE DESPISED REMNANT, IX-XV.
    1. Existence of the Eternal and the Enemy, ix.-x.
    2. Experiences of the Evil and the Enemy, xi.-xv.

N.B.—In this section we get the godly remnant's exercise of soul and experience
of suffering at the hands of Antichrist and the apostates of Israel. Their tribulation,
however, is seen to end in triumph.

III. RECORD OF THE DIVINE REDEEMER, XVI-XLI.
    1. The Redeemer, xvi.-xxiv. Source of Salvation.
    2. The Remnant, xxv.-xxxix. Exercise and Experience. Subjects of
       Salvation.
    3. The Redeemer, xl.-xli. Saviour and Sinners.

N.B.—"Christ is seen in the midst of His people manifesting God to them and
sanctifying them to God." In Ps. xxv. sins are acknowledged for the first time in
the Psalter.

Book One. I. Revelation of the Divine Ruler, i.–viii.

1. The Ruler, i.–ii. Son of God.

PSALM I.   CONTRASTED CHARACTERS

I. THE GODLY APPROVED (1–3).
    1. Consistent Conduct (1–2).
    2. Consequent Character (3*abc*). Fig. TREE.
    3. Confident Conclusion (3*d*). Enduring Prosperity.

II. THE GODLESS ABANDONED (4–5).
    1. Consistent Conduct (4*a*). "Not so" (antithesis 1–2).
    2. Consequent Character (4*b*). Fig. CHAFF.
    3. Confident Conclusion (5). Eventual Perdition.

III. THE GOAL ATTESTED (6).
    Two ways—two ends, cf. Matt. vii. 13–27.

PRIMARY ASSOCIATION.—Date unknown, but the authorship is almost certainly David's. Distinguished from most of the psalms in Book I in having no title. Note affinity with Pss. xxvi. and cxii.

PROPHETIC ANTICIPATION.—Pattern and promise for Israel's remnant especially in the last days. Christ as the true Israelite. Personal character of God's anointed King, cf. Deut. xvii. 19. See notes Ps. ii. Israel has never yet been a true "assembly of the righteous" (5) but the nation will be eventually, cf. Isa. lx. 21–22.

PERSONAL APPLICATION.—Shows the characteristics of the godly man, emphasis being laid upon individual faithfulness in days of declension. Man's true happiness is found only in a life of fellowship with God. Godly conduct has a positive side (2) as well as a negative one (1). In Book I three psalms open with a beatitude, (*a*) The Obedient Man—Godward aspect, (i); (*b*) The Forgiven Man—Selfward aspect, (xxxii.); (*c*) The Compassionate Man—Manward aspect, (xli.). The Counsel of the Self-willed—heed not; the Conduct of the Sinners—imitate not; the Company of the Scorners—seek not; Evil Principles—Evil Practices—Evil Partnerships, (1). Unfading Foliage—our confession; Unfailing Fruit—our character, (3).

VERSE NOTES

1. "Blessed," or, "Happy" (R.V.M.), lit. happinesses, Heb. plural of magnitude, here indicates great or complete happiness. First of the many beatitudes found in the Psalms, cf. Matt. v. The Book of Genesis, too, begins with a divine blessing upon man, Gen. i. 28. Ps. i. opens with a beatitude, Ps. ii. closes with one. Mark the threefold parallelism in this verse: walking, standing, sitting, counsel, way, seat; wicked, sinners, scornful; indicating a course leading to a climax. "Wicked," Heb. means "lawless," those who own no authority but their own will, who recognise no law but their own desires. The word is commonly found in the Psalms. "Sinners," Heb. intensive indicates habitual offenders. "Seat of the scornful," br. session of scoffers, *i.e.* a class of cynical free-thinkers who mock at holy things; such are frequently referred to in the Book of Proverbs.

2. "Law of Jehovah," here practically syn. with the Word of Jehovah, *i.e.* the whole divine revelation. "Meditate" or, muse; cf. Jos. i. 8.

3. Fig. of vitality, beauty and fertility, cf. Jer. xvii. 7-8. In Scripture the vegetable kingdom furnishes the great types of production; the animal kingdom, the great types of consumption. "Planted," fig. of the tender care and ministry of the Holy Spirit acting through the Word of God. "Water-streams," *i.e.* artificial channels seen upon irrigated land. (*d*) *i.e.* he carries it through to a successful issue.

4. "Not so," (emph.) sums up the character of the wicked (*i.e.* lawless, s.H.w. 1, 5, 6). He is the very antithesis of the godly man. In this verse is a figure familiar to all acquainted with threshing-floors in the East. Chaff is worthless and wind-driven; indic. character and destiny. Judgment will drive such out of the Kingdom, cf. Matt. iii. 12; Luke xvii. 34-35.

6. Each clause implies the supplement of its antithesis in the other clause, a form often found in the psalms. Jehovah knows (or, acknowledges) the way of the righteous, who is preserved. Jehovah equally knows the way of the lawless, who perishes.

PSALM II.   THE MESSIANIC MONARCHY

I. REVOLT OF THE NATIONS (1-3). WORLD INSURRECTION. OPPOSITION TO GOD'S ANOINTED. GENTILE DEFIANCE.

1. World Commotion (1).
2. Wrongful Meditation (1).
3. Wicked Association (2).
4. Wily Machination (2).
5. Wilful Proposition (3).

II. REACTION OF THE LORD (4-6). WRATHFUL INTERVENTION. ACCESSION OF GOD'S ANOINTED. DIVINE DISPLEASURE.

1. Uncompromising Deity (4-5). Ever-watchful God.
2. Unshakable Kingdom (6). Everlasting Realm.

III. RESPONSE OF THE KING (7–9) WONDERFUL INTIMATION.
DOMINION OF GOD'S ANOINTED. MESSIANIC DECREE.
1. Unique Relation (7).
2. Universal Possession (8). Subjugation by Power.
3. Unsparing Administration (9).

IV. RECOMMENDATION TO THE NATIONS, (10–12). WISE INJUNC-
TION. SUBMISSION TO GOD'S ANOINTED. PERSONAL
DIRECTION.
1. Well-advised Attention (10).
2. Worthy Occupation (11).
3. Warning Admonition (12ab).
4. Weighty Conclusion (12c).

PRIMARY ASSOCIATION.—Authorship of this psalm is determined
by the quotation at Acts iv. 25, where it is attributed to David.
Date is less certain, but it probably belongs to a late period of David's
reign, maybe to the time when Solomon was first appointed king
and a revolt of subject nations threatened as well as domestic troubles.
The psalm is undoubtedly based upon the great promise of 2 Sam.
vii. 12 ff. The structure is dramatic in form, different speakers being
heard; the psalmist (1–2), the conspirators quoted (3), the psalmist
(4–5), the Lord quoted (6), the Anointed (7a), the Lord quoted
(7b–9), the psalmist (10–12).

PROPHETIC ANTICIPATION.—One of the better known Messianic
psalms, see "Notes on the Messianic Psalms," Appendix I. Here we
find the counsels of God concerning His Christ, rejected by earth
but owned by heaven. Verses 1–2 are applied to the coalition of
Jews and Gentiles against our Lord at His first advent (Acts iv.
25-28). There will be a more compete fulfilment when the remnant
of Israel in the last days will meet the full fury of the final storm
of opposition to God, the nations then attempting to throw off the
last semblance of the Christian yoke. Besides other quotations in
the New Testament the language of this psalm is frequently
borrowed in Revelation in connection with the fierce conflict and
final triumph of Christ's Kingdom, xii. 5; xiv. 15; xxi. 26–27.

Pss. i. and ii. again seen to be complementary, showing Israel's
two great sins in rejecting God's double testimony to the nation,
(i) Disobedience to His Law, i.; (ii) Disownment of His Son, ii.
Law emphasised, i.; Prophecy emphasised, ii.—two great divisions
of the Old Testament.

PERSONAL APPLICATION.—Perhaps best summed up in outline. (a) Fact of Rebellion (1-3), (b) Fury of rebellion (1), (c) Focus of rebellion (2), (d) Folly of rebellion (4), (e) Failure of rebellion (5-6), (f) Frustrator of rebellion (7-9), (g) Forgiveness for rebellion (10-12). The world to-day is very restive under divine restraint (1-2). It is madness for the many to stand against the Mighty. It is better to have God for us than against us, Rom. viii. 31. God ever watches the course of events on earth (4). There is a limit to divine patience (9). Submission to the Son is the only way to escape destruction (10-12). Happy indeed are all who take refuge in Him, especially during the period of His rejection (12), cf. David as type (1 Sam. xxii. 1-2). Distinguish the true kiss of homage and the false kiss of betrayal (12 with Luke xxii. 48.)

VERSE NOTES

1. "rage," see margin—"peoples," or, races (of men)—"imagine" or as marg., s.H.w., i. 2, but here in bad sense. Note outward tumult and inward thought.

2. "kings . . . earth" ctr. "My King" (6); expression occurs nine times in the Book of Revelation.

3. Language refers to the yoke of subjection and the reins of restraint—note (a) the Preparation (2a); (b) the Plotting (2b); and (c) the Proposal (3).

4. Translate verbs in present tense, "laugheth . . . derideth . . ." dramatic description of divine displeasure, cf. vbs. in 1-2; fig. anthropopatheia (App. III, 9) human language used to describe God's attitude and actions without fear of lowering Him to a human level.

5. "sore displeasure" lit. fiery wrath.

6. br. "And I (emph.) have established . . ." Jehovah answers the rebels' words (3); men set Him on a cross—His title "King of the Jews" was His condemnation. "Zion" was the name of the ancient stronghold which became the City of David (2 Sam. v. 7) consecrated by the presence of the ark till the temple was built; poetical and prophetical name for Jerusalem in the character of the Holy City, the earthly dwelling-place of Jehovah. In the glorious future the Messiah's throne will be set in this centre of the millennial metropolis.

7. "decree," cf. 2 Sam. vii. 12 ff.—"My Son" (cf. Matt. iii. 13) = Messiah's divine nature—"Jehovah's Anointed" (3) = Messiah's divine office; "Son", i.e. "Only-begotten" in His relation to God—"Firstborn" in His relation to man. "Messiah" (Christ) and "Son of God" are titles freq. assoc. in New Testament, so in this Psalm. "This day," prophetically of Messiah's ascension, corresponding to the king's adopted sonship in the rite of anointing, see App. I. The decree, recorded also at I Chron. xvii. 11-13, looks beyond Solomon to David's greater Son, Messiah. The contexts of quotations in the N.T. seem to cover Messiah's history including His incarnation, resurrection, exaltation and ascension upon His earthly throne at the second advent; see Acts ii. 30-33, xiii. 33, Heb. i. 5, v.5.

8. Our Lord has not yet asked, cf. Jno. xvii. 9. Dominion over the nations is not expressly mentioned in 2 Sam. vii., but cf. Ps. lxxxix. 27.

9. br. "Thou shalt shepherd them with a rod (or, sceptre) . . ."—even a shepherd's rod can smite with severity, *e.g.* Moses' rod in Egypt; so Rev. ii. 27; xii. 5; xix. 15. "Thou shalt shatter . . ." fig. of easy and complete destruction.

10. "Be admonished ye judges . . .", *i.e.* rulers generally.

11. This is the "everlasting gospel" of Rev. xiv. 6–7. Rejoicing is to be tempered with reverence.

12. "Son," word in original unusual in Old Testament not same as in 7, but refers to same person. For the kiss of homage, see 1 Sam. x. 1; 1 Kings xix. 18, etc.—"lest He", meaning same whether ref. to Jehovah or to the Son—"in the way" = primarily, "lest you find your proposed expedition lead only to ruin," but the spiritual application must not be passed over—br. "For quickly may His anger blaze forth." Note the closing beatitude, as margin.

Book One. I. Revelation of the Divine Ruler, i.–viii.

2. The Remnant, iii.–vii. Exercise and Experience.

PSALM III.   GUARDED BY GOD

I. THE PRESSURE OF DAVID'S FOES (1–2).
   1. Their Increase (1*a*).
   2. Their Insurrection (1*b*).
   3. Their Inference (2). That his cause was hopeless! Selah.

II. THE PROTECTION OF DAVID'S GOD (3–4).
   1. God his Shield. The rebels had attacked his person.
   2. God his Glory. The rebels desired his crown.
   3. God his Uplifter. The rebels sought his downfall.
   4. God his Sanctuary. The rebels had driven him from Zion. Selah.

III. THE PEACEFULNESS OF DAVID'S SLEEP (5–6).
   1. His Confidence (5). Trustfulness.
   2. His Courage (6). Fearlessness.

IV. THE PETITION OF DAVID'S HEART (7–8).
   1. His Appeal for Himself (7).
   2. His Aspiration for the People (8), (R.V.). Selah.

SUPERSCRIPT.—A Psalm of David, when he fled from Absalom his son.

SUBSCRIPT.—For the Chief Musician; upon Neginoth.

PRIMARY ASSOCIATION.—Pss. iii. and iv. are obviously connected. Both are by David and both belong to the same crisis of his life, referred to in the title of Ps. iii., but while iii. is a morning hymn "after a night spent in the midst of danger," iv. is "an evening hymn written on a somewhat later occasion when the danger, though less imminent has not yet passed." Cf. the graphic account of the circumstances, 2 Sam. xv.–xvii. David had gratified his own heart's desire in bringing back his son in unrighteousness. From that moment, Absalom became a thorn in David's side, and plotted to wrest the kingdom from his father. A series of crises overwhelmed David at this time, namely, the treachery of his beloved son, the perfidy of his trusted counsellor and the revolt of a disaffected party in the nation. It is amid such circumstances that David retires into the presence of his God. Having committed his cause to God, he rested in perfect peace. Regarding subscript, see Introduction V. "Neginoth" from "nagan," to strike, is primarily connected with striking the strings of an instrument with a plectrum. It seems also to suggest a deeper meaning, (a) a "smiting" with words—the trials of the saints (lxix. 12, Lam. iii. 14, 63; Job xxx. 9), and (b) a "smiting" of foes—the triumphs of the saints (iii. 7, etc.).

This is the first psalm in which "Selah" occurs and its threefold use is well illustrated; (a) Lively Contrast—the enemy falsehood of (2) and the established fact of (3); (b) Logical Consequence—the comfort (5–6) following the cry (4), peace the answer to the prayer; (c) Literary Connection—between Pss. iii. and iv. (8).

In the superscript "Psalm" may be rendered "melody" and so throughout the five books.

PROPHETIC ANTICIPATION.—Some of David's experiences are in measure anticipatory of Messiah's. In this connection it is interesting to note that the company with David passed over by the same path as our Lord took to Gethsemane, 2 Sam. xv. 23, 30. We here see also the Spirit of Christ in the faithful Jewish remnant suffering oppression by the apostate majority of the nation, especially in the last days when the usurping Antichrist is temporarily in power. Refer to Analysis, Book I. In Pss. i. and ii. we saw the Lord's Anointed and His kingdom threatened from without; in iii. and iv. we see them threatened from within.

PERSONAL APPLICATION.—In Pss. iii. to vii. we get the attitude and experiences of faithful ones amid failures and trials. There are many precious lessons for the people of God in these days. "When the waves of trial rise, the soul is driven up higher upon its Rock of Refuge." Our past experiences of divine deliverances afford us ground for confidence in the present and hope regarding the future.

Human plots are powerless to frustrate God's purposes. Whatever men may say God never forsakes His own (2, 4). Calmness in the face of danger is a practical proof of faith. Distressed saints should be able, not only to lay themselves down, but to sleep (5). "One with God is a majority." David was as peaceful and secure on the open plain as he was in his own palace.

VERSE NOTES.

1. "mine adversaries," lit. "they that distress me"—"increased," cf. 2 Sam. xv. 12–13—"Many (or, multitudes) are rising up. . . . Many (or multitudes). . . ." cf. 2 Sam. xviii. 31–32. See 6.

2. A thought possibly expressed by Shimei, 2 Sam. xvi. 5, 8—"soul," emphatic for the man's self, a freq. expression in the Psalms—"help" (or, salvation, 8) primarily in a physical sense.

3. No partial defence—"shield," cf. Gen. xv. 1; Deut. xxxiii. 29—"glory," for it was from God that David derived his royal dignity and honour.

4. Heb. impf. tense often denotes repeated action or habit, so here—"whenever I call . . . He answereth"—"holy hill," i.e. Zion, seat of the Ark, viewed as the centre from which God exercised His earthly sovereignty, cf. 2 Sam. xv. 31.

5. Present experience also justifies confidence. "I" (emph.), i.e. even I notwithstanding my present circumstances. His sleep was not that of exhaustion, but of possessed peace—"sustaineth," s.H.w., xxxvii. 17b, 24b; cxlv. 14 ("upholdeth"), ctr. xxvii. 2b.

6. "I will not," cf. xxvii. 3—"ten thousands," (lit. myriads) see 1–2. "That have set . . ." 2 Sam. xvii. 1–2.

7. "Arise," cf. opening words of Israel's ancient marching song, Num. x. 35. "For . . ." past experience the basis for present appeal. A buffet on the cheek was the height of insult against a beaten foe; it showed that all spirit and power for resistance were gone, 1 Kings xxii. 24—"broken the teeth" i.e. the ungodly portrayed as fierce wild beasts rushing upon their prey, but suddenly deprived of all power to harm.

8. "salvation" in the Psalms denotes deliverance generally, but "as revelation grows it becomes of deeper significance until it gains an inexhaustible fulness of spiritual meaning in the New Testament." (8b). The welfare of his people is more to David than his own personal safety; he intercedes on behalf of the rebels, cf. Luke xxiii. 34. The whole nation is still Jehovah's people, though in revolt against His anointed.

PSALM IV.   PILLOWED IN PEACE

I. ENTREATY (1). Addressed to God.
II. EXPOSTULATION (2–3). Addressed to Rebels.
    1. Concerning their Attack upon David (2). **Selah.**
    2. Concerning the Anointed of Jehovah (3).

III. EXHORTATION (4–5). Addressed to Rebels.
    1. Concerning their Attack upon David (4). Selah.
    2. Concerning their Attitude to Jehovah (5).

IV. ENTREATY (6–8). Addressed to God.
    1. Patronage Entreated (6).
    2. Portion Enjoyed (7).
    3. Peace Experienced (8).

SUPERSCRIPT.—A psalm of David.

SUBSCRIPT.—For the Chief Musician; upon Nehiloth.

PRIMARY ASSOCIATION.—An evening psalm. See corresponding notes to Ps. iii. The structure of both psalms is similar, namely, four stanzas of two verses each, and "Selah" omitted at the end of each third stanza. The "Selah" at the end of Ps. iii. marks a further point of connection between the two psalms, for it indicates the same historical setting.

"Nehiloth" (in subscript) is generally taken to mean "wind instruments," but ancient versions suggest vocalisation "nehaloth" = inheritances. It seems therefore better to read here "concerning inheritances." This suits the tenor of the psalm, which emphasises God our portion (7). Two inheritances are spoken of, (a) Jehovah's in His people, Deut. xxxii. 9, and (b) their inheritance in Jehovah, Ps. xvi. 5, etc. Spiritual inheritances are more precious than temporal ones, cf. Heb. x. 34 (R.V.). The rebels sought to drive David out of his possessions; they might succeed so far as material ones were concerned, but they could never separate him from God. See also Analysis, Ps. iii., section II.

PROPHETIC ANTICIPATION.—Belongs to same prophetic period as Ps. iii. National apostasy is not yet consummated; there is yet time for repentance. The Spirit of Messiah in the remnant speaking as in the midst of their enemies.

PERSONAL APPLICATION.—Some advance in experience shown; in iii., God is the saint's protection; in iv., God is the saint's portion. What He does for us (iii.); what He is to us (iv.). When you feel "hemmed in" God will "make room" (lit.) for you (1). Man ever seeks what he loves (2). Rebels should reflect and repent (4). "It is better to trust Jehovah to remedy national evils, than to start a revolution" (5). "One beam of sunshine from God's face dispels all gloom" (6). Peace may be independent of outward circumstances (7-8). Heavenly joys are better than earthly joys (7). Material prosperity cannot compensate for spiritual poverty (7). Commune with conscience on your couch (4).

VERSE NOTES

1. (a) cf. 3 and iii. 4. Confident of the integrity of his heart and justice of his cause, David calls upon God for vindication; (b) i.e. "made room" for him when he was in a "strait," still another instance of past experience as a ground of present appeal; (c) better as margin.

2. A remonstrance with the leaders in the rebellion—"glory," i.e. his personal honour and royal dignity as Jehovah's representative. 2b. Rebellion is (a) vain: because doomed to failure, cf. ii. 1; (b) false: bec. based upon false principles—it never fulfils the promise it gives.

3. "him . . . godly;" cf. margin. Hebrew word denotes one whom God has "graced" (favoured) and whose character conforms, i.e. is "gracious" to others.

4. "Stand in awe," or, tremble. In Eph. iv. 26 the line is quoted from LXX. The words here are a warning to the rebels generally; "be still," i.e. desist.

5. "Offer . . . righteousness," ctr. hypocritical sacrifices of the rebels, 2 Sam. xv. 12; cf. Deut. xxxiii. 19; Ps. li. 19.

6. "Many say," cf. iii. 2; indic. the attitude of the waverers. With last clause cf. Num. vi. 24-26; Pss. xxxi. 16; lxxx. 3, 7, 19.

7. Ponder these words in light of David's experiences at the time, 2 Sam. xvii. 27-29. Joy in Jehovah is more than the joy of harvest or vintage.

8. Cf. iii. 5 notes. "For Thou . . ." may mean "It is Thou, Jehovah, who makest me dwell apart in security," i.e. isolated from his foes in God's safe keeping. He claims God as his sole protector.

PSALM V.   MORNING MEDITATION

I. APPEAL. REQUEST FOR AUDIENCE (1-3).

II. ARGUMENT. REASONS FOR CONFIDENCE (4-7). "For."
    1. Jehovah's Repugnance to the Wicked (4-6).
    2. Jehovah's Reception of the Worshipper (7). Loving-kindness shown.

III. APPEAL. REQUEST FOR GUIDANCE (8).

IV. ARGUMENT. REASONS FOR CONCERN (9).
    David's Risks among the "Watchers."

V. APPEAL. REQUEST FOR VENGEANCE (10ac).

VI. ARGUMENT. REASONS FOR CONFIDENCE (10d-12).
    1. The Wicked have rebelled against Jehovah (10d).
    2. The Worshippers shall rejoice in Jehovah (11-12). Favour shown.

SUPERSCRIPT.—A psalm of David.

SUBSCRIPT.—For the Chief Musician, upon Neginoth; relating to the Sheminith.

PRIMARY ASSOCIATION.—This psalm is ascribed to David and it almost certainly belongs to the period of Absalom's rebellion, but rather later than the preceding psalm. There the psalmist pleads *with* the rebels; here he pleads *against* them because they remain unrepentant despite his loving appeals. The time for repentance having passed, nothing can follow but righteous judgment. A morning hymn. On Hebrew word "Neginoth", see Ps. iii. notes. "Sheminith," = eighth or octave, *i.e.* bass—the male choir.

PROPHETIC ANTICIPATION.—Looks forward to the days of the faithful Jewish remnant upon the eve of the outpouring of God's judgment against the apostate nation and their Gentile abettors, guilty of the persecution of the true people of God.

PERSONAL APPLICATION.—Note the strong contrast between the ungodly and the godly in their talk and walk. David started the day with prayer and meditation; do we? Pray as you meditate, and meditate as you pray. "An infant has no language but a cry, but it is enough for a mother and for God (2). A look may say more than words." When we have prayed, do we "watch" for the answer? An "ordered" prayer does not mean a formal prayer, nor does it indicate a hurried extempore one. Our thinking builds our character, see Prov. xxiii. 7; Phil. iv. 8. Do we really pray to God like David (2), or with ourselves like the Pharisee (Luke xviii. 11)? David prayed (*a*) early, (*b*) audibly, (*c*) thoughtfully, (*d*) earnestly, (*e*) orderly, (*f*) expectantly, and (*g*) reverently (7). His was a definite request—for guidance. The holiness of God necessitates the judgment of evil. They can truly rejoice, who can take refuge in the Lord. Whoso takes refuge in Him soon learns to love His name.

VERSE NOTES

1. Not only our words, but our thoughts should be acceptable to God, xix. 14.

2. "cry" Heb. word used specially of a call for help; "King . . . God," cf. lxxxiv. 3. King David acknowledges Jehovah as his Sovereign Overlord.

3. "in the morning" repeated for emphasis; "order" = arrange; note suggestive use of the word, Gen. xxii. 9; Lev. i. 7–8; Exod. xl. 4, 23, etc., and cf. Ps. cxli. 2; "keep watch," *i.e.* for the answer, cf. Hab. ii. 1; Micah. vii. 7, marg. 4–5. Cf. the ideal of the King's court, Ps. ci.

4. "God" = El, Mighty One. Note significant use of the title here. Power without goodness is the heathen conception of deity. Not so is our God, Who is both mighty and good. (*b*) rather as margin. Divine holiness is a consuming fire which the wicked cannot endure, xxx. God cannot entertain as privileged guests,

entitled to protection according to the laws of oriental hospitality, such as are here classed as evil, 5–6; cf. David's prayer, 2 Sam. xv. 31, and God's answer, xvii. 14–23.

5–6. Note classes of evildoers mentioned.

5. "arrogant," or "boasters;" "stand . . ." *i.e.* no place for them in the presence of God, cf. Absalom and his lying promises, 2 Sam. xv. 3–5.

6. "speak lies," lit. "actors of a lie;" (*b*) lit. "men of bloodshed and deceit," *i.e.* those who do not shrink from murder and that by treachery; cf. Ahithophel's character, 2 Sam. xvii. 1–4.

7. "But *I* . . ." (emph.); "multitude," ctr. the "multitude" (10); "fear," *i.e.* true reverence; "worship" = primarily to prostrate oneself—the oriental attitude of reverence or supplication; then, signifies the corresponding attitude of heart. David worships facing the sanctuary, outward symbol of Jehovah's presence among His people. Against the Davidic authorship of this and similar psalms, critics have urged the use of the words "House of God" and "Temple." But the argument does not stand for the former term is used of the Tabernacle, Exod. xxiii. 19; xxxiv. 26, etc.: also of the Tent pitched by David for the Ark on Mt. Zion, 2 Sam. xii. 20. The Heb. word for temple is applied to the Sanctuary at Shiloh (1 Sam. i. 9; iii. 3) and doubtless remained in use for the Ark-Tent. Note close juxtaposition of the words in Ps. xxvii. 4–6. By the use of the inspired terms in these passages, the Holy Spirit thus makes them fit into the prophetic programme yet to be fulfilled in the experiences of the remnant.

8. "in Thy . . ." *i.e.* because Thou art righteous; "enemies" = an unusual word, see marg., or "them that watch me;" "plain" Heb. = both "level and straight."

9. "no faithfulness," cf. marg. (*b*) cf. marg.; "throat" here regarded as an organ of speech. Smooth words cover deadly designs.

10. Cf. 2 Sam. xv. 37; "thrust them out (or down)"; cf. xxxvi. 12; "rebelled," = revolt against the king (God's anointed) is rebellion against God Himself.

11. Render "So shall all them that take refuge in Thee rejoice,
They shall ever shout for joy while Thou protectest them,
And they that love Thy name exult in Thee."   (Kirkpatrick).

"name" stands for God's revealed character.

12. "shield" = buckler, *i.e.* a large shield protecting the whole body and usually double the size of the ordinary shield.

PSALM VI.   SOLACE FOR THE SICK

I. ARDENT APPEAL (1–5). "O Jehovah," Five times.

1. For the Shewing of Mercy (1–3).
2. For the Sparing of Life (4–5).

II. ACUTE ANGUISH (6–7).

1. Weariness (6*a*).
2. Weeping (6*b*). (Inverted Parallelism.)
3. Wasting (7).

III. ASSURED ANSWER (8–10). "Jehovah," Three times.
    1. Persecutors Admonished (8).
    2. Prayer Accepted (9).
    3. Persecutors Ashamed (10).

SUPERSCRIPT.—A psalm of David.

PRIMARY ASSOCIATION.—Date cannot be fixed with any certainty, but probably belongs to the period between David's sin with Bathsheba and Absalom's rebellion. Note the writer's three-fold distress; he was suffering: (a) the Scourge of Dangerous Illness; (b) the Sense of Divine Displeasure; and (c) the Scoffs of Delighted Foes. There is no explicit confession of sin as in xxxviii., which opens with similar words. Suffering and misfortune were popularly regarded as evidences of commensurate guilt on the part of the sufferer (vide Book of Job), hence when the godly suffered he became an object of scorn to the ungodly; see Ps. xxx. which appears to be a corresponding thanksgiving. Our present psalm is first of the "penitential" psalms so called from early Christian times. The others are Pss. xxxii., xxxviii., li., cii., cxxx., and cxliii.

PROPHETIC ANTICIPATION.—Here we get the soul exercise of the suffering Jewish remnant in the last days. Naturally clinging to their covenant privileges, they must be brought to realise that they can expect nothing but the covenant curse. Nothing is left to plead but the mercy of God (4). In this they are upon common ground with the despised Gentile. While the assurance comes that the prayer is heard, there is as yet no entering into the full joy that comes from the knowledge that their sins are put away through the atoning work of Messiah. This comes out in later psalms. Our Lord's appropriation of 3a (cf. John xii. 27) and 8a (cf. Matt. vii. 23) warrants us in regarding the psalm, at least in part, as Messianic, but we must ever remember that our Lord's sufferings at the hand of God were entirely vicarious and only as identifying Himself fully with His sinful people; see Gal. iii. 13.

PERSONAL APPLICATION.—The displeasure of God against sin is revealed (Rom. i. 18) equally with the fact of His love for sinners (Rom. v. 8). One truth must not be over-emphasised to the detriment of the other. Those who augment the sufferings of saints under discipline shall suffer shame. In the experience of God's saints, the sun always breaks out after the showers. Do we often thank God that we live in the Christian age with the glory light of Christ's resurrection dispelling the uncertainties and gloom of the departed state? See 2 Tim. i. 10.

VERSE NOTES

1. Emphasis is upon "Not in anger neither . . . in . . . displeasure," *i.e.* "do not deal with me beyond the requirements of love's discipline."

2. Br. "Be gracious unto me," cf. iv. 2; "bones" prob. synecdoche for his whole body.

3. He was suffering in mind as well as in body, "vexed," = dismayed; "How long" = fig. aposiopesis.

4. "Return" for he feels as if God had forsaken him (4*b*). Plea based upon Jehovah's declaration concerning Himself, Exod. xxxiv. 7–8.

5. A further plea. God would lose rather than gain by his death. Translate, "...no commemoration (or, memorial) of Thee, *i.e.* in the "unclothed" state there *is* remembrance, but no memorial of God's praise before those still living in the body. Hezekiah alludes to this psalm, Isa. xxxviii. 18–19. For Christians enjoying the light of New Testament revelation, it is hardly possible to realise what the life-long slavery to the fear of death (Heb. ii. 15) meant to the faithful Israelite, and the bold struggles of his faith to break the fetters." With him to die was not gain, but real loss (ctr. Phil. i. 21). The Old Testament saints were granted but a very partial revelation of the state after death. They viewed it as a condition in which they were cut off from the blessings which to God's people were the token of His favour. "Sheol" = Gk. *Hades*, = abode of the spirits of the dead.

6. Br. "every night," as R.V.

7. The appearance of the eyes is a sure indication of the state of one's mental and bodily health; "adversaries"=them that distress me, cf. iii. 1; iv. 1; vii. 4, 6.

8. The shadow now passes from the soul of the psalmist.

9. Note the repeated assertion of faith and in 10, the reasonable assurance concerning foes.

10. "vexed" = dismayed, cf. 2–3. The assailants shall suffer what they caused him to suffer—a just retribution.

PSALM VII.   A SORELY SLANDERED SAINT

   I. APPEAL FOR DELIVERANCE (1–2). Prayer.

       1. Expression of Confidence (1*a*).
       2. Entreaty for Rescue (1*b*).
       3. Extremity of Need (2).

   II. ASSERTION OF INNOCENCE (3–5). The Slandered. Protestation. Selah.

   III. ASSIZE OF JEHOVAH (6–13). The Judge.

       1. Application for Justice (6–8).
       2. Anticipation of Succour (9–10).
       3. Administration of Justice (11–13).

IV. ARREST OF WICKEDNESS (14-16). The Slanderer. Punishment.
  1. Plot devised 14.
  2. Pit dug (15a).
  3. Plotter discomfited (15b-16).
V. ASCRIPTION OF PRAISE (17). Praise.
SUPERSCRIPT.—Shiggaion of David, which he sang unto Jehovah, on account of the words of Cush, a Benjamite.
SUBSCRIPT.—For the Chief Musician; upon Gittith.

PRIMARY ASSOCIATION.—Writer and circumstances are stated in the title. "Shiggaion," Heb. occurs only here and plural in Hab. iii. 1; most probably derived from a Heb. verb generally translated "to roar," and means to cry out, *e.g.* in trouble or danger or pain, also as a challenge and in triumph or joy; here, a loud cry of distress to Jehovah his Refuge and Rescuer. Cush (="black" or "sunburnt") not mentioned in the historical record, but was probably a close adherent as well as a fellow-tribesman of Saul, and prominent among those who made slanderous insinuations against David (1 Sam. xxii. 8), further inflaming Saul's already irritated mind. Of such men David complains (1 Sam. xxiv. 9; xxvi. 19). Some think the name "Cush" is a symbolic one referring to Saul himself, whose character was morally "black" (his father's name was Kish). At any rate he was the chief offender by listening to the calumnies against David, and acting thereon. The psalm, then, belongs to the period when David was hunted from place to place by Saul who sought his life. "Gittith," *i.e.* winepresses; cf. subscript to Pss. lxxxi. and lxxxiv. These psalms were for use at the autumn Festival of Ingathering, or Tabernacles, which took place at the close of the vintage, the last harvest of the year. It may also have been sung as a chant by those who trod the grapes at the winepresses. This is a psalm of judgment; cf. Rev. xix. 15; Isa. lxiii. 3.

PROPHETIC ANTICIPATION.—A "remnant" psalm pointing on to the time when a *darker* power will have risen up against God and His people, even Antichrist, oppressor of the faithful few. We hear the utterance of the remnant that shall be. The Spirit of Christ has again anticipated the need and provided words easily appropriated to express the feelings of the sufferers, especially during the days of the Great Tribulation.

PERSONAL APPLICATION.—Shows how we should conduct ourselves under unjust accusations or when attacked by the malice and envy of others. The righteous should leave their defence in the hands of God (1 Peter iv. 19). Those who invoke judgment must themselves submit to judgment, for God is no partial Judge. God has His arrows as well as the wicked (xi. 2) and the wicked one (Eph. vi. 16). Against sin, holiness can only manifest itself as anger. Wickedness works to its own woe, unrighteousness to its own undoing. Do we sigh for the end of all wickedness on the earth? (v. 9); this corresponds to the pattern prayer (Matt. vi. 10). "Gittith"—sorrow and suffering are like the trodden grape-clusters, fruitful in producing the wine of holy joy.

VERSE NOTES

1. Br. "In Thee (emph.) have I taken refuge"; (b) see 1 Sam. xxiii. 28; xxiv. 14; xxvi. 18; they sought his life, 1 Sam. xx. 1, 31; xxiii. 15, etc; "deliver" = rescue.

2. The chief persecutor here specified; "my soul"=a Heb term generally indicating the person himself considered as a living entity.

3. Refers to the crime of which he was falsely accused; for the calumny, see 1 Sam. xxiv. 9, 11; xxvi. 19; for protestation of innocence, cf. language, 1 Sam. xx. 1; xxiv. 10–11; xxvi. 18, 23–24; "iniquity" = wrong, what is crooked and distorted, not same Heb. word as in 14.

4b. His conduct had been the very reverse of that which was attributed to him, 1 Sam. xxiv. 4 ff.; xxvi. 8 ff. ctr. Saul's spirit, 1 Sam. xxiii. 21 with 2 Sam. ii. 5; David's Ps. xxxv. 12–13.

5. David invokes a violent death by an enemy hand if he be guilty. "Selah" connects the crisis with the cry.

6. i.e. it might seem as if God were an indifferent spectator of His people's plight, or as if He were a negligent sentinel asleep at His post, yet the psalmist knew it was not really so ; cxxi. 3-4.

7. A judgment scene. David prays that a general summons be issued to all the peoples to attend the tribunal; (b) as R.V., but a change in vowel points (which did not appear in the earlier text) makes the sense "over it (the assembly) take Thy seat on high," cf. ix. 4, 7. Language of this verse suits the prophetic programme of the last days.

8. The Judge having taken His seat the assize opens and the psalmist comes forward with his plea, "Do me justice." He claims a decision based upon his conscious innocence of the charge of treachery brought against him ; cf. 1 Sam. xxiv. 10-11 ; xxvi. 23. See App. VIII.

9. David recognizes that his own case is but a part of the great cause of right against wrong. First line is an aspiration, "Oh, that the evil of wicked men might come to an end and that Thou wouldest establish the righteous"; (b) argument, or ground upon which the hope is based, "For a trier of hearts and reins is God the righteous"; "heart" in Old Testament regarded as organ of thought and will; "reins," (kidneys) as seat of emotions.

10. (a) i.e. it rests with God to defend him (11a); "God" = Elohim; (b) "God" = El, Mighty One.

12-13. God described under fig. of a warrior armed with sword and bow as executor of vengeance upon the wicked. (13) Br. "Yea, at him hath he aimed deadly missiles, making His arrow fiery." (Kirkpatrick). God's arrows are His lightnings, xviii. 14; Zech. ix. 14; perhaps an allusion to the fire-darts of ancient warfare—arrows with inflammable material attached, lighted and discharged into a besieged city to set it on fire.

14-16. The punishment of the wicked here, viewed from a different angle, namely that which inevitably follows as result of his own action. It is remarkable to find that Saul was smitten by the arrows of the very Philistines by whom he had hoped to destroy David, and by his own sword, 1 Sam. xviii. 17-21 with xxxi. 3-4. David instead of being killed by the Philistines was actually saved by them, 1 Sam. xxvii. 1-3.

15. Kirkpatrick renders "He hath dug a pit and delved it deep, and is fallen into the ditch he was making"; fig. used is that of pitfalls such as are made by hunters of wild animals.

16. Evil recoils upon the head of the evil-doer; 1 Sam. xxv. 39.

17. Closing Doxology; an acknowledgment of righteousness manifested in judging the wicked. Note title, Jehovah Elyon, suited to One who is Supreme Governor of the World.

Book One. I. Revelation of the Divine Ruler, i.–viii.

3. The Ruler, viii. Son of Man.

PSALM VIII. THE CROWN OF CREATION

I. ASCRIPTION OF PRAISE (1-2).

    1. The Invocation (1).
    2. The Inspiration (2).

II. MAN'S COMPARATIVE FRAILTY (3-4). His Insignificance.
    In Relation to the Heavens.

III. MAN'S CONFERRED DIGNITY (5). His Eminence.

    1. Made lower than Heavenly Beings.
    2. Set highest of Earthly Creatures.

IV. MAN'S CONSTITUTED AUTHORITY (6-8). His Influence.
    In Relation to the Earth.

V. ASCRIPTION OF PRAISE (9).

SUPERSCRIPT.—A Psalm of David.

SUBSCRIPT.—"For the Chief Musician; concerning the Death of the Champion (= Muth-labben)."

PRIMARY ASSOCIATION.—David is the writer and the circumstances seem to connect themselves with the victory over Goliath, in which the despised shepherd boy overcomes the mighty Philistine, cf. 2 with 1 Sam. xvii. 14, typical of a mightier victory when David's Son and Lord conquered our great adversary. The victory of the Cross will issue in the blessed results set forth in this psalm. Instead of being lifted up with pride at his achievement, David, in a spirit of true humility, ascribes all the glory to Jehovah. He sees in the circumstances an exemplification of the truth that God has chosen the weak things of the world to confound the mighty. He is then led on to the more general theme of the dignity and destiny of man in the original purpose of God—the marvel of God's choice of man to be a revelation of Himself and to be His representative on earth. As a reflection of God's glory, nature is indeed wonderful, but man is more wonderful still.

PROPHETIC ANTICIPATION.—In Ps. ii., Messiah is seen as King of Israel (cf. John i. 49); in viii. He is seen as Son of Man (cf. John i. 51) in which character His rule is more extensive, in fact universal (John v. 27; Heb. ii. 4-6; Eph. i. 10; 1 Cor. xv. 27-28; 45-47; see also Ps. lxxii.). Adam, first representative of the human race, failed to maintain the eminent place given him by the Creator. By his sin, he lost for mankind the lordship of creation. The purpose of God, however, is not thereby frustrated, for Christ, the Second Man and Last Adam (1 Cor. xv. 45), in resurrection becomes representative of a "new race" and, because of His perfect obedience even unto the death of the Cross, receives the highest and fullest honours designed for man. In Him, man regains more than ever Adam lost; cf. the millennial consummation, Isa. xi. 1-9; Rom. viii. 16-23.

PERSONAL APPLICATION.—Here are the mystery and the mastery of man. David begins (1) and ends (9) with the glory of God; do we? The mystery of man is greater than the mystery of the skies. The spiritual ever transcends the material. Mindfulness is more than mere memory (4). The Eternal has enemies. The Almighty has adversaries, those who oppose His purpose and question His providence. The "overcomer" will share world rule with the Lord Jesus (Rev. ii. 26-27). Even "children" may be the Creator's chosen champions. Children confounded the carping critics in our Lord's days (Matt. xxi. 16). His witnesses are mostly the "weak" ones of the world. Christ is the only complete answer to the question, "What is man?"

VERSE NOTES

1. Cf. 9: exclamation of reverent wonder; lit. "Jehovah our Adonai" (Sovereign Lord). Jehovah manifest in Christ the Son of Man; "excellent" = majestic; "Thy name," *i.e.* Thy character as expressed in the works of creation and providence; "above," or "upon the heavens," *i.e.* God has clothed them with a glory which manifests His own. Connect this line with verse 2, marking the contrast between God's revelation of Himself in the glory of the heavens and his revelation of Himself in the feeblest representatives of humanity. Connection of the two verses as such must still be preserved.

2. "children (infants) . . . founded strength . . . adversaries . . . to quell the . . ." First line quoted Matt. xxi. 16 (from the LXX.) which foreshadows the subjects of the Kingdom and their praises, Matt. xviii. 3; "avenger" = one who usurps in his own interests a judgment function belonging to God alone, Deut. xxxii. 35; Nah. i. 2.

3. No mention of the sun suggests that David is contemplating the skies by night as doubtless he often did in his shepherd days; "fingers," God is viewed under the fig. of a clever handicraftsman.

4. (*a*) "man" = Heb. enosh = frail man, see App. x ; (*b*) "man" = Heb. adam; "visitest" refers to the Creator's constant care for His creatures ; 4-6 quoted Heb. ii. 6 ff.

5. Note difference between A.V. and R.V. Former follows the LXX., etc. Heb. = elohim (see App. II, 6). The language here significant in its very ambiguity. God has come down (in Christ) to be lower than God yet ever remains God—a striking paradox (cf. Phil. ii.); see Gen. i. 26-27; "glory and honour (majesty)" are attributes of God Himself, Ps. cxlv. 5, 12; and of His royal representatives on earth, Ps. xxi. 5; xlv. 3.

6. "dominion," cf. Gen. i. 26, 28; see 1 Cor. xv. 27. Such dominion given only to (*a*) Adam with his consort Eve, and (*b*) to Christ and His consort the Church. After the Fall rule was granted to Noah over the beasts of the field (Gen. ix. 2); to Nebuchadnezzar over men, beasts and birds (Dan. ii. 38), but to Messiah the rule is extended to all things, including the fish, etc., *i.e.* universal rule, see Matt. xvii. 27.

7. (*a*) Domestic animals; (*b*) wild animals.

9. This closing exclamation of reverent wonder repeated for emphasis (1).

Book One. II. Response of the Despised Remnant, ix.–xv.

1. The Theme Epitomised. Existence of the Eternal and the Enemy, ix.–x.

PSALM IX.   JEHOVAH IS JUDGE

I. INTENTION OF THE PSALMIST. PRAISE TO JEHOVAH (1-2). Personal.

II. INTERVENTION OF JEHOVAH (3–6). Reason for Praise.
  1. Execution of Judgment (3–4). Just Inquisition.
  2. Extirpation of the Wicked (5–6). Godless for ever forgotten.

III. INTIMATION BY THE PSALMIST. MANIFESTATION OF JEHOVAH'S PRESENCE (7–12).
  1. Expectation. Messiah's Righteous Rule (7–8).
  2. Explanation. Saints' Certain Confidence (9–10).
    (a) Spoken of Jehovah.
    (b) Spoken to Jehovah.
  3. Exhortation. Messiah's Praising People (11–12).

IV. IMPLORATION BY THE PSALMIST. PRAYER TO JEHOVAH (13–14). Personal.
  1. Petition (13).
  2. Plea (14).

V. INTERVENTION OF JEHOVAH (15–18). Reason for Praise (14).
  1. Execution of Judgment (15–16). Just Retribution.
  2. Extirpation of the Wicked (17–18). Godly never forgotten.

VI. INVOCATION BY THE PSALMIST. MANIFESTATION OF JEHOVAH'S POWER (19–20). Selah.

SUPERSCRIPT.—A psalm of David.

PRIMARY ASSOCIATION.—Pss. ix. and x. are closely related. In some ancient versions they are found as one. Note the absence of a title to Ps. x. and the incidence of "Selah" at the end of ix. (similar to Pss. iii.–iv.). The psalms are united by an irregular alphabetical acrostic running through both, ix. ending the first half of the Hebrew alphabet, while x. with a significant omission of certain letters, completes it. There is a similarity in the language used, but a marked difference in tone corresponding to the two parts of the one theme exhibited. A key phrase appears in both, "in times of trouble" (ix. 9 and x. 1) and is found nowhere else. David is undoubtedly the writer of both psalms, but the occasion is fixed with less certainty. Ps. ix. probably celebrates his general victories recorded, *e.g.* 2 Sam. viii., while Ps. x. seems to refer rather to the nation's domestic troubles. It must be remembered that during his reign, David had great difficulty in controlling his powerful nobles (2 Sam. iii. 39; xv. 2 ff.), and the contest with Ishbosheth left a legacy of disorder (1 Sam. xxii. 1–2; 2 Sam. iii. 1, 22; iv. 2). Ps. ix. views the enemy without, Ps. x. the enemy within the nation. David sees the age-long conflict between righteousness and evil waged in two fields; first, between the people of God and the Gentiles (ix.), then between the ungodly oppressors within the nation and their godly victims (x.). PROPHETIC ANTICIPATION.—Pss. ix. and x. both belong prophetically to the great crisis in the history of Israel and the world, when evil shall have reached its climax in the manifestation of the Man of Sin. This culminating point will be immediately followed by an open demonstration of divine control in the coming of Jehovah-Jesus as rescuer of Israel and ruler of the world. There will be a grand renewal for both. The "times of trouble" referred to is the period of "Jacob's trouble" (Jer. xxx. 7), the Great Tribulation. We see here a beautiful confirmation of divine inspiration of the Scriptures in the very irregularity of the structure, which has so puzzled the critics and many devout commentators. There is no "unsolved literary problem" as they assert. Alphabetical structure symbolises governmental order which is here broken by a gap of *six* letters near the beginning of Ps. x. in the very section that gives a description of the Man of Sin. This broken order agrees with the "troubled times." The number "6" is the number of man (see Rev. xiii. 18). It falls short of divine completion "7" and is the culminating point of evil yet limited by God. As soon as Jehovah comes into the psalmist's view again at x. 12, the alphabetical order is resumed. Moreover the Hebrew letter *daleth*, fourth in the alphabet and standing for the number "4," is the symbol of world order and is significantly dropped from the alphabetical arrangement in Ps. ix., leaving just ten letters ("10" is the symbol of man's responsibility and recompense).

PERSONAL APPLICATION.—The four-fold "Thou hast" of God's providence should be followed by the four-fold "I will" of our praise, 1–2. Thanksgiving should be whole-hearted not half-hearted, and with the heart and not merely the lips, 1. To the saints of God it is both a duty and a delight to tell out· the wonderful works of God, 1. Who has such cause for joy as the child of God? 1–2, 14*c*; cf. Ps. v. 2 and Phil. iv. 4. Do we daily realise the truth of 7*a*? The "face" (presence) of Jehovah brings peace to His people, but panic to His enemies. Other kingdoms rise and fall, but Jehovah's Kingdom, like Himself, abides for ever, 7. His rule will be true service, His throne an ever-accessible court of appeal, 8–9. The saints are safe in their "high tower" the while sinners sink in their own pit, 9 with

15. Faith generally precedes knowledge; knowledge generally precedes trust, 10. Knowing the Name leads to loving the Name, 10. People forget God, but God does not forget His people, nor does He forsake them, 10, 12, 18. Those who trust will soon testify, 10–11. Pondering the providence of God promotes praise and prayer, 11–14. The sinner is snared and slain by his own sin, 15. Mighty peoples are but mortal men, 20.

VERSE NOTES

1–4. Show close connection with Ps. vii., closing words of which here expanded.

2. "Most High" = Elyon; Jehovah's millennial title.

3. "Because . . . (and) stumble . . ." graphic picture of a fleeing and frightened foe.

4. Br. "Thou didst take Thy seat on the throne . . ."

5. (b) Cf. language at Deut. ix. 14; xxv. 19; Exod. xvii. 14.

6. Br. "The enemy . . . (his) desolations are come to a perpetual end, and cities—Thou didst uproot—The very remembrance of them (i.e. the enemy) is perished."

7. "But the Lord sitteth enthroned for ever," in strong contrast to the enemy (6).

8. "He" emph. His administration is both upright and universal; "peoples" Heb. = races; "uprightness," or equity; cf. Acts xvii. 31.

9. A good uplift for the downtrodden; "trouble," Heb. indicates extremity of need, destitution or dearth.

11. "Sing praises," lit. psalm, or make melody; "dwelleth," The cherubim overshadowing the Ark formed the throne of the shekinah (glory), the earthly counterpart of heaven; cf. viii. 1; xcix. 1; "people," margin correct; "doings," i.e. mighty works in delivering Israel.

12. Br. "hath remembered . . . hath not forgotten"; "poor" = meek, or afflicted. Jehovah is the "Goel" = the Avenger of blood.

13. Br. "Be gracious unto me." Faith has viewed the future as revealed in the prophetic word and now supplicates in the actual circumstances.

14. "in the gates," in the East the place of common concourse and business, hence here = with the greatest publicity; implied contrast with 13b is obvious; "daughter of Zion," a poetic personification of the city of Jerusalem itself; "salvation," for Israel this will be both physical and spiritual.

15. cf. vii. 15.

16. (b) Br. "Snaring the wicked one in . . ." "Higgaion" = meditation; "Selah," see Introduction V. It here points the connection between the fate of Antichrist and that of his followers; cf. Rev. xix. 19–21.

17. "Sheol" ref. still to judgment as far as this world is concerned and not eternal judgment (Rev. xx.) when Sheol (Hades) must deliver up its dead (i.e. the spirits of the departed wicked) to final judgment. For the wicked death as the legal penalty of sin shuts them out of the millennial kingdom, for only the Lord's own will be raised prior to its establishment. The judgment of the great white throne takes place after the thousand years and will shut the wicked out of the

new heavens and new earth for ever. The doom of those that forget God is that of being cast into the outer darkness during the earth's joyous day under the rule of the Prince of Peace; the A.V. gives the true sense.

18. "alway" = perpetually; "poor," *i.e.* afflicted, see 12.

19. "man" = Heb. enosh *i.e.* frail man; "prevail," = wax strong.

20. *i.e.* by some awe-inspiring exhibition of power such as in Egypt; "men," Heb. enosh = frail men.

PSALM X.   THE WAYS OF THE WICKED

I. INTERROGATION. The Psalmist Expostulates (1). Jehovah.

II. IMPUTATION. The Psalmist Exposes (2-11). The Lawless One.
  1. Accusation of Pride and Recklessness (2-6).
      (i) Oppression of the Meek (2-3).
      (ii) Glorification of Self (4-5).
      (iii) Occasion of Pride (6). Vain Thoughts.
  2. Accusation of Perfidy and Ruthlessness (7-11).
      (i) Deception in his Words (7).
      (ii) Description of his Wiles (8-10).
      (iii) Occasion of his Perfidy (11). Vain Thoughts.

III. INVOCATION The Psalmist Entreats (12-18). Jehovah.
  1. Petition for Remembrance (12).
  2. Parenthesis. The Wicked One (13).
  3. Anticipation of Response (14).
  4. Petition for Recompense (15).
  5. Parenthesis. The Anointed One (16).
  6. Anticipation of Response (17-18).

SUBSCRIPT.—For the Chief Musician.

Primary Association.—See Notes to Ps. ix.

Prophetic Anticipation.—See Notes to Ps. ix.

Personal Application.—God is never an indifferent or indolent spectator of His people's sufferings, 1. Faith and appearances often conflict, but true faith ever sees the invisible, 1. Few indeed are the saints who have never cried to God during trial, "Why—Why," 1. Countenance often corresponds to character, 4. He who defies God and derides man is a wicked (lit. lawless) one, 5. "I shall not be moved" may be the language of folly (6) or of faith, 8. Man without God becomes like a wild beast, 8-10, see Dan. iv. 24-25, 33; of the World Powers, Dan. vii.; of the Man of Sin and Antichrist, Rev. xiii. 1, 2. Folly judges by appearances, while faith triumphs over appearances, 4. In his own proper time, and only then, God takes matters in hand, 14. The helpless saint "abandons" (so lit.) himself to God Who never abandons him, 14, with ix. 10. The time comes when God must interpose in judgment; further patience would be no longer forbearance but weakness. That Jehovah is King for ever and ever (16) is a fact that brings comfort to the saints, but may well cause consternation to sinners. Faith realises and enjoys what is yet to be, 17–18. This psalm presents perils of the pilgrim.

VERSE NOTES

1. God is said to be "far off" when He remains apparently indifferent to the distress of His people. Conversely He is said to be "near" when He manifests His power on their behalf; (b) lit. "Why mufflest Thou?"—as if God covered His eyes from seeing and His ears from hearing, cf. Pss. lv. 1; Isa. i. 15; Lam. iii. 56. The preceding psalm, ix. 9, had declared God to be a stronghold in just such seasons.

2. The cause of the cry; (b) br. "They (the poor) are being taken in the plots, that they (the wicked) have devised."

3. "wicked (= lawless) one boasteth . . ." i.e. of having his own way; (b) or, "And in his rapacity renounceth . . ."

4. "The lawless in his disdain (saith), 'He will not make requisition;'" "thoughts," = lit. plots, s.H.w. (2); see xiv. 1; liii. 1.

5. His plans appear to succeed; cf. lxxiii. 3-5. The possibility of divine retribution does not enter his calculations; "puffeth at," i.e. by open gestures expresses contempt for them ; colloquially, he pooh, pooh's them. Compare another contemptuous gesture, "sniff," Mal. 1. 13.

6. Contrast the arrogance of the godless with the assurance of the godly, xvi. 8.

7. "deceit," lit. deceits; "oppression" abetted by fraud. lxx. quoted Rom. iii. 14; (b) i.e. wickedness is thoroughly to his taste, he rolls it under his tongue like a delicious morsel; Job xx. 12.

8-10. A threefold description of the wicked one; (a) as a lawless bandit; (b) as a lurking lion; (c) as a luring hunter.

8. "lurking places" = in ambush; "helpless," = wretched or unfortunate, an obscure Hebrew word peculiar to this psalm, 10, 14.

9a. ". . . the poor, dragging him off in his net."

11a. "God," = El (Mighty One). Experience seems to confirm his assumption in 4; ctr. the faith of the saints, ix. 12, 18.

12. "Arise," cf. iii. 7; vii. 6; ix. 19; "God" = El; "lift . . . hand" = attitude of action; (b) and so disprove the calumny of the wicked, 11; see ix. 12.

13. "wicked" = lawless one, significantly mentioned six times in these two psalms, viz. ix. 5, 16; x. 3, 4, 13, 15.

14. "Thou hast seen," whatever the wicked may think (11); "spite," = misery, or vexation; (c) is an appeal to experience; "orphan" mentioned as a typical example of one friendless and helpless; cf. Exod. xxii. 2 ff.; Mal. iii. 5.

15. Paralysing thus his power for mischief; "seek out" = require, s.H.w., 4, 13, and ix. 12. Evil will be exterminated from the Messiah's Kingdom, Matt. xiii. 41.

16. May be allusion to 2 Sam. iv. 6–7, and to the expulsion of the Philistines, mentioned, 1 Sam. xxxi. 7. The Canaanites were never wholly exterminated from the land till David's day; "his land," cf. Lev. xxv. 23; Joel ii. 18.

17. "heard" as well as "seen," 14; "desire of the meek," ctr. the desire of the wicked, 3; (b) or, "Thou confirmest . . . causest . . ."

18. (b) i.e. in defying God and destroying men; "man" = enosh (frail man).

Book One. II. Response of the Despised Remnant, ix.–xv.

2. The Theme Expanded. Experiences of the Evil and the Enemy, xi.–xv.

PSALM XI.   THE TRIUMPH OF TRUST

I. CONFESSION. THE FEARLESSNESS OF FAITH (1–3). Jehovah the Refuge of the Righteous.

   1. Answer of the Psalmist (1). To the Advice of the Friends.
   2. Advice of the Friends (2–3). Violence of the Wicked manifested.

II. CONFIDENCE. THE FOUNDATION OF FAITH (4–6). A Further Answer.

   1. Authority of Jehovah. His Sovereignty (4a).
   2. Administration of Justice. Its Equity (4b–6). Violence of the Wicked punished.

III. CONCLUSION. THE FRUIT OF FAITH (7). Jehovah the Rewarder of the Righteous.

   1. Attribute of Righteousness (7a).
   2. Approval of Righteousness (7b).

SUPERSCRIPT.—David's.

SUBSCRIPT.—For the Chief Musician; relating to the Sheminith.

PRIMARY ASSOCIATION.—Written by David almost certainly during the period of his life spent at the court of Saul. There he became in imminent danger of his life, but because he held a position of responsibility, he felt he could not abandon his post without clear guidance from God. Notwithstanding the earnest advice of fainthearted friends and conscious of his rectitude, he resolves to face the danger assured that God would protect him. The time for flight did come later. On subscript, see Ps. v. note; cf. 1 Chron. xv. 21.

PROPHETIC ANTICIPATION.—In the history of the godly Jewish remnant of the future belongs to that period known as the first half of Daniel's seventieth "week." The usurper, Antichrist, is upon the throne, but the Great Tribulation has not yet broken out (midst of the week); the time for the godly ones to flee is not yet, (Matt. xxiv. 15 ff.).

PERSONAL APPLICATION.—If the saint of God has taken refuge in the Lord, why should he try to seek an asylum elsewhere, 1. The well-meant advice of our friends is not always in line with the will of God, 1-4. The sorely-tried saint can flee for refuge to God while still remaining at his post of duty, 1. When the foundations of the state and of society seem to be crumbling, the people of God take refuge in Him, 3-4. The godly are "God-like" in loving righteousness (7) and hating evil, 5. The eyes of faith are upon the unseen Protector in the heavens rather than on the unseen foes in the dark, 2. The righteous (a) have taken refuge in God—past; (b) now endure testing,—present; (c) shall behold His face,—prospect, 1, 5, 7. Fellowship here leads on to the fellowship hereafter, 7.

VERSE NOTES

1. Br. "In Jehovah have I taken refuge," cf. vii. 1; "my soul," i.e. emph. for "me"; "as a bird," graphic picture of those in persecution, who have no resource but in flight; "mountain," i.e. hill country, which with its caves was a natural place of retreat for fugitives.

2-3. Fainthearted friends urge their reasons for the advice.

3. "foundations," i.e. the fundamental principles of law and order, which were being subverted.

4. "eyelids," these are contracted when one wishes to examine an object closely.

5. The form of the Heb. word indicates "trieth (and approveth) the righteous," and (b) (trieth and) hateth (i.e. rejecteth) the wicked (= lawless one); "His soul hateth," i.e. God's essential nature is antagonistic to evil; cf. Isa. i. 14.

6. The fate of Sodom is the typical example of judgment upon gross and defiant sin; with Ezek. xxxviii. 22 cf. Luke xvii. 28-30, 32; "snares," bec. the judgment will take the wicked unawares; "brimstone," Heb. word may cover any kind of mineral pitch or oil, and possibly sulphur as well. Sir Wm. Dawson has shown that the instrument of divine judgment upon Sodom and the cities of the plain was almost certainly a bitumen or petroleum eruption, when burning showers of ignited gas and oil rained down upon the doomed cities. The valley of the Dead Sea is known to be a rich oil district. This valley may have been in view when David wrote the psalm.

7. "righteousness," i.e. righteous acts. The ungodly are destroyed, but the upright are admitted to Jehovah's presence, cf. Rev. xxii. 4.

PSALM XII.   PRAYER AND PROMISE

I. APPEAL TO JEHOVAH.   A PRAYER FOR HELP (1-2).
1. The Petition of the Psalmist (1a). Because of the prevailing corruption.
2. The Provocation by the Wicked (1b-2).

II. AFFIRMATION BY DAVID. PUNISHMENT OF THE WICKED (3-4).
Their mendacious words quoted.

III. ANSWER FROM JEHOVAH. A PROMISE OF HELP (5).
His veracious words quoted.

IV. ASSURANCE OF DAVID. PROTECTION OF THE RIGHTEOUS (6-8).
1. The Perfection of the Word (6).
2. The Preservation of the Righteous (7-8). In spite of the prevailing corruption.

SUPERSCRIPT.—A psalm of David.

SUBSCRIPT.—For the Chief Musician.

PRIMARY ASSOCIATION.—Writer is David: time, probably while he was at Saul's court or during his outlaw life. Prophecy and psalmody meet in this psalm, for we hear the writer addressing God and God answering through the writer. Note, three voices heard, (a) the psalmist's, (b) the oppressors', and (c) the Lord's.

PROPHETIC ANTICIPATION.—Belongs to the same period as the previous psalm. If, as we believe, all true believers are caught away (1 Thess. iv.) immediately preceding the commencement of Daniel's seventieth "week" then particular point is given to the complaint of the psalmist-prophet recorded in first and following verses. How truly will this psalm express the feelings of the godly Jewish remnant at that time.

PERSONAL APPLICATION.—Note that in 1-4, man is spoken of, in 5-8, God. Their words are strongly contrasted. Men's words are the weapons of the wicked; Jehovah's words are the safety of the saint. The words of the wicked are worthless, the words of Jehovah are weighty. The words of the wicked manifest vanity (2), flattery (2), duplicity (2) and audacity (3). The words of the Lord are pure (6), proved (2), and preserved (7). The devil uses words to ensnare and slay men; the Lord uses words (the gospel) to enlighten and save men. Remember that our words, too, are powerful for good or for evil. Three great mistakes made by the wicked in their statements (4) namely, (*a*) their tongue shall *not* prevail; (*b*) their lips are *not* their own; (*c*) they are *not* their own masters (Rom. vi. 16). Even God's people need to remember that their tongues, their lips and themselves altogether belong to Another. The foolish attitude of the men of to-day is, "The untrue is true because we pronounce it true," 3–4. The Word of God is true currency, the best medium of exchange in all human dealings.

VERSE NOTES

1. Br. "Save, Jehovah, for . . ." note connection with 5*c*; "godly," see note on iv. 3; "ceaseth . . . fail"; graciousness and trustworthiness seem to have quite disappeared; a calamity for any country.

2. cf. 1 Sam. xxiv. 9. Hypocrisy and duplicity are universal; cf. 2 Tim. iii.; "vanity" or, falsehood; their words are hollow and unreal; (*b*) their lips and heart are neither consistent nor constant, ctr. the men of Zebulon, 1 Chron. xii. 33; see Prov. xxvi. 24 ff.

3. Or, "May Jehovah . . ."

4. "Who is lord," *i.e.* they deceive themselves into thinking that no one can call them to account for all the falsehoods by which they seek to attain their evil ends.

3–4. See James iii. 1–12.

5. "For . . . for," br. "because of . . . because of . . ."; the moment for action has at last come; here is the answer to iii. 7 and vii. 6; (*c*) see x. 5 note.

6. In Jehovah's words, no dross, no alloy of falsehood or flattery, ctr. words of men, 2–4; (*b*) omit "as,"; silver is the emblem of purity and preciousness, cxix. 40; "seven times purified," *i.e.* again and again until no trace of dross is left; seven is the number of completeness and perfection.

7. Br. "Thou (emph.) Jehovah wilt preserve them," *i.e.* the poor and needy of 5; "Thou wilt guard him . . ." *i.e.* each one of the sufferers is singled out as the object of divine care; "this generation," from denoting people of some particular age, the expression comes to indicate a *class* of persons in a good or bad sense; this usage is frequent in Scripture, *e.g.* Matt. xvii. 17.

8. When vile men are raised to positions of authority, the wicked swagger everywhere unabashed and unrestrained. This will be truer still of the last days; see xi. 3.

PSALM XIII. SINGING SUCCEEDS SIGHING

I. THE PLAINT. EXPOSTULATION AT APPARENT DELAY (1–2).
"Me . . . My enemy." *David Sighs.*

II. THE PRAYER. ENTREATY IN ACUTE DISTRESS (3-4).
"Me . . . My enemy." *David Supplicates.*

III. THE PRAISE. EXULTATION IN ANTICIPATED DELIVERANCE
(5-6).
"Thou (Jehovah) . . . Me." *David Sings.*

SUPERSCRIPT.—A psalm of David.

SUBSCRIPT.—For the Chief Musician.

PRIMARY ASSOCIATION.—Expresses David's emotions when he had
been for some time a hunted fugitive from Saul's presence. His
powers of endurance are almost spent; he feels that unless God comes
speedily to his deliverance, he must succumb, and his enemies will
then triumph, see 1 Sam. xxvii. 1. One powerful and relentless
enemy is singled out above the rest of his adversaries; cf. 1 Sam.
xviii. 29.

PROPHETIC ANTICIPATION.—A "remnant" psalm belonging to
the period of Daniel's seventieth "week." Saul, the king of Israel's
own choice, is again seen as a type of the coming Antichrist,
accepted by the mass of the apostate nation, but oppressor of the
godly remnant; cf. 1 Sam. viii. 4-9, 19-22; xii. 13; with John v.
43, etc.

PERSONAL APPLICATION.—The whole psalm expresses the common
experience of saints in distress passing out of the shadow into the
sunshine. Convert complaint into prayer and confidence will come.
"How long?" indicates not hopeless despair but heart-agonising
desire, 1-2. God's seeming delays are designed to test the reality of
our faith, 1-2. Protracted prayers are not proportionately powerful.
Brevity is born of urgency, 3. David's prayer was precise and con-
cise, 3. Enlightened eyes are those that have looked upon the glory
of His face, 3; they cannot but reflect the Light, cf. Pss. iv. 6; xxxi. 16;
xxxvi. 9. Every believer should be deeply concerned lest the enemy
sin should triumph over him, 4. The shadow passes, but the sun
abides, 5-6. Faith relies upon God's loving-kindness (grace) and
rejoices in His salvation, 5-6. Faith turns weights into wings, 5-6.
As we pray, hope is rekindled and faith revived, 5-6. Note the close
relations between the psalmist and his Saviour expressed in the
pronouns of each line, 5-6. Every believer can surely join with
David, 6.

VERSE NOTES

1. See Isa. xlix. 15 ; liv. 8 and Mark iv. 38.

2. *i.e.* devising one plan after another, but all in vain ; "mine enemy," for the phrase, see 1 Sam. xxiv. 4 ; xxvi. 8 ; "exalted," *i.e.* in authority and having the upper hand. David has Saul in mind.

3. Br. "Behold, answer me," instead of hiding Thy face and forgetting my need; "lighten mine eyes," *i.e.* the eyes are an index of vital energy; see note on vi. 7 and cf. 1 Sam. xiv. 24–29; Ezra ix. 8. David desired restoration of declining strength and drooping spirits. Remember the spiritual application.

4. *i.e.* and thus Thine own honour will suffer.

5. Br. "But as for me, in Thy loving kindness do I trust." (*b*) or, "Let my heart rejoice . . . let me sing;" "rejoice" = exult. Faith at last triumphs over fears.

PSALM XIV.   THE RUINED RACE

I. HUMAN CORRUPTION (1–3).

    1. Sweeping Accusation (1).

    2. Divine Inspection (2).

    3. Solemn Conclusion (3).

II. HEARTLESS OPPRESSION (4–6).

    1. Strong Expostulation (4).

    2. Divine Interposition (5).

    3. Scornful Denunciation (6).

III. HOLY ASPIRATION (7).

    1. Sublime Manifestation.

    2. Divine Restoration.

    3. Sanctified Exultation.

SUPERSCRIPT.—David's.

PRIMARY ASSOCIATION.—The writer is David; the historical occasion is not so clear, but the mention of Zion and of the "captivity" seems to suggest that it belongs to the period between the taking of the stronghold of Jebus (1 Chron. xi.) and the bringing back of the Ark from its captivity, the event referred to, 7 (1 Chron. xv.–xvi.). For this sense of "captivity" cf. Judges xviii. 6; 1 Sam. iv. 10–11; vii. 14, and Ps. lxxviii. 60–61. The "restoration" began with the return of the Ark to Beth-shemesh and Kirjath-jearim, but was not completed until it was brought to Zion with great rejoicings, 1 Sam. vi.–vii. 2; 1 Chron. xiii. 1–3; xv. 25; 2 Sam. vi. 12–14; cf. Ps. liii. David probably altered Ps. xiv. to make it more suited to the public service of the sanctuary; see title and subscript to liii.

PROPHETIC ANTICIPATION.—Here we find the oppressed remnant of the last days encouraging themselves in the remembrance of divine deliverances in the past history of the nation. They also express their intense longing for the manifestation of the Messiah as their Salvation. The universal corruption of those days accompanied by a practical denial of God will parallel that of the antediluvians. The ambiguous term for "captivity" seems designed by the Spirit of God to cover not only past events but future circumstances. The greatest of all "fools" is the person referred to in 2 Thess. ii. 4.

PERSONAL APPLICATION.— Universal corruption follows the denial of God. He also is an "atheist" who, while not denying the existence of God, yet denies Him a place in the ordering of his life, cf. Luke xii. 16–20. The "fool" has many followers, 1a with 1b. Man is astray from God and become "abominable," 3. Prayerlessness is practical atheism, 4c. Where there is no God, there can be no good, 1, 3. God desires men to "understand" and "seek Him," 2. Character is reflected in conduct. Do we long for the coming of Christ, 7? God can soon put His fear into the heart of the self-confident atheist, 5.

VERSE NOTES

1-3. Quoted Rom. ii. 10–12 in proof of the universal depravity of man; supplemented by further quotations from other Old Testament passages; "fool," Heb. "nabal" denotes moral perversity rather than mere ignorance or weakness of reason; s.H.w. Isa. xxxii. 5–6 (A.V. = vile person—villany). Nabal seems to have been just such a man, 1 Sam. xxv. 25 (R.V. m.); 36–38; note repeated "my" 1 Sam. xxv. 11; Luke xii. 17–18.

"said in his heart," i.e. deliberate conclusion, the basis of his conduct; "no God" (cf. x. 4), not mere theoretical denial of God's existence, but a practical disbelief in His moral government; see Jer. v. 12; Zeph. i. 12; Rom. i. 28 ff.

1. (c) Br. "They corrupted their doings, they made them abominable, there was none doing good"; cf. Gen. vi. 5, 11–12. Ref. no doubt primarily to antediluvians.

2. Cf. Gen. xi. 5; xviii. 21; fig. anthropopatheia (see App. III); br. "that did seek God"; witness of conscience and of creation both rejected.

3. "All were turned aside, together had they become tainted"; "filthy"; this word, which in a material sense is applied to a state of putrefaction, is here used in a moral sense, s.H.w. Job xv. 16 ; note positive and negative aspects.

4-6. Man's corruption exemplified in the oppression of God's people.

4. "Were not all . . . made to know?" i.e. taught by sharp experience to know

their error. Verse 5 is the answer; cf. Judges viii. 16 where "taught" lit. "made to know."

(b) i.e. they live by devouring God's people; ref. is to oppressors of Israel from Egyptians (Exod. i.–x.) down to the Philistines (1 Sam. vii. 2–3); (c) "call not . . ." cf. Exod. v. 2.

5. God's intervention in the overthrow of the Egyptians was repeated many times in the history of Israel. David may also have in mind, 1 Sam. vii. 10; see Exod. xiv. 24–25.

6. David taunts the enemy, "You would have frustrated if possible the counsels of the afflicted, but . . ."

7. "bring back . . . captivity" Heb. idiom for "restore prosperity," see Job xlii. 10, but also used in sense given, see note under "Primary Association." (c) or, "Let Jacob rejoice and Israel be glad." The early rejoicing of Israel in connection with the return of the Ark to Beth-shemish, etc. was short-lived. 1 Sam. vii. 2 with vi. 13 ; more complete 1 Chron. xv. 25-28. Prophetically points to the out-gathering from the nations of the *diaspora* (the scattered of Israel) and their return to Palestine under the righteous rule of Christ, their acknowledged king.

PSALM XV.   FITNESS FOR FELLOWSHIP

I. FERVENT APPEAL. A PRAYER IMPLIED (1).

II. FITTING ANSWER. A PATTERN INDICATED (2–5a).
   1. Positive Aspect (2).
   2. Negative Aspect (3).
   3. Positive Aspect (4).
   4. Negative Aspect (5b).

III. FINAL ASSURANCE. A PROMISE IMPARTED (5b).

SUPERSCRIPT.—A psalm of David.

PRIMARY ASSOCIATION.—Composed by David and probably in connection with the Ark's translation to Zion, 2 Sam. vi. 12–19. Psalm is closely connected with xxiv.

PROPHETIC ANTICIPATION.—A "remnant" psalm in which the godly Jews of the last days are instructed as to the character befitting the citizens of Messiah's metropolis, when He shall be manifested and shall dwell in their midst.

PERSONAL APPLICATION.—Much for the Christian to ponder here; although the ground is Jewish, moral principles are unchanging. Here is a standard for the saints. If God be among the generation of the righteous (Ps. xiv.) then their character must be conformed to His requirements of holiness. Ps. xiv. shows the natural man; Ps.

xv. the spiritual man; Ps. xiv. God with His people; Ps. xv. God's people with Him. To be a citizen of Zion is a high privilege, to be a citizen of heaven is higher still, Eph. ii. 19; Phil. iii. 20; Heb. xii. 22–24. Those among whom Jehovah dwells must be a holy people. 1 Peter i. 15–16; Heb. xii. 14, 28–29. Fellowship with God and the fruits of the Spirit go together. Righteousness has a negative aspect as well as a positive: it not only consists in what one does, but what one does not do, 3 and 3a. Grace alone makes one a guest of God but a guest is bound by the laws of hospitality no less than the host: while security is recognised, sincerity is required. Note walk, works and words in 2. Holiness is exhibited not by emotion, but by character; it affects feet, hands, heart (2), tongue, ears (3) and eyes (4).

VERSE NOTES

1. "Tabernacle," *i.e.* tent. R.V. m. refers here to the Tent which David pitched for the Ark on Mt. Zion; "sojourn," or "be guest," Heb. usually denotes a temporary stay, but not necessarily so, as is seen from the parallel in next line and other passages. In Eastern lands the guest enjoys the protection of his host as well as entertainment. The Jews were prone to assume that God's presence among them was a guarantee of their security, forgetting that it demanded holiness on their part, Micah iii. 11; "hill," *i.e.* Zion.

2. "in his heart," br. "with his heart," *i.e.* he is not double-hearted, xii. 2.

3. "friend," br. "fellow"; (c) *i.e.* he does not make the faults and failings of others an object of his ridicule or sarcasm.

4. His estimate of men shows the essential truthfulness of his character. (c) "Though he hath sworn to his own hurt he changeth not," see Num. xxx. 2.

5. "reward," *i.e.* "a bribe." This verse exposes two of the commonest and worst offences against justice, Isa. xxxiii. 15. Both have always been a curse in the East.

(c) Not only shall he dwell in the presence of Jehovah, but he shall enjoy an unshaken position of blessing, iv. 8.

Book One. III. Record of the Divine Redeemer, xvi.–xli.

1. The Redeemer. Source of Salvation, xvi.–xxiv.

PSALM XVI. THE PATH OF THE PERFECT PILGRIM

I. THE PSALMIST'S PRACTICE (1–7). Expression of Messiah's Faith.
   1. The Prayer of Faith (1). For Preservation. Petition and Plea.
   2. The Profession of Faith (2).

    3. The Partnership of Faith (3). The Saints.
    4. The Pledge of Faith (4). The Apostates.
    5. The Provision of Faith (5a).
    6. The Possessions of Faith (5b–6).
    7. The Praise of Faith (7). For Instruction.

II. THE PSALMIST'S PROSPECT (8–11). Expression of Messiah's Hope.
    1. The Purpose of Heart (8a). Messiah's Life summarised (8).
    2. The Presence of Power (8b).
    3. The Pervasion of Joy (9a). Messiah's Death implied (9).
    4. The Preservation from Death (9–10).
    5. The Pathway of Life (11a). Messiah's Resurrection indicated (10).
    6. The Perfection of Bliss (11b).
    7. The Permanence of Pleasures (11c). Messiah's Ascension signified (11).

SUPERSCRIPT.—Michtam of David.

PRIMARY ASSOCIATION.—Written by David (Acts ii. 25 ff.) during his exile period. Verses 4–6 have considerable significance in light of the circumstances mentioned, e.g. 1 Sam. xxvi. 19 (R.V. m.). Driven from his material inheritance he claims Jehovah Himself as his true portion and he strongly repudiates any suggestion of serving another god, a temptation with which he was doubtless faced when among the Philistines and other idolaters. The prophetic character, especially of the latter part of the psalm, does not exclude the primary reference to David's own faith and hope, but we must carefully distinguish between the faint and incomplete shadows of the psalmist's experiences and the complete fulfilment of the prophecy in the experiences of the Son of God. This psalm is closely related to the next. On "Michtam" see Introduction V.

PROPHETIC ANTICIPATION.—For the Messianic message, see analysis and verse notes. The psalm is cited by both Peter and Paul as referring to our Lord Jesus Christ. They quote the LXX version. See Acts ii. 25–28; xiii. 35. Note Messiah's (a) prayer, 1; (b) place, 2–3; (c) pledge, 4; (d) portion, 5–6; (e) praise, 7; (f) path, 8–9; (g) prospect, 10–11.

PERSONAL APPLICATION.—A psalm of the satisfied soul. Ponder the pattern Pilgrim and press after Him. If the Saviour's delight is with His saints, ought we not to delight in one another? 3. Many professed Christians not only "mention" but pay honour to the names of the founders of certain heathen religions, men who are now worshipped as gods, 4. Let.Jehovah Himself be my joy, 5. Covetousness is just the craving of a heart unsatisfied with its portion. The desired thing then becomes a god; Col. iii. 5; Phil. iii. 19, where "the belly" = the seat of craving. Be in happy possession of the heavenly portion, 5–6, see Eph. i. 3. Daily counsel comes by (a) Direct message revealed by the accepted Word; (b) Discriminating judgment resulting from the assimilated Word, 7. Led by Jehovah and learning from Him, we shall not go astray, 7. Night is ordained of God, not for sleep alone, but as a season of quiet for meditation, 7. Note the "always," 8; for ourselves dare we change it to "sometimes"? The path of life (11) leads to the Source of life. The joy of heaven is to be with the Lord. The glorified One is the crucified One; we shall see Him as He is only to find Him just what He was. Note the pilgrim's (a) Preceptor, "Thou"; (b) Person, "me"; (e) Path; and (d) Prospect, "life" (11).

VERSE NOTES

1. "Preserve me, O El (Mighty One), for in Thee have I taken refuge," cf. vii. 1.

2. ff. A.V. to be preferred here. Messiah's absolute obedience before God would entitle Him to a place far different from the death of the cross. His "goodness" was for the saints, hence it was an obedience unto death, Phil. ii. 8; cf. Matt. xiii. 44. On the two verses note that Christ's life as man was a true life of faith, cf. Heb. ii. 13; xii. 2. He completed the whole course. The glory of His Godhead must not obscure for us the truth of His perfect Manhood. He is able to sympathise with us in every sinless human experience, Heb. iv. 15.

3. In grace Christ thus accounts His people; made saints by His calling (1 Cor. i. 2). He views also the time of perfect consummation, when the glory of His workmanship will be seen in them.

4. (b) cf. Isa. lxvi. 3; (c) "their names," i.e. of the false gods; see Exod. xxiii. 13; Hosea ii. 17; Zech. xiii. 2. The special sin of the legal dispensation, idolatry, is here denounced by Messiah. Idolatry was not unknown in the days of our Lord, esp. in "Galilee of the Gentiles" where so much of His life was spent; e.g. among the Herods and their many heathen courtiers, governors, soldiers, etc.

5. lit. "Jehovah is the measure of my portion (of food) and my cup," i.e. He is all I need to satisfy both hunger and thirst, John vi. 35. "Portion" is what belongs to a person, whether he enjoys it or not; "cup" indicates actual enjoyment. With our Lord, His portion and His joy were one—Jehovah was the measure of both; He had nothing beside, He wanted nothing beside; ctr. two evils, Jer. ii. 13. The Lord was a true Levite, Deut. x. 9 ; xviii. 1 ; Num. xviii. 20. Note that the inheritance, is a pleasant possession, and a permanent possession (6).

6. "lines" = portions of land measured by line and distributed by lot; language

here still figurative; (b) "Yea, fair (or, lovely) is (my) heritage to me"; see Eph. i. 18 and cf. above, verse 3.

7. Cf. xxxii. 8; lxxiii. 24; see 1 Sam. xxx. 7–8; xxiii. 2, 4, 6, 9; ctr. Saul, who by slaying the priests (1 Sam. xxii. 18–20) bereft himself of those through whom he might have consulted Jehovah, hence 1 Chron. x. 13; 1 Sam. xxviii. 6–7; (b) "Yea, that in the night seasons my reins (= inmost self) admonish (lit. bind) me," cf. Matt. v., where the Lord insists upon this secret life before God.

8. Here is "the practice of the presence of God," (b) "at my right hand," i.e. as advocate (cxix. 31) or champion (cx. 5 ; cxxi. 5). (b) "right hand,"

9. "heart," here = soul; "glory," = spirit; "flesh," = the body. Man is a tripartite being, 1 Thess. v. 23. The spirit is the highest part of man, and seat of the intelligence. It distinguishes him from the lower animals and links him with God Who is Spirit, cf. Gen. ii. 7; Job xxvii. 3; xxxiii. 4. The soul is both the life principle and the seat of the emotions, whereby spirit and body are linked. The body is the organism through which the soul expresses itself. It links man with the lower creation. The spirit makes man God-conscious; the soul makes him self-conscious; the body makes him world-conscious. Both soul and spirit are said to rejoice in God, see Luke i. 46–47; Ps. xxxv. 9; Isa. lxi. 10; Hab. iii. 18, and elsewhere. Our rejoicing is to be not only emotional (soulful) but spiritually intelligent. (b) "dwell in safety," or, rest secure; for the phrase cf. Deut. xxxiii. 12, 28; Jer. xxiii. 6; "corruption" sometimes=the pit, the grave. Of David, the passage primarily means preservation *from* death; of Christ it certainly means preservation *through* death, see citations in Acts.

10. "Holy One" = Godly, or Beloved One.

11. lit. "Thou wilt cause me to know . . ." cf. cxliii. 8. He who descended also ascended; (b) lit. "Fulness of joys—Thy presence," cf. Heb. xii. 2; (c) "right hand" = place of approbation; cf. close of next psalm where a similar promise is for the saints. Whatever special rewards are given, there will be approbation for all. The fruit of *our* work can never equal the fruit of our Lord's work, hence the common joys we shall share above will be the deepest. Note: (a) Pleasures of sin for the wicked, Heb. xi. 25 ; (b) Pleasures of this life for the worldly, Luke viii. 14 ; (c) Pleasures for evermore for the wise, Ps. xvi. 11.

PSALM XVII.   PRAYER FOR PROTECTION

I. INVOCATION (1–6).   "Attend, O Jehovah."

    1. Petition (1).
    2. Pleas (2–5).   (a) Equity of Jehovah (2).
                 (b) Integrity of the psalmist (3–5).
    3. Petition (6).   Confident Persuasion. "Thou wilt . . . "

II. INTERCESSION (7–12).   The Saviour and His Saints.   "them," (7); "us," (11).

    1. Prayer for His People (7–8). Deliverance desired.
    2. Plaint against His Persecutors (9–12). Doings described.

III. INVOCATION (13-15).   "Arise, O Jehovah."
   1. Petition (13).
   2. Pleas (14).   (a) Instrumentality of the Enemy.
                (b) Prosperity of the Enemy.
   3. Prospect (15).   Confident Persuasion. "I shall . . . "

SUPERSCRIPT.—A prayer of David.

SUBSCRIPT.—For the Chief Musician.

PRIMARY ASSOCIATION.—Historical occasion is the period of David's outlaw life; see *e.g.* 1 Sam. xxiii. 25-29. This "prayer" is one of the five psalms so entitled. Note many links with xvi. The two psalms, however, differ in tone, consequent upon the different circumstances. Ps. xvi. shows the danger in the background and the psalm "breathes a spirit of calm repose and joyous serenity"; in xvii. "the danger is pressing and help urgently needed."

PROPHETIC ANTICIPATION.—Belongs to the period of the persecuted Jewish remnant in the closing days of this age and with millennial days in immediate prospect. Messiah is seen as their Intercessor associating them with Himself. He makes appeal against the enemies of His people, based upon His own personal perfection.

PERSONAL APPLICATION.—Let there be no hypocrisy in my prayer, 1. Will all my ways bear the divine scrutiny? 3. Do I know by experience the preserving power of the Word of God? 4. The "reflection" in my eye will be a miniature of that upon which I gaze. As He looks into my eyes, does the Lord see a small likeness of Himself? 8. If the Perfect One needed the Word for His path down here, how much more do we need it? 4. The "works" of men are diametrically opposed to the Word of God, 4. Both the might and the mercy of God are manifested on behalf of those who take refuge in Him, 7. Divine power delivers from deadly peril, 7. Wicked men may be the instruments of discipline, 13-14, but their triumph is short, Job xx. 5. When the voices of the world are hushed in the night season, the truth makes itself more clearly heard, 3. Worldly men are satisfied to see themselves reflected in their sons; Christians will be satisfied to see God in the person of His Son, 14.

VERSE NOTES

2. "sentence" = judgment, *i.e.* vindicate the justice of my cause. (b) br. as R.V. m. His prayer is based upon the known character of God.

c

3. "proved" = tried. For the blessing of the quiet night season, cf. xvi. 7;
(*bc*) br. "Thou hast proved (refined, or assayed) me and findest no evil purpose
in me; my mouth doth not transgress."

4. "I have shunned the paths of the violent," *i.e.* avoided both their society
and their example; ctr. the path of life, xvi. 11; "violent," Heb. = one who breaks
through all restraint.

5. "paths," Heb. = beaten tracks such as made by wheeled traffic; "slipped,"
s.H.w. "moved," xvi. 8.

6. "I" (emph.); "God" = El (Mighty One).

7. (*a*) *i.e.* by some signal intervention of divine power; "trust" = "take refuge
in" xvi. 1.

8. (*a*) "keep" = preserve, s.H.w. xvi. 1 ; "apple" *i.e.* the part of the eye forming
the pupil, emblem of that which is tenderest and dearest, and therefore guarded
with jealous care; cf. Deut. xxxii. 10; Prov. vii. 2; Zech. ii. 8; word lit. = the
little man, that is, the reflection seen in the pupil. Heb. here adds "daughter," cf.
Lam. ii. 18.

(*b*) "Hide . . . wings," a favourite figure of speech with the psalmist, taken
from the care of the mother bird for her young, xxxvi. 7; lvii. 1; lxiii. 7; xci. 4;
in light of lxi. 4 may also be a reference to the wings of the cherubim which
patterned all the beautiful curtains and the veil of the tabernacle sanctuary. These
were to be seen by the ministering priests above and all around them, except the
way of entry to the Holy Place.

9. "deadly," *i.e:* they sought his life, 1 Sam. xxiv. 11.

10. or as R.V. m.; (*b*) cf. x. 2; xii. 3–5.

11–12. cf. x. 8–9.

12. "He," one adversary (Saul) is conspicuous for ferocity and craftiness.

13. "cast . . . " or, make him crouch (in abject submission).

13–14. A.V. on the whole here preferable.

14. Cf. New Testament language, Luke xvi. 8; Luke xx. 34–35; Phil. iii. 19,
R.V.; "whose portion," see R.V. m.; ctr. xvi. 5; "Thou fillest," cf. cvi. 15;
"children" = sons; in Eastern lands the great desire is to see the family
perpetuating its name; "rest of their substance," br. their superabundance.

15. Or as R.V. m., expressing the psalmist's aspiration in ctr. with that of the
"men of the world," cf. xvi. 11. (*b*) cf. Num. xii. 6–8; Exod. xxxiii. 18–23 for
the psalmist's desire (*i.e.* a waking sight and not a mere dream or vision). For
the christian application to the joyful hope, see John xiv. 9; 1 John iii. 2; Rev.
xxii. 4; see also of men in the old creation, 1 Cor. xi. 7, shadow of the ultimate
purpose of God for redeemed man. Christ is now the perfect expression of it.
Man is satisfied with sons, the believer with the Son.

PSALM XVIII.   A PERSONAL PRAISE

I. EXPRESSION OF DIVINE PRAISE (1–3). The Deliverer.

II. EXPERIENCE OF DIVINE POWER (4–19). The Deliverance.
    (Passive and Personal—"my enemy".)

   1. Strong Appeal (4–6). The Cause of the Storm.

2. Sudden Advent (7–15). The Coming of the Storm. *Divine Interposition.*
3. Satisfying Answer (16–19). The Consequence of the Storm.

III. EXAMPLE OF DIVINE PROCEDURE (20–24). (God's Reaction to Personal Integrity.)

IV. EXPLANATION OF DIVINE PRINCIPLES (25–26). (Central.)

V. EXAMPLE OF DIVINE PROCEDURE (27–31). (God's Reaction to Personal Trust.)

VI. EXPERIENCE OF DIVINE POWER (32–48). The Deliverance. (Active and National—"mine enemies".)
  1. Specific Acknowledgment (32–34). "It is God . . . "
  2. Surpassing Achievement (35–45). *Divine Invigoration.*
  3. Specific Acknowledgment (46–48). "It is God . . . "

VII. EXPRESSION OF DIVINE PRAISE (49, 50). The Deliverer.

SUPERSCRIPT.—(A psalm) of David the servant of Jehovah, who spake unto Jehovah the words of this song in the day that Jehovah delivered him out of the hand of all his enemies, and out of the hand of Saul; and he said:—

SUBSCRIPT.—For the Chief Musician.

PRIMARY ASSOCIATION.—This is the Thanksgiving Hymn of David, the Warrior King. Found also 2 Sam. xxii. Differences here due doubtless to revision by David himself in preparing the psalm for the chief musician for use in the public services. Belongs to the middle of his reign, when he was at the zenith of prosperity and power. David acknowledges that Jehovah alone has made him what he is. While the important qualifications of physical strength, martial courage and skilful generalship are recognised as gifts of God, yet he owns that victory is due to Jehovah's direct intervention; cf. 1 Sam. xvii. 37, 46. In the title David is styled "Jehovah's servant"; cf. Ps. xxxvi. title, and see 2 Sam. iii. 18; vii. 5, 8, etc. As a distinctive title it is used of only a few whom God chose for special service, or who were in a special relation to Himself, *e.g.* Moses, Joshua and Job, and notably of Christ. In using it of himself, David would seem to imply recognition of divine authority of his words as inspired. Note distinction between "enemies" and Saul, the latter a private foe, the former public foes. The personal enmity of Saul singles him out from the rest.

PROPHETIC ANTICIPATION.—Here we see God manifesting His power on behalf of Messiah in delivering Him out of death and exalting Him above all His foes.   As His people's representative Messiah associates them with Himself.   The psalm is connected particularly with Jewish hopes and promises.   As Son of Man exalted, Christ still maintains His place of dependence and loving service in carrying out all the will of God.

PERSONAL APPLICATION.—Let us recognise the reality of our Rock. Begin and end with praise like David.   God is both Defender and Deliverer, 2.   Be both a fugitive and a fighter, 2; cf. 1 Tim. vi. 11–12. Note: Appeal, 6; Assurance, 6; Answer, 7 ff.   Creation senses the slightest movement of its Creator, and there is an intimate relation between the natural realm and the spiritual, 7–15.

God delivers His persecuted saints from perilous straits into perfect security, 16–19.   Jehovah's character is unchangeable, but His attitude towards men necessarily changes according to their attitude to Him, 25–26.   Unswerving fidelity to God meets unswerving faithfulness in Him, 25–26.   Be pitiful, be "perfect," be pure and be not perverse, 25–26.   God's Way (30), Work (Deut. xxxii. 4) and Word (Ps. xix. 7) are all "perfect," i.e. both flawless and finished.   Equipment for victory, 32–36; Experience of victory, 37–42; Effect of victory, 45.   Where else is a Rock worthy of all our confidence, 31? God, whose way is perfect, makes perfect the way of His servants, 32. Remember that God Himself is often in *our* storms, 13.

VERSE NOTES

1. Br. "Fervently do I love Thee."   "This is one of the noblest utterances in the Old Testament."   In it the psalmist touches the highest peak of personal devotion.   Note multiplication of divine titles (1–2), nine in all.   Imagery derived from natural features very familiar to David.

2. "Rock," Heb. sela = a cleft rock, mountain crag or cliff, cf. *e.g.* 1 Sam. xxiii. 25-28 m.; implies height and inaccessibility; "fortress" or stronghold, see 1 Sam. xxiii. 29; "God" = El; br. "My Rock in whom I take refuge."   Here Rock = Heb. tsur; implies strength and immovability; first occurrence in the Psalter, but freq. used in Old Testament to express God's firmness and faithfulness.   Sela = security as a refuge; tsur = security as a resting-place; or, sheltering power and supporting power; "buckler," or shield (for defence); "horn . . ." (for attack) a fig. taken from the wild ox; "high tower," cf. ix. 9.

3. Br. "(Whensoever) I call upon Jehovah, the object of my praise, then am I saved."

4. "cords," or toils; (*b*) br. "torrents of ungodliness," Heb. belial = worthlessness, generally ref. to moral mischief, but sometimes to physical mischief; freq. of what is obstructive and destructive in attitude towards God and men.   Of Messiah we

must ever remember that sin was a positive horror to His holy nature in His daily contact with it. With 4, 5, cf. of David, 1 Sam. xx. 3.

5. Death and Sheol like hunters with noose and net.

6. "called . . . cried," Heb. = kept calling . . . kept crying out; "temple," cf. 16a; (d) br. as A.V. Between 6 and 7 prophetically is the interval of the present day of grace.

7ff. Outpouring of Jehovah's judicial wrath, accompanied by extraordinary natural phenomena; note graphic description. No record of such an event in David's life, but he may have experienced something similar to 1 Sam. vii. 10; prophetically, see Isa. xxix. 6; xxx. 27-33; Rev. xvi. 17-21. Wrath is that attitude of God's character that moves Him to righteous judgment.

8. Bold fig. suggested by the panting and snorting of an infuriated animal, cf. 15; (b) fire is a constant emblem of God's consuming wrath.

10. "cherub," cf. Ezk. i. etc. Cherubim are always connected with divine government and here with judicial action; (b) "Yea, he swooped," figure of speed and power.

11. In judgment God's power is displayed, but not His personality, for it is His "strange work," Isa. xxviii. 21. Here we see the side He presents to man in judgment, viz. darkness, though He Himself is Light.

12. Br. "From the brightness before Him there passed through His thick clouds hailstones . . ."

13. "Most High" = Elyon; omit line (c).

14. "arrows," i.e. the lightnings; "them" = the enemy; (b) Br. "yea, lightnings . . . discomfited," Heb. indic. sudden panic, e.g. 1 Sam. vii. 10; Exod. xiv. 24.

15. cf. Exod. xv. 8; Nah. i. 3-5; (d) cf. 8.

16. Br. "He reached forth from on high," cf. cxliv. 6-7; "drew me," Heb. verb elsewhere only Exod. ii. 10. As Moses was drawn out of the Nile waters to be Israel's deliverer, so Messiah out of death to be His people's Saviour.

17. Historically of Saul. 19b. cf. xxii. 8; xli. 11; cf. David, 2 Sam. xv. 26; of Messiah, Matt. iii. 17.

20-23. Of David this language is relative only, see 1 Kings xiv. 8; of Messiah language is absolute. In 21-22 note order, positive—negative—positive—negative.

23. "mine iniquity"; the ref. is not to indwelling sin; "from being perverse," gives the true sense.

25. "merciful" = gracious, or kind; see note at iv. 3.

26. "with the pure," i.e. one who purifies himself, cf. 1 John iii. 3; Matt. v. 8; "shew . . . froward," i.e. obstructive, frustrating. God must needs be at cross purposes with those who work contrary to His will, Lev. xxvi. 23-24; Job v. 12-13; e.g. history of Balaam.

27. "afflicted," or lowly, i.e. those who have learned humility in the school of suffering; (b) cf. Prov. vi. 17.

28. "wilt," br. "dost." (b) "Jehovah my God enlighteneth my darkness." A burning lamp is the emblem of continuance of life and prosperity, cf. 2 Sam. xxi. 17; of Christ ref. to the darkness of desertion on the cross.

29. Prob. reminiscence of 1 Sam. xxx.; (b) 2 Sam. v. 6-8; victory over all enemies and obstacles indicated.

30. "God" = El; "word," = promise; "tried" = no dross of uncertainty or insincerity, xii. 6; "shield," cf. 2; quot. Prov. xxx. 5.

31. "For who is a God save Jehovah," God = Eloah; Rock = tsur, as in 2.

32. "The God (El) . . . " cf. 39; (b) i.e. by removing all obstacles, cf. 2 Sam. vii. 9; viii. 6, etc.

33. (a) i.e. surefooted and swift; indispensable qualities in ancient warfare; (b) metaphor of the hind continued.

34. cf. cxliv. 1; (b) sign of unusual strength ; "brass" = bronze.

35. "gentleness" = meekness; but marg. gives the sense here.

36. "enlarged . . ." i.e. made a way for him, cf. 19.

37-38. Verbs best rendered as pasts not futures, 38, cf. Heb. i. 13.

40. Br. "Yea, mine enemies hast Thou made to . . . and as for them that hated me, I cut them off," i.e. they were put to flight and then destroyed.

41. (a) the cry of despair.

43. (a) ref. to rebellious Israel; (b) to recalcitrant nations; internal and external opposition respectively; of David, 2 Sam. viii.; of Messiah, Ps. ii. 8; (c) " . . . knew not did serve."

44. " . . . obeyed me . . . strangers came cringing unto me," margin gives the sense; see also lxvi. 3; lxxxi. 15.

45. " . . . faded . . . and came . . . their fastnesses," i.e. surrendered at discretion.

47. Render verbs in past tense; cf. 1 Sam. xxiv. 12; xxv. 29.

48. Br. "My deliverer (2) from . . . Yea, Thou didst set me on high from them that rose up against me; from the man of violence didst Thou rescue me"; (c) historically of Saul.

49. Cited Rom. xv. 9 in proof that Old Testament anticipated Gentile admission to the blessings of salvation; "sing praises" = lit. psalm, or make melody.

50. See 2 Sam. vii. 18-29; xxiii. 5; a grand anticipation to be fulfilled only in Messiah.

PSALM XIX.   WITNESS OF THE WORLDS AND THE WORD

I. THE MEANING OF THE SKIES (1-6).
"EL" the Creator-God.   His Grandeur.

1. The Power of the Witness (1-4).
2. The Path of the Sun (5-6). "in them," Heb. "bahem."

II. THE MESSAGE OF THE SCRIPTURES (7-11).
"JEHOVAH" the Covenant-God. His Grace.

1. The Power of the Word (7-10).
2. The Path of the Servant (11). "in them," Heb. "bahem."

III. THE MEDITATION OF THE SOUL (12-14). Response to the Witness of I and II.
"GOEL" the Kinsman-Redeemer. His Guarantee.

1. The Prayer of the Writer (12–14*b*).
2. The Profession of the Saint (14*c*).

SUPERSCRIPT.—A psalm of David.

SUBSCRIPT.—For the Chief Musician.

PRIMARY ASSOCIATION.—Occasion of this psalm is unknown. The shepherd king had studied the book of nature and the book of the Law, and the contemplation of both led to deep exercise of soul. It is interesting to note that many of the Heb. words used in the first six verses are ancient astronomical terms used elsewhere in Scripture in connection with the sun and the heavens.

PROPHETIC ANTICIPATION.—The great witnesses for God before the advent of Christ are seen pointing on to Him; cf. Heb. vi. 1 (A.V.m). The psalm begins with the Creator and ends with the Redeemer, the Sun of Righteousness who will arise with healing in His wings for Israel, Mal. iv. 2.

PERSONAL APPLICATION.—God has His testimony in the skies, the Scriptures and the soul. The witness of His works and of His Word are complementary not contrary, modern critics and scientists with their theories notwithstanding. "Jehovah" is seen seven times in the psalm. In the skies we trace the path of the sun, in the Scriptures the path of the Son. The sun is a type of the Son (*a*) Light—photic rays; (*b*) Love—thermic rays; (*c*) Life—actinic rays; absence of the sun spells darkness, desolation and death. Note the seven-fold service of the Scriptures to the soul, 7–11. There is grace to purge, to preserve and to perfect, 12–13. Note the appeal and the assurance (14). The words of the mouth should match the meditation of the heart. "My Rock" answers to I; "My Redeemer" answers to II. Resulting from the two-fold witness come consciousness of sin and cognizance of the Saviour, 12–14. God's Word is better than the best, 10. Sovereignty and service both combine in the Christ of God. Love for the Lord (xviii.) involves love for the Word (xix.).

VERSE NOTES

1. The words of both the Nicene Creed and the "Apostles' Creed" ascribe the work of creation to God the Father alone. Scripture does not, Col. i. 16; John i. 3; "declare," cf. Rom. i. 20.
2. Day and night; each has its own message.
4. "Their line,"—the measuring line marks out limits; see quotation from the LXX, Rom. x. 18. The witness of nature and the witness of the gospel are

both universal. The witness of the heavens is (*a*) Initiatory (1), not a complete revelation of God; (*b*) Incessant (2); (*c*) Inarticulate (3), yet real; (*d*) Inclusive (4), the whole world.

5. Two similes; (*a*) the bridegroom exquisite in his apparel and (*b*) the champion exultant in his ability. To us, Christ is both.

7. "law," see on i. 2; for the various synonyms, cf. Ps. cxix.; "wise," cf. 2 Tim. iii. 15; "simple," *i.e.* inexperienced.

8. "right," or equitable; "enlightening," and (10), cf. 1 Sam. xiv. 24–29.

9. "ordinances," *i.e.* judicial decisions or regulations.

10. "honeycomb," lit. as marg. *i.e.* the purest and sweetest honey. Here are riches to be coveted and a repast to be enjoyed Possession and Pleasure, (10), Protection and Profit, (11).

12–13. The ceremonial law provided atonement for sins of ignorance (error), Lev. iv., v.; Num. xv. 22 ff., but for presumptuous sins there was none, Num. xv. 30–31; Deut. xvii. 12–13. The rebellious sinner was cast upon the forgiving mercy of God alone.

13. "transgression," *i.e.* the deadly sin of rebellion or apostasy.

Psalms xx. and xxi. are a closely related pair. In structure and contents they are similar and both are liturgical, the former a prayer, the latter a praise. The former breathes the spirit of expectation, the latter of exultation.

PSALM XX.   BLESSING BEFORE BATTLE

I. ADDRESS TO THE KING (1–5).   Before Sacrifice.

II. ASSURANCE OF THE KING (6–8).   After Sacrifice.
1. Individual Confidence (6).   "I."
2. National Confidence (7–8).   "We."

III. APPEAL FOR THE KING (9).

SUPERSCRIPT.—A psalm of David.

SUBSCRIPT.—For the Chief Musician.

PRIMARY ASSOCIATION.—Writer is David; the occasion uncertain, but belongs probably to the period of his wars recorded 2 Sam. viii–x. Before going forth to meet the enemy, sacrifice is offered (cf. 1 Sam. vii. 9–10; xiii. 9–12) and the national cause committed to Jehovah. Verses 1–5 apparently were sung by the congregation, or their representatives the Levite singers. The king himself or the presiding priest or prophet speaks in 6–8, and the psalm concludes with a prayer by the congregation. In Pss. xx. and xxi. Israel's king is seen in his double character as representative of Jehovah and as a representative of Jehovah's people. Note that confidence is in God

Himself rather than in the proved skill, the personal strength and the past successes of the king.

PROPHETIC ANTICIPATION.—The Holy Spirit adopts and adapts the language of both psalms with prophetic purpose, hence fulfilment is found only in Christ. We see the faithful remnant associating themselves with their Messiah. Note the appeal of xx. 4 finds the answer in xxi. 2, *i.e.* resurrection, xxi. 4. The day of Messiah's "strait" is the day of His offering of Himself. He is now "set on high." In His deliverance is involved the salvation of *all* His people, though xx. 2 looks on to millennial days when Christ shall be "a priest upon His throne." After the order of Melchizedek, He is even now our Great High Priest exercising His office in the heavenly sphere of priesthood and in the seat of royal power of which the earthly sanctuary and the earthly Zion are the types, 2.

PERSONAL APPLICATION.—Devotionally, believers may regard 1-4 as a divine benediction and the remaining verses as our dutiful response. Let "the Name" be our watchword and .our ward, 5-7. Note: (*a*) Deliverance from foes through "the Name," 1; (*b*) Defiance of foes in "the Name," 5; and (*c*) Defence against foes by "the Name," 7. We are victors in Christ's victory, 5. "God save the king!" 1 Peter ii. 17, and "God save the King!" Matt. xxv. 34.

VERSE NOTES

1. "God of Jacob," Who promised everything to one having nothing and deserving nothing. Title practically = God of all grace; cf. Gen. xxxv. 3.

2. "strengthen" = uphold, s.H.w., xviii. 35.

3. "offerings," see marg. The meal offering always accompanied the burnt offering; both typify Christ, the former in His devoted life and the latter in His devoted death.

4. "counsel," *i.e.* in the war.

5. "thy"; the king recognized as Jehovah's chosen instrument for delivering the people, cf. 2 Sam. iii. 18. (*b*) banners," *i.e.* the tribal standards; see Num. i. 52; ii. 2 ff.

6. Note the assurance of faith, so also 8; "His anointed," this title implies on the king's part a pledge of obedience to Jehovah and is at the same time the plea for help from Jehovah; "answereth," or keeps answering; "holy heaven," = the true sanctuary; for earthly type, see 2.

7. "chariots," cf. 2 Sam. viii. 3–6; 1 Chron. xviii. 3–5. For the verse, cf., *e.g.* 2 Chron. xvi. 8–9; 1 Sam. xvii. 45.

8. "bowed down," s.H.w., xviii. 39*b*. Here still the anticipation of faith.

9. Render as R.V. m. Short concluding prayer, cf. xxi. 13.

PSALM XXI.   BLESSING AFTER BATTLE

I. ACKNOWLEDGMENTS TO THE LORD (1-7).
Infinite Loving-kindness. The King exults in Jehovah's strength.

II. ADDRESS TO THE KING (8-12). Inescapable Judgment.

III. ASCRIPTION TO THE LORD (13). Intended Praise. Jehovah exalted in
His own strength.

SUPERSCRIPT.—A psalm of David.

SUBSCRIPT.—For the Chief Musician; relating to Aijeleth-hash-Shahar.

PRIMARY ASSOCIATION.—This seems originally to have been
written as a coronation hymn or national anthem, and later used as
a thanksgiving for victories granted in answer to prayer; see notes to
preceding psalm.   The Heb. words found in the subscript mean
"The Hind of the Morning," a poetical expression for the dawn of
day.   The first rays of the rising sun are likened to the horns of a
deer appearing above the rising ground before its body comes into
view.   The phrase is traditionally linked with the dawn of redemption
for Israel.   It brings to mind "the last words of David," 2 Sam. xxiii. 4;
cf. Pss. lxxii. 19, 20; cxxx. 5, 6; Luke i. 78; 2 Pet. i. 19.

PROPHETIC ANTICIPATION.—Messiah the King is seen in glory
following the victory of the Cross.   Being now "set on high" (xx. 1)
as Son of Man, He confidently awaits the fulfilment of the promise,
Ps. cx. 1 and 1 Cor. xv. 25.   The psalm looks back to His finished
work and on to His future triumphs over all His enemies and those
of His people.   He sought not exaltation for Himself, for He needed
it not (Phil. ii. 6 ff), but as Son of Man He has taken the highest
place in order to fulfil all the divine counsel of grace and blessing
to His creatures.

PERSONAL APPLICATION.—As believers we rejoice in God's
salvation, 1.   Christ's is the perfect pattern of prevailing prayer,
for He ever sought the will of God, 2.   By prayer, impotence can
set Omnipotence in motion.   "God does not always wait for our
petitions, He comes beforehand with His gifts," 3.   Christian warfare and Christian worship go together.   The "countenance"
(presence) which delights the faithful (6) destroys the foe, 9 marg.
Our trust is answered by God's loving-kindness, so that we shall not
be moved, 7.   "God overtakes, outflanks and overthrows His
enemies, 12."   Exalt our God and exult in Him, 13.

VERSE NOTES

2. **Answer** to the prayer of xx. 4. "Selah" precedes the prayer and follows the answer, thus pointing the connection.

3. "**preventest**," *i.e.* comest to meet; (*b*) cf. 2 Sam. xii. 30.

4. Of David, must be taken in the sense of 2 Sam. vii. 29; of Messiah, in the sense of the resurrection life, Heb. vii. 24–25.

5. These divine attributes reflected in Jehovah's representative, the king; of Messiah, cf. Heb. ii. 9.

6. Lit. "**makest Him blessings**," *i.e.* the king was both the recipient of divine favours and the medium of blessing to others; "in thy presence," the recent victory was a pledge of divine favour and fellowship, cf. xvi. 11; see also Acts ii. 28.

7. The ground of blessing: (*a*) David's trust, (*b*) Jehovah's loving-kindness.

8. The recent victory a pledge of future victories; of David, see 2 Sam. viii.; 1 Chron. xviii.

9. *i.e.* consume them as fuel in a furnace, Mal. iv. 1 ; "anger," see marg.; of Messiah, the word "presence" suggestive of His Coming (Gk. parousia = presence), in connection with which see 2 Thess. ii. 8 R.V. m.

10. "**fruit . . . seed**," *i.e.* their posterity, see Rev. xi. 18.

11. "**intended**," or threatened; "imagined a device . . ." *i.e.* devised a plot they could not carry out." Malice against God and His Christ is often shown in the persecution of God's people, Acts ix. 4.

12. "**turn . . . back**," *i.e.* in flight from the victor; (*b*) render, "Against their face, aiming with thy bowstrings."

13. Short concluding praise uttered in a spirit of prayer (*a*) and promise (*b*); cf. xx. 9, "strength" returns to the thought in verse 1; "power," or might, shown in mighty acts of deliverance, cf. xx. 6.

A Trilogy of Ps. xxii.–xxiv. forms a fitting close to this section of Book I. These psalms present the Saviour in three notable aspects: xxii. the Saviour; xxiii. the Shepherd; xxiv. the Sovereign. In them we view respectively: the Cross, the Crook and the Crown; or, Grace, Guidance and Glory; the Past, the Present and the Prospect.

PSALM XXII. FROM GLOOM TO GLORY

I. MESSIAH'S GRIEF. HIS AGONISING PRAYER. WOES EMPHASISED (1–22). Humiliation in the midst of His Enemies.

    1. APPEAL (1–2). "Why so far." The Crowning Anguish—"Thou answerest not."

    2. PLEA (3–5). The Fathers. Their trust. "But Thou."

    3. ADVERSARIES (6–8). Their Ridicule. "But I." The Gibes.

    4. PLEA (9–10). The Sufferer. His trust. "But Thou."

    5. APPEAL (11). "Be not far." The Central Accent. *The Sufferer alone.*

    6. ADVERSARIES (12–13). Their Rage. The Gaping.

    7. PLEA (14–15). The Sufferer. His torture.

8. ADVERSARIES (16–18). Their Ruthlessness. The Gazing.
9. APPEAL (19–21). "Be not far." The Closing Assurance—"Thou hast answered."

II. MESSIAH'S GLORY.   HIS ABOUNDING PRAISE.   WORSHIP EMPHASISED (22–31). Exaltation in the midst of His Elect.
   1. NATIONAL WORSHIP (22–26). The Earthly Seed. Israel.
      i. Precentor and People (22–23). "I," "Ye." General.
      ii. Reason (24). "For."
      iii. Precentor and People (25–26). "I," "the meek." Particular.
   2. UNIVERSAL WORSHIP (27–29b). The Gentiles. Millennial Nations.
      i. Peoples (27). General.
      ii. Reason (28). "For."
      iii. Peoples (29). Particular.
   3. SPIRITUAL WORSHIP (29c–31). The Heavenly Seed. The Elect.
      i. The Redeemer (29c). (See note.)
      ii. The Regenerate (30–31).
      iii. The Reason (31). "For"—It is finished.

SUPERSCRIPT.—A psalm of David.

PRIMARY ASSOCIATION.—Written by David the inspired prophet, Acts ii. 30–31. While the psalm may have its roots in his own deep soul exercise during the period of Saul's persecution, its language reaches far beyond this to the atoning sufferings of Christ, 1 Peter i. 2, is well illustrated here. The Spirit of God is not bound by the limits of the human instrument He is pleased to use, hence the Messianic references entirely eclipse the Davidic.

PROPHETIC ANTICIPATION.—The New Testament applies the psalm in a most positive and exclusive way to the Lord Jesus. Its distinctive character is that it brings out by way of marked contrast the experiences of Messiah and those of the godly. The latter in their suffering have been and will be delivered when they cry to God, but Messiah, "perfect in the fullest sorrow," was not. Many graphic details of His death on the Cross are given. The whole psalm formed the subject of His meditation during those hours of agony. While the Gospels record His more apparent sufferings, the psalms record the more hidden sorrows. This psalm begins with the Cross and ends with the Crown. Note the interval of silence to be understood between 21–22 indicating that death and resurrection have taken place.

In Ps. xxii. we see Christ as the Sin Offering; in xl. as the Burnt Offering; in lxix. as the Trespass Offering. In Ps. xxii. section 1,

Prayer unanswered; section 2, Prayer answered; section 1, the centre; section 2, the circumference. In both sections the same voice, but on a different note.

PERSONAL APPLICATION.—Let us approach this psalm with unshod feet for the place whereon we stand is holy ground. The unique sufferings of Christ on the Cross are revealed as far as may be for the full satisfaction of our conscience and the adoring worship of our hearts. It is good exercise to trace out all the prophetic details given here in their fulfilment on the Cross. Here is the crisis of the conflict between good and evil. The orphan cry is never for the redeemed. Power can create stars but cannot cancel sin; love could not act at the expense of righteousness, Prov. xvii. 15. In their antagonism to the Christ of God men become like beasts, 12-13, 16, 21. Commit to (Heb. = "roll upon") the Lord: (a) Woes, 8; (b) Way, xxxvii. 5; (c) Works, Prov. xvi. 3. The glory of the Redeemer's Crown is in the cross. He who was alone in His sorrow is accompanied in the song, 22. The last sentence in the psalm touches the keynote of the Gospel.

VERSE NOTES

1. "God" = El. cf. 10; "forsaken,"—Christ the believing sinner's substitute was abandoned to the full curse of the broken law. The very height of His essential majesty made the horror of His cross infinite. Such desolation no soul but His could experience; for us it will ever remain an unfathomable mystery; "roaring," i.e. the groaning of the holy Sufferer is likened to sounds made by a distressed lion.

2. (b) Br. as marg.

3. In the supreme agony of His soul He yet justifies God. Here is no trace of reproach against God or bitterness towards man, Luke xxiii. 34; "But . . .," cf. Isa. lii. 6 and Hab. i. 13; line br. as margin; the praises of Israel ascending like clouds of incense form as it were the throne upon which Jehovah sits; or may be fig. metonymy for the place to which the national praises were directed, viz. the Sanctuary.

4-5. Emphasis throughout is on "Thee,"—deliverance for the fathers not for Him. His, then, was not merely the death of a martyr, Heb. xi. 35-37. No suffering at the hands of man could make atonement with God; "ashamed" = put to shame.

6. "worm" = one despised, defenceless and downtrodden, cf. Isa. liii. 3; "no man," Heb. ish, Appendix X.

7. Cf. Luke xxiii. 35; (b) i.e. in contempt and feigned abhorrence, Matt. xxvii. 39.

8. Lit. "Roll it upon Jehovah." Trust in God was the ruling principle of Messiah's life. Unable to upbraid Him with sin, His enemies taunted Him with that which was characteristic of His moral glory. He alone realised what Job professed, Job xiii. 15; (b) "He (Jehovah) delighteth in Him (the Sufferer)," cf. xviii. 19; Isa. xlii. 1.

9. Br. "Yea, Thou . . .," their mocking words were true, and He turns them into a potent plea.

10. "Upon *Thee* have I been cast . . ."

12. "bulls," fig. of reckless power and rebellious pride; "Bashan" (see Bible map) a district famous for its rich pastures and magnificent cattle.

13. Cf. xxv. 21.

14. Token of utter weakness, cf. 1 Sam. vii. 6; 2 Sam. xiv. 14; "melted," *i.e.* grown faint.

15. Cf. xxxii. 4; lxix. 3; (c) br. "Thou art laying me in . . ." Behind man's persecution He sees the hand of God, Acts ii. 23.

17. Br. "I can count . . ."; (b) "while *they* (the tormentors) gaze . . .," *i.e.* they look on with malicious delight.

19. "But *Thou*, O Jehovah, keep not Thou far off."

20. "my soul" = myself, Num. xxiii. 10; "my darling" = term primarily used of an only child, Gen. xxii. 2; Judges xi. 34; here denotes his one precious life, cf. xxxv. 7; in each case the parallelism shows it syn. with "soul."

21. There is a sudden transition from earnest appeal to calm assurance in this verse; after the word "oxen," instead of "rescue me" or some similar prayer, comes a break, best indicated by a hyphen.

22. "Declare . . .," cf. John xx. 17, where note the important distinction, not "our Father" but "My Father and your Father;" "name," *i.e.* all that God had proved Himself to be, Heb. ii. 12; public proclamation and praise.

23. "Ye that fear . . ." indic. an inner circle of faithful ones.

24. Ctr. the attitude of men, 6; see Heb. v. 7.

25. Jehovah is both the object and the source of praise; "vows," *i.e.* thank-offerings vowed in time of trouble.

26. The thank-offering was in the nature of a peace-offering, see Lev. vii. 11–18; here the offerer invites "the meek" as His guests; (c) the host invokes a blessing on the guests.

27. "kindreds," or families. The patriarchal promise fulfilled, Gen. xii, 3; xxviii. 14.

28. The fact of Jehovah's universal sovereignty recognized in millennial days; br. "He ruleth among , . ."

29. *i.e.* the mighty and the mean; all classes share the blessings of His reign and acknowledge His supremacy; "bow" = kneel. (c) A new verse should begin here and read, "As for Him that caused not His soul to live (= Messiah) His seed shall serve Him. It shall be told unto a generation that shall come; His righteousness shall be declared unto a people that shall be born; for He hath done (it)." See Pss. xlviii. 13; cii. 18.

31. "Righteousness," *i.e.* faithfulness to His covenant; "For He . . .," cf. lii. 9; Isa. xliv. 23.

PSALM XXIII.   THE SHEPHERD SONG

I. THE SHEPHERD'S ABUNDANT PROVISION (1–3). "Jehovah."
Pastures and Waters. My Supplies.

II. THE SHEPHERD'S ABLE PROTECTION (4). "Thou."
Rod and Staff. From Death. My Safeguards.

III. THE SHEPHERD'S ABLE PROTECTION (5). "Thou."
Table and Cup. From Enemies. My Society.

IV. THE SHEPHERD'S ABUNDANT PROVISION (6). "Jehovah."
Goodness and Loving-kindness. My Servants.

SUPERSCRIPT.—A psalm of David.

PRIMARY ASSOCIATION.—This "Pearl of Psalms," the simplest and sweetest song ever sung, was written by David the shepherd-king, but at what period of his life is not known.

PROPHETIC ANTICIPATION.—The voice of Messiah, as the truly dependent Man in His daily life down here, is heard expressing His satisfaction in Jehovah. In this He identifies Himself with Israel's godly remnant. In another view, this psalm, coming as it does between xxii and xxiv., *i.e.* the Cross and the Glory, may be the subject of Christ's meditation in Hades (Paradise), cf. Luke xxiii. 43, in which case several expressions gain point.

PERSONAL APPLICATION.—The sheep are safe and satisfied. Little need be said here as so much has been written about this precious portion of God's Word. There is no doubt that multitudes of saints have lived by it and in the faith of it multitudes have died. We cannot fail to note the intense individuality of the psalm and that, while the Shepherd's gracious provision is detailed, the emphasis is upon the Giver rather than upon the gifts; the Person is greater than the provision. Our Lord takes up the beautiful figure and applies it to Himself, John x. Guardianship and guidance are assured us until home is reached. The unfailing Presence preserves from unknown perils. The world is a scene darkened by the sentence of death—the stamp of death is upon everything, but for the believer the sting has gone even from death itself, only the "shadow" remains. On the "other side" is everlasting sunshine. There may be gloom all around, but upward is ever the blue sky. At the end of the way is an eternal welcome. God is no niggardly supplier; He provides for the joys of life as well as for its necessities, civ. 15. Peace and plenty are our portion—do we enjoy them? Our Shepherd knows the way for He Himself has trodden it alone. Right paths may lead through perilous regions,

All my resources are in Him: (i) Rest, (2); (ii) Refreshment, (2); (iii) Restoration, (3); (iv) Regulation, (3); (v) Rescue, (4); (vi) Reassurance, (4); (vii) Reception, (4); (viii) Rejoicing, (5); (ix) Retainers, (6); (x) Residence, (6).

VERSE NOTES

1. Jehovah is often referred to as the Shepherd of Israel and Israel as His flock, especially in this Book of Psalms, e.g. lxxx. 1.

2. Br. "pastures of tender grass"; rest in the noontide heat here pictured. The sheep is a ruminant (hence "clean" according to the Law); it does not simply swallow its food. While the sheep is lying down at rest, the gathered food is regurgitated and deliberately and thoroughly masticated ready for assimilation. So should the believer enjoy the soul-satisfying treasures of God's Word ministered by His Spirit. (b) "still waters," ref. to wells and cisterns upon which shepherds depend, rather than upon the streams, which often fail in time of need; "leadeth," Hebrew word suggests gentle guidance (cf. Isa. xl. 11), the shepherd graciously accommodating his pace to the strength of the sheep. In Eastern lands the flock is never driven; see Gen. xxxiii. 14. Water is a daily necessity, especially in a hot and dry climate.

3. "He restoreth . . .," i.e. rescues my life from forbidden and fatal places. There are private fields, gardens and vineyards, upon which if a sheep stray, its life is forfeit to the owner of the land; "paths of righteousness," or right paths; "for His Name's sake," i.e. to prove Himself what He has declared Himself to be. Jehovah ever cherishes and upholds His good name—here as Shepherd. He desires to be fully known by us, so that we may fully trust Him and delight ourselves in Him.

4. "valley . . .," i.e. a deep ravine in which lurk wild beasts, natural enemies of the flock; "shadow of death" = a Heb. idiom for intense darkness; "rod," for counting and controlling the sheep, Lev. xxvii. 32; Jer. xxxiii. 13; "staff," used to defend the sheep from its enemies, 1 Sam. xvii. 37, 40.

5. "table," to find a good and safe feeding-place for the sheep often calls for the highest skill and heroism on the part of the shepherd. He must study the nature of the grass, note the presence or absence of poisonous plants and reptiles, search out the lairs of predatory animals, stopping up their dens with stones, and if necessary, attacking and destroying the animals themselves. At the close of the day the shepherd stands at the door of the fold "rodding the sheep," i.e. controlling them with his rod, and not only counting them as they pass in, but closely examining the condition of each sheep. Using olive oil and cedar tar, he anoints wounds, scratches and bruises, and refreshes the worn and weary by making them drink out of a large two-handled cup, brimming with water from cisterns provided for the purpose. "Oil" typifies the refreshing and restoring ministry of the Spirit of God; "cup" speaks of actual enjoyment of His abundant provision. It runs over; no element is lacking to make the joy complete.

6. Br. "Only (= nothing but) goodness and loving-kindness . . .," here is assurance that the Shepherd's care will be unremitting day by day; "dwell," for

not only long life, but intimate fellowship is indicated; '·for ever," cf. margin; also xxi. 4. Thus the song ends with the sheep settled and safe in the sheepfold. The end is seen to be a glorious beginning. For many of these "Verse Notes" the writer is indebted to the well-known book, "The Song of the Syrian Guest."

PSALM XXIV. THE COMING OF THE CONQUEROR

I. THE CONQUEROR'S APPROACH (1–6).
    1. The Sublime Confession (1–2). Chant. Jehovah's Universal Sovereignty.
    2. The Solemn Consideration (3). Question.
    3. The Searching Conditions (4–6). Response. Selah.

II. THE CONQUEROR'S ARRIVAL (7–10).
    1. The Summoning Cry (7). Chant.
    2. The Sentinel's Challenge (8a). Question.
    3. The Soul-stirring Chorus (8bc). Response.
    REPEAT. 4. The Summoning Cry (9). Chant.
          5. The Sentinel's Challenge (10a) Question.
          6. The Soul-stirring Chorus (10bc). Response. Selah,

SUPERSCRIPT.—David's.

PRIMARY ASSOCIATION.—Written by David most probably for the inauguration of the newly captured fortress of Zion as the final resting-place of the ark, Jehovah's earthly throne, 2 Sam. vi. Dramatic in form the psalm pictures the procession bearing the ark in its approach and arrival; cf. lxviii., the procession setting out; lxxxvii., the joyful entry; cv., the subsequent celebrations. This psalm is antiphonic and later was appointed for the first day of the week in the temple services.

PROPHETIC ANTICIPATION.—Primarily, not the ascension of our Lord, but His future coming in glory to His millennial metropolis is foretold. He will then appear as the mighty Victor after the overthrow of His and His people's enemies. God has chosen Zion to be the place of His rest for ever, Ps. cxxxii. 13–14; cf. Micah iv. 7. The city will be canopied with a cloud of glory, sign of Jehovah's presence, Isa. iv. 5, like the camp in the wilderness. It must be remembered that the history of Israel and that of the earth are inseparably bound up together. In that nation's blessing is involved the welfare of the nations at large.

PERSONAL APPLICATION.—The character of God determines the

character of His worshippers (3–5). His worshippers must be holy in hand and in heart, in deed and in thought. The psalm begins with Jehovah as Sovereign-Owner of the world and ends with Him as Sovereign-Owner of the heavens. Note, (a) His World; (b) His Worshippers; (c) His Welcome. Have the gates of our hearts been opened with joy for the entrance of the Conqueror of sin and of Satan?

VERSE NOTES

1. Br. as Heb. order, "Unto Jehovah belongeth the earth . . ." Though He deign to dwell in Zion, His presence and power are not limited thereto; cf. 1 Chron. xxix. 11–16; words cited 1 Cor. x. 26.

2. "He" (emph.); "floods," or streams.

3–6. Cf. Ps. xv. These verses gain emphasis in view of the disaster which for a while deferred the ceremony, 2 Sam. vi. 9.

3. "ascend," i.e. for worship; "stand," i.e. stand his ground, cf. i. 5; 1 Sam. vi. 20.

4. (b) i.e. faithful to Jehovah; (c) i.e. true to his neighbour.

6. "generation" indic. a class of people, as in xii. 7; xiv. 5.

6. (b) A.V. correct; "O Jacob," i.e. those who seek after Jehovah will seek also the favour of Jehovah's people, among whom He dwells; the descendents of Jacob they are called, because they will owe everything to grace, not to any goodness in themselves. Line (a) then, contemplates Israel and (b) Gentiles, Isa. lvi. 6–7.

7. "Lift up" as though these ancient gates of Zion were too low and mean for the entrance of "the high and lofty One;" "everlasting," i.e. in the sense (primarily at least) that they were of unknown antiquity.

8. The Ark was the symbol and pledge of Jehovah's presence among His people, Num. x. 35–36; ctr. 1 Sam. iv. 21. (bc) cf. past, Exod. xv. 2–3; future, Rev. xix. 11 ff.; "King," cf. Exod. xv. 18; He is here proclaimed Victor.

10. The climax. Right of entry is based upon (a) Undisputed victory; (b) Universal sovereignty. "Jehovah of Hosts," first occurrence of this title in the Psalter. He commands the stars of the skies, the myriads of angels and the armies of Israel.

Book One. III. Record of the Divine Redeemer, xvi.–xli.

2. The Remnant. Subjects of Salvation, xxv.–xxxix. Their Exercises and Experiences.

In this series of "remnant" psalms we see the reaction to the revelation of the Redeemer; the testimony of faith to the salvation announced. Compared with the previous series, note the fuller yet still imperfect apprehension of divine grace.

PSALM XXV. A PLEA FOR PARDON

I. APPEAL FOR DELIVERANCE (1–7). Supplication to Jehovah. Fragrance of Faith. Seven Petitions. "Let me not be ashamed."

II. AFFIRMATION OF GUIDANCE (8–10). Declaration concerning Jehovah. The Teacher. "He will teach."

III. ACKNOWLEDGMENT OF SIN (11). Confession to Jehovah. Poignant Prayer and Powerful Plea.

IV. AFFIRMATION OF GUIDANCE (12–14). Declaration concerning Jehovah. The Taught. "Him will He teach."

V. ASSURANCE OF SALVATION (15). Expectation from Jehovah. Praiseworthy Posture and Positive Persuasion.

VI. APPEAL FOR DELIVERANCE (16–21), Supplication to Jehovah. Faltering of Faith. Seven Petitions. "Let me not be ashamed."

VII. AMPLIFICATION OF PRAYER (22). Supplementary Petition. Prayer for the Nation. Conclusion.

SUPERSCRIPT.—David's.

PRIMARY ASSOCIATION.—Writer: David; period, probably time of Absalom's rebellion. One of the nine acrostic psalms, this one is irregular with the omission of two Hebrew letters. Double Aleph at the beginning with a double Resh at 18–19 "connects the uplift of the soul to Jehovah with the downlook of Jehovah upon the sufferer." Close study will show much other interweaving of thought between the sections. This psalm is related to xxxiv. which has a similar alphabetical construction. The imperfect alphabet is in keeping with the yet imperfect apprehension of divine grace; the irregularity is suited to the troublous times in which it was penned.

PROPHETIC ANTICIPATION.—Shows the godly remnant cast upon God in entire confidence to find the fullness and sufficiency of Divine grace. The work of Christ being completed (Pss. xxii.–xxiv.), we now meet for the first time in the Psalter, a full, unreserved confession of sin. The true character of the remnant people is seen as "meek," cf. Matt. v. 5. See concluding notes to preceding paragraph.

PERSONAL APPLICATION.—Like David we cannot plead our merits, only God's mercies (6). Jehovah's secret counsels are more than a match for the enemies' secret plots (14). The glory of God is His goodness (7) with Exod. xxxiii. 18–19.   God remembers the sinner, but not his sins—if he is a subject of salvation (7). Humility of heart is an essential condition to being taught of God (9); we need to remember both our littleness and our sinfulness. The greatness of the iniquity only magnifies the grace that puts it away (11). Faith anchors itself in God's faithfulness (2). God's tender mercies and loving-kindnesses (6) should be met by our integrity and uprightness (21). Note David's three pleas: (a) Mercies of his faithful God; (b) Misery of his own soul; (c) Malignity of his many foes.

VERSE NOTES

1. Positive aspect; for negative, cf. xxiv. 4.
2. cf. 20.
3. (b) i.e. faithless desertion of God.
4. Lit. "Make me to know Thy way," cf. Moses' prayer, Exod. xxxiii. 13 = not merely ways in which we should walk, but the divine principles of action.
5. "truth" = faithfulness.
6. (b) lit. ". . . for they . . . from everlasting."
7. "sins"; the thoughtless offences of youth; "transgressions"; the deliberate offences of later years; "goodness," cf. Rom. ii. 4; xi. 22.
9. "judgment," i.e. wise discernment coupled with right practice.
10. (a) cf. Exod. xxxiv. 6; (b) "testimonies," i.e. His commandments as witnesses to His holy will.
13. Blessings temporal; (b) cf. Matt. v. 5.
14. Blessings spiritual; "secret," Hebrew word denotes the confidential intercourse of intimate fellowship; a privy council, cf. Gen. xviii. 17; Amos iii. 7. David frequently consulted Jehovah through the high priest and the ephod, 1 Sam. xxii. 15 indicating his practice; see also 1 Sam. xxiii. 6–9; xxx. 7–8; 2 Sam. ii. 1. Saul's impatient selfwill would not wait for divine counsel, 1 Sam. x. 8; xiii. 8, 14; xiv. 18-19; (b) lit. "make them to know," note Persuasion, 3 ; Prayer, 4.
16. Br. "Be gracious unto me"; cf. iv. 1, etc.; "desolate" = solitary, without other friend or helper.
17. Br. "The straitnesses of my heart enlarge Thou, and bring . . ."
18. "Consider" = behold; the downlook is to be in response to the uplook of 15; "forgive," lit. take away; sin here regarded as a heavy burden. Cf. 2 Sam. xvi. 5–12. Shimei's charge seems to have found an echo in David's conscience, hence the nature of his reply to Abishai; cf. his spirit of meekness there and that shown in our psalm.
19. "Consider" = behold, as 18; behold (a) my Affliction; (b) my Adversaries; "cruel" = violent.
20. "Oh, keep . . . oh, preserve . . . for I have taken refuge in Thee."
21. "preserve," = guard. As so often in the psalms two divine principles here interwoven, namely confidence in God (20) with integrity of heart (21).
22. The psalmist here links the redemption of Israel with his own.

PSALM XXVI. A PLEA OF PROBITY

I. TERSE PETITION (1a). Prayer for Vindication.

II. TELLING PLEA (1b). The Psalmist's Walk. Practice Hitherto.

III. TERSE PETITIONS (2). Prayer for Examination.

IV. TELLING PLEAS (3-8). The Psalmist's Walk. Practice.
    1. Jehovah's Loving-kindness (3a).
    2. Psalmist's Life (3b). Shown by
        (i) Shunning the Society of the Sinful (4-5). "I hate."
        (ii) Seeking the Service of the Sanctuary (6-8). "I love."

V. TERSE PETITION (9-10). Prayer for Preservation.

VI. TELLING PLEA (11a). The Psalmist's Walk. Purpose Hereafter.

VII. TERSE PETITION (11b). Prayer for Redemption.

VIII. TELLING PLEA (12). The Psalmist's Worship. Purpose.

SUPERSCRIPT.—David's.

PRIMARY ASSOCIATION.—Writer is David. Occasion cannot be fixed with certainty, but it seems to have been a period of national calamity. Conscious of his personal integrity, David appeals for deliverance from a fate which threatens to overwhelm both wicked (9) and righteous in a common judgment. This psalm bears a relation to the preceding one. Ps. xxv., Confession of Sin; xxvi., Profession of Sincerity. In the former, David contrasts his character with the character of God; in the latter he contrasts it with the character of the godless. On the psalmist's claim to personal integrity, see Appendix VIII.

PROPHETIC ANTICIPATION.—Strikingly appropriate as the future utterance of the godly remnant in the last days, when the righteous judgments of God fall upon the apostate nation.

PERSONAL APPLICATION.—Integrity is the fellow and fruit of faith. Separation from evil is with a view to separation unto God, *i.e.* sanctification. Attachment to the good must be accompanied by detachment from the evil. "Leaven changes its environment into its own substance and likeness." Our companions are an index to our own character. A sanctified walk is a necessary preparation for sanctuary worship. Resolve should be complementary to request. Homage only of holy hands and hearts is acceptable to God. Worship

(7a) should always be followed by witness (7b). Public acknowledgment may well follow answered prayer (12).

VERSE NOTES

1. "Judge me" = vindicate my integrity, cf. vii. 8. Sincerity of purpose and conformity of practice were his rule of life.

2. Attests a clear conscience, but acknowledges need of cleansing from unknown sin. Here is the language of the refiner of precious metal: (a) "Assay" me = test for quality; (b) "Prove" me = test for reality; (c) "Smelt" me = for removal of impurity; (b) i.e. the inmost thoughts, vii. 9.

4. Cf. i. 1; "go in" = associate with.

5. Ctr. the "congregations" of the saints (12).

6. Ref. to preparation of the priests before drawing near to minister at the brazen altar, Exod. xxx. 17-21; cf. Ps. xxiv. 4; may be ref. also to Deut. xxi. 6; (b) In order to complete the prescribed ritual in the offering of the daily sacrifices the ministering priest did in fact "compass (i.e. encompass) the altar." What the priests did in symbolic rite, the psalmist would do in spiritual reality.

8. (b) lit. "the place of the tabernacle of thy glory"; Jehovah's glory here = His manifested presence of which the Ark was the outward symbol.

9. "gather not" = take not away; i.e. Let me not share a common doom with those whose society and practices I have ever shunned.

9-10. The wicked here described as those who (a) Plan murder; (b) Perpetrate crimes, and (c) Pervert justice; men in authority seem to be indicated, Micah vii. 2 ff.

11. "redeem me," i.e. from the doom of the wicked.

12. Faith anticipates the answer to its prayer; "even place" = the upland pastures, so often connected with the inheritance of Reuben.

8. David's love for God's house may be gathered from such scriptures as Ps. xxvii. 4; lxix. 9; and 2 Sam. xv. 25; 1 Chron. xxix. 2-3.

PSALM XXVII. SEEKING THE SANCTUARY

I. REJOICING CONFIDENCE (1-6). Faith's Testimony.

    1. Assurance (1-3).

        As to i. Present (1); ii. Past (2); iii. Prospect (3).

    2. Aspiration (4-6).

        i. Request (4); ii. Reason (5); iii. Result (6).

II. REVEALED CONCERN (7-12). Faith's Testing.

    1. Prayer (7).

    2. Plea (8). "For."

    3. Prayer (9).

    4. Plea (10). "For."

    5. Prayer (11-12a).

    6. Plea (12b). "For."

III. RENEWED CONFIDENCE (13-14). Faith's Triumph.
   1. Assurance (13). The Acknowledgment of Faith.
   2. Advice (14). The Encouragement to Hope.

SUPERSCRIPT.—David's.

PRIMARY ASSOCIATION.—David is the writer; historical occasion is uncertain, but tradition assigns it to the period before his anointing as king over all Israel (so LXX.), probably that of the wars during the first seven years of his reign. Note the sudden transition from the confidence of (I.) to the concern of (II.), characteristic of so many psalms and confirmed so often in the experience of the saints.

PROPHETIC ANTICIPATION.—Again the soul exercise of the faithful remnant, amid the deep trials of the last days, is portrayed.

PERSONAL APPLICATION.—A psalm of sunshine and shade. The believer enjoys (a) Light which dispels darkness; (b) Liberty which delivers from distress; (c) Life which defeats death. Light reveals not only myself and my environment, but it is also self-revealing. Purpose must not be parted from pursuit; right desire is good, but should be followed up by spiritual energy (4). To learn God's secrets, we must live near to Him (4). The godly are God's guarded guests (5). The sanctuary provides security from spiritual foes, as well as from human adversaries. Note the three-fold security: (a) Sheltered from calamitous storm; (b) Secreted from unseen danger; (c) Saved from open assault (5). Those who are safe should sing (6). Fear often lies very near to faith (7). Every believer has experience of mountain and valley. Severe storm shakes not the saints' sure support (10). We are in constant need of: (a) Divine Grace (7); (b) Divine Gathering (8-10); (c) Divine Guidance (11); and (d) Divine Guard (12). If not—what then? Have you considered this (13)? Wait, yea, wait (14) on the Lord.

VERSE NOTES

   1. Cf. Rom. viii. 31; "my salvation," cf. 9; "strength," see marg.
   2. "eat . . . flesh"; assailants compared to wild beasts waiting to devour.
   3. Cf. iii. 6.
   4. The climax of all his petitions, cf. Phil. iii. 13; ctr. James i. 8. (c) may be rendered as margin. David desired to know the inner meaning of these symbols of heavenly realities; see Heb. x. 19-22; "beauty," or graciousness.
   5. (b) Br. "in the hiding-place (or secrecy) of His tent."

6. Present triumph anticipated; (*b*) "in His tent," 2 Sam. vi. 17; "sacrifices of joy," *i.e.* thank-offerings.

7. "Be gracious unto me."

8. A peculiar Heb. construction here, but A.V. and R.V. give the general sense. David pleads Jehovah's own invitation to His people, *e.g.* Deut. iv. 29; and similar scriptures.

9. Prayer based upon promise (*a*) and experience (*c*).

10. Though friendless and forsaken like a deserted child, he will be adopted by Jehovah Himself, whose love is stronger than that of the nearest and dearest human relationships; cf. Ezk. xvi. 4–6; Isa. xlix. 15; "take me up," or gather me.

11. (*a*) cf. xxv. 4, 12. "false witnesses," *i.e.* slanderous calumniators.

13. Br. with LXX. etc., "I believe that I shall see," *i.e.* experience and enjoy; "land of the living," = this life in contrast to the next.

14. David addresses himself. His faith rebukes his faintness.

PSALM XXVIII. RECOURSE TO THE ROCK

I. INVOCATION TO JEHOVAH (1–3). APPROACH IN PRAYER. Feared Silence.

1. Prayer for Hearing (1–2). "Voice of supplications—hear."
2. Prayer for Help (3). Discrimination desired.

II. IMPLORATION AGAINST THE PERVERSE (4–5). APPEAL FOR THEIR PUNISHMENT.

1. Petition (4).
2. Prediction (5).

III. INTERVENTION OF JEHOVAH (6–7). ASCRIPTION OF PRAISE. Fervent Song.

1. Praise for Hearing (6). "Voice of supplications—heard."
2. Praise for Help (7). Protection provided.

IV. INTERCESSION FOR THE PEOPLE (8–9). APPEAL FOR THEIR PRESERVATION.

1. Profession (8).
2. Petition (9).

SUPERSCRIPT.—David's.

PRIMARY ASSOCIATION.—Written by David, apparently during a time of national calamity. The psalm is a companion of xxvi., but here the danger seems more pressing. In xxvi. the plea is the integrity of the righteous, here it is the iniquity of the wicked.

PROPHETIC ANTICIPATION.—The faithful remnant in the last days, surrounded by enemies and evil-doers and with the shadow of death upon them, have recourse to their unchangeable "Rock."

PERSONAL APPLICATION.—David knew the joy of answered prayer, do we? He could say, "The Lord is *my* strength and shield," because he had proved this truth in personal experience. Notice how often the psalmists burst into song; their songs far outnumber their sobs and sighs. See the conviction, then the consequences (7); and the moral order of the latter, trust—help—joy—praise. Happy the people who are saved—blessed—shepherded (lit.)—carried by the Lord (9). Note of the wicked: (a) treachery against their fellows (3); (b) trifling with their God (5).

VERSE NOTES

1. Jehovah Himself is the ground of David's confidence; "like," he does *not* say "among"; "them that . . .," *i.e.* the dying and the dead.

2. "cry," *i.e.* for help; (b) the attitude of prayer, cf. 1 Tim. ii. 8; "toward . . . oracle," *i.e.* the Holy of Holies where the Ark stood, cf. 1 Kings. viii. 30 ff.

3. Cf. xxvi. 9, but Hebrew here is stronger, being used of condemned criminals dragged away to execution. The psalmist prays that he may not share the doom of those now incurring the judgment of God; (cd) cf. xii. 1-2.

4. See notes on the so-called "imprecatory" psalms, Appendix IV.

5. Ctr. the Lord's works with those of the wicked (4).

7. "greatly rejoiceth" = exulteth.

8. (a) prob. should read with LXX., etc., "Jehovah is strength to His people"; cf. xxix. 11.

9. Note the four-fold petition; "feed" = shepherd; "lift up" = bear, or carry.

PSALM XXIX.   THE THEOPHANIC THUNDERSTORM

I. DIRECTION TO THE HEAVENLY THRONG (1-2).   Greatness and Glory. "The Lord" (objectively) four times. Summons to the "Strong."

II. DESCRIPTION OF THE HEAVY THUNDERSTORM (3-9).
"The Voice of the Lord" seven times. It is Pervading—Powerful—Penetrating.

III. DECLARATION OF THE HAPPY THEME (10-11).   Government and Grace. "The Lord" (subjectively) four times.
Solace for the Saints.

1. God's Government (10).
2. God's Gifts (11).

SUPERSCRIPT.—A psalm of David.

PRIMARY ASSOCIATION.—Written by David, but at what point in his history is uncertain. The psalm forms a fitting sequel to xxviii., the "voice" of Jehovah responding to the "voice" of David, xxvii. 2. Both psalms end similarly. Pss. xxv.–xxix. form a connected series, the "integrity" of xxv. 21 is the main theme of xxvi.; xxvi. 8 links with xxvii. 4–5; the exhortation of xxvii. 14 becomes the experience of xxviii. 6–7; the predicted judgment of xxvii. 4–5 with its manifestation and results seen in xxix. "To the devout Israelite . . . all the terrible phenomena of the sub-tropical thunderstorm were an expression of the majesty of the Eternal Sovereign of the Universe," cf. xviii. Note the: (*a*) Visible Approach (3); (*b*) Violent Outburst (in the north) (4–6); (*c*) Vivid Lightnings (7); (*d*) Vast Sweep (towards the south) (8–9); (*e*) Vibrant Chorus (9*c*). The progress of the storm is thus graphically described. The "Voice of Jehovah" here is like seven successive peals of thunder, cf. Rev. x. 3–4.

PROPHETIC ANTICIPATION.—Here we see depicted in typical language the great judgment-storm of Jehovah in which He will break down all opposition in the world (the focal point being the land of Palestine). He will then sit enthroned as universal ruler receiving the homage of earth's mighty ones, to which 1–2 may prophetically refer. Verse 9 seems to hint at the re-birth of the Jewish nation hastened by God's awful visitation. There will be a "stripping of the forest," but a remnant delivered. The outcome, not only for Israel but for the world, is seen to be perfect blessing and abiding peace (11). In prophetic language "trees" symbolise individual potentates, and "mountains" represent earthly governments.

PERSONAL APPLICATION.—A song of the storm. Here we find solace for the storm-tossed soul. The storms pass, but God ever remains the Governor in His universe and the Guardian of His people. To the saints the God of Power is finally manifested as the God of Peace (11). There is a rainbow in the storm-cloud (11). He gives strength during the storm and peace after the storm. The true viewpoint for the saints is ever that of heaven (9*c*). Link the marginal reading of xxix. 9 with that of xxvii. 4.

VERSE NOTES

1. Cf. 1 Chron. xvi. 28–29, also the three-fold ascription, Isa. vi. 3. The manifestation of divine glory on earth is the occasion of the summons to worship: see note under "Prophetic Anticipation"; "give," *i.e.* ascribe.

2. "glory . . . name," *i.e.* His glory as revealed in the world, here primarily in nature; "in holy array," or adorning, *i.e.* like the priests (Exod. xxviii. 2), but in spiritual reality, not mere outward symbol; cf. xcvi. 9.

3. "voice," trans. "thunder" at Exod. xx. 18; 1 Sam. xii. 17-18, cf. Ps. xviii. 13; "many waters," *i.e.* those collected in the dense masses of storm-clouds. God often interposed on behalf of His people by sending a terrible thunderstorm, see Exod ix. 23-25, Josh. x. 11, cf. Rev. viii. 7; xvi 17-21; (*c*) br. as A.V.

4. Seven thunders, see Isa. ii. 19.

6. "Sirion," *i.e.* Hermon.

7. (*a*) *i.e.* the forked lightnings.

9. (*a*) *i.e.* prematurely in fear: an observed fact; (*c*) or, "While in His temple, all are saying, Glory," or, ". . . all of it uttereth glory."

10. "Jehovah sat enthroned at the Flood," cf. Gen. vi.–xi. The Noahic flood was a typical example of divine judgment in which God overwhelmed the wicked and preserved His remnant people. World judgment will be repeated in a coming day, cf. Luke xvii. 26 ff.

11. Cf. xxviii. 8–9.

PSALM XXX. DELIVERANCE FROM DEATH

I. EXPRESSION OF PRAISE (1). DAVID'S THANKSGIVING.

    1. The Resolve (1*a*).

    2. The Reasons (1*bc*).

II. EXPERIENCE OF PRESERVATION (2-5). DAVID'S TESTIMONY.

    1. Appeal (2*a*). Addressed to Jehovah.

    2. Answer (2*b*-3). Divine Healing (Physical).

    3. Acknowledgment (4-5). Addressed to Saints.

III. EXPRESSION OF PENITENCE (6-7). DAVID'S THOUGHTS.

    1. Folly exhibited (6). Confession of Pride and Presumption.

    2. Fallacy exposed (7).

IV. EXPERIENCE OF PRESERVATION (8-12*a*). DAVID'S TESTIMONY.

    1. Appeal (8-10). Addressed to Jehovah.

    2. Answer (11). Divine Healing (Spiritual).

    3. Acknowledgment (12*a*). Appertaining to himself.

V. EXPRESSION OF PRAISE (12*b*). DAVID'S THANKSGIVING.

    1. The Purpose.

    2. The Perpetuity.

SUPERSCRIPT.—A psalm. A song at the dedication of the House. David's

SUBSCRIPT.—For the Chief Musician.

PRIMARY ASSOCIATION.—Written by David for the occasion mentioned. "The House" is an emphatic designation of the house of God, not that of David; so the Chaldean paraphrase. Before the building of "Solomon's" temple, Jehovah's acceptance of the special sacrifice, 2 Sam. xxiv. and 1 Chron. xxi. marked the place already as the house of God, cf. Gen. xxviii. 17. David repeatedly calls the temple prospectively, "the house of my God," 1 Chron. xxix. 1–3. The Jews still use the psalm in their ritual at the Feast of Dedication, John x. 22. Following the sin of numbering the people, it seems not improbable that David himself fell grievously sick, and upon recovery wrote the psalm, which read in this light is very illuminating indeed. Note the several antitheses.

PROPHETIC ANTICIPATION.—In the series of Psalms xxx.-xxxiv., the blessings of Israel's salvation are more particularly specified. In this psalm we see the deliverance of the godly Jewish remnant at the last critical moment when all hope will seem gone. Their deplorable condition is acknowledged as due to sin.

PERSONAL APPLICATION.—A psalm of grace and gratitude. Thanksgiving to God is followed by testimony for God. God's order is first the evening, then the morning (5); cf. Gen. i. After the night's sorrow comes the morning song. Sorrow is generally associated with darkness, and singing with the daylight, but there are times when the saint can sing songs in the night, xlii. 8; lxxvii. 6. The grief of the godly shall always be turned to gladness (11); cf. John xvi. 20. God may have to shake to its foundations our "strong mountain" in order that we may cling the closer to Himself. God's presence is better than worldly prosperity (6–7). The latter is perilous and precarious; if it does not leave us, we must leave it.

VERSE NOTES

1. "raised up," *i.e.* drawn up as from a deep pit; "rejoice over," *i.e.* by his death.

3. His recovery was as one delivered from the very jaws of death.

4. Lit. "psalm unto," or make melody.

5. Note margin; cf. ciii. 8 ff.; Isa. liv. 7–8; Micah vii. 18.

6. A perilous approach to the attitude of the wicked, x. 6.

7. "mountain," emblem of the Davidic kingdom with its divinely appointed seat at Mt. Zion. David was in danger of putting confidence in it instead of in God Himself; "troubled," a strong Hebrew word denoting helpless terror, as in vi. 2, 3, 10.

9-10. The words of his supplication. His plea is that if he dies, God will miss his voice from the chorus of praise, a bold approach, cf. Isa. xxxviii. 18-19; "dust," *i.e.* the grave, or rather those in it, cf. vi. 5; "truth" here equivalent to "faithfulness," as in xxv. 5.

10. Br. ". . . and be gracious unto me."

11. Br. "Thou didst turn . . . didst loose . . . and gird"; "sackcloth," the garb of mourning; "gladness," like a festal garment, cf. Isa. lxi. 3.

12. "my glory," to be understood possibly as "soul" or "spirit," see vii. 5 note.

PSALM XXXI. DELIVERANCE FROM THE DESTROYER

I. SUPPLICATION FOR DELIVERANCE (1-6). PRAYER. To the Lord.
  1. Petitions (1-2). "Deliver me . . . Let me not . . ."
  2. Pleas (3-4). Threefold "for." Jehovah's trustworthiness.
  3. Professions (5-6). Trust, "My spirit . . . into Thy hand."

II. SONG OF DELIVERANCE (7-8). PRAISE.
  1. Resolve (7*a*).
  2. Reasons (7*b*-8).

III. SUPPLICATION FOR DELIVERANCE (9-18). PRAYER.
  1. Pleas (9-13). Threefold "for." David's trouble.
      (i) Consequences (9-12).   (*a*) Upon Himself (9-10).
                                 (*b*) Upon Others (11-12).
      (ii) Causes (13).
  2. Professions (14-15*a*). Trust, "My times . . . into Thy hands."
  3. Petitions (15*b*-18). "Deliver me . . . Let me not . . ."

IV. SONG OF DELIVERANCE (19-22). PRAISE.
  1. Rendition (19-20).
  2. Reasons (21-22).

V. SUMMONS TO DEVOTION (23-24). PROMISE. To the Saints.
  1. Exhortation (23*a*).
  2. Explanation (23*bc*).
  3. Exhortation (24).

SUPERSCRIPT.—A psalm of David.

PRIMARY ASSOCIATION.—Written by David apparently during the period of Saul's persecution, and most probably refers to his experiences at Keilah, 1 Sam. xxiii.; cf. "shut up" (5) with s.H.w. at

1 Sam. xxiii. 7; "into the hand," (8) with same chapter (7, 11-12); "men (lit. baali) of Keilah" denotes the Canaanite portion of the city's inhabitants; (6a) refers to these Baalites; "strong city" (21), cf. 1 Sam. xxiii. 7. Such was Keilah against which the Philistines sent up not a band but "armies." It consisted of two strongholds separated by a valley. The psalm exhibits the ebb and flow of faith during a period of deep distress.

PROPHETIC ANTICIPATION.—Again we see Israel at the time of the end. As with David so with them, a signal deliverance by Jehovah gives promise of final triumph. Note that 5a affords another instance of our Lord taking up and adapting words used long before in the Scriptures which He knew so well. The fact that He quoted this line on the Cross warrants us in looking closer at this psalm as setting forth the holy exercise of His soul. We shall find that much, if not most of its language is suited to the circumstances of His humiliation. David was betrayed by those whom he came to save; so with the great Antitype, 1 Sam. xxiii. 5, 12.

PERSONAL APPLICATION.—Even shadows may be shot with sunbeams. Have you ever known your faith to fight with your feelings? Let us commit both ourselves and our "times" into God's hand (5, 15), cf. 1 Peter iv. 19. What a blessed ground of confidence— "Thou hast redeemed *me*, O Jehovah (Covenant God) El (Mighty One) of faithfulness." When God delivers us He always sets us in a roomy place to enjoy real freedom (8). The voice of the violent will soon be silent (17). There is a great storehouse of goodness in God (19). Both the provision and the person are *kept* one for the other by Jehovah; cf. 1 Peter i. 4-5, with 19-20 here. The waves of the storm fling us higher upon the Rock (14). Be strong and let *your* heart take courage (24).

VERSE NOTES

1. Br. ". . . have I taken refuge; . . . never be ashamed," *i.e.* by finding my trust vain and hope crushed.

2. (*b*) lit. "Become to me . . ."; the plea in 2-3 is "show Thyself to be what I know Thou art."

5. The context shows that David has in view the preservation of his life; cited by our Lord (Luke xxiii. 46) in connection with His departing life; "redeemed," prim. = delivered, cf. 2 Sam. iv. 9; 1 Kings i. 29.

6. We should prob. read with LXX and some other versions, "Thou hatest," (*b*) "But as for me, I . . ."; "lying vanities," *i.e.* false gods.

7. "mercy" = loving-kindness; "known . . ." *i.e.* taken knowledge of the straits of my soul."

8. (*b*) cf. xviii. 19, xxvi. 12.

9. "Be gracious unto mė . . . in strait"; (*b*) cf. vi. 9 note.

12. (*b*) *i.e.* viewed with contempt as being worthless.

13. Jeremiah often takes upon his lips the language of the psalms known in his day, even as Christ did with deeper understanding. This is why so many critics ascribe the composition of certain psalms to Jeremiah's pen, in spite of the superscriptions. Saints of this age continue to use the language of the psalms in a similar way, as applying to their own circumstances; see Jer. xx. 10.

14. "But as for mė, I have trusted . . . have said . . ."

17. Cf. xxv. 2-3.

19. " . . . those taking refuge in Thee"; (*d*) "before the sons of men" should be connected with "wrought."

20. Cf. xxvii. 5.

21. Cf. xvii. 7; "strong," *i.e.* "fenced."

22. "But as for me, I . . ."; he confesses his want of faith in the hour of trial; "I said . . .," cf. cxvi. 11; "haste," *i.e.* alarm, or agitation.

23. Cf. xxx. 4; xxxii. 11.

24. Cf. xxvii. 14. Note parallels in last two verses. Persons addressed (23*a* and 24*b*); Proposal made (23*a* and 24*a*); Preservation of the faithful (23*b*) with the Punishment of the froward (23*c*).

PSALM XXXII. THE PARDONED PENITENT

I. DAVID'S COMMENDATION (1-2).
> Happiness of the saints extolled.

II. DAVID'S CONFESSION (3-7). Way of Restoration.
> 1. His Affliction (3-4). Selah.
> 2. His Admission (5).
> 3. His Absolution (5). Selah.
> 4. His Admonition (6).
> 5. His Appropriation (7). Selah.

III. JEHOVAH'S COMMUNICATION (8-9).
> 1. Affirmation, "I will" (8).
> 2. Admonition, "Be not" (9).

IV. DAVID'S CONVICTION (10). Warning against Rebellion.
> 1. Misery for the Rebellious (10*a*) The contrasted lot.
> 2. Mercy for the Righteous (10*b*).

V. DAVID'S CONCLUSION (11).
> Happiness of the saints expressed.

SUPERSCRIPT.—David's. Maschil.

PRIMARY ASSOCIATION.—Second of the seven so-called "penitential" psalms. First of the thirteen "maschil" psalms. "Maschil," Heb. = "for instruction," see next paragraph. Written by David almost certainly after his great sin, recorded 2 Sam. xi.-xii. For nearly a year he obstinately resisted the accusations of conscience and possibly also ailment of body (3-4), until Nathan's message cut him to the heart. Ps. li. is probably David's first prayer for pardon, this psalm being written later for the instruction of others in fulfilment of his resolve, li. 13. The reality of David's repentance is seen in that he, a king, should commit to the chief musician for the use of the temple choir at public services, a psalm relating his own sin and shame; see subscript to Ps. li. Tested by the action of other kings, David's is probably unique in history.

PROPHETIC ANTICIPATION.—Sets forth Israel's repentance in the days of their final tribulation, which God uses to bring the nation to Himself. Significantly it is the middle psalm of the "remnant" series we are now studying, xxv.-xxxix. It teaches the nation God's way of forgiveness for its long backsliding, which culminated in the crucifixion of the Messiah and the rejection of the Holy Spirit's testimony, Acts vii. "Maschil" is connected with "maschalim" trans. "those that understand" (Dan. xi. 33, 35) and "they that be wise" (Dan. xii. 3). The word means also "those who make (others) to understand" = teachers (R.V. m.). These "maschil" psalms therefore seem intended to provide special instruction for the godly Jewish remnant in the last days. This view is supported by our Lord's words concerning this very time (Matt. xxiv. 15), an appeal to "men of understanding." Rev. vi.-xix. deals with the same period, another noteworthy connection with Daniel's prophecy, see Rev. xiii. 18. As Noah and his family in the ark so the remnant will be preserved (6-7); cf. Isa. xxvi. 20; xxv. 4.

PERSONAL APPLICATION.—The psalm begins with happiness as the fruit of forgiveness, and ends with fullness of joy as the fruit of fellowship. Great guilt is met by greater grace—a great lapse by greater love. Through grace, backsliding issues in blessing, God overruling David's fall to the lifting-up of many.

In a believer, unconfessed sin causes unabated suffering (3). Frank and full confession meets with instant pardon (5). When the believer ceases to hide his sin, God will hide it for ever (5). An essential condition of forgiveness is absolute sincerity; there must be no attempt to deceive either self or God (2*b*, 5). Personal experience aids powerful exhortation (6). Only the pardoned soul can enjoy true security (6*b*). The godly are not exempt from trouble, but they are preserved in it, that is, from any evil consequences (7*a*). God's everwakeful eye is upon the godly (8); cf. xxxiii. 18-19; xxxiv. 15. Only the pardoned can truly praise (7*b*). By the use of force does the brute creation learn to submit to man's will; in the exercise of free-will should man learn to submit to God's will (9). Bit and bridle keep the horse near its master; trials and troubles are designed to keep us near our Lord (9). Ours is not merely a marked-out path, God Himself is with us as our Companion-Guide (8). Calamities and chastisements are the lot of the contumacious (10). All kindred spirits should share the joy of the forgiven sinner (11). There are times when our joy should be demonstrated (11). The sweetest song on human lips is the song of forgiveness. Public crime should be followed by public confession, Ps. li. (subscript). General lessons, see Prov. xxviii. 13; 1 John i. 8-9. Note the triple expressions throughout this psalm.

VERSE NOTES

1-2. Cited Rom. iv. 6 in support of the doctrine of righteousness apart from works; "blessed" = happy; ctr. Gal. iii. 10. Note three terms for sin: (*a*) "transgression," Heb. = an act of revolt; (*b*) "sin," Heb. = a wandering from the way; (*c*) "iniquity," Heb. = moral crookedness. Note also three terms for forgiveness: (*a*) "forgiven" (more lit. "lifted off"), Heb. denotes the removal of the burden of sin; (*b*) "covered" = the hiding of the stain of sin; (*c*) "imputeth not" = the cancelling of the debt of sin. Remember that the fact only is stated, the method or basis (atonement by blood) is not viewed here, though certainly implied. Compare the threefold confession (5).

3-4. David's experience of God's chastening hand. While his sin remained unconfessed, his suffering with complaining was not prayer, and did not bring any relief, Hosea vii. 14; "bones," cf. vi. 2.

5. "*Thou*" (emph.); "forgive," see note (1-2).

6. "For this" = therefore; "time," cf. lxix. 13.

7. "hiding-place," s.H.w. xxvii. 5; xxxi. 20; xci. 1; "songs" = shouts (11).

8. Note the triple assurance. This necessarily involves nearness, a close walk with God. He would not have His people constantly curbed and guided by circumstances, but rather have us enjoy holy intimacy with Himself like Abraham; cf. of Moses, "Show . . . that I may know," Exod. xxxiii. 13; cf. John xvii. 3; Col. i. 9-10; iii. 10; Phil. i. 9-11.

10. "mercy" = loving-kindness.

11. Note triple expression of joy; "rejoice—exult—shout in triumph."

D

PSALM XXXIII. COUNSELS OF THE CREATOR

I. CALL TO PRAISE (1–3). The United Tribute.

II. CAUSES FOR PRAISE (4–19). The Universal Testimony.
    1. Jehovah's Word and Work in Creation (4–9). Omnipotence.
        i. Reason for Praise, "For" (4–7).
        ii. Recommendation (8).
        iii. Reason for Praise, "For" (9).
    2. Jehovah's Counsel and Care in Providence (10–19). Omniscience.
        i. Relation to States (10–12).
            (a) The Rebellious Nations (10–11).
            (b) The Chosen Nation (12).
        ii. Relation to Souls (13–19).
            (a) The World's Inhabitants (13–17).
            (b) The God-fearing Individuals (18–19).

III. COMPLEMENT OF PRAISE (20–22). The United Trust.
    1. Reliance (20).
    2. Rejoicing (21).
    3. Request (22).

PRIMARY ASSOCIATION.—A congregational hymn of praise closely linked with xxxii. The absence of a title confirms this and suggests also that David is the writer (so LXX). The historical occasion is not known, but it is probably connected with some national deliverance. Compare xxxii. 11 with xxxiii. 1, invitation and answer.

PROPHETIC ANTICIPATION.—Shows the joy of the forgiven remnant expressed following the experience of Ps. xxxii. Israel's praise finds an echo in all creation, Jehovah the God of redemption being also the God of creation.

PERSONAL APPLICATION.—A psalm of power and providence, and in praise of praise. Every fresh exhibition of grace demands a fresh expression of gratitude (3). Our God is Creator, Controller and Consummator. The heavens and their host teach us our littleness and dependence. Many delight in the wonderful works of God who, alas, despise the God of wonderful works. Contemplation of Jehovah's power should move us to reverence (8); consideration of His providence to reliance (20–22). God's counsel stands firm like His creation (11, 9). Host, hero and horse are all alike impotent if God be not our trust. Is our trust false (16–17) or true (20–21), vain or victorious? Jehovah's knowledge is not only universal but individual. In the mouth of the upright alone is praise seemly (1).

VERSE NOTES

1. "Rejoice" = shout for joy, s.H. verb xxxii. 11*b*.

3–4. Same Heb. at 1 Sam. xvi. 17.

4. "right" = upright, s.H.w. (1). (*b*) "All His work is in faithfulness," *e.g.* the fixed laws of nature upon which man has learned to rely.

5. Righteousness is the principle of justice; judgment is its application.

6. Cf. Gen. i. Here is found the germ of the doctrine of the Word, John i.; "host of them" = the stellar system.

7. Present tense of the verbs expresses continual control as well as the original creation; "as a heap," all the ancient versions have "as in a bottle (wineskin)."

8–9 The emphasis is upon the wonder of creation by simple divine fiat. Hebrew more tersely, "*He* (emph.) spake and it was; *He* (emph.) commanded and it stood forth," Gen. i.; Isa. xlviii. 13.

10–11. Note the parallelism here, emphasising contrast between God and men. "Counsel . . . thoughts . . . counsel . . . thoughts."

12. "Blessed" = happy.

15. All are in some way subservient to God's plan and purpose.

17. "horse"; cavalry formed in the psalmist's day the most formidable part of an army, Prov. xxi. 31.

18. See xxxii. 8, note; br. "that wait for His loving-kindness."

19. "death," *i.e.* violent death.

20. Br. "hath looked for," s.H.w. found again in the Psalter only at cvi. 13.

22. "mercy" = loving-kindness.

PSALM XXXIV. A SONG OF THE SAVED

I. THANKSGIVING FOR A SAVED LIFE (1–10). Devotional.
   Grateful Celebration—The Song.
   1. Intention (1–2). The Vow of Praise.
   2. Invitation (3). (General). "Oh, magnify."
   3. Inspiration (4–7). The Divine Deliverance. The Voice of Experience.
      Personal (4). General (5).
      Personal (6). General (7).
   4. Invitation (8*a*). (Individual). "Oh, taste." The Venture of Faith.
   5. Inspiration (8*b*).
   6. Invitation (9*a*). (General). "Oh, fear."
   7. Inspiration (9*b*–10). The Divine Providence.

II. TEACHING FOR THE SANCTIFIED LIFE (11-22). Doctrinal.
   Golden Counsel—The Sermon.
   1. Invitation (11).
   2. Interrogation (12).
   3. Injunction (13-14).
   4. Instruction (15-22). The Divine Deliverance.
       i. The Righteous (15).
       ii. The Wicked (16).
       iii. The Righteous (17-20).
       iv. The Wicked (21).
       v. The Righteous (22).

SUPERSCRIPT.—David's; when he changed his behaviour before Abimelech, who dismissed him and he departed.

PRIMARY ASSOCIATION.—An acrostic psalm related to xxv., under which see notes. Certain expressions also connect the psalm with the preceding and the following ones. David is the writer and the occasion is mentioned in the title. Both this and lvi. belong to the period when David was fugitive at the court of Achish of Gath. He was twice with the Philistines. On the first occasion he had but a small band of young men with him, 1 Sam. xxi. 4-5, 10-15. He then feigned madness. On the second occasion, six hundred men were with him. He was welcomed by Achish and stayed a year and four months, 1 Sam. xxix. The title, "Abimelech," lit. "father of a king," implies an hereditary monarch, and is evidently a dynastic title like Pharoah and Agag. Achish was the King's personal name. Ps. lvi. is the prayer for deliverance, and our present psalm the praise for deliverance; note esp. 4, 6, 7, 17, 19.

PROPHETIC ANTICIPATION.—The trials of the godly remnant are seen producing fruit in the breaking down of all national pride (18), and the experience of certain deliverances results in praise, not yet perfect (hence incomplete acrostic) until the final great deliverance. Nevertheless Jehovah is seen as the perpetual praise of His redeemed people.

PERSONAL APPLICATION.—Blessed experience leads to bold exhortation. God's acts and man's are interrelated (15-16). *At all times* bless the Lord (1). It is a good thing to join others in magnifying the Lord (3). Are we delivered from *all* our fears? (4). God delivers from the troubles as well as from the terrors (4, 19). The Angel of

Jehovah has angelic legions at His command, 2 Kings vi. 16 ff.;
Heb. i. 14. If we are not happy, it is because we do not trust (8).
Not "any thing," but "any good thing" is the promise (10). The
tongue ever needs a special guard (13). Each man himself determines
God's attitude to him (15–16). Between good and evil, right and
wrong, there is a clear line of demarcation (14). The righteous are
not exempt from evils, but they are extricated out of them (19).
Evil exacts its own penalty. Sin itself will slay the sinner (21), the
Saviour alone can save him. The faithful are called saints (9), sons
(11) and servants (22).

VERSE NOTES

2. In the Hebrew order "In Jehovah" stands at the beginning of the line
for emphasis; "meek" = those who have learned humility in the school of
suffering.

5. David's experience is common to all who look to Jehovah; "They" = men;
"be confounded," *i.e.* be abashed, or blush (for shame).

6. "poor" = "afflicted"; read " . . . called . . . his straits."

7. "The Angel of Jehovah," cf. xxxv. 5, 6; Gen. xlviii. 16, *et. al.* This mysteri-
ous Being who appears in the Old Testament as Jehovah's representative in His
intercourse with man is undoubtedly the second person in the Trinity, the Son of
God of the New Testament. A study of the passages where the title occurs
("*the* Angel," not "*an* angel") is most instructive. These theophanies prepare us
for the incarnation of the Son of God. In the phrase here, there may be an allusion
to the words of Achish, 1 Sam. xxix. 9.

8. "taste" = make trial of; (*b*) br. "Happy is the man that taketh refuge in
Him"; "man" = Heb. geber = strong man (hero).

9. "saints" = holy ones, those whose character corresponds to calling, Lev. xi.
44, 45.

11. "fear of Jehovah" = true reverence for Him; the phrase is characteristic of
the Book of Proverbs.

12. (*b*) explains and emphasises (*a*); "good," see 10.

13. "keep" = guard; "guile" = deceit.

14. (*a*) recurs at xxxvii. 27.

15. Lit. " . . . are toward their cry (for help)."

17. br. "Men cried . . .," cf. the construction at verse 5.

20. In a general sense denotes the safe preservation of the whole being. Jehovah's
care for the righteous was exemplified in the absolutely righteous One as a prophecy
which must needs be literally fulfilled, John xix. 36.

21, 22. "condemned," s.H.w. Ps. v. 10; br. ". . . And none that take refuge
in Him shall be held guilty," cf. Rom. v. i.

Psalms xxxv.–xxxix. form a group which may be analysed as follows:
>xxxv.–xxxvi. God's dealings with the wicked.
>xxxvii. Contrasted lot of the righteous and the wicked.
>xxxviii.–xxxix. God's dealings with the righteous.

PSALM XXXV.   THE PLAINT OF THE PERSECUTED

I. INTRIGUE OF THE ENEMY (1–10).
>1. Imploration (1–3). Prayer for Protection.
>2. Imprecation (4–8). Plea against Persecutors. "Them that devise my hurt."
>>i. Requests (4–6). "Let them."
>>ii. Reason (7). "Without cause."
>>iii. Requests (8). "Let him."
>3. Intention (9–10). Promise of Praise

II. INGRATITUDE OF THE ENEMY (11–18).
>1. Incrimination (11–16). Plaint against Persecutors.
>>i. Accusation (11–12). Evil for good. False Witness. "Things I know not."
>>ii. Affirmation (13–14). Good for evil.
>>iii. Accusation (15–16). Evil for good. Base Slander. "Whom I know not."
>2. Imploration (17). Prayer for Protection.
>3. Intention (18). Promise of Praise.

III. INHUMANITY OF THE ENEMY, 19–28.
>1. Imploration (19–25). Prayer for Protection.
>>i. Requests (19). "Let them not."
>>ii. Reason (20–21a). Without cause (19).
>>iii. Requests (22–25). "Let them not."
>2. Imprecation (26). Prayer against Persecutors. "Them that rejoice at my hurt."
>3. Intention (27–28). Promise of Praise.
>>i. The Saints (27).
>>ii. The Psalmist (28).

SUPERSCRIPT.—David's.

SUBSCRIPT.—For the Chief Musician.

PRIMARY ASSOCIATION.—Written by David most probably during the period of Saul's persecution. Saul's enmity was fomented by the malicious slanders of courtiers jealous of David's sudden rise. Among these were men with whom he had been on friendly terms at court. In this and similar psalms, it is mainly against such men that David directs his appeals to Jehovah. Again and again he solemnly protests his innocence of the charge of disloyalty levelled against him. Jeremiah seems to have borrowed the language of this and other psalms. Note points of contact with Pss. vii.; xxii. 37–40; lix. On the "imprecatory" psalms, see Appendix IV.

PROPHETIC ANTICIPATION.—This is an appeal of the godly remnant amid the persecution of the last days. Beloved of God, their sufferings bear features like that of the chief Sufferer Himself, God's Well-beloved, hence much of the language is applicable to our Lord's sufferings for righteousness' sake.

PERSONAL APPLICATION.—A psalm of the adversary and the Advocate. Have you heard God say to your soul, "I am thy salvation" (3)? Spiritual foes are ever spreading nets and digging pits to catch unwary believers, therefore watch and pray (7–8). Rejoice in the Lord as well as in His salvation (9–10). Base ingratitude is an ancient sin and a very modern one (13–16). To return evil for good is demon-like; to return evil for evil is man-like; to return good for evil is God-like (12–16). In the midst of trouble David was enabled to give thanks to God (28). In Ps. xxxiv. the Angel of Jehovah is seen protecting the saints; in Ps. xxxv. the Angel of Jehovah is seen pursuing the spoilers. True prayer always brings back a blessing to the praying one.

VERSE NOTES

1. "Plead my cause with them that implead me," better represents the original.

2–3. These verses expand the idea of Jehovah as a "man of war," Exod. xv. 3; cf. Deut. xxxii. 41 ff.

2. Cf. Ps. v. 2; br. "Arise as my help."

3. (b) prim. ref. to temporal, not spiritual salvation.

4. ff. Prayer for the repulse and rout of his enemies.

5. Picture of a pell-mell rout; "the Angel," cf. xxxiv. 7 note.

7. The insidious nature of the enemy's secret plots is indicated; "net" and "pit" are frequent figures in the Psalter. They were methods anciently used to catch wild creatures.

8. (c) br. as R.V. marg. but "destruction" must be understood to mean the pit that he hath dug.

10. "All my bones," *i.e.* the whole being; "poor" = afflicted.

11. Cf. 1 Sam. xxiv. 9; "unrighteous," the Hebrew denotes those who do violence to the truth; cf. Exod. xxiii. 1; Matt. xxvi. 59 ff.

12. Cf. 1 Sam. xxiv. 17 ff.

15. (*b*) Br. "the slanderers . . . ere I knew," or as R.V. marg.

16. Br. "with profane babblers for bread," *i.e.* sycophants who earn their entertainment at carousals by foolish and unwholesome jests.

17. See marg. = my precious life; cf. xxii. 20.

18. Cf. xxii. 22, 25.

19. Latter part of (*b*) cited by our Lord of Himself, John xv. 25.

21. Br. "And they open . . . they say . . . have seen it," *i.e.* their desire in the fall of the one they hate.

22. Note how the psalmist turns the taunt of the enemy into a plea with God.

24. *i.e.* "Do me justice," cf. vii. 8.

25. Or, "Aha (this is) to our mind," *i.e.* according to our desire.

PSALM XXXVI. GOD AND THE GODLESS

I. THE LAWLESS; HIS EVIL-DOING (1-4). Rebellion.
    1. His Guiding Principle (1-2). Character.
    2. His General Practice (3-4). Conduct.

II. THE LORD; HIS LOVING-KINDNESS (5-11).
    1. The Psalmist's Acknowledgments (5-9). Praise.
        i. God's Attributes (5-6*a*).
        ii. God's Activities (6*b*).
        iii. God's Attributes (7*a*).
        iv. God's Activities (7*b*-8).
        v. God's Attributes (9*a*).
        vi. God's Activities (9*b*).

    2. The Psalmist's Appeal (10-11). Prayer.
        i. Request (Positive) (10).
        ii. Request (Negative) (11).

III. THE LAWLESS; THEIR END (12). Ruin.

SUPERSCRIPT.—"(A psalm) of David the servant of the Lord."

PRIMARY ASSOCIATION.—Writer is David, historical occasion unknown. Only other psalm with this title is xviii., cf. xxxv. 27.

PROPHETIC ANTICIPATION.—Here are found instructive truths for the saints of all ages, but particularly suited to the circumstances of the godly remnant in the last days.

PERSONAL APPLICATION.—As a message for to-day we may note: (a) the Wickedness of the Wicked (1-4); the Graciousness of God (5-9); (c) the Confidence of the Christian (10-12); or, the Sinner, the Saviour, and the Saint, respectively. Contemplate the total contrast between the character of God and that of the godless. The wicked deny God's providence and defy His powers (1). Words are an index to the heart (3); cf. Luke vi. 45. God's changeless character is displayed in His creation (5). Summits, sea and sky all declare His greatness and goodness (5-7). He is Protector of and Provider for all peoples (7-8). Let us drink deep of the "river of His pleasures," delighting in the things that delight Him; so shall our souls be truly satisfied (8). God is the true source of light and life (9). The overthrow of the wicked will be complete and final (12).

VERSE NOTES

1. "transgression" = revolt; "saith," Heb. = utters as an oracle. A somewhat difficult verse. If the A.V. is correct, the sense is that the action of the wicked speaks to the psalmist as surely as a divine message, the truth given in the next line. But LXX and other ancient versions read "his heart" in which case the meaning is that *sin* is the oracle of the wicked; *i.e.* he is servant to it, and its suggestions hold a place in his heart that God's word holds in the heart of the servant of Jehovah. Sin is thus a "lying spirit" within the lawless heart, persuading it that there is no need to be in terror of God's judgments; "fear" = terror; cited, Rom. iii. 18.

2. (b) br. as margin; "found" = detected with a view to punishment.

4. "Upon his bed"; cf. the time for repentance for sin, iv. 4; for recollection of God, lxiii. 6, not for the ripening of evil; (b) indicates deliberate choice.

5. "is in" = (reacheth) to; God's loving-kindness is immeasurable.

6. (a) *i.e.* God is immovable and unchangeable in His faithfulness to His character and covenant; "God" = El.

6. (b) *i.e.* inexhaustible and unfathomable; cf. Rom. xi. 33.

7. "God," a significant change of title, for His loving-kindness extends beyond the people of the covenant to all peoples.

8. (a) as marg. or, lap up; (b) "river" lit. torrent.

12. The doom of those mentioned in 1-4 is foreseen by the eye of faith.

PSALM XXXVII. TEACHING FOR TROUBLOUS TIMES

I. GOOD COUNSEL (1-11). Exhortations and Encouragements.

    1. The Recommendations (1). *The Commencing Admonition.*

    2. The Reasons (2). "For."

3. The Recommendations (3-4a).
4. The Recompense (4b).
5. The Recommendations (5ab).
6. The Recompense (5b-6).
7. The Recommendations (7-8).
8. The Reasons (9-10). "For . . . for."

II. GREAT CONTRASTS (12-26).   Reasons and Reflections.

1. The Rebellious (12-15).
2. The Righteous and the Rebellious (16-17).
3. The Righteous (18-19).
4. The Rebellious (20).
5. The Rebellious and the Righteous (21-22).
6. The Righteous (23-26).

III. GOOD COUNSEL (27-28).   Exhortations and Encouragements.

1. The Recommendations (27).
2. The Reasons (28). "For."

IV. GREAT CONTRASTS (28-33).   Conduct and Consequences.

1. The Rebellious and the Righteous (28b-29).
2. The Righteous (30-31).
3. The Rebellious and the Righteous (32).

V. GOOD COUNSEL (34).   Exhortations and Encouragements.

1. The Recommendation (a).
2. The Recompense (b).

VI. GREAT CONTRASTS (35-40).   Individualities and Issues.

1. The Rebellious (35-36).
2. The Righteous and the Rebellious (37-38).
3. The Righteous (39-40). *The Closing Assurance.*

SUPERSCRIPT.—David's.

PRIMARY ASSOCIATION.—Written by David at some late period in his life (25). It is acrostic in structure, antithetic in style and didactic in substance. Note that the voice of prayer is here silent. Acrostic arrangement nearly perfect. Instead of the usual couplet, the letters Daleth, Kaph and Koph have each a triplet, while Cheth, Nun and Tav have five lines each. The Aleph stanza gives the theme of the psalm and the Tav stanza a fitting conclusion. The same fundamental ideas recur throughout with somewhat complex alternations and introversions. Pss. lxxiii. and xlix. should be compared, also the Books of Job and Proverbs. See additional note, Appendix V.

PROPHETIC ANTICIPATION.—Still the remnant in the last days,

when a very distinct line of cleavage is seen between the lawless ones and the loyal ones, the way of apostasy and the way of allegiance to Jehovah. Here is counsel for the coming crisis. Note the characteristic promise for the remnant; they shall dwell in the land (Canaan) (3, 9, 11, 22, 34). This looks on to millennial days and beyond. The slight irregularities in the acrostic suggest that the perfect state is not yet reached though it is seen approaching.

PERSONAL APPLICATION.—A psalm of the rule of recompense. Note the positive and negative exhortations, the former predominating. All may be summed up in the phrase "exercise faith and patience." Compare the three-fold "Fret not" (more lit. "Do not get heated") and the three-fold "Be not envious." The prosperity of the ungodly is precarious and not permanent (1-2). Let our souls feed upon the faithfulness of our God (3). The antidote to envious discontent is patient trust and persistent well-doing (3-4). Such discontent is not only foolish and useless but dangerous, as it may lead to evil-doing (8). The loyal must not copy the tricks of the lawless (8). Disappointment and destruction are the destiny of the destroyers (19-20). The fate of the wicked has been foreseen and foreordained from the first (13). The enemies of Jehovah's people are enemies of Jehovah (20). While the wicked rave (12) the righteous rest (7). The principle of retribution may be traced in human history (14-15). The truly "strong man" gets his strength from the Lord (23a). The steps and the stops of the saint are all ordered of God (23). His failures are not fatal or final (24). There is a definite relation between our walk and our talk (30-31). Not only *keep* God's way (34) but *delight* in it (23). It is the end of the way that matters (37-38).

VERSE NOTES

2. "grass . . . green herb," common figures in Scripture for what is transient and perishable.

3. "land" = Canaan, the land of promise; "follow after . . ." lit. "feed on faithfulness," *i.e.* Jehovah's.

4. "desires" = petitions.

5. Note margin; cf. Prov. xvi. 3, 1 Peter v. 4; (*b*) lit. "and *He* (emph.) will do (it)." The result of the "doing" seen in next verse, *i.e.* "thy cause will be vindicated."

11. Cf. Matt. v. 5.

12. Br. "doth laugh . . . for He hath seen."

13. "day," *i.e.* the appointed day of retribution.

14. "poor" = afflicted or oppressed; "upright . . .," lit. "upright of way."

16. Note word "many."

17. *i.e.* their misused power rendered of no effect.

19. "evil" = calamity.

20. (*b*) as A.V. and R.V. m. The meaning is that they who would not be consecrated to God in life shall be "devoted" to Him in their death, consumed by the fire of His wrath, even as sacrificial animals under the ban.

21. The greediness of the wicked and the graciousness of the righteous contrasted.

22. "him . . . him," *i.e.* Jehovah.

23. Read, "When a man's (Heb. geber, Appendix X.) steps are made firm by Jehovah, and he (the man) delighteth in His (Jehovah's) way; though he . . ."

24. (*a*) *i.e.* shall not lie prostrate; cf. Prov. xxiv. 16; (*b*) br. as R.V. m.

25. An appeal to experience. The righteous is never deserted by God, despite appearances.

27. (*a*) cf. xxxiv. 14; (*b*) cf. 3b, 29.

28–29. Cf. Prov. xi. 31.

35. Another appeal to experience (25). (*a*) or ". . . lawless one" = ruthless.

36. Br. "And I passed by . . ."

37–38. "end . . . end," or "future . . . future"; "transgressors" = rebels; "wicked"=lawless men.

PSALM XXXVIII.   SIN, SUFFERING AND SUPPLICATION

I. MOVING APPEAL TO JEHOVAH (1).   Commencing Prayer, "Rebuke me not."

II. MANIFEST ASSOCIATION OF SIN AND SUFFERING (2–10). "for."

III. MEAN ACTION OF FRIENDS AND FOES (11–12).

IV. MEEK ATTITUDE OF THE SUFFERER (13–16).
   1. Silence Manward (13–14).
   2. Confidence Godward (15–16).

V. MANIFEST ASSOCIATION OF SIN AND SUFFERING (17–18).

VI. MEAN ACTION OF FRIENDS AND FOES (19–20).

VII. MOVING APPEAL TO JEHOVAH (21–22).   Closing Prayer, "Forsake me not."

SUPERSCRIPT.—A psalm of David to bring to remembrance.

SUBSCRIPT.—For the Chief Musician, for Jeduthun.

PRIMARY ASSOCIATION.—Third of the so-called "penitential" psalms. Written by David; historical occasion uncertain, but probably the period of Absalom's revolt. The sin referred to in the psalm may be the folly of indulging his children, which led to such dire consequences for himself, his family and the people generally, cf. 1 Kings i. 6. The two groups of Pss. xxxviii.-xli. and lxix.-lxxii. have much in common and seem to belong to a late period in David's reign. This psalm bears a close relation to vi. and xxxix. Superscript, "to bring to remembrance," is prefixed also to lxx; s.H.w. is found, 1 Chron. xvi. 4, "celebrate." David's intention may be to remind God of His covenant promises, 2 Sam. vii. (cf. Isa. xliii. 26; lxii. 6-7), or of His people's needs. Subscript, "For Jeduthun," appears again at the end of lxi. and lxxvi. This man was a Levite and chief singer and director of the temple music, see 1 Chron. ix. 16; xvi. 38 ff.; xxv. 1 ff.; 2 Chron. v. 12; xxix. 14; and Neh. xi. 17. He was at first called Ethan.

PROPHETIC ANTICIPATION.—By reason of their suffering in "the Tribulation" period, Israel's faithful ones (the remnant) are brought to a confession of sin and an acknowledgment that their punishment was justly inflicted by Jehovah. Recognising their utter helplessness and worthlessness, they cast themselves upon Jehovah's mercy.

PERSONAL APPLICATION.—Our sins may be like an overwhelming flood and a crushing burden, but there is help in God (4). Sin is essentially foolishness (5). While friends stand aloof, foes often draw near (11-12). While the righteous meditates wisdom (xxxvii. 30) his enemies "meditate" (s.H.w.) deceits (12). Consciousness of his own guilt (13) and recognition of divine chastening (xxxix. 9) keep the sorrowing saint silent. When in distress we need not despair (15). The sombre depths of repentant confession lead to the sunny heights of restored communion. Our kindred are not always kind (11). The fickleness of friends is often harder to endure than the fierceness of our foes (11). Sin necessarily involves suffering to the saint now, 1 Cor. xi. 32. Knowledge of some specific sin may co-exist with a consciousness of innocence in our actions towards men generally; 17-18 are not contradicted by 19-20. Let us be sincerely sorry for our sin (18). Anchor your soul in God; He will answer for you (15). The wicked rejoice at the guilt of the believer, but rage at his goodness (16, 20). Note: (a) Shadow of divine displeasure; (b) Sorrow of divine estrangement; (c) Supplication of divine favour.

VERSE NOTES

1. The emphasis is upon "in wrath" and "in hot displeasure." David desires God to deal with him, not in the character of an angry Judge, but as a loving Preceptor.

2. "arrows," a fig. for divine judgments in general, but more particularly here = pain and prostration.

3. Cf. Isa. i. 5, 6, of Israel's condition nationally; "rest" = peace, or health.

5-10. Physical and mental sufferings graphically described.

6. Br. as margin.

8. "roared" = the utterance of sounds of distress.

10. (b) cf. vi. 7; xiii. 3 note.

11. "my plague," or stroke; Hebrew word specifically used of leprosy. His friends treated him as a leper.

12. Cf. Shimei's cursings, 2 Sam. xvi. 7-8.

14. He had nothing to say in his own defence.

15. "Thou (emph.) wilt answer," may be taken in the sense of "answer my prayer," or "answer for me" (to my detractors). The former sense, of course, involves the latter.

16. (b) cf. xxxv. 26.

18. "sorry" = troubled.

20. "good," that is, the good which he wrought towards them, cf. xxxv. 12-13.

21-22. "my God . . . my salvation"; this closing appeal contains in itself the assurance of acceptance and answer.

PSALM XXXIX.   LAMENT ON THE LIMIT OF LIFE

I. SUPPRESSED EMOTIONS (1-3).   Confession of inward strivings.
    1. The Resolve (1).
    2. The Results (2-3).

II. STRONG ENTREATY (4-5).   Supplication for greater enlightenment.
    1. The Prayer (4).
    2. The Plea (5). *The Vanity of Man. His Fleeting Days.* Selah.

III. SOLEMN EMPHASIS (6).   Assertion of sober facts.
    The Folly and Futility Man's Efforts.

IV. STRONG ENTREATY (7-8).   Supplication for complete deliverance.
    1. The Profession (7).
    2. The Prayer (8). Positive and negative petitions.

V. SIGNIFICANT   EXPLANATION   (9).   Manifestation of becoming humility.

VI. STRONG ENTREATY (10-11). Supplication for speedy relief.
    1. The Prayer (10).
    2. The Plea (11). *The Vanity of Man. His Failing Delights* (R.V.m.). Selah.

VII. SOULFUL ENDING (12-13). Conclusion in tearful importunity.
    1. The Prayer (12*a*).
    2. The Plea (12*b*).
    3. The Prayer (13).

SUPERSCRIPT.—A psalm of David.

SUBSCRIPT.—For the Chief Musician.

PRIMARY ASSOCIATION.—Written by David possibly during the period of Absalom's rebellion. It is a sequel to xxxviii. and related to lxii. with many parallels also in the Book of Job. Said to be the most beautiful elegy in the Psalter. David speaks throughout as one failing in strength and perplexed by the mystery of the continued impunity of ungodly men, as Shimei, Joab, etc. For this reason some assign the psalm to the time of Adonijah's revolt.

PROPHETIC ANTICIPATION.—Prophetically belongs to the same period as the preceding psalms; the godly remnant still seen in deep exercise of soul.

PERSONAL APPLICATION.—Keep ward and watch over words and works (1). It is better to be absolutely silent than to say the wrong thing (1-2). Our days have a measure, therefore let us measure our days (4). Suppressed feelings feed the fire (3). We *are* frail but do we face the facts? (4) Human life and earthly treasures are fleeting (6). Man's only sure stay is in God (4-7). Human frailty should drive us and divine faithfulness draw us into the loving arms of God (7). There is hope for one whose hope is in God (7). Sin is the sole cause of the frailty of human existence and the futility of human efforts (8). It is only the foolish who regard the sufferings of the godly as a mark of God's wrath (8). The Christian, too, is a stranger and sojourner (12); cf. 1 Peter ii. 11. Only by "looking away" from the sinner and "looking upon" the face of the Saviour can a holy God regard man with favour, lxxxiv. 9.

VERSE NOTES

    1. Cf. xxxviii. 13-14 and note marg. He would avoid complaining while waiting for God to "cut off" the wicked.

    2. *i.e.* he kept absolute silence, but the suppressing of his emotions aggravated his sufferings, cf. xxxii. 3.

4. He desires to know not so much how long he has to live, but to realise how surely life must end, and how brief life is at best.

6. Kirkpatrick renders, "Only as a phantom doth each walk to and fro; Only for vanity do they turmoil; One heapeth . . ." Ctr. Nabal's self-aggrandisement with David's gathering of wealth for the Lord's House, 1 Sam. xxv. 11; 1 Chron. xxii. and xxix. 2–5.

9. Indicates his resignation to the will of God, 2 Sam. xvi. 10; cf. Aaron, Lev. x. 3, and, still more, David's Antitype, Isa. liii. 7.

10. "stroke," s.H.w., xxxviii. 11.

11. (a) cf. xxxviii. 1; (b) As the larva of the clothes moth destroys the beauty of garments, so easily does God's chastening destroy all that in which man prides himself. (c) "Nought but vanity are all men," cf. lxii. 9; "surely" represents the Hebrew particle "ak" characteristic of this psalm and lxx. It occurs here four times in the sense of "only," or "nought but."

12. Israelites were taught to regard themselves as strangers and sojourners in the land of promise, which belonged to Jehovah Himself, Lev. xxv. 23. Thus as a stranger (or guest) he pleads clemency according to the rule, Exod. xxii. 21, etc.; cf. David's words recorded 1 Chron. xxix. 15. In passing, it may be pointed out that man generally is but a temporary tenant in the earth which is the Lord's, cxix. 19.

13. Br. as margin, *i.e.* avert Thy frowning countenance.

Book One. III. Record of the Divine Redeemer, xvi.–xli.

3. The Redeemer. The Saviour and Sinners, xl.–xli.

These two psalms stand in emphatic contrast to one another. In the former we see the heart of Christ, the Saviour; in the latter, the heart of men, saints and sinners (again a contrast).

PSALM XL. THE SECRET OF SACRIFICE

I. GRATEFUL ACKNOWLEDGMENT (1–4). *Record of Past Deliverance.*
   1. The Experience (1–3a).
   2. The Effect (3b).
   3. The Encouragement (4).

II. GLAD AVOWAL (5–10). *Resolve of Personal Devotion.*
   1. Declaration of Jehovah's Works (5). Testimony before God.
   2. Declaration of the Psalmist's Obedience (6–8).
   3. Declaration of Jehovah's Attributes (9–10). Testimony before men.

III. GREAT APPEAL (11–17). *Request for Present Deliverance.*
   1. The Expectation (11).
   2. The Extremity (12).

3. The Entreaty (13). "Make haste . . ."
4. Imprecation (14–15). Against soul-seekers.
5. Intercession (16). For God-seekers.
6. The Extremity (17*a*).
7. The Expectation (17*b*).
8. The Entreaty (17*c*). "Make no tarrying . . ."

SUPERSCRIPT.—A psalm of David.

SUBSCRIPT.—For the Chief Musician.

PRIMARY ASSOCIATION.—Written by David probably during the period of Absalom's rebellion, or that of Adonijah. Both these sons of David commenced their open revolt by a sacrificial feast, 2 Sam. xv. 7–12; 1 Kings i. 9, 41; cf. Ps. lxix. 30–31 and David's warning to Absalom's faction (Ps. iv. 5), who cloaked their evildoing under a show of religion. Ceremonial observance was confounded with cordial obedience to the will of God, a common error in Israel and, alas, in Christendom to-day. In this psalm we find another instance of the deliverance celebrated, followed by a description of the circumstances preceding that deliverance. Note that in lxx. part of this psalm recurs, but in perfect harmony with the context; there, as following the trespass offering, lxix.; here, in the burnt offering psalm.

PROPHETIC ANTICIPATION.—Long recognised as Messianic, this psalm represents the burnt offering aspect of the Cross; cf. xxii. and lxix. The writer of the Hebrews Epistle quotes the LXX version of 6–8 at x. 5–7, where the efficacy of Christ's perfect obedience in sacrificing Himself is contrasted with the inefficacy of the legal sacrifices, now set aside in the "once-for-all" offering of the body of Jesus Christ. The difference in the words of the Old Testament and the New Testament are not a contradiction but an explanation. The inspired writers of the New Testament often explain as they quote the Old Testament Scriptures. The Holy Spirit surely has the right to explain His own words. "Digged ears" and "prepared body" both indicate readiness for service. The burnt offering characterised the brazen altar and gave it its more frequent name, Exod. xxxviii. 1–7. This offering was tried fully by the fire of divine holiness and nothing found but a sweet savour, all ascending to God. It is interesting to notice that the number of our psalm is the representative number of perfect trial, forty. From the Messianic standpoint, we may analyse the psalm thus: (a) Confident Confession, 1-4; (b) Crowning Obedience, 5-13; (c) Contrasted Consequences, 14-17. Verse 12 was true of Christ only in His vicarious sufferings as the Sin-bearer, hence the close association of this verse with the preceding one. The depths into which His holy soul sank are represented in verse 2.

This psalm has also a prophetic relation to the faithful remnant and their soul exercise in the days of the coming crisis. Verse 6, for instance, while expressing a general truth, seems to apply expecially to them in the days of the last great national apostasy, dark days referred to also in 2 Thess. ii. We have already seen that the sufferings of Messiah in certain aspects are closely related to those of His people.

PERSONAL APPLICATION.—Patient waiting for God always meets its due reward (1). For the believer there is a firm footing and strong stepping (2). He has exchanged a slippery place for a secure place, no footing for sure footing (2). The God who has delivered, does deliver and will yet deliver, 2 Cor. i. 10. Remembrance of our salvation is always an occasion for a new song (3). Study the beatitudes in the Psalter; here is one (4). God's thoughtfulness for "us" (5) is individualised for "me" (17). Try counting our blessings; it is good exercise, but we shall not succeed (5). Let us constantly remind ourselves of the solemn words recorded in 1 Sam. xv. 22. What delights God should delight His servants (8). Gratitude to God is best expressed by willing obedience (8). Public declaration and private desire should be complementary and consistent (8-9). The Lord "withholds not" His tender mercies (11), then "withhold not" your testimonial message (9). The best qualification for a preacher of righteousness is the practice of it (9). For Messiah, man's guilty pleasure insisted upon the Cross, and God's good pleasure involved the Cross. We love God's salvation, because in it we see His character (= personality, power and purpose) so wonderfully displayed (16); we love *His* appearing also, because it will bring the consummation of God's salvation, 2 Tim. iv. 8. Let us make 17*b* our very own to-day.

VERSE NOTES

2. Quagmires are common in Palestine.

4. "Happy is the man that hath made Jehovah his trust; and hath not turned aside to the arrogant and apostates"; "man" = strong man.

5. "Thou," (emph.); (*b*) or, "... and Thy thoughtfulness for us"; br. (*c*) as margin.

6-8. Contrast Saul's selfwill with David's self-devotion, 1 Sam. xv. 22.

6. Note mention of principal offerings to show that all those given in the Levitical code are included; "sacrifice" (Hebrew = zebach) a general term for all eucharistic sacrifices—peace, votive and thank-offerings; "offering" (Heb. mincha) is the meal offering with which is connected the drink offering; "burnt offering," (Heb. olah); "sin offering" (Heb. chatath) refers to the expiatory sacrifices, *viz.* sin and trespass offerings. All pointed to Christ and found their full realisation in Him, consequently were no more required after He appeared. It is significant that the very generation which saw His rejection, saw also the Jewish priesthood abolished and the sacrifices taken away. Since then the Jews have had no opportunity for offering sacrifices according to the legal code. As typifying Christ's perfect offering, we may briefly mention:(*a*) the Sin Offering, Expiation for sin; (*b*) the Trespass Offering, Restitution for sin; (*c*) the Meal Offering, Perfection of life; (*d*) the Burnt Offering, Devotion unto death; (*e*) the Peace Offering, Reconciliation effected and enjoyed.

6. (*b*) Placed between (*a*) and (*c*) apparently for poetic effect introductory to 7-8. True in measure of David, Messiah was the supreme and only perfect example of obedience. The meaning is not the same as in Exod. xxi. 6, though there is a connection. There perpetual service is denoted; here, perfect service; both are realised in Christ; cf. Isa. l. 4-5.

7. "Then"; of David, expresses the ready response of the servant to his master's summons, Num. xxii. 38; 2 Sam. xix. 20; cf. Isa. vi. 9; of Messiah, it is to be referred to the time after His assumption of manhood (Heb. x. 5). Note tense of verb in R.V. (*b*) cf. John v. 39; Luke xxiv. 44; but here specifically the institution of the sacrifices mentioned, verse 6; as much as to say, "My work is the fulfilment of these." Only blind critics could ever take verse 6 to mean that sacrifices were never instituted of God. David did not neglect their use (1 Chron. xxix. 21), though he did condemn the rebel's abuse of them, cf. Isa. i. 10-17. See Appendix VII.

8. (*a*) Ctr. the "delight" of the wicked (14), s.H.w.; (*b*) Such was God's demand of Israel, Deut. vi. 6, and such is the characteristic of the righteous, Ps. xxxvii. 31. Such also is to be the condition of those under the New Covenant, Jer. xxxi. 33.

9. (*a*) Br. as marg., xxxv. 18. Public declaration of a paramount theme. (*b*) br. "I did not restrain ...," not a prayer, but an expression of confidence in the divine response.

11. (*b*) As he has not ceased to acknowledge God's loving-kindness and truth, so loving-kindness and truth will not cease to guard him.

12. "evils," *i.e.* afflictions; "so that" ... br. "And I cannot see"; cf. xxxviii. 10.

13-17. Passage recurs as Ps. lxx. with a few variations. 13*b*. cf. xxxviii. 22.

14ff. Recall passages in Ps. xxxv.

15. *i.e.* be discomfited because of the defeat of their malevolent plans; "Aha, aha" = exclamation of malicious pleasure.

17. "But" or though.

PSALM XLI. TRUST, TREACHERY AND TRIUMPH

I. ASSURANCE OF JEHOVAH'S FAVOUR (1-3).

II. APPEAL TO JEHOVAH'S GRACIOUSNESS (4).

III. ARRAIGNMENT OF DAVID'S FOES (5-9).
1. The Adversaries; their Conspiracy (5). Words quoted.
2. The Archtraitor; his Hypocrisy (6). *Scene.* The Sufferer's Sickroom.
3. The Adversaries; their Conspiracy (7-8). Words quoted.
4. The Archtraitor; his Treachery (9). *Scene.* The Rebels' Council Chamber.

IV. APPEAL TO JEHOVAH'S GRACIOUSNESS (10).

V. ASSURANCE OF JEHOVAH'S FAVOUR (11-12).

DOXOLOGY (13). (END OF BOOK ONE).

SUPERSCRIPT.—A psalm of David.

SUBSCRIPT.—For the Chief Musician.

PRIMARY ASSOCIATION.—Written by David perhaps at the period of Absalom's rebellion, like the preceding psalms, but some would refer the group to the time of David's last sickness, when Adonijah sought to seize the kingdom. Although the historical records are silent on the point, there are indications supported by the language of several psalms that David suffered a serious illness between the time of his great sin with Bathsheba and the outbreak of Absalom's revolt. It is otherwise difficult to account for his apparent laxity in attending to his official duties, which Absalom's words seem to imply (2 Sam. xv. 3) and the strange failure of his natural courage which led to his flight from the capital at the very first sign of open rebellion. Note that this last psalm of Book I begins, like the first, with a beatitude; moreover the last *two* psalms, like the first two, both contain a beatitude.

PROPHETIC ANTICIPATION.—Portrays Messiah as the Suffering One. Verse 4 sees Him as the Sin-bearer; the true force of "I have sinned" here may be gathered by the use of the same Hebrew word, *e.g.* by Judah, Gen. xliv. 32 = "bear the blame (sin)." Note that verse 1 does not teach (as commonly supposed from the language of A.V. and R.V.) deliverance from calamity as a reward for mere benevolence.

The words are somewhat enigmatical, "who considereth (or, understandeth as to) the Weakened One," *i.e.* Messiah. Taken thus, the teaching is quite clear and in perfect harmony with the rest of the psalm as well as with the preceding one; cf. cii. 23, 2 Cor. xiii. 4. Faith discerns the glory of Christ under the veil of His sufferings and there is especial blessing for those of the godly remnant who shall understand the mystery of Messiah crucified through weakness (1–3).

PERSONAL APPLICATION.—Blessed is the man who even to-day understands the holy mystery of the crucified Christ (1). That God makes the bed of His saints in sickness is a striking thought, but that He changes their sickness into health is more the meaning of the text (3). The saint often needs healing no less than the sinner (4). "Jesus Christ maketh *thee* whole," Acts ix. 33–34. A faithless friend is worse than a frank foe, a treacherous ally worse than a tenacious adversary (9). Christians must not be surprised if they are called to share with their Lord the sorrows of false friendship (9); cf. John xv. 20. God delights in the obedient saint (11). What sort of friends are we to Christ? cf. John xv. 14. The Divine existence is an eternal present (13). Let us bless the Lord God of Israel; He who is faithful to His ancient people, will be faithful to all His people (13).

VERSE NOTES

1. "Blessed . . .," br. "Happy . . . who considereth (or rather, understandeth as to) the weak (or, Weakened One)"; "poor" not same Hebrew word as in xl. 17.

2. "blessed . . ." = "made happy in the land"; (*b*) read as A.V.

3. (*b*) lit. "Thou has turned his lying down," *i.e.* changed his sickness into health. "Enemies" (2) and "sickness" (3) are both referred to in 5–9.

4. "I, even I, have said . . ."; "have mercy . . .," br. "be gracious to me"; "Heal my soul," equivalent to the New Testament phrase "make whole," refers to the healing of the whole man, body and soul.

6. "he" = "one (of them) . . ."; verse refers to hypocritical professions of sympathy, the while he is gathering matter for malicious retail to others.

8. Lit. "a thing of Belial clingeth . . . ," cf. Shimei's taunt, 2 Sam. xvi. 7. (*b*) *i.e.* now that he has taken to his bed, he will never leave it.

9. (*b*) *i.e.* violently spurned me. Words are quoted by Christ of the treachery of Judas, John xiii. 18. Note that the fate of Ahithophel was very similar to that of Judas.

10. Br. "be gracious unto me"; "raise me up . . .," *i.e.* contrary to the expectation of the enemy (8); (*b*) *i.e.* in his official capacity as chief judge of the nation.

11. Cf. xxxv. 27; 2 Sam. xv. 26.

12. "integrity" is not synonymous with sinlessness; see Appendix VIII; (b) ctr. 5b, the expectation of his enemies.

13. Doxology. Not original part of the psalm, but marks the close of Book I, cf. 1 Chron. xxix. 10-11, 20. "Amen and amen,"=the response of the congregation in the temple services.

Book Two. *Israel's Ruin and Redemption, Pss. xlii.-lxxii.*

Prophetically, much of this Book is occupied with the faithful remnant of Israel driven out of the land, crying out for God and solacing themselves with the future. There is a special reference to the last days, when the distressed remnant, having fled to the mountains (Matt. xxiv. 16), appeal to God for deliverance. Deprived of the covenant blessings, but not destitute of faith, they longingly await Messiah's coming to rescue the nation. Compare Peter's second epistle, where we find this apostle and a remnant in exile, Jews outcast for Christ, suffering but awaiting the advent of the Lord. We must ever remember that God's relationship with Israel as a nation is connected with His dwelling-place in the sanctuary, hence to be driven out of Jerusalem is a loss of immense significance. Having lost the covenant title as a nation, the faithful ones are led at last to cast themselves wholly upon the mercy of God. In Book II, therefore, the covenant name "Jehovah" is dropped in favour of "Elohim," by which title God is displayed in His own essential nature. When "Jehovah" is used, there is generally a special reference to the future of Israel, when covenant relationship is restored. "Remnant" psalms furnish expressions of faith which will be the comfort and stay of loyal hearts in the days of trial preceding their deliverance. Three persons are prominent: (*a*) the King (Messiah) typified by David, Solomon, etc.; (*b*) the ten-horned and the two-horned "Beasts" of Rev. xiii., typified by Absalom and Ahithophel respectively. It is noteworthy that in this the "Exodus" book of the Psalter, most if not all the illustrations are from Exodus, as those of Book I were from Genesis. Redemption is seen in its twofold character:

> 1. Redemption by Blood—the Ransom Paid. This buys back the condemned slave. Life given.
>
> 2. Redemption by Power—the Release Perfected. This breaks off the cruel shackles. Liberty given.

Book II, therefore, begins with the sufferings of the moaning remnant, and ends with the splendours of the Messianic reign. The first nine psalms form an epitome of the latter day history of Israel.

Analysis.

I. DELIVERANCE OF THE EXILED REMNANT, XLII-LI.
    1. The Redemptive Power, xliii.-xlix. From External Evil. Eight Korahite Psalms.
    2. The Restored People, l.-li. From Internal Evil.

II. DISCLOSURES CONCERNING THE ENEMY REPROBATE, LII-LX.
    1. The Apostates and the Remnant, lii.-lv. (Maschils). The Antichrist Identified. Instruction concerning the Lawless One.

2. The Afflicted and their Refuge, lvi.–lx. (Michtams). The Almighty Invoked. Inspiration for the Loyal Ones.

III. DOMINION OF THE ENTHRONED REDEEMER, LXI–LXXII.
    1. The Returned King, lxi.–lxviii.
    2. The Restored Kingdom, lxix.–lxxii.

Book Two. I. Deliverance of the Exiled Remnant, xlii.–li.

1. The Redemptive Power, xlii.–xlix. Deliverance from external evil.

This section consists of eight Korahite Psalms and may be subdivided as follows:
    i. The Distress, xlii.–xliv.
    ii. The Deliverer, xlv. Permanence of His Glory.
    iii. The Deliverance, xlvi.–xlviii.
    iv. The Desolators, xlix. Passing of their Glory.

NOTE.—The Korahites were the posterity of Korah (Num. xvi.), who with his company suffered condign punishment for rebellion. His children however were spared (Num. xxvi. 11), divine judgment being tempered with mercy. The descendants were appointed sentinels of the camp of the Levites, and warders of the sacred tent erected by David on Mt. Zion. (1 Chron. ix. 17–19; xxvi; Neh. xi. 19). They were also leaders of Israel's praise in the temple services, 1 Chron. vi. 22–27. Heman, one of David's three principal musicians, was a Korahite and his sons became leaders of fourteen out of the twenty-four courses of temple musicians, 1 Chron. xxv. 4–31; see further allusions, 2 Chron. xx. 19; xxix. 14. Psalms dedicated to these "Sons of Korah" are all characterised by a deep spiritual tone. Divine loving-kindness so markedly displayed in their history, becomes a constant theme of their praise. Their very presence in the sanctuary was a continual witness to Israel of the grace of God.

Psalms xlii. and xliii. are best taken together as they form a preface to Book II, and are so closely linked in structure and language that in some ancient versions they appear as one. Absence of any title to xliii. suggests the same connection.

PSALM XLII. A SIGH OF THE SOLITARY SOUL

I. INVOCATION. "O God." LONGING FOR THE LIVING ONE (1–4).
    1. Thirst of the Soul (1–2). Aspiration.
    2. Thrust of the Enemy (3). Humiliation. "Where is thy God."
    3. Thoughts of the Past (4). Retrospection.

II. INTROSPECTION. LANGUAGE OF THE LOYAL HEART (5). Self-rebuke. Refrain.

III. INVOCATION. "O my God." LONGING FOR THE LIFE-GIVER (6–10).

    1. Realisation of Exile (6). Depression.
    2. Reality of Distress (7). Affliction.
    3. Recognition of Mercies (8). Retrospection.
    4. Resolve in Perplexity (9). Expostulation.
    5. Reproach of Adversaries (10). Humiliation. **"Where is thy God?"**

IV. INTROSPECTION. LANGUAGE OF THE LOYAL HEART (11).
    Self-rebuke. Refrain.

PSALM XLIII.

V. INVOCATION. "O God." LONGING FOR THE LIGHT-BRINGER (1–4).

    1. Entreaty for Deliverance (1). Supplication.
    2. Echo of Perplexity (2). Expostulation.
    3. Entreaty for Guidance (3). Supplication.
    4. Expectation of Praise (4). Anticipation.

VI. INTROSPECTION. LANGUAGE OF THE LOYAL HEART (5).
    Self-rebuke. Refrain.

SUPERSCRIPT.—Maschil for the Sons of Korah.

SUBSCRIPT.—For the Chief Musician.

PRIMARY ASSOCIATION.—Written by one in exile and in great distress, perhaps David himself or one of his loyal followers, who crossed the Jordan with him (6), a Levite accustomed to conduct companies of pilgrims up to Jerusalem for the great festivals (4). Obviously belongs to the period of the monarchy and may best be referred to the time of Absalom's rebellion at a point in David's flight later than that of Ps. lxiii. This is the second "Maschil" psalm, see note to xxxii. Compare lxiii. and lxxxiv. which are also "wilderness" psalms, all expressing a thirst after God, though the circumstances differ.

PROPHETIC ANTICIPATION.—Voices the deep yearning of the godly remnant in exile, cast out of the land of which they had enjoyed but brief possession. The title "Maschil" confirms the interpretation as belonging to the great tribulation period. Significantly "Jordan" is the river of death (separation), while Hermon is connected with a Hebrew root denoting the ban or banishment.

PERSONAL APPLICATION.—Every saved sinner should become a servant of the sanctuary. We are preserved from perishing to be promoters of praise (title). Note (*a*) Past Experience of Worship (4); (*b*) Present Exclusion from Worship (6); (*c*) Positive Expectation of Worship, xliii. 3–4. "Christ is the answer to the cry of the human heart for God. Without Him God is invisible and incomprehensible." Note "Why?" ten times; four times addressed to God, six times to self. Do we not sometimes experience conflicting emotions such as find expression in these psalms? Fears and faith, doubt and devotion, sorrow and song may intermingle. Even when men do not, the tempter taunts with "Where is thy God?" (3, 10). The loyal saint ever longs to join the assembly in worship, xliii. 3; cf. Heb. x. 25. God is not only "El Chay"—the Living God, He is "El Chayyay"—God of my life (2, 8). First the billows then the blessings, first the sigh then the song, first the mourning then the morning (7–9). Keep hoping in God for you shall yet praise Him (5, 11, 5). Is God *my* exceeding joy? xliii. 4. They who begin by "panting" (1) will surely end by "praising" (11), xliii. 5. Facts often appear to contradict faith. "The darkest night has its star, the longest night, its morning.

VERSE NOTES

1. "hart," br. hind; "panteth," *i.e.* suffering in a period of prolonged drought; "waterbrooks," typical of the Spirit of God who both awakens and satisfies these holy desires.

2. "the Living God," Heb. El Chay, elsewhere only Josh. iii. 10; Hosea i. 10 and Ps. lxxxiv. 2; (*b*) *i.e.* at the three great festivals.

3. (*b*) These taunts were the bitterest ingredient in his cup of sorrow.

4. (*b*) Tense of the verb indicates that it was his custom to conduct pilgrims up to Jerusalem for the feasts.

5. (*c*) The psalmist immediately acts upon his own advice; (*d*) probably reading "Who is the help of my countenance and my God," as in 11 and xliii. 5; "help," lit. salvations; plur. indicates manifold character of salvation.

7. "roar of thy cataracts," one trouble following another until he feels utterly overwhelmed; br. "all thy breakers and rollers have . . .," the swiftly flowing waters of the nearby Jordan probably supplied the figure.

8. Kirkpatrick and others render the verbs in this verse in the past tense, "used to command," etc.; "Day . . . night," *i.e.* continually; refers to both clauses (*c*) Prayer often denotes any form of communion with God; "God" = El.

9. "God" = El; br. to use capital "R" in Rock; (*b*) an expression of perplexity, not a complaint demanding explanation.

Ps. xliii.

1. "Judge," *i.e.* vindicate; lit. "from a nation without loving-kindness."
2. Lit. "my stronghold God."
3. *e.g.* as at the exodus from Egypt; (*c*) "tabernacles" = Heb. plur. of majesty.
4. Or, "That I may come . . ." (*b*) God is Himself the goal of the pilgrimage; (*c*) "praise" = give thanks; "God, my God," Heb. Elohim Elohay.

PSALM XLIV. THE PEOPLE'S PRAYER IN PERPLEXITY

I. PRAISE FOR DELIVERANCE (PAST). (1-3).
    1. The Success (1-2).
    2. The Source (3).

II. PROFESSION OF FAITH (4-8).
    1. Personal (4).
    2. National (5).
    3. Personal (6).
    4. National (7-8).   Selah

III. PLAINT AFTER DISASTER (9-16).
    1. National (9-14). Divine Rejection and its Results.
    2. Personal (15-16). Psalmist's Shame and its Source.

IV. PROTESTATION OF FIDELITY (17-22).
    1. The Avowal (17-18).
    2. The Adversity (19).
    3. The Avowal (20-21).
    4. The Adversity (22).

V. PRAYER FOR DELIVERANCE (PRESENT) (23-26).
    1. The Appeal (23-24). "Awake."
    2. The Affliction (25).
    3. The Appeal (26). "Arise."

SUPERSCRIPT.—For the Sons of Korah, Maschil

SUBSCRIPT.—For the Chief Musician; upon Shoshannim (= Lilies).

PRIMARY ASSOCIATION.—The language of the psalm shows that Israel had just sustained a serious reverse in an encounter with foreign foes. The most probable occasion is an event which took place during David's war with Syria and Zobah, cf. Ps. lx. At that time Edom took advantage of David's absence with his main forces in the north and invaded Palestine as far as the south end of the Dead Sea, inflicting great slaughter on the Israelites; see 1 Kings xi. 16-17 where "bury the slain," *i.e.* Israelites; and "every male," *i.e.* capable of bearing arms. Edom subsequently took also territory once occupied by Amalek (south of Palestine), the desert of El Tih.

for only in David's time could Israel truly make such a plea. Yet verses 9–16 might suggest the crisis in Hezekiah's day, 2 Kings xviii. The psalmist looks back to the deliverance of Israel from Egypt and is encouraged to pray for a similar divine interposition. The subscript indicates that the psalm was to be used for the temple sevices during the spring festival of Passover. Call for God on the part of the individual, xlii.; Call for God on the part of the nation, xliv.

PROPHETIC ANTICIPATION.—While the prayer was answered in the psalmist's day, a more exhaustive fulfilment awaits the faithful Jewish remnant at the future return of Christ. "Maschil" (= instruction) also indicates that the psalm has special reference to the last days.

PERSONAL APPLICATION.—Reversals of fortune are not necessarily due to specific sins (cf. Job) but are a necessary part of our discipline and bring greater profit than material success. Facts of the past often afford joy for the present, and hope for the future (1–3). Divine grace, not our goodness, gives the inheritance; God's power not our proficiency gains us our possessions (3). We must use the weapons, but the victory is His (6–7); cf. 2 Cor. x. 3–4. A study of Israel's history encourages prayer (4), trust (5–6), and praise (8). Note the sixfold "Thou" (9–14) recognising that Israel's circumstances were due to God's disciplinary action. If we suffer, let us be sure it is for Christ's sake and not our own sin (22); cf. 1 Peter iii. 17; iv. 15–16. If Christ suffered "as a sheep" (Isa. liii.) it is no wonder that Christians must suffer (22); "the servant is not greater than his Lord," John xv. 20. Suffering drives the saint to supplication in the sanctuary (23–26). Our God is a searcher of hearts (21). Faith may flourish even amid the fury of the foe.

VERSE NOTES

1. (c) br. "even the days . . ."
2. Note alternation, 2b and 2d; "them" = Israel.
3. Jehovah's favour not Israel's fitness, His grace not their greatness gained them the land; cf. Deut. iv. 37; viii. 17–18; ix. 4–6; (c) cf. Exod. xiii. 21. The Pillar of cloud and of fire was a visible emblem of the invisible presence of God.
4. May be rendered, "Thou are He (the Same), my King, O God," i.e. the One who appeared to Moses and manifested Himself so wonderfully on behalf of Israel at the exodus, is still their God. (b) "deliverance" = Heb. plural of amplitude.
5. Language borrowed from the animal world; Heb.=to thrust with the horns, Exod. xxi. 29.

10. (b) or, "plunder at their will."

11. *i.e.* some butchered like sheep, others sold as slaves.

12. *i.e.* gave them away as worthless; fig. anthropopathy, see Appendix III. God gets no glory from Israel while the nation is given up to the Gentiles. Instead of being honoured. God's name is reproached because of them, Rom. ii. 24.

13. *i.e.* neighbouring nations ever ready to rejoice at Israel's humiliation.

14 "byword," or proverb.

16. "Because of . . ."; (b) "Because of . . ."; "avenger," hence one who usurped a function belonging to God alone; cf. Rom. xii. 19.

18. "declined" or, swerved.

19. Br. "That thou shouldest have crushed us into a haunt of jackals"; seems to imply that historically there was then no national apostasy to account for such sore punishment; prophetically true only of the remnant; (b) "shadow of death," a Heb. idiom = deathly gloom; cf. xxiii. 4.

22. "Nay, but for . . ."; quoted Rom. viii. 36.

23. This is the boldness, not of impudence, but of earnestness; not irreverence, but confidence; cf. Heb. iv. 16; the cry of the "slaughtered" sheep to their shepherd.

25. *i.e.* they lie utterly prostrate.

PSALM XLV.   MESSIAH'S MILLENNIAL MARRIAGE

I. INTRODUCTION (1).   THE POET'S ARDOUR.
   "Touching the King"—His Matters Penned.

II. ADDRESS TO THE ROYAL BRIDEGROOM (2–9).   The Poet's Admiration.
   1. His Personal Attractions (2).
   2. His Victorious Advent (3–5).
   3. His Righteous Administration (6–7).
   4. His Fragrant Apparel (8).
   5. His Regal Assemblage (9).

III. ADDRESS TO THE ROYAL BRIDE (10–11).   The Poet's Admonition.

IV. ADDRESS TO THE ROYAL BRIDEGROOM (12–16).   The Poet's Admiration.
   1. The Wealthy Aspirants (12).
   2. The Bride's Adornment (13–14a).
   3. The Virgin Attendants (14b–15).
   4. The Princely Administrators (16).

V. CONCLUSION (17).   THE POET'S AIM.
   "Touching the King"—His Memory Perpetuated.

SUPERSCRIPT.—For the Sons of Korah. Maschil. A Song of (surpassing) Love.

SUBSCRIPT.—For the Chief Musician; for the Sons of Korah; relating to Alamoth.

PRIMARY ASSOCIATION.—An inspired epithalamium generally thought to have as its historical basis the marriage of Solomon with Pharoah's daughter, 1 Kings iii. 1, but is more probably that of Hezekiah with Hephzibah, cf. 2 Kings xxi. 1 with Isa. lxii. 4. Solomon is named also Jedidiah (= Beloved of Jah), 2 Sam. xii. 25, and the title here is rendered in the LXX, "A Song of the Beloved." The Messianic aspect of the psalm, however, quite overshadows the historic, and alone exhausts its true import, Pss. xlv. and lxxxvii. are the only two distinguished by having the title "For the Sons of Korah" repeated in the subscript. The word "love" in the title is a Hebrew plural of amplitude or excellence and is always used in Scripture of high and noble affection, and especially of Jehovah's love to His people. "Alamoth" (see subscript) lit. maidens, i.e. for maiden's voices, the treble choir; cf. 1 Chron. xv. 20.

PROPHETIC ANTICIPATION.—Portrays Messiah's happy reunion with His people Israel. The figure of marriage is frequently used in the Old Testament to express God's relation to that nation. Here is the answer in person to the cry of xliv. "Maschil" links it with the last days. Owing to national unfaithfulness the relations between Jehovah and His ancient people have been suspended, Isa. l. i.; Hosea ii. 2, but will be gloriously renewed in a coming day, Isa. lxii. 5. There is teaching for the Church to-day, but we must clearly distinguish between *application* and *interpretation*. The latter here belongs to Messiah and Israel. The earthly may be a figure of the heavenly, though both are distinct; see *e.g.* two Jerusalems (Gal. iv. 25-26); so Ezek. xlvii. 1-2; xlviii. 8-35, with Rev. xxi. and xxii.

PERSONAL APPLICATION.—Meditation upon the relationship between Christ and His New Testament Bride should stir in our hearts emotions not inferior to those of the psalmist. This great theme generates glad thoughts. Christ is true Son of Man, but He far transcends all the sons of men (2). Note that Christ gains His kingdom not by invitation, as so many Christians think, but by subjugation (3). Worldly "righteousness" is proud, true righteousness is meek (4). Righteousness, peace, joy—this is ever the true sequence (7); cf. Rom. xiv. 17. Contemplation rather than comment, meditation rather than ministry befit this psalm. The more we gaze upon the beauty of "the King" the more we gain in blessing to our souls. "Words of men have never accomplished such miracles of grace in transforming the lives of their followers, bringing pardon to the penitent, hope to the disconsolate, guidance to the perplexed, peace and goodwill to the outcast and downtrodden (2)." How suitable that such a psalm should be set to an accompaniment of maidens' voices!

VERSE NOTES.

1. "overfloweth" (or, bubbleth over) with goodly words"; "made," *i.e.* composed.

2. "fairer far"; the beauty is not merely physical, but moral and spiritual; cf. Cant. v. 9–16; 2 Cor. iv. 6; "grace," word occurs twice only in Psalms; here grace displayed; lxxxiv. 11, grace given; cf. Prov. xxii. 11; Luke iv. 22.

3. Grace now exchanged for a sword of judgment, Rev. xix. 15; (*b*) = "(Gird on) Thy majesty and Thy splendour."

4. "And in Thy splendour, prosper, ride on; In the cause of truth and meekness of (or, suffering) righteousness"; victorious progress depicted.

5. "arrows," cf. Zech. ix. 14. (*b*) This clause should be in parenthesis. Messiah's weapons are not carnal, but the Word of Truth, Isa. xi. 4.

6–7. Fulfilling the promise of eternal dominion to the house of David, 2 Sam. vii. 13, 16; qtd. Heb. i. 8–9, to show the essential difference between the Son and the angels. Note (*a*) the Excellency of His Person; (*b*) the Eternity of His Throne; and (*c*) the Equity of His Rule; the character of the Kingdom is determined by the character of the King; "anointed," other kings were anointed with oil, Messiah with the Holy Spirit; the anointing mentioned is not that of consecration to office, but rather that accorded to an honoured guest; see also Isa. lxi. 3. Ctr. 2 Sam. xii. 20; xiv. 2. The rejoicing of the marriage festival is here indicated. "O God," indic. Messiah's deity; "thy fellows," indic. Messiah's humanity; "fellows" refers prophetically to the remnant.

8. The fragrance of Messiah's character and conduct gladdens both God and man, Isa. xlii. 1; Matt. iii. 17. In Scripture "garments" symbolise conduct before men; "spices" symbolise spiritual graces; (*b*) Music greets the bridegroom as he enters the palace. Stringed instruments symbolise man's power over inanimate nature. In the divine purpose, his hand was to produce the harmony of praise on earth. Hitherto, alas, mostly discords have been heard, but redeemed man shall yet bring forth that which gladdens the heart of the King.

9. Psalmist here seems to anticipate (14–15); "king's daughters," prophetically points to representatives of the Gentile nations attendant upon the Lord of the whole earth; "queen," Heb. = shegal, a queen by marriage, a queen consort, not one who is queen in her own right; prophetically refers to Jerusalem as representative city of the nation; "gold of Ophir" = the choicest gold, symbolical of divine righteousness.

10. This and the next verse are addressed to the bride while still in her father's house.

11. "reverence Him," or "do Him homage."

12. Tyre was the leading city of commerce; here she comes not with a price, but with a bridal offering. (*b*) "Yea, the richest of the people . . ." These entreat for the greater riches.

13-15. Description of the bridal procession in eastern lands, always an important part of the marriage ceremony. The bride, gorgeously arrayed in her wedding dress, waits in her father's house (13). At the appointed time she is conducted in solemn and stately manner to the palace of her husband. A train of attendants accompanies her with songs, music and dancing, and every mark of rejoicing. This bride is of royal birth as well as a king's bride; symbolises the new Israel as born of God.

14. "In raiment of embroidery," cf. Ezek. xvi. 10-14; Israel will be clothed with garments of His salvation, robed in His righteousness and adorned with the ornaments of His grace, Jer. ii. 2; Hosea ii. 14, 18, 21, 22; "broidery," s.H.w., Ps. cxxxix. 15 may suggest another line of thought.

14. (b) Typical of Gentile nations won for Messiah by Israel's testimony, Isa. xii. 4-5; Ps. lxxii. 10-11; Zech. xiv. 16; Micah iv. 2.

16. It seems better to refer this verse to the King; the Hebrew pronouns are all masculine. Fruit of Messiah's union with Israel; rulers established throughout the whole earth. Messiah's spiritual descendants will eclipse in numbers, greatness and glory His human progenitors. Men boast in their ancestry, Christ rejoices in His "seed." Isa. liii. 10-11.

17. Unlike Solomon or Hezekiah there will be nothing to tarnish forever the fair name and spotless character of our Lord.

Psalms xlvi.–xlviii. form a trilogy of praise celebrating the signal deliverances of Jerusalem from powerful enemies. The Seat of Jehovah, xlvi.; the Sovereignty of Jehovah, xlvii.; the Security of Jerusalem, xlviii.

PSALM XLVI.   MESSIAH'S MANIFESTED MIGHT

I. HIS ASSURED PROTECTION (1-3). UNFAILING HELP.
    1. The Protector Extolled (1).
    2. The Peace Experienced (2-3).   Selah.

II. HIS ABIDING PRESENCE (4-7). UNSHAKABLE HABITATION.
    1. The Generous Provision (4).
    2. The Gracious Presence (5a).
    3. The Glad Prospect (5bc).
    4. The Glorious Proof (6). REFRAIN (7). Selah.

III. HIS ACKNOWLEDGED PRE-EMINENCE (8-11). UNIVERSAL EXALTATION.
    1. The Power Exhibited (8-9). "In the earth."
    2. The Person Exalted (10). "In the earth." REFRAIN (11). Selah.

SUPERSCRIPT.—A Song.

SUBSCRIPT.—For the Chief Musician.

PRIMARY ASSOCIATION.—Historical occasion of this psalm most likely was the great deliverance of the capital from the army of Sennacherib in the reign of Hezekiah, 701 B.C. See 2 Kings xviii.-xix. Pss. lxxv. and lxxvi. seem to refer to the same event. The writer was evidently an eye-witness of the stirring events portrayed. There are many coincidences of language and thought with the prophecies of Isaiah. The poet may have been the prophet himself or even Hezekiah. If the psalm be viewed in its dramatic form, the following interesting introversion appears:

> i. Israel's Colloquy among themselves (1-7).
> ii. Israel's Call to the Gentile peoples (8-9).
> iii. God's Call to the Gentile peoples (10).
> iv. Israel's Colloquy among themselves (11).

PROPHETIC ANTICIPATION.—Pss. xlvi.-xlviii. are triumphal songs describing in progressive form events to take place at the return of God's anointed King (Isa. xxiv. 23), whose glorious person has already been seen in xlv. Ps. xlvi. refers to Armageddon and Messiah's triumph; xlvii., the coronation scene to follow; xlviii., the establishment of Messiah's kingdom on Mt. Zion. Our present psalm shows the Refuge of the Rescued Remnant; (a) their Confidence amid mighty devastations and desolations (1-3); (b) their Consolation in rest and retrospection (4-7); (c) their Contemplation of Messiah's triumph and testimony (8-11). Verses 2-3 depict Tribulation terrors with the whole world in convulsion, government overthrown, lawlessness and apostasy rampant, Rev. viii. 8, etc. Mountains in Scripture symbolise empires raised on high.

PERSONAL APPLICATION.—Here is special comfort for days of war and calamity. Read the psalm again and again. It was Luther's favourite one on which he based his famous hymn, "A mighty stronghold is our God." Our God in time of trouble is tried and true (1). Confession inspires confidence and courage (1-3). Vivifying streams of the Spirit ever flow from the presence of God. In Him is the secret source and the sufficient supply (4). All the redeemed have recourse to this river now. In God is our all sufficiency as well as abiding shelter, ample provision as well as assured protection (1-4). The divine presence is ever a pledge of protection (5). To Christians also, God is a God of might and a God of mercies, a great God and a gracious God (7). Let us avail ourselves of our

E

"High Retreat" (7). The dawn of deliverance succeeds the night of distress (5). "God is the God of all Jacobs that He may make them all Israels" (7). The Lord Jesus will one day make war against war (9); cf. Zech. xiv. 3-4; Joel iii. Note, (*a*) His Works seen; (*b*) Wars ended; (*c*) Weapons destroyed (8-9). Men need to be taught the folly of resisting God (10). Even Christians sometimes find "Be still" a hard lesson to learn.

VERSE NOTES

1. Cf. similar language, Joel iii. 16; ctr. Isa. xxviii. 14-17; xxx. 1-3; "very present," *i.e.* immediately at hand, soon found.

2. The reasoning of faith; cf. xxiii. 4; Job xxxiv. 29.

3. "Selah" emphasises the contrast between the raging of the enemy like a flood, and the working of God against the enemy, silent and secret like the rock-hewn watercourse which ministered to the needs of the besieged. God's purposes are hidden; "roar," s.H.w. trans. "raged," 6.

4. "river," *i.e.* the silent-flowing stream in Hezekiah's secret channel; cf. 2 Kings xx. 20; 2 Chron. xxxii. 3, 4, 11, 30. It is contrasted with the raging of the Assyrian hosts (3); cf. also Isa. viii. 6 ff. Rock-cut conduits formed part of the defences of the ancient city of Jebus, affording a secret water supply which, combined with the precipitous approach, made the citadel well-nigh impregnable. "Gutter," 2 Sam. v. 8 refers to such a channel. During the siege of Jerusalem, Hezekiah availed himself of an older conduit system and modified it to suit his own purposes. This and other channels have been discovered within the last seventy years. Br. "the rivulets (or, watercourses) thereof..." Prophetically refers to an actual river with a symbolic meaning, Joel iii. 18; Zech. xiv. 18; Ezek. xlvii. 1-12; Rev. xxii. "City of God," = Zion; only the mother city remained, Isa. xxxvi. 1. (*b*) br. "the holy dwelling-place of the Most High."

5. (*b*) "... at the early dawn," lit. "at the turn of the morning"; cf. Isa. xxxvii. 36; also Exod. xiv. 27; Isa. xvii. 14; prophetically, see Isa. lxvi. 24; Rev. xix. 19-21, etc.

6. "raged," cf. ii. 1; and the cry of the Edomites, cxxxvii. 7. In Heb., seven words describe the whole power of the oppressors, and seven words their complete overthrow.

7. Zion's watchword is "Immanuel," Isa. vii. 14; viii. 8, 10; 2 Chron. xxxii. 7-8. "Jehovah of Hosts" = God as ruler of all the heavenly powers, the supreme Sovereign of the universe; title occurs frequently in Isaiah; see also 2 Kings vi.15-17; "refuge," see marg., s.H.w., ix. 9; xviii. 2; xlviii. 3; Isa. xxxiii. 16; "God of Jacob" occurs about twenty-two times in Scripture, see Ps. xx. 1, note. Despite constant failure and distrust, God was still his refuge. In the life of the patriarch may be traced the fitful history of the nation. "Selah" connects faith in the promise (7) with fulfilment of the promise (8-9).

8-9. Never yet has there been a point of time in the world's history to which these words could possibly apply in a literal sense.

8. "Behold," = gaze with discerning eyes; see Isa. xxxvii. 36; Ps. lxvi. 5.

9. cf. Isa. ix. 5; ii. 4; Zech. ix. 10; "chariots" or, baggage-wagons; however, armoured vehicles of some kind seem to be indicated; cf. 2 Kings xix. 23.

10. or, "let be," or "desist"; Heb. = to let go, to drop the hands in inactivity; here = submit, for resistance is useless; cf. 2 Kings xix. 19.

11. "Selah" points the connection between this psalm and the next. They have a common theme—the exaltation of God, cf. xlvi. 10 with xlvii. 9.

PSALM XLVII. MESSIAH'S MILLENNIAL MONARCHY

.I. EXHORTATION TO PRAISE (1-2).
>   1. The Rejoicing (1). Universal Summons.
>   2. The Reason (2). Universal Sovereignty.

II. EXHIBITION OF POWER (3-4).
>   In the Restoration of Israel.   Selah.

III. EXALTATION OF GOD (5).

IV. EXHORTATION TO PRAISE (6-8).
>   1. The Rejoicing (6). Universal Summons.
>   2. The Reason (7a). Universal Sovereignty.
>   3. The Rejoicing (7b). Universal Summons.
>   4. The Reason (8). Universal Sovereignty.

V. EXPRESSION OF ALLEGIANCE (9abc).
>   By the Representatives of Gentiles.

VI. EXALTATION OF GOD (9d).

SUPERSCRIPT.—A psalm for the Sons of Korah.

PRIMARY ASSOCIATION.—See introductory notes, xlvi. Many, however, think this psalm and the next historically celebrate the overthrow of the heathen confederacy against Judah in the days of Jehoshaphat, 2 Chron. xx. It was perhaps sung on the battlefield of Berachah after the victory, II Chron. xx. 2b; cf. Ps. lxxxiii which may possibly anticipate the victory. Several references appear to bear out this conclusion. The grace of God averted two disasters, the hostile invasion from without and the ungodly alliance within, 2 Chron. xx. 27, 37. It is quite possible that Hezekiah made use of this earlier composition as suiting the circumstances of the crisis in his days. The thought in xlvi. 10 is expanded. This is new year's day psalm in the Jewish synagogue. It is then sung seven times before the "blowing of trumpets."

PROPHETIC ANTICIPATION.—See notes, xlvi. Here note Messiah's Victory Celebrated (1-4) and Messiah's Reign Inaugurated (5-9). The remnant has become the new nation, a kingdom of priests, Exod. xix. 6. Representatives of the Gentile nations gather to the coronation of the universal King to render due homage and to join in the joyous festivities to follow (9). Through Israel favour will be shown to the Gentiles, but this is more a matter of priority than of superiority, Gen. xii. 2-3.

PERSONAL APPLICATION.—A song of sovereignty; the Lord is sovereign (*a*) in power (3), (*b*) in wisdom (4), (*c*) in holiness (8). "Crown Him Lord of all" in our lives. Praise awakens praise. "Don't stop praising." To praise God aright needs spiritual intelligence (7). What God has performed is proof and promise of what He can and will yet do (3-4). He subdues by love as well as by power (3). What an inheritance God has chosen for the Christian (4) with 1 Peter i. 3-5. The once Crucified Victim will be seen as the Crowned Victor.

VERSE NOTES

2. "Most High" = God's millennial title; br. ". . . is to be revered;" (*b*) theme of the psalm = the Great King; title was arrogantly assumed by the Assyrian king, Isa. xxxvi. 4.

3-4. cf. Deut. xxxii. 8; Exod. xix. 5; "nations," br. "races (of men)."

4. cf. 2 Chron. xx. 11; "glory" or, pride; cf. sim. phrases, Nah. ii. 2; Jer. xiii. 9-10. Israel's inheritance was "excellent" or, exalted—better than any other in the earth.

5. God is said to "come down" when He manifests His presence by active interposition in the affairs of the world, and to "go up" when His work is finished. Prophetically this refers to His intervention in the person of Messiah; (*b*) the sound of recall from the victorious battlefield.

6. "sing praises," throughout the verse, more lit. "psalm ye."

7. (*b*) more exactly, "Psalm ye understandingly" or, "Psalm ye an instruction," Heb. maschil; Israel are to instruct the nations in this manner; see Introduction V*e*.

8. br. "God hath proclaimed Himself King over . . . God hath taken His seat upon . . .," the Heb. verbs express an act not merely a fact.

9. br. "The nobles . . .," lit. willing-hearted ones; Heb. connects with cx. 3. These persons gather in their representative capacity; see Gen. xlix. 10; Isa. lx. 3-7. (*b*) omit words in italics; here is the climax of Messianic hopes, Rom. ix. 25; Gen. xii. 2 ff.; xvii. 4. Grace will gather the great ones of the Gentiles. (*c*) "shields" = the princes as protectors of their people. Messiah will be their great Overlord.

PSALM XLVIII. MESSIAH'S MILLENNIAL METROPOLIS

I. THE GREATNESS OF GOD (1). Praised "in the City."

II. THE GLORIES OF ZION (2). Her Beautiful Situation.

III. THE GREATNESS OF GOD (3-8). "For."
Demonstrated by His Performance. Zion established "for ever." Selah.

IV. THE GRACIOUSNESS OF GOD (9-11). Praised in the Temple.

V. THE GLORIES OF ZION (12-13a). Her Basic Strength.

VI. THE GRACIOUSNESS OF GOD (13b-14). "For."
Declared by His People. Israel guided "for ever."

SUPERSCRIPT.—A Song. A Psalm for the sons of Korah.

SUBSCRIPT.—For the Chief Musician.

PRIMARY ASSOCIATION.—Writer unknown, but historically seems connected with preceding psalm, which was sung probably after the rout of the enemy, xlviii. being sung at the thanksgiving service later in the Temple, 2 Chron. xx. 19. Title, "A Song," *i.e.* for celebration; "A Psalm," *i.e.* for musical accompaniment. In the temple services this psalm was later appointed for recitation by the Levites on the second day of the week.

PROPHETIC ANTICIPATION.—Celebrates the final victory over the enemies of Israel, the event prophesied Ezek. xxxviii., not that of Zech. xiv. which precedes. The circumstances are very different. In Zechariah, Jerusalem is seen in the very extremity of distress, already partly in the hands of the enemy and on the verge of destruction, when the Lord intervenes by His personal appearing from heaven to deliver the people and the city. The attack by Gog is somewhat later and against a city already enjoying peaceful conditions under the beneficent rule of the Prince of Peace, whose presence is sufficient guarantee of security. It is the presence of the King that makes the city glorious, Zech. ii. 10-11; Isa. xii. 6; Zeph. iii. 15-17. He graciously imparts to her His own attributes and characteristics, Ezek. xlviii. 35; Jer. xxxiii. 16. Note Zion (a) the dedicated city (1); (b) the delivered city (4 ff.); (c) the delightsome city (12, 13).

PERSONAL APPLICATION.—Citizens of the "Jerusalem on high" may well rejoice in her unseen yet eternal realities. They should feel a true patriotism and pride in her glories as the dwelling-place of God; Heb. xii. 22-23; Rev. xxi. 10 ff. God is (a) "most surely" present in adversity, xlvi. 1; (b) "most surely" exalted as King, xlvii. 9; and (c) "most surely" worthy of praise, xlviii. 1. Frustration of our cherished plans may be a matter for praise (7). A greater danger arises from an alliance with evil-doers than from an attack by the enemy, (7) with 2 Chron. xx. 35-37. It is in the sanctuary that we really come to know the greatness of God's goodness (9). Think and thank (9). What God has been to His people for a moment, He can and will be for a millennium (14). He who delivers also directs (14). This God is our God, a Guide for ever (14). Note in 14 (a) Confession of faith; (b) Claim of relationship; (c) Celebration of goodness; (d) Confidence in (Divine) faithfulness.

VERSE NOTES

1. "greatly," Hebrew emphatic adverb describing intensity; occurs three times in this group of psalms, see notes above.

2. "Zion" here stands for the whole city of Jerusalem; "joy of . . . ," same Hebrew phrase Lam. ii. 15; Isa. lx. 15; (c) cf. xlvii. 2 note. Some suggest reading, "Zion, on the northern sides is the city . . ." Prophetically may indicate the new situation resulting from the earthquake cleavage; see Zech. xiv. 4.

3. Br. "God is in her palaces known as a high fortress"; see s.H.w. xlvi. 7, 11; Zion (2) is a symbol of God Himself.

4. Describes the coming of the enemy; next verse describes their going; cf. lxxxiii. 3-8; 2 Chron. xx. 16-20; mutual distrust led to internecine slaughter; cf. also Exod. xiv. 25; (b) "passed over," i.e. uniting their forces, they crossed the frontier against Judah.

7. Br. "With an east wind Thou didst . . . ," cf. 1 Kings xxii. 48-49; 2 Chron. xx. 35-37. Psalmist here alludes to a more insidious danger, to which Jehoshaphat and Judah were exposed; doubtless there will be a future fulfilment also.

8 ff. Cf. 2 Chron. xx. 7, 14-17 with Exod. xiv. 13; "heard and seen," cf. xliv. 1, which has "heard" only, hence the two deliverances are here combined; recent experience confirming tradition.

9. Cf. 2 Chron. xx. 27-28; example of true worship. Not only the glory, but the grace engages the thoughts; "have thought," i.e. rested in the thought.

11. "daughters of Judah," see 2 Chron. xx. 4, 18, 27-28, for the prayer; here is the praise; "daughters," = common term in Scripture for cities or towns.

12. ". . . Zion, yea, go round . . . count . . ."

13. "Consider . . . contemplate . . ."

14. Or, "For such is God our God . . ."; more lit. ". . . guide over death," i.e. raising out of its reach. LXX has "guide for evermore."

PSALM XLIX. WARNING TO WEALTHY WORLDLINGS

I. PRELIMINARY SUMMONS (1-4).   Universal Scope Contemplated.
   1. Pressing Invitation (1-2).
   2. Particular Intention (3-4).

II. PROVERBIAL SPEECH (5-12).   False Confidence of the Foolish Rich.
   1. Self-reproving Expostulation (5).   Why fear the Wealthy Worldling?
   2. Solemn Explanation (6-12).
      i. The Power of Wealth—Its Limitation (6-9).
      ii. The Possession of Wealth—Its Termination (10-11).
      iii. Sad Refrain (12).

III. POSITIVE STATEMENT (13-15).   Ultimate States Contrasted.
   1. Man's Delusion (13).   His Folly during Life. Selah.
   2. Man's Destiny (14-15).   His Fate after Death. Selah.
      i. The Ungodly (14).
      ii. The Upright (15).   (cf. 14b).

IV. PROVERBIAL SPEECH (16-20).   Final Condition of the Foolish Rich.
   1. Salutary Exhortation (16).   Fear not the Wealthy Worldling.
   2. Solemn Explanation (17-20).
      i. The Possession of Wealth—Its Termination (17).
      ii. The Power of Wealth—Its Limitation (18-19).
      iii. Sad Refrain (20).   (cf. and ctr. 12).

SUPERSCRIPT.—A psalm for the Sons of Korah.

PRIMARY ASSOCIATION.—No clue to the writer or occasion, but probably belongs to Isaiah's day. Close parallels of thought with the Books of Job, Proverbs and Ecclesiastes. Compare also Pss. xxxvii. and lxxiii. where the wickedness is prominent, here it is the worldliness of men; see Luke xii. 1-34 and xvi. 1-31. This is a didactic poem presented with musical accompaniment (4). An enigma is expounded. Refer again to the analysis of this section for its relation to the group. This is one of the few psalms having a separate introduction (1-4). In this section note the many alternations and introversions.

PROPHETIC ANTICIPATION.—While containing truth for all time, the psalm has special reference to the Gentile oppressors of the Jewish nation in the last days of distress "with deliverance assured but not yet accomplished, though about to come." The psalmist is representative of the nation and has in view the morning of the millennial day rather than that of resurrection. In application as distinguished from interpretation, we see the germ of the latter truth.

PERSONAL APPLICATION.— The voice of God ever claims priority over the voices of others (1). Before speaking to men it is wise to listen to God (4). The godly man need not fear the godless rich (5, 16). Not the possession of wealth, but trust in wealth is here condemned as folly (6); not money, but the love of money is a root of all evil, 1 Tim. vi. 6-10, 17-19. Not its use but its misuse is sinful. Riches do not make a man wicked, nor does poverty make a man good. Failure to distinguish between false wealth and the true is fatal folly. In this life, wealth has tremendous influence and may become a terrible weapon of oppression. Riches are powerless to prolong this life and cannot profit in the next. The grave is the limit of material possessions. They cannot redeem the soul (7). Wisdom is better than wealth, yet it, too, cannot deliver from death (10). Death knows no class distinction (10). For the godless, Death is their shepherd and Sheol (Hades) their fold (14). The word "perish" does not mean extinction of being (14). Self-confident fools have many sycophant followers (13). Posterity perpetuates the folly of its fathers (13). The godly of the old covenant were not delivered from the grave, but were delivered from its power, cf. believers in this age, 1 Cor. xv. 55-57, etc., with 15 here. Death baffles the wealthy worldling (17). The tenure of earthly treasure is insecure and impermanent (17). It is far better to find our wealth in God than to make wealth our God; see Luke xvi. and xii. Dives trusted his gold, Lazarus trusted his God.

VERSE NOTES

1. "world," Heb. = world as transitory, this age; specially significant in this Psalm.

4. "parable" or, proverbial speech; the psalmist first receives by revelation what he desires to teach, cf. lxxviii. 2; "dark saying," or enigma.

5. Br. as margin.

7. According to the Law, in exceptional cases, wealth could deliver from death in man's relationship with man (e.g. Exod. xxi. 30), but never in cases where life was forfeited to God; see also Num. xxxv. 30 ff.

8. A parenthesis; br. " . . . is costly and must be let alone for ever"; or, "it (the life) must be given up for ever," i.e. the rich man has no alternative but to give up the attempt to redeem the life, ctr. 15.

9. Br. "... should live on perpetually."

10. "For one seeth . . ."; (c) "leave," = "abandon," not "bequeath."

11. Cf. Isa. v. 8; wealthy worldlings are wilfully blind.

13. "This is the way of them that are self-confident; And of their followers (or, posterity) who approve their sayings." Connect with verse 11.

14. "like sheep," i.e. herded helplessly toward their end; Sheol (= Gk. Hades) and the grave must not be confounded, and are not confounded here. The former received their spirits, the latter their bodies; but since Sheol retained the spirit, the body left behind necessarily wasted in the grave until it disappeared in dust and needed no more a habitation. Contrast the thoughts of these worldlings during their lifetime (11); "morning," prophetically = the "day" when Israel is restored, Mal. iv. 1; Isa. xiv. 2.

15. The wicked perish in Sheol, the psalmist is preserved from Sheol. Prim. ref. to deliverance from death of those who appeared doomed to die at the hands of their oppressors.

16ff. The thought in 10 is here resumed; from self-encouragement the poet now turns to encourage others; "afraid," cf. 5.

18. (a) self-gratulation; "his soul" = himself.

19. (b) Br. "... no more shall they see light"; significant expression concerning the doom of all that forget God.

Book Two. I. Deliverance of the Exiled Remnant, xlii.–li.

2. The Restored People, l.–li. Deliverance from Internal Evil.

(i) Adjudication of Jehovah, l. Condemnation of Sin.
(Principles and Pronouncements).

(ii) Attitude of Israel, li. Confession of Sin.
(Root and Results).

PSALM L.   INQUISITION UPON ISRAEL

I. GENERAL ANNOUNCEMENT BY THE PSALMIST (1–6). INTRODUCTION.

1. Concerning Jehovah's Advent (1–3).
2. Concerning Jehovah's Assize (4–6). Selah.

II. JEHOVAH'S ADDRESS TO ISRAEL (7–15). The Godly Remnant. Their worship analysed. First table of the decalogue violated. Formalism denounced.

1. Act approved (7–8). Negative side.
2. Attitude reproved (9–13).
3. Admonition uttered (14–15). Positive side—Praise; Prayer; Promise.

III. PSALMIST'S ANNOTATION (16a).

IV. JEHOVAH'S ADDRESS TO ISRAEL (16b–22). The Graceless
Renegades. Their works arraigned. Second table of the decalogue
violated. Hypocrisy denounced.
  1. Attitude considered (16b–17).
  2. Acts condemned (18–21).
  3. Admonition uttered (22). Duty—Danger.

V. GENERAL ANNOUNCEMENT BY JEHOVAH (23). CONCLUSION.
Summary of the Psalm.
  1. Concerning Acceptable Worship and Result (23a). See 7–15.
  2. Concerning Acceptable Ways and Result (23bc). See 16–22.

SUPERSCRIPT.—A psalm of Asaph.

SUBSCRIPT.—For the Chief Musician.

PRIMARY ASSOCIATION.—Writer is Asaph; historical occasion almost
certainly connected with 1 Chron. xv.–xvi. Asaph took a prominent
part in this great procession (1 Chron. xv. 17, 19) and here seems to
allude to things seen and heard, 1 Chron. xvi. 4–5. David himself
composed a hymn of praise for the occasion. Asaph (= "the
gatherer," cf. 5) was one of the three choral leaders, 1 Chron. xv.
17–19; chief minister before the Ark, 1 Chron. xvi. 4–15; a seer
(= prophet), 2 Chron. xxix. 30; and poet. This is the only Asaphic
psalm in Book II; eleven others are found in Book III. In all his
writings the holiness of God is a prominent theme. Our present
psalm is didactic in purpose and dramatic in form. It is a solemn
scene of judgment; Israel is indicted, God appears as complainant,
witness and judge, and the inhabitants of the whole universe are
spectators.

PROPHETIC ANTICIPATION.—This psalm shows there will be a
sessional judgment of Israel after the appearing of Christ in glory,
a judgment answering to that of the Gentiles depicted Matt. xxv.
Those who are really Jehovah's in that day will be separated from
the rest and addressed in similar fashion to the "sheep" and the
"goats" of Matt. xxv. God's "controversy" with the nation here,
has respect to the Law; in Ps. li. it has respect to the rejection of
Messiah.

PERSONAL APPLICATION.—Note the emphasis on the righteousness
of the Judge and the righteousness required by Him. God has
spoken through His servants and through His Son, Heb. i. He will

speak again, not in grace but in judgment, and all will hear His voice (1). His long silence will soon be broken by His open intervention in the affairs of men (2–3). Judgment must begin with God's own people (3); cf. 1 Peter iv. 17. In the place where they crucified their Messiah, Israel will be judged; where the Gentiles crucified the Son of God, they, too, will be judged, Matt. xxv. Guilt is in proportion to privilege (7); cf. Amos iii. 2. God is spirit (John iv.); He is not dependent on man (9–11), nor is He materially sustained (12–13); ctr. pagan notions. Ritual without righteousness is abomination to God. To hold the form of godliness (2 Tim. iii. 5) whilst denying the power thereof is severely denounced (16–17). In Christianity profession without practice is far too common. Prayer is a proof of trust (15). The voice of slander often sounds like the voice of righteousness. Recounting another's evil with inward relish is scandal-mongering (19–20). The world misinterprets the silence of God (21). God's silence does not spell licence to sin, but long-suffering towards the sinner (21). The execution of the sentence upon sin is not always summary, but it is sure (21); cf. Eccles viii. 11. "Human nature loves posing and posturing; hypocrisy is the art of making up" (16 ff.). God listens to the language of the life, not of the lip (16).

VERSE NOTES

1. The combined title befits One who is universal Judge (occurs elsewhere only Josh. xxii. 22); El Elohim Jehovah emphasises God's personal attributes of might, majesty and mercy respectively. Other titles also appear, Eloah (22) and Elyon (14); see App. II.

3. The Coming predicted and described; note phenomena suiting God's august presence, Exod. xix. 16; xx. 18–19; Deut. xxxiii. 2; (a) cf. Isa. xlii. 13–15; (bc) these signs show that "God as yet cannot manifest His holiness in the serenity of complacent love."

4. Inhabitants of both spheres summoned to witness the judgment of Israel; cf. Matt. xxv. 31; Mark viii. 38; Luke ix. 26. The Lord will be accompanied by myriads of angels as well as multitudes of saints.

5. "saints," Heb. = godly, or favoured-ones; the recipients of God's loving-kindness and exhibiting the same to their fellows. (b) prim. ref. to Exod. xxiv.; shows how the title "saints" was obtained; lit. = "cut a covenant"; for the expression see Jer. xxxiv. 18–19, which explains and confirms Heb. ix. 15–18. The Noahic, Abrahamic and Mosaic Covenants were all made over sacrifice, Gen. ix. 9; with viii. 20–22; xv. 10–18; Exod. xxiv. 8; also the New Covenant, Matt. xxvi. 27–28, etc.

6. The justice of the Judge declared by those in the heavens, probably includes

the raptured saints of our present age. (*b*) br. " . . . for God is about to judge."
"Selah" connects the call to judgment (1–6) with the grounds for judgment (7 ff.).

7. The trial opens; (*c*) cf. Exod. xx. 2.

8. Cf. Num. xxviii., xxix. and 1 Chron. xvi. 40; xxiii. 31.

14. Refers back to Lev. vii. 12–15; xxii. 29–30. The sacrifice of thanksgiving was in the nature of a peace offering; (*b*) the "vows" or votive offerings (Lev. vii. 16) were of "a higher character than the thanksgiving sacrifice as expressing a more positive faith in God under the pressure of circumstances"; cf. for the spiritual application, Heb. xiii. 15–16 with faith as exhibited in Heb. xi.-xii.

15. The LXX inserts a "Selah" at the end of this verse. Prayer is based upon the assurance of acceptance implied in the peace offering.

16. "wicked" = lawless, ctr. "saints" (5), the loyal ones; lawless ones are not in true covenant relationship with God.

17. See margin.

18. Br. " . . . thou didst delight thyself . . . "

19. More lit. "Thou has let loose thy . . . "

20. Sin against the fifth commandment; moral degeneracy in which the closest ties of kinship are ignored.

21. (*b*) or, "Thou thoughtest Ehyeh (s.H.w. Exod. iii. 14) such an one as thyself"; (*c*) the limit of divine patience is reached; "set in order," *i.e.* the various counts of the indictment.

22. This warning to the careless shows God's yearning love over sinners.

23. Sums up the teaching of the psalm; (*b*) *i.e.* to him who orders his way as taught here; (*c*) shows that despite the material sacrifices, salvation is still needed.

PSALM LI.   PRAYER OF THE PENITENT

I. INVOCATION WITH DAVID'S CONFESSION (1-5). DAVID'S CAUSE.
1. Impassioned Cry (1-2).
2. Intense Contrition (3-5).

II. INDICATION OF THE DIVINE REQUIREMENT (6).
God's Desire—A Sincere Heart.

III. IMPLORATION FOR DIVINE PARDON (7-15).
1. Resulting in joy (7-8).
2. Resulting in Testimony (9-13).
3. Resulting in Praise (14-15).

IV. INDICATION OF THE DIVINE REQUIREMENT (16-17).
God's Desire—A Surrendered Heart.

V. INTERCESSION FOR ISRAEL'S CONSECRATION (18-19). ZION'S CAUSE.

1. Inspired Request (18).
2. Important Results (19).

SUPERSCRIPT.—A psalm of David, when Nathan the prophet came unto him, after he had gone in to Bathsheba.

SUBSCRIPT.—For the Chief Musician.

PRIMARY ASSOCIATION.—This is the fourth "penitential" psalm. For writer and occasion see title; cf. 2 Sam. xi.-xii. Read again the corresponding notes to Ps. xxxii. David was visited by Nathan almost a year after the sin was committed. In such a case the typical sacrifices all failed; they did not avail for wilful sin (Deut. xvii. 12) particularly deliberate murder. David could only cast himself upon the sovereign mercy of God. The one supreme sacrifice of the Cross accomplished what the types could never do. The latter pointed on to Christ and thus expressly disclaim any virtue in themselves. Verses 18-19 were probably added by David himself when handing his composition to the precentor for liturgical use.

PROPHETIC ANTICIPATION.—See notes to preceding psalm. This points to the time of Israel's national repentance and restoration. Though David was guilty of other sins, it is significant that the only one specified here is that of bloodguiltiness, hence the psalm is particularly appropriate to the nation guilty of the death of Messiah. That the future repentance will be national yet intensely individual is shown by later prophets, e.g. Zech. xii. 10-14. Thus we find the Spirit of God again using the various experiences of David to express all that the godly remnant of Israel will pass through before they can enter the millennial rest. An interesting point is that in some Jewish forms of ritual, this psalm is recited on the Day of Atonement, type of a yet greater "Day" when Israel with adoring wonder will learn that the Crucified One was indeed the Lamb of God's providing, whose once-for-all sacrifice of Himself laid the foundation of their national redemption and restoration.

PERSONAL APPLICATION.—A psalm of repentance and restoration, of penitence and pardon. Sin is here regarded as: (a) a blotted record to be expunged; (b) a polluted robe to be washed; (c) a fatal disease to be cured. It is "transgression" = law violated; "iniquity" = morals perverted; "sin" = mark missed; or, disobedience, distortion and declension. Note: (*a*) Manifold character of sin presented; (*b*) Manifold cleansing· of soul portrayed; (*c*) Manifold compassions of God pleaded (1-3). Repentance contains the element of faith, remorse the element of despair. True confession makes no excuse or apology; it makes no attempt to delude self, deceive men or dissemble with God (3-4). There is a wide difference between sorrow for the consequences of sin and sorrow for its cause (3). The sin may be forgiven, but certain consequences remain. Sin is a personal responsibility (1-3), note the "my" repeated; we must not blame heredity or society or necessity. Sin against man is primarily sin against God, for at every point that we touch God's creature, we touch God Himself (4). Man's sin and God's ways of dealing with it bring into clearer light the justice and holiness of God. "Modern" theologians hate verse 5; they like to talk about the "God in man" instead of the "sin in man." The source of sin is in our souls, not in our surroundings; evil acts proceed from an evil nature, (5). Man is born with a moral twist (5). God ever looks through to the heart (6). Though man has a corrupt nature, he has an inner conscience (5-6). Sin needs washing white, not white-washing; man often does the latter, but God alone can do the former (7). The redemptive work of Christ for us must be accompanied by the regenerative work of the Spirit in us (10). For the believer in this dispensation to pray as David does (11) would be sheer unbelief, John xiv. 16-17; Gal. iv. 1-7; 1 Cor. xii. 13, etc. Heaviness of heart enfeebles walk and work (12). The "pleasures of sin" cost David the joy of salvation (12). Sin shuts the saint's lips, pardon opens them for testimony and praise (13, 15). God rejects cold-hearted sacrifice (16) but accepts whole-hearted sacrifice (19). The former speaks of self-will, the latter of self-surrender. The pardoned one becomes a pleader for others (18-19).

VERSE NOTES

1. Br. "Be gracious unto me according . . . according to the abundance of Thy compassion . . ." The prayer for pardon is based upon God's revelation of His own character, Exod. xxxiv. 6-7; "transgressions" = revolts, so 3.

2. "wash," Hebrew word used of washing the clothes of the leper, Lev. xiv. 4, 7-9; "iniquity" = perversity, so 5.

3. "I" (emph.). Long known to God, the sins are at last "known" to David and acknowledged by him.

4. Cf. Gen. xxxix. 9; ctr. Saul's concern for "face" before the people, 1 Sam. xv. 30; (b) cf. 2 Sam. xi. 27; xii. 9, 13; (c) "speakest," i.e. givest sentence; "justified," i.e. divine righteousness vindicated; "clear," i.e. divine holiness vindicated. God is vindicated whether He punishes or pardons. LXX cited Rom. iii. 4. Note context.

5. "sin"; this seems to be the only occurrence in Old Testament of this word in the absolute sense; cf. Rom. v. 12; all other refs. are to *acts* of sin. David is not finding an excuse for sin, for see 6.

6. "wisdom," i.e. application of knowledge gained through the Word of God to the discrimination of good and evil.

7. Fig. borrowed from the ceremonial law, Exod. xii. 22; Lev. xiv. 6–7; Num. xix. 6 ff.; Heb. ix. 19; "purify," or, sin-cleanse; (b) cf. Isa. i. 18; "iniquities," = perversities.

8. Purification of the unclean was followed by re-admission to the joys of fellowship with God and with His people in the sanctuary.

9. "blot out" see 1.

10. See marginal readings.

11. David doubtless has in mind, 1 Sam. xvi. 13–14; see Hagg. ii. 5. He desires the renewal and maintenance of fellowship.

12. "And let a willing spirit sustain me," i.e. a spirit of prompt obedience.

14. "bloodguiltiness," Heb. "bloods"; Others besides Uriah had been slain at the time, 2 Sam. xii. 9; xi. 17; but David may have in mind the truth expressed in Ezk. iii. 17 ff; "righteousness," here = God's faithfulness to His character and word in pardoning the sincere penitent, even as in punishing the impenitent, 1 John i. 9.

16–17. Alludes to 1 Sam. xv. 21–28.

17. i.e. a heart in which sorrow and affliction have done their beneficient work, changing the obstinacy of pride into the humility of penitence. A broken spirit—a crushed heart are not the true antitypes of the sacrifices, but in cases where the legal offerings failed, the only suited moral condition that God could accept is here declared.

18–19. Confirms the prophetic character of the psalm as the national confession which is the necessary prerequisite to national blessing.

18. Cf. 1 Chron. xi. 5–8. David was probably afraid lest, as a result of his personal sin, the crowning work of his kingdom (the completion of Israel's capital city with its protective walls) might be impeded, 1 Kings iii. 3; ix. 14–15.

19. Shows that the cessation of animal sacrifices is not implied in 16–17. In millennial days they will be offered as memorials of the perfect sacrifice already once offered, Ezek. xliii. 18–27; xlv. 15–25. Remember that millennial conditions have not the perfection of the eternal state. (a) "Then . . .," i.e. sacrifices offered in the right spirit; (b) two Hebrew words here used of the burnt offering; the first denotes the sacrifice as ascending to God, the second, as being wholly consumed. Both are types of Christ's utter devotion to God in His death; (a) of its *intent*; (b) of its *extent*; or, (a) its motives, (b) its measure.

Book Two.   II. Disclosures concerning the Enemy Reprobate, lii.-lx

1. The Apostates and the Remnant, lii.-lv. (Maschils).   The
   Antichrist Identified.

   (i) The Faithless Ones, lii.-liii.
   (ii) The Faithful Ones, liv.-lv.

PSALM LII.   DENUNCIATION OF THE DECEIVER

I. CONDEMNATION OF DOEG (1-5).   The Deceiver Addressed.
  1. His False-heartedness Denounced (1-3).   Selah.
  2. His Fate Described (4-5).   Selah.

II. CONTEMPLATION BY THE RIGHTEOUS (6-7).
  1. Their Reverence for God—The "Strong One" (El) (6a).
  2. Their Ridicule of "Geber"—The "Strong man" (6b-7).

III. CONFESSION OF DAVID (8-9).   The Deliverer Addressed.
  1. His Faith Declared (8).   "me."
  2. His Fervour Displayed (9).   "Thee."

SUPERSCRIPT.—Maschil of David; when Doeg the Edomite went and told
Saul and said unto him, "David is come to the house of Ahimelech."

SUBSCRIPT.—For the Chief Musician; relating to Mahalath.

PRIMARY ASSOCIATION.—Writer and occasion clearly indicated in
title; see 1 Sam. xxi.-xxii. Doeg as chief of Saul's herdsmen was a
man of importance and of substance. With malicious intent he
reported facts which seemed to support Saul's unjust suspicion that
David was plotting against his life. The results to Ahimelech's
family were fatal. Subscript indicates that David later handed his
composition to the precentor for liturgical use, probably in further
celebration of his victory over the Philistine. "Mahalath" according
to ancient vocalisation should read "m'holoth" = dancings or the
great dancing, in reference to Goliath's death, 1 Sam. xviii. 6-7.
It was "the great dancing" that led to the jealousy of Saul, the slander
of Doeg and the massacre of the priests. In the psalm there appears
to be a double reference, to Goliath and to Doeg.
PROPHETIC ANTICIPATION.—See Book Analysis above. "Maschil"

points to special instruction for the last days. Behind the historical Doeg we see the more sinister figure of Antichrist, whose true character is displayed in these psalms; cf. Dan. xi. 36; Isa. xxx. 33; lvii. 9; Rev. xiii. In Book I the character of Christ is seen by way of contrast.

PERSONAL APPLICATION.—A Psalm of the Tongue—the treacherous and the truthful. Moral indignation against evil is better than meditated indifference. Mercy characterises the Mighty One (El) (1). Note contrast between the malice of man and the mercy of God (1). Some men boast in devilish mischief, others in divine mercy (1). Human guile does not disannul divine goodness (1). Deceit is really a confession of defeat (2). Malice is a matter of motive; truth may be told with malicious intent (2). The malicious tongue is often denounced in Scripture, see e.g. James iii. Watch your tongue! "A razor is for shaving not for slaying; the tongue is for use not abuse." The heart is a fountain, language is the flow, James iii. 11. Praise best suits the saint's tongue (9).

VERSE NOTES

1. "mighty man," Heb.=geber, see Appendix X. (4); or, "O thou hero!" (ironically); "continually" lit. all the day; God = El.

2. (b) Br. "O thou worker of deceit!"

3. Ctr. of Christ, xlv. 7; "more than," br. "rather than."

4. "Deceitful" because while the statement was true (see superscript) the implication was false.

5. Doom of the miscreant's house described in forcible figures; "thy dwelling-place," lit. tent, or tabernacle. Ahimelech was cut off during his ministry in the Tabernacle, so God repays in kind; the word "tent" being applied also to Doeg's dwelling, see xlix. 11; cf. 1 Sam. xxi. 7.

6. Not the malicious satisfaction of the evil-minded, but satisfaction at the vindication of divine justice; cf. ii. 4. What the righteous see (6); what they say (7).

7. Note the negative followed by the positive aspects of sin; "man" Heb. = strong man, here ironical; akin to the Heb. word in 2; "abundance," see 1 Sam. xxii. 7-9 with viii. 11, 12, 15; "wickedness," Heb. = sing. form of that trans. "mischiefs" (2) = deep practice; (b) connects with xlix. 6.

8. Ctr. the fate of the evil-doer in 5. The olive is an evergreen and its fruit contains the oil which is in Scripture typical of the Holy Spirit; "house" in ctr. with "tent" (5).

9. "Thou hast done it." For sim. use of this phrase, cf. xxii. 31; xxxvii. 5; "saints" = favoured ones.

PSALM LIII.   FOLLY OF FREE-THINKERS

I. HUMAN CORRUPTION (1-3).
   1. Sweeping Accusation (1).
   2. Divine Inspection (2).
   3. Solemn Conclusion (3).

II. HEARTLESS OPPRESSION (4-5).
   1. Strong Expostulation (4).
   2. Divine Interposition (5a).
   3. Smitten Opposition (5b).

III. HOLY ASPIRATION (6).
   1. Sublime Manifestation (6a).
   2. Divine Restoration (6b).
   3. Sanctified Exultation (6c).

SUPERSCRIPT.—Maschil of David.

SUBSCRIPT.—For the Chief Musician; upon Neginoth.

PRIMARY ASSOCIATION.—A recension of Ps. xiv. adapted to public use (see subscript). The marked variation in the text at verse 5 was made in order to suit new circumstances, in all probability the destruction of Sennacherib's army in the days of Hezekiah; compare 5 with 2 Kings xix. 35-36. See corresponding notes to Ps. xiv. "Neginoth," see Ps. iii. notes.

PROPHETIC ANTICIPATION.—"Maschil" again points to special instruction for the remnant in the last days. The character, conduct and confounding of Antichrist and his followers are shown. While godless at heart, they outwardly own a political "god" for their own ends, 2 Thess. ii. 4; Dan. xi. 36-37, 38; Rev. xiii. 15. The remnant is here associated with the execution of the divine judgment (5). In keeping with the general character of Book II and the prophetic theme of the psalm, the divine title "Elohim" occurs seven times instead of three times and "Jehovah" four times in Ps. xiv. Alternative title, "The Atheism of the Antichrist."

PERSONAL APPLICATION.—The Scriptures of Truth are adapted to our ever-changing conditions. These ancient words always suit modern needs. Men seek everything but God (2). The Lord's search for (a) Seekers after God (2); (b) Sinners lost from God, Luke xix. 10.; (c) Saints to worship God, John iv. 23. God despises those who deny Him (5). Neglect of God is the cause of moral corruption. While men regard not God, He ceases not to regard them. Note the sevenfold affirmation of God in the presence of the ungodly multitude. See also Ps. xiv.

VERSE NOTES

See Notes to Psalm xiv.

PSALM LIV. UPHOLDER OF THE UPRIGHT

I. PRAYER FOR DELIVERANCE (1-3). THE APPEAL OF FAITH.
    1. The Requests (1-2).
    2. The Reason.(3). Designs of the Enemy. Selah.

II. PROFESSION OF DEPENDENCE UPON GOD (4-5a). THE ANCHOR OF FAITH.

III. PETITION FOR DESTRUCTION OF ENEMIES (5b). THE ARGUMENT OF FAITH. "In Thy faithfulness."

IV. PRAISE FOR DELIVERANCE (6-7). THE ANTICIPATION OF FAITH.
    1. The Rendition (6).
    2. The Reason (7). Defeat of the Enemy.

SUPERSCRIPT.—Maschil of David; when the Ziphites came and said unto Saul, "Doth not David hide himself with us?"

SUBSCRIPT.—For the Chief Musician; upon Neginoth.

PRIMARY ASSOCIATION.—The title indicates both writer and occasion, see historical record 1 Sam. xxiii. 14-15, 19-24; xxvi. 1-4. Ziph was a small town fifteen miles S.E. of Hebron in the territory of Judah. It seems that its inhabitants displayed treachery on two occasions, see xxxi., notes. "Neginoth," see Ps. iii. note.

PROPHETIC ANTICIPATION.—Here is further instruction (Maschil), for the last days, days of fierce persecution for the Jewish remnant. Like David, many of these godly ones will meet treachery while being hunted and harassed by Antichrist and his followers (cf. Luke xxi. 16 ff.), yet faith triumphs in the anticipation of divine deliverance.

PERSONAL APPLICATION.—Might is one attribute of "the Name" (1). If men set God before them, they would never persecute the godly (3). Can you say, "God is *my* Helper?" (4). He helps by upholding (4). We have a present God for present needs (4). God's character is pledged to fulfil His word (5*b*). All our worship should be voluntary (6). God is good (6). Where there is no trouble, there is no triumph (7). Faith sees the future as the present (7). God leads His people out of the turmoil of trouble into the "pastures of peace" (7).

VERSE NOTES

1. Salvation here is external, *i.e.* from enemies; (*b*) *i.e.* "Do me justice . . . "

3. Cf. 1 Sam. xxiii. 15; "strangers" prob. ref. to the men of Keilah, who were Canaanites by race; "seek" ctr. the seeking, liii. 2.

4. (*b*) Br. "Adonai (the Lord) is the Upholder of my soul."

5. See marg.; "enemies," s.H.w. elsewhere in Psalter only v. 8; xxvii. 11; lvi. 2; lix. 10; (*b*) br. "In faithfulness destroy Thou them."

6. Note the title "Jehovah" in contrast to the general usage in Book II.

7. "he" or, "it," *i.e.* the Name, = Jehovah Himself revealed as the covenant-keeping God of His people; "trouble" or, strait; (*b*) "hath seen" = looked upon the defeat of his foes.

PSALM LV.   ODE OF THE OPPRESSED

I. PLAINTIVE SUPPLICATION (1-8).   David contemplates himself. The dominant note is depression.

1. Prayer (1-3). The Cry and its Cause.
2. Plight (4-5). The Foes and the Fears.
3. Plaint (6-8). The Cry and its Cause. Rest desired.

II. PORTENTOUS DENUNCIATION (9-15).   David contemplates his foes. The dominant note is indignation.

1. Prayer (9-11). The Cry and its Cause.
2. Parenthesis (12-14). The Friend and his False-heartedness. (The Arch-traitor—central point of psalm).
3. Prayer (15). The Cry and its Cause. Retribution discerned.

III. PATIENT ANTICIPATION (16-23).   David contemplates his God. The dominant note is consolation.

1. Prayer (16-19). The Appeal and the Assurance.
2. Parenthesis (20-21). The Friend and his False-heartedness.

3. Persuasion (22–23). The Appeal and the Assurance. Reliance displayed.
    (a) Men addressed (22).
    (b) God addressed (23).

SUPERSCRIPT.—Maschil of David.

SUBSCRIPT.—For the Chief Musician; upon Jonath-elem-rechokim.

PRIMARY ASSOCIATION.—Written by David most probably during the period of Absalom's rebellion, 2 Sam. xv.–xvii. Ahithophel is doubtless the false friend referred to. He was the mainstay of the revolt. It is instructive to trace the motive of Ahithophel's treachery, for the record shows some of the evil fruits of David's great sin. See 1 Chron. iii. 5; 2 Sam. xi. 3 with xxiii. 34, 39. Eliam (or Ammiel) father of Bathsheba was son of Ahithophel and Uriah's brother officer in the king's bodyguard. Ahithophel nursed a sense of wrong towards the corrupter of his grand-daughter and the murderer of his grandson by marriage. David thus placed a powerful weapon in the hands of his enemies. His only safe course lay in prayer, committing his cause to a faithful and merciful God, 2 Sam. xv. 31. For subscript see R.V. m.; connects with 5–8.

PROPHETIC ANTICIPATION.—Here we see the deep soul exercise of the much persecuted Jewish remnant in the last days which precede the nation's final deliverance from the power of Antichrist. Further details concerning the latter's character come into view. He is here seen as (a) a Professor of the worship of his fathers' God (14) though an atheist at heart, liii.; (b) a Profaner of his solemn covenant (20), cf. Dan. ix. 27; (c) a Persecutor of the godly remnant (3). His doom is also predicted (15, 23); cf. Rev. xix. 20. This psalm also foreshadows the experiences of our Lord, who when on earth fathomed the depths of human baseness, cruelty and ingratitude to an extent that none else ever did. Judas the apostate, in many salient features, foreshadows the Antichrist as the lying deceiver yet to come.

PERSONAL APPLICATION.—A psalm of trust amid trouble and treachery. Our troubles may be caused by ourselves or by others, as a result of our failure or as the result of our faith. In either case God alone is our true resource. Even Christians are sometimes caught in a maze of mingled emotions. The Redeemer is the true refuge of the restless (2); cf. Matt. xi. 28–30. Security is not always found in solitude; wickedness may be found in the wilderness (6). God may not grant us the wings of a dove to escape troubles, but we may have the wings of an eagle to soar above them; (6) with Isa. xl. 31. Note the sevenfold form of rampant evil (9–11). The attitude of an unfaithful friend is worse to bear than the antagonism of an unremitting foe (12–13). If tempted to flee from the foe, fly to the faithful God (6, 16). David, like Daniel, prayed three times a day (17). A word of comfort is here for saints in war-stricken countries (18). There is peril in prosperity (19). Material plenty often brings spiritual poverty (19). Changes challenge the character of our Christianity (19). In our change let us turn to the Changeless One (19). "No change Jehovah knows." If God does not remove the burden He gives strength to bear (22). The righteous are some-times moved *on*, but never *from*, their foundation (22). David's advice was born of experience (22); cf. 1 Peter v. 7. "I will put my trust in Thee," is the saint's watchword for all time (23). Scorn to be disloyal to your King (12–14).

VERSE NOTES

2. "moan," or, am distracted; cf. Isa. xxviii. 14; Ezek. vii. 16.

3. *i.e.* hurling insults, calumnies and threats is like casting stones or firebrands upon an enemy; "wicked" = lawless one.

4. "sore pained," or, writhes.

7. Cf. Jer. ix. 2.

9. Jerusalem having become as Babylon (Babel), he prays for a confusion of counsels, Gen. xi.

11. "wickedness," s.H.w. lii. 2 = deep practices; "streets," lit. broad places, *i.e.* the place of public concourse at the city gates, where justice was administered and business transacted.

12. (*b*) Br. "might have . . ."

14. Br. "we were wont to take . . . to walk . . ."; habitual intimacy and confidential intercourse in private, and fellowship in the public worship of God; "throng," *i.e.* of worshippers.

15. This prayer is a prediction; cf. the death of the apostates in the wilderness, Num. xvi. 31–35, and cf. Rev. xix. 20.

19. The Heb. text is not corrupt as some allege. Read, "God shall hear, and answer them (*i.e.* with judgment), even He that sitteth enthroned eternally. Selah—(the men) who keep not their oath (*i.e.* of allegiance to David), and who fear not God." The "selah" points on to the character of "them" in first line.

22. Note how the name of the covenant-keeping God, Jehovah, shines out in this section in marked contrast with 20, 21; cf. xxxvii. 5; 1 Peter v. 7.

23. *i.e.* by a premature death. Ahithophel destroyed himself, 2 Sam. xvii. 14, 23. Absalom came to an early end and his body was cast into a pit; Judas hanged himself, and Antichrist's doom is foreseen, Rev. xix. 20.

Book Two. II. *Disclosures concerning the Enemy Reprobate, lii.–lx.*

2. The Afflicted and their Refuge, lvi.–lx. (Michtams). The Almighty Invoked.

PSALM LVI.   FAITH FETTERS FEARS

I. PRAYER. PLEA FOR DELIVERANCE (1–4).
   1. Appeal (1–2). The Cry and the Cause.
   2. Assurance (3).
     Profession of Trust (4). Refrain.

II. PLAINT. PERIL OF DEATH (5–11).
   1. Appeal (5–8). The Cause and the Cry.
   2. Assurance (9).
     Profession of Trust (10–11). Refrain.

III. PLEDGE. PRAISE FOR DELIVERANCE (12–13).
   1. Acknowledgment (12). The Consecration and the Cause.
   2. Anticipation (13).
     (a) Preservation.
     (b) Purpose.

SUPERSCRIPT.—Michtam of David; when the Philistines seized him in Gath.

SUBSCRIPT.—For the Chief Musician. Al-tashheth (= Destroy not).

PRIMARY ASSOCIATION.—Title gives writer and occasion, see 1 Sam. xxi. 10–15; xxvii. 4; xxix. 2–11. Verse 13 seems to suggest the crisis of David's second flight to Gath. Closely related to Ps. xxxiv. which see for notes on the two psalms; connected also with lvii. Refrain gives the theme. Ps. lvi. is the Prayer for Deliverance, and xxxiv. the Praise for Deliverance, here anticipated by faith. For meaning of "Michtam," see Introduction V. (f).

PROPHETIC ANTICIPATION.—This group of "Michtam" psalms shows the true path of the godly during the coming period of the Great Tribulation. The pattern for God's people is found in Ps. xvi. Towards the end they come to a realisation that their sufferings are God's disciplinary measures to bring them to a full confession of their sins, particularly their guilt in rejecting Messiah. The lowest point in their humiliation proves to be the turning point in their salvation, lx.

PERSONAL APPLICATION.—Since Elohim (God) is for us what can "enosh" (frail man) do unto us? (1) Those who "fear" God need fear no one else; then face the foe without fear (2-3). "Trust in Him at all times" (lxii. 8), but especially when you feel afraid (3). Faith receives, rests on and rejoices in the Word of God (4, 10). God's faithfulness inspires the saint's faith. Let us always praise God for His Word (4). Contrast the tenderness of God with the tyranny of the enemy (5-8). God takes note of your every tear and will one day wipe all tears away with His own gracious hand (8); cf. Rev. xxi. 4. He sees every sorrow of His saints. God is on your side (9); cf. Rom. viii. 31. None who work iniquity shall escape (7). The life as well as the lips should render a thank-offering (13); cf. Heb. xiii. 15-16. Past experience confirms present expectation (13). He who has delivered our souls from death will surely deliver our feet from falling (13). Our steps will be right if we walk in the light (13).

VERSE NOTES

1. "Be gracious . . . man (= enosh) panteth after me," so 2; note threefold "all day long" character of the persecution, 1, 2, 5.

2. "enemies," as margin.

3. Faith overcomes fear. "I" (emph.). For the only time on record that David was afraid of man, see 1 Sam. xxi. 12.

4. "flesh," here = man as a frail and short-lived creature in contrast with God the Eternal Spirit.

5. See 1 Sam. xxiv. 9. Calumniators sought to poison Saul's mind against David.

6. "hide themselves," or set an ambush; cf. 1 Sam. xxiii. 22-23; (b) i.e. they dogged his heels intent on his life; (c) "As they wait for . . ."

8. "tears . . . bottle" ref. to ancient custom of mourners for the dead who collected their tears in a bottle (lachrymatory), which was later buried with their loved one; a bold figure; "book," cf. Mal. iii. 16.

9. "Then" (emph.), i.e. in the very day that he calls the enemy is turned back.

12. "Vows upon me," i.e. they are now due to be fulfilled, for faith tells me my prayer is already granted; in xxxiv. we see the vows fulfilled.

13. (c) i.e. in ctr. with the shades of Sheol; cf. John viii. 12; Job xxxiii. 30.

PSALM LVII.   A FUGITIVE'S FAITH

I. THE PRAYER OF FAITH (1-5).
Cause of the Cry—Remorseless Cruelty.

 1. Faith's Request (1).   Fig. epizeuxis.
 2. Faith's Resolve (2).   "Unto God."
 3. Faith's Reward (3).   "Loving-kindness and truth sent from heaven."
  Selah.
 4. Faith's Repose (4).   "I will lie down."
 5. Faith's Refrain (5).   "Be Thou exalted, O God."

II. THE PERSPECTIVE OF FAITH (6).   Selah.
 Result of preceding prayer and Reason for succeeding praise.

III. THE PRAISE OF FAITH (7-11).
 Consequence of the Cry—Recovered Calm.
 1. Faith's Resoluteness (7).   Fig. epizeuxis.
 2. Faith's Rejoicing (8).   "I will awake."
 3. Faith's Response (9).   "Unto Thee."
 4. Faith's Reason (10).   "Loving-kindness and truth reach unto heaven."
 5. Faith's Refrain (11).   "Be Thou exalted, O God."

SUPERSCRIPT.—Michtam of David; when he fled from Saul into the cave.

SUBSCRIPT.—For the Chief Musician. Al-tashheth (= Destroy not).

PRIMARY ASSOCIATION.—Writer and occasion as title, most probably the event recorded 1 Sam. xxiv. 1-8. Seems to be an evening hymn (4, 8). Closely related to the preceding psalm but has a more triumphant tone. It is also characterised by the figure epizeuxis (emphatic repetition of words). Pss. xxxiv.; lvii. and cxlii. are all "cave" psalms. Verses 7-11 appear again in cviii. Note corresponding members in sections I and III of the analysis, but slightly different order.

PROPHETIC ANTICIPATION.—See corresponding notes to preceding psalm. David again seen as the representative of the nation in the last days. Though still surrounded by "fiery" foes, the faith of the godly remnant anticipates the intervention of God from heaven. Their hopes will be fulfilled by the manifestation of Messiah in glorious power for their deliverance, because of God's loving-kindness and truth (= faithfulness to His word). Israel will become the heralds of salvation to the nations and the leaders of universal praise (9).

PERSONAL APPLICATION.—Faith is not always inconsistent with fears, nor does faith excuse us from taking reasonable precautions. The difference between a brave man and a coward is that one yields to his fears, while the other overcomes them. There is safe shelter under the shadow of El Shaddai (1). In the day of calamity the sheltering wings of the divine love (1) are better than the swift wings of the fleeing dove, lv. 6. His wings provide a place of rest as well as of refuge (4). God is a safe place in sore peril (4). God is for me (lvi. 9) and He accomplishes for me (2). Not only my person, but my affairs are safe with Him. The night of trouble ends in the dawn of deliverance (8). It is a good thing to awake the dawn with praise (8). When "the Sun of Righteousness shall arise" the beams of His glory will cover the earth (5, 11).

VERSE NOTES

1. "Be gracious . . . be gracious . . . hath taken refuge . . . refuge." Note the significant change of tenses; "calamities," s.H.w. lii. 2; lv. 11.

2. "call unto Elohim Elyon," see Appendix II.; combination of titles elsewhere only lxxviii. 56.

3. "Selah," points on to the just retribution, 6d.

4. "I will lie down to rest among fiery foes, even the sons . . ."

5. The poet desires the manifestation of God's majesty in defeating the murderous machinations of the enemy.

6. Here is the eternal law of retribution; see xxxv. 7, note. "Selah" looks back to 3.

7. "fixed," i.e. steadfastly resolved; note, "fixed . . . fixed . . . sing . . . sing"; fig. epizeuxis; "sing praises" or (as so often in the Psalter) "make melody"; lit. psalm (used as a verb).

8. "my glory," probably = the soul or spirit; (b) br. as margin.

9. "nations," br. races (of men).

PSALM LVIII.   CORRUPT COURTS CONDEMNED

I. JUDGES EXPOSED (1-5). THE SIN PROBED. The Unrighteous Judges.
    1. Accusation of Judicial Corruption (1-2). By the Psalmist.
    2. Assertion concerning the Wicked (3-5).

II. JUSTICE EXPECTED (6-9). THE SENTENCE PREDICTED.
    1. Appeal to the Lord (6-8). Invocation.
    2. Address to the Lawless (9). Intimation.

III. JUDGMENT EXECUTED (10-11). THE SATISFACTION PRODUCED.
    The Righteous Judge.
    1. Approbation by the Righteous (10).
    2. Admission of Just Retribution (11). By the Peoples.

SUPERSCRIPT.—Michtam of David.

SUBSCRIPT.—For the Chief Musician. Al-tashheth (= Destroy not).

PRIMARY ASSOCIATION.—Composed by David probably during the period of Absalom's rebellion, 2 Sam. xv.–xvii. This view clears up the difficulty generally experienced in understanding the language of verse 1, for the reference will be to the boastful claims of the leaders of that revolt. Note that David blames others rather than his own son. In contrast to what is generally found in the psalms, the last verse gives the theme.

PROPHETIC ANTICIPATION.—During the days of Antichrist's rule, corruption will characterise the judicial systems, and godly ones suffer injustice and oppression to a degree unknown hitherto. This will lead to deep exercise of heart and great longing for the manifestation of God in judgment upon the oppressors. The remnant's divinely inspired prayers will be answered—their hopes abundantly fulfilled. The poet-seer describes the utter defeat of Israel's enemies by direct divine interposition in seven bold figures: (a) Power broken (6a); (b) Attacks fail (6b); (c) Forces routed (7a); (d) Weapons futile (7bc); (e) Resources exhausted (8a); (f) Hopes blighted (8b); (g) Destruction completed (9). The meaning of this last verse sorely puzzles many commentators because they do not perceive the prophetic significance; see Rev. xix. 20–21.

PERSONAL APPLICATION.—Fair words of false-hearted flatterers always fail of fulfilment (1). The hands work the will of the heart (2). The scales of injustice weigh out violence (2). He who stops his ears to the voice of God must be classed with the wicked (4). It is evident that a time must come when evil can no longer be tolerated in the earth, but must be extirpated (6–9). The now silent righteousness will one day reign; (1) with Isa. xxxii. 1. Despite what men now say, they will soon be forced to acknowledge that wickedness does not pay and that there is a God who judges righteously (11).

VERSE NOTES

1. Br. "Will ye indeed utter long silent righteousness . . . ?" See 2 Sam. xv. 2–6.
2. (b) "Throughout the land your hands weigh out violence"; so LXX, etc.
3. "estranged," i.e. from God; cf. Gen. viii. 21; Eph. iv. 18; Col. i. 21.
4. Worthy children of the Old Serpent! Snake-charming is alluded to Eccles. x. 11; Jer. viii. 17.
5. The serpent typifies subtlety, i.e. insidious evil; the lion, ferocity, i.e. rampant evil; the adder, utter indifference to the voice of God.
6–9. According to the Heb. text the verb forms imply denunciation, but in the LXX they are predictive.

7. Ref. to the hostile armies; "apace," or run off; (b) i.e. the arrows have their heads severed and are harmless.

8. The slug or snail is alluded to in connection with the observed fact that myriads of these creatures in Eastern lands shrivel and perish during seasons of drought.

9. (b) Br. "He shall sweep them away with a whirlwind, living and in wrath."

10. i.e. rejoicing in the triumph of good over evil, and in the vindication of God's righteousness; (b) cf. lxviii. 23. i.e. ride over the corpses of slain enemies; see Rev. xix.

PSALM LIX.   TRUST TRIUMPHS OVER TROUBLE

I. PRAYER FOR RESCUE (1-5).   SUPPLICATION.
    The Psalmist's Deliverance.
    1. Request (1-2).   Against Personal Enemies.
    2. Reasons (3-4a).
    3. Request (4b-5).   Against National Enemies.   Selah.

II. PORTRAYAL OF ENEMIES (6-7).   SIMILE.
    Like Prowling and Howling Dogs.   "At evening they return"—The Threatening Foes.

III. PORTENT OF DEFEAT (8).   SCORN.
    REFRAIN. *Profession of Trust* (9). "God my High Tower." "I will watch unto Thee."

IV. PROSPECT OF TRIUMPH (10). SATISFACTION. (Central Thought).

V. PRAYER FOR RETRIBUTION (11-13).   SUPPLICATION.
    The Persecutors' Destruction.
    1. Request (11).
    2. Reasons (12).
    3. Request (13).   Selah.

VI. PORTRAYAL OF ENEMIES (14-15).   SIMILE.
    Like Prowling and Howling Dogs.   "At evening let them return."— The Thwarted Foes.

VII. PRAISE FOR DELIVERANCE (16-17).   SONG.
    1. Rendition (a).
    2. Reason (b).
    REFRAIN. *Profession of Trust* (17). "God my High Tower." "I will sing unto Thee."

SUPERSCRIPT.—Michtam of David; when Saul sent, and they watched the house to kill him.

SUBSCRIPT.—For the Chief Musician; relating to Shushan Eduth (= Lily of Testimony).

PRIMARY ASSOCIATION.—Clue to writer and occasion is in the title, see 1 Sam. xix. 11–18. "Watched" (title) s.H.w. 1 Sam. xix. 11. Subscript indicates that the psalm was to be used in the temple liturgy at the spring festivals.

PROPHETIC ANTICIPATION.—This is clearly shown by verse 5. Here are prayer for and prediction of judgment upon the nations gathered against the city (Jerusalem) in a final effort to exterminate the people of God, cf. Zech. xiv. The godly in Israel recognise that the presence and removal of Gentile enemies are signs respectively of divine anger and its passing away.

PERSONAL APPLICATION.—Despite danger and difficulty our doubts may be dispelled. God scatters those who gather against the saints (3, 11). The ungodly often charge the righteous with the very sin of which they themselves are guilty, 1 Sam. xxii. 8, 13 with 3, 5. In great need be bold enough to claim the great resources of God (5), cf. Heb. iv. 16. What a challenge to the living God? (7c). It is not only wicked but absurd to plot against Him (8). Those at whom He laughs are irretrievably lost (8). Our enemies may be strong (3), but God is our strength (9). Whoso has God as his "high tower" is placed far above the reach of the enemy's rage (9). A better example of the bitter fruit of sin may be furnished by the lives of the wicked than by their deaths (11). Men are apt to forget God's lessons (11). It is a solemn thought that God often allows the wicked to live on for a time that His people the better may see His righteous dealing in the present life (11); cf. Exod. ix. 16. God makes men's own sin their punishment; the statement (6), the sentence (14); cf. Jer. ii. 19. The foes may howl at night (14), but the saint's "Hallelujah" is to be heard in the morning (16). "Beware of the dogs," cf. (14) with Phil. iii. 2 R.V.

VERSE NOTES

3. "For, lo, strong ones have laid wait for my life, they gather . . ."; "transgression," *i.e.* the sin of treachery of which he had been falsely accused, 1 Sam. xxiv. 11.

4. "prepare" or "station"; "for no iniquity (of mine). . .," *i.e.* the hostility was, unjust and unprovoked; br. "Arouse Thee to meet me . . ."

5. Br. "Yea, do Thou, O Jehovah of Hosts, the Eloah of Israel"; (*b*) Not the psalmist, but the adversary and his many abettors were the real transgressors, cf. xxv. 3; (*c*) "Show not grace to any treacherous workers of iniquity," cf. lvii. 1; "nations," here introduced with prophetic significance.

6. Enemies compared to a pack of half-wild, savage and hungry dogs, such as still infest cities in the East; cf. xxii. 16, 20.

8. Cf. ii. 4.

9. Br. "O my strength, unto Thee will I watch; For God is my High Tower, the God of my loving-kindness," so 17. David's enemies watch the house (see title), but he will watch for God's help.

10. Continue, "He shall come to meet me . . .," cf. iv. 3; "enemies," see margin; cf. liv. 7.

11–13. Three reasons are given for this prayer: (a) that the sin of the enemy might be punished (12); (b) that the sovereignty of God might be recognised (13); (c) that the soul of the saint might be exercised (11).

11. (a) ref. to the leaders who will be made a living example, cf. Rev. xix. 20; (b) refers to their many followers.

13. Br. ". . . let men know . . .," cf. 1 Sam. xvii. 46.

14ff. or, "And though they return at evening, howl like dogs . . . though they wander . . . Yet as for me I . . . "; "tarry," or (with LXX) whine.

17. "sing praises" = psalm (as verb) or, make melody.

PSALM LX.   THE LAND FOR THE LOYAL

I. GOD'S PEOPLE CHASTENED (1–4).   PENITENT LAMENTATION.
   "Thou hast cast us off."   Divine Displeasure Apprehended.

II. GOD'S PROTECTION CRAVED (5).   POWERFUL SUPPLICATION.
   "Thy beloved ones . . . save!"   Divine Deliverance Asked.

III. GOD'S PROMISE CLAIMED (6–8).   PERTINENT CITATION.
   "God hath sworn by His holiness."   Divine Declaration Adduced.

IV. GOD'S   POWER   CONTEMPLATED   (9–12).   PRAYERFUL ANTICIPATION.
   "Thou . . . who didst cast us off."   Divine Deliverance Assured.

SUPERSCRIPT.—Michtam of David, to teach; when he waged war with Aram-naharaim and with Aram-zobah; when Joab returned and smote of Edom in the Valley of Salt twelve thousand.

SUBSCRIPT.—For the Chief Musician; upon Neginah.

PRIMARY ASSOCIATION.—Writer and occasion as title; cf. notes to xliv., which may belong to the same period; and cviii. of which verses 5–12 of the present psalm form part. Aram-naharaim = Syria of the two rivers (i.e. Euphrates and Tigris) identified with Mesopotamia. Aram-zobah refers to the region between Tigris and

Orontes, N.E. of Damascus. By collating 2 Sam. viii.; 1 Chron. xviii. 12–13; 1 Kings xi. 15–16, etc., we gather that while David was engaged in his first Syrian campaign in the far north-east, the Edomites seized the opportunity to invade Palestine and inflicted a serious reverse upon the Israelites. When David heard of it, he immediately despatched a strong force under Joab and the enemy was crushed in the Valley of Salt (south of the Dead Sea on the ancient border between Judah and Edom).* By his skilfulness and promptitude in meeting this great crisis, David gained considerable renown, 2 Sam. viii. 13. He himself defeated the Syrians, Abishai (Joab's lieutenant) the Edomites, while Joab remained six months in Edom to complete the conquest, 1 Kings xi. 16. In the encounter with Abishai, the Edomites lost eighteen thousand men slain, and Joab accounted for another twelve thousand. There is therefore no discrepancy as some allege. "Neginah "(subscript) = smiting, see Ps. iii. The plural "Neginoth" generally appears.

PROPHETIC ANTICIPATION.—Points to the time when Israel will at last realise that the long period of dispersion and suffering comes from God's chastening hand. We see here some of the fruits of this divine discipline. Israel will be then in a condition to receive the full inheritance which has never yet been hers in actual possession. The fulfilment of divine promises such as Deut. xxx. 1–3 will be claimed by a newly exercised faith on the part of the godly ones. Verses 6–7 suggest a fresh apportionment of the land which can hardly refer to the period of David's wars, and the reference to a standard (4) indicates that Israel (prophetically) is once more acknowledged by God as His people. The ambiguous language of verse 4 is probably to suit both historical and prophetical aspects.

PERSONAL APPLICATION.—The psalm expresses confidence in a crisis. Despise not divine discipline nor despair under it; cf. Heb. xii. Men's passions are like volcanic fires ever ready to discharge molten lava in a destructive stream; when God's restraining hand is removed, these passions, ever seething under the surface of society, belch forth with disastrous effect (3). God sometimes punishes the wicked by intoxicating them with success (3). Our Lord Jesus is the true Benjamin (5), see verse notes. God's essential nature makes it impossible for Him to break a promise (6). Restoration brings men back to the path their faithful fathers trod (6). Mere profession

*Scene also of Amaziah's victory later, II Chr. xxv. II.

(Moab), the old nature (Edom), and fleshly religion (Philistia) all come under the judgment of God (8). 11*b* contains a truth frequently urged upon our attention. Compare 12*b* with Phil. iv. 3. When God's people sin, they are no longer invincible, cf. Josh. vi.–viii. Sin makes wide breaches in the saint's defences (2). There is great lack to-day of long-sighted leaders (9). The Lord is the true Leader (10).

VERSE NOTES

2. The disaster is compared to an earthquake, a common figure in Scripture for social convulsions.

3. "Hard" = calamitous. (*b*) A common metaphor for divine judgments; like a drugged potion in its virulent effects.

4. "Banner" = standard; (*b*) the LXX perhaps represents a better reading, "That they may betake themselves to flight from before the bow," *i.e.* God had summoned them to the battle only to put them to flight before the enemy archers; the line is expostulatory; for similar thought, cf. Deut. i. 27.

5. Seems an allusion to Benjamin's name (Son of my right hand) as representing the whole people, cf. Deut. xxxiii. 12; "beloved (ones)"; "us," br. me, as A.V.

6–8. God is the speaker; possibly an actual oracle quoted or it may be inspired comment on the great promise to David, 2 Sam. vii. The Lord is here represented as a victorious warrior portioning out the land to His people. "Shechem . . . Succoth" the former representing territory west of Jordan, the latter that east of Jordan. Both places are connected with patriarchal history and here appear also with prophetic significance. Shechem (= shoulder) was the first place where Abraham received promise of the land. References show that it typifies the spirit of obedience; this will characterise Israel in the land under the New Covenant. Succoth (= booths) connects with the meaning of the Feast of Tabernacles, which commemorates the end of wilderness wanderings and foreshadows the millennial day of final rest in the promised land. Other historic names in this psalm also have prophetic meaning.

7. (*a*) Ref. to that section of the nation which settled east of Jordan; (*bc*) these two tribes represent those who settled west of Jordan; "defence," Ephraim was numerically the strongest tribe and here represented as a warrior's helmet.

8. Neighbouring nations reduced to servitude in ctr. to the honour placed upon Israel. Proud Moab becomes like the slave who bears the vessels for washing the conqueror's feet; while Edom will be like the slave to whom the conqueror flings his sandals to be carried or cleaned (margin); the action may also signify transference of possession, Ruth iv. 7; Josh. x. 24. Philistia will raise the shout of acclamation acknowledging the conqueror as king lest she too be destroyed.

9. "city" probably refers to Sela, or Petra, the capital of Edom and famous for its inaccessibility, Obad. 3; (*b*) pref. as marg., so 10*a*.

12. This prayer of faith anticipating victory, refers back to Ps. xliv. 5.

Book Two. III. Dominion of the Enthroned Redeemer, lxi.–lxxii.

1. The Returned King, lxi.–lxviii.

(i) Sighs for the Sanctuary, lxi.–lxiv. Prayers.
(ii) Songs of the Salvation, lxv.–lxviii. Praises.

PSALM LXI.   VOWS OF THE VICTOR

I. PRELIMINARY PRAYER (1).   The Psalmist's Invocation.

II. PURPOSE AND PETITION (2).   "I will cry."

III. PARTICULAR REASON (3).   "For."   Confidence based upon Experience.

IV. PERSONAL PETITION (4).   "Let me . . . let me."   Selah.

V. PARTICULAR REASON (5).   "For."   Confidence based upon Experience.

VI. PROSPECT AND PETITION (6-7).

VII. PROMISED PRAISE (8). The Psalmist's Intention. "I will psalm."

SUPERSCRIPT.—David's.

SUBSCRIPT.—For the Chief Musician. To Jeduthun.

PRIMARY ASSOCIATION.—Written by David almost certainly when he was at Mahanaim still away from home, but with Absalom's revolt already crushed, 2 Sam. xviii. His heart is overwhelmed at the loss of his son, but faith triumphs over sorrow for the sake of the kingdom restored to him in the goodness of God. As the representative head of the nation he cannot but rejoice. "To Jeduthun" (subscript) see notes under Ps. xxxviii. Alternative title, "Expectation of the exalted exile."

PROPHETIC ANTICIPATION.—Messiah the King as representative of His people, identifies Himself with them in their experiences. He takes up and fulfils on their behalf the vows which they failed to carry out. The historical notes show how suitably this psalm is placed as introductory to the section. With 6-7 cf. Luke i. 32–33. The words "tent" and "for ever" seem to be inapposite until we compare the expression in Rev. xxi. 3 (Gk.) which speaks of final earthly blessing.

PERSONAL APPLICATION.—Many people pray only when pressed or in pain (2). Perplexity provokes prayer (2). Faith ever views the fulfilment of divinely inspired hopes. Prayer, praise and purpose form an ideal trio. When in trouble man needs One greater than himself (2). Christ is the Rock, 1 Cor. x. 4. The saints are the Saviour's precious possession (5). God's loving-kindness and faithfulness are constant guardians of His people (7). Those who have proved God will praise Him (3, 8). Let those who purpose also perform (8). The presence and protection of God are much to be desired (4).

VERSE NOTES

2. "earth," or land; (b) as margin, or "is wrapped in gloom"; (c) i.e. too high to reach by unaided effort.

3. (b) For lit. sense cf. Judges ix. 51.

4. Cf. 2 Sam. xv. 25. This verse is better regarded as a prayer, "Let me sojourn . . . let me take refuge . . ."; (b) probably alludes to the wings of the cherubim embroidered on the beautiful curtains and inner veil; cf. xxvii. 5; xxxi. 20; Targum has "in the shadow of Thy presence" (lit. shechinah).

5. (b) Margin pref.; answer to the vows of (a).

6. Cf. 2 Sam. vii. 16; Ps. xxi. 4. David refers to himself in his representative capacity as king, and delights to dwell on this theme.

7. Br. "He shall sit enthroned before God . . ."; (b) prepare = appoint; "preserve," or guard.

8. Note and compare "for ever" with "daily."

PSALM LXII.   THE OMNIPOTENT ONLY

I. EXPRESSION OF FAITH (1-2).

    1. Silent Attitude (1).
    2. Sure Defence (2).

II. EXPOSTULATION WITH FOES (3-4). Faithlessness Exposed.

    1. Their Violence (3). "Ye."
    2. Their Dissimulation (4). "They." Selah.

III. EXHORTATION TO FAITH (5-8).

    1. His Soul Enjoined (5-7). "My Refuge is God."
    2. His Subjects Enjoined (8). "Our Refuge is God." Selah.

IV. EXPOSTULATION WITH FOLLOWERS· (9-10). Fallacies Exposed.

    1. The Vanity (9). "They."
    2. The Dissuasion (10). "Ye."

V. EXHIBITION OF FAITH (11–12).
  1. Spoken Word (11). "Unto Him (Elohim)." Strength.
  2. Special Attributes (12). "Unto Thee (Jehovah)." Loving-kindness.

SUPERSCRIPT.—A psalm of David.

PRIMARY ASSOCIATION.—There is little doubt this psalm was written by David during the period of Absalom's rebellion. Like Ps. xxxix. it is characterised by the use of the Hebrew particle "ak" which occurs at the beginning of verses 1, 2, 4, 5, 6, 9 in the original text. The word generally means "only." David saw that waverers might be influenced by the numbers joining the revolt and the men of distinction among the leaders of Absalom's faction, hence the language in the latter part of the psalm.

PROPHETIC ANTICIPATION.—After the introductory psalm (lxi.) we are now taken back somewhat earlier in time to the breaking out of open hostility to Messiah and His people, such as will characterise the last days of Gentile dominion. Enjoying but a short triumph, man will be shown to be what he has ever been, in reality nothing but a "breath." It will be universally recognised that "power belongeth unto God."

PERSONAL APPLICATION.—David's relation with God was intensely personal; note the oft repeated "my." The saint's strength often lies in silence (1, 5). Many trust in God who do not trust in Him *only* (1–2). "Waiting is but prolonged trust and lengthened hope" (1). From God is my salvation (1) and my expectation (5). Confidence in Him should grow (2, 6), and confession of what He is to our souls helps it to grow. If the "Rock" supports the tottering fence it cannot fall (3); cf. 2 Cor. iv. 8–9. The defence of His people's honour with the deliverance of their persons rests with God (7). Trust in Him at all times and trust in Him only (8). God is a refuge "for us" (8) and "for *me*" (7). Let us not be faint-hearted followers of the King. Sadly misplaced is the trust that trusts in riches (10). Place all men in the scale against God and they do not weigh so much as a breath (9). Man needs reminding again and again of the most elementary truths (11). In God loving-kindness and justice are associated with power (12). He is never kind at the expense of justice (12). The harvest of idleness is an empty barn; God gives increase to the ploughed land and the sown seed (12).

VERSE NOTES

1. Lit. "Only (or, surely) to God is my soul silence"; *i.e.* towards God silence (becometh) my soul.

3. Cf. xxxvii. 24; (*b*) br. "Battering him all of you . . . " *i.e.* calamitous blows have already taken effect and the enemy hoped to complete his destruction.

4. *i.e.* from his high dignity as God's anointed king. David was the principal object of attack; cf. 2 Sam. xvii. 1 ff.

6. (*b*) cf. 2*b*. but "greatly" is omitted here. Is this a sign of David's growing faith?

7. "with" lit. = upon.

8. "ye people," cf. 2 Sam. xvii. 2 ff.

9, 10. "Only vanity are men, (only) a lie are great men." The rebels instead of trusting God, relied upon (*a*) the number of their adherents—"sons of Adam"= ordinary men (9*a*); (*b*) the eminence of their leaders—"sons of ish" = men of distinction (9*b*); (*c*) methods of oppression (10*a*); (*d*) material wealth thus amassed (10*b*); but all was "vanity."

10. (*c*) br. "increase . . . pay no regards . . ." Social discontent was a factor in the revolt; cf. iv. 6.

11. "once . . . twice . . ." *i.e.* repeatedly, cf. Job xxxiii. 14.

12. "For" br. "But . . . ;" qtd. Rom. ii. 6 ff. "Lord," prim. text "Jehovah."

PSALM LXIII.   SONG IN THE SOLITUDES

I. ATHIRST FOR GOD (1-2) ASPIRATION.

    1. Expression of Desire (1).
    2. Experience of Communion (2).

II. ATTENDANT UPON GOD (3-8).   OCCUPATION.

    1. Praising (3-4).
    2. Rejoicing (5).
    3. Pondering (6).
    4. Rejoicing (7).
    5. Pursuing (8).

III. ASSURED IN GOD (9-11).   ANTICIPATION.

    1. Extermination of Enemies (9-10).
    2. Exultation of Saints (11).

SUPERSCRIPT.—A psalm of David; when he was in the wilderness of Judah.

SUBSCRIPT.—For the Chief Musician.

PRIMARY ASSOCIATION.—Writer and occasion stated in superscript. It was the time of Absalom's revolt, 2 Sam. xv.–xviii. David with his loyal followers left Jerusalem by the Jericho road, which led through the northern part of the wilderness of Judah. He lingered awhile at "the fords" before crossing the Jordan. David was deeply troubled by the infamy of his favourite son, the treachery of his trusted counsellor and the insurrection of his beloved people, and pours out his heart to God. Grace enabled him to rise above circumstances. In his hasty flight from the capital, David suffered many privations, 2 Sam. xvi. 2, 14; xvii. 29, but mourns most his enforced separation from the sanctuary. His faith, however, was not focussed upon the visible symbol of God's presence and power, see 2 Sam. xv. 24–25; ctr. the more superstitious Israelites in Eli's days, 1 Sam. iv. David took great delight in the tabernacle worship. He it was, who under God, arranged the order of the services and the ministry of the priests and Levites in their various courses, 1 Chron. xxiii.–xxiv. He accompanied with his musical instruments the Levites in singing his own inspired compositions, and it was he who prepared the plan and provided most of the wealth for building the Temple. The language of our psalm suggests it was composed at night (1*b*, 6). In the circumstances David was not likely to sleep restfully, yet his soul found rest in communion with God. For similar intense longing for God, compare Pss. xlii. and lxxxiv.

PROPHETIC ANTICIPATION. — David's circumstances foreshadow the experiences of Christ, as rejected by the nation yet having a few devoted followers, betrayed by a familiar friend and later to be recalled and reinstated after a most notable triumph over the rebels, 2 Sam. xix. 9–10, ("were at strife," *i.e.* with themselves as feeling very conscience-stricken and blameworthy). We hear the voice of Messiah as representative of the godly remnant in their yearning after God and in the anticipation of final triumph over all their foes. The words of verse 4 are particularly suited to One who is not only the anointed King, but also the anointed Priest. The whole life of our Lord on earth was also a prolonged benediction and it reached a characteristic close, Luke xxiv. 50.

PERSONAL APPLICATION.—This is a song of the satisfied soul. God often manifests Himself in desert places, *e.g.* to Moses, Israel, Elijah, etc. In the hush of the wilderness we may hear better the voice of God. We need the Mighty One (El) to help us in a crisis (1). David had personal dealings with a personal God (1). God alone can slake our soul thirst and satisfy our soul hunger (1). The

Christian has access to the heavenly sanctuary at all times; cf. 2 with the Hebrew Epistle. Visions in the sanctuary should brighten our view of the solitude (2). "Gazing" upon God is great glory (2). Distinguish between our blessing God and God blessing us; the former is expressed in acts of homage and worship (adoration); the latter is accompanied by tangible benefits (impartation); for the double aspect see Eph. i. 3. Let us bless God in our lives (4) as well as by our lips (3). The Saviour alone can give supreme satisfaction (5). All God's gifts are characterised by rich abundance (5). The seeking soul (1) shall be satisfied (5); cf. Matt. v. 6. In a new crisis remember past mercies (6). When sleep fails, copy the psalmist's example (6). In the divine shelter the saint finds refuge (lxi. 4) and rejoicing (7). The redeemed have reason to rejoice (7). Those who hang upon God will be holden up by Him (8); our part is to cleave, His part to uphold. While the saint's path leads ever upward, that of the rebellious leads downwards (8–9). "Pursued yet pursuing (8)." The mouth of the sinner prevaricates (11), the mouth of the saint praises (5). Contrast the destiny of the King and His followers with that of Antichrist and his adherents (9–11).

VERSE NOTES

1. More lit. "Elohim, Thou are my El (Mighty One)"; cf. 1, 15; "earnestly," or early; Hebrew suggests communion with God at dawn; "soul" = whole self; "thirsteth," cf. 2 Sam. xvi. 2 for the material refreshment; "longeth" represents strong Hebrew word occurring only here = languisheth, or pineth; (c) metaphor suggested by actual circumstances.

2. (b) "Thus have I . . ." i.e. according to my soul yearning.

3. "praise" = laud, not s.H.w. in 5.

4. (b) Jewish attitude of prayer; but here may refer to the priestly benediction; cf. Num. vi. 22–24. It was the prerogative of the priests thus to bless the people, see Deut. xxx. 5; 1 Chron. xxiii. 13; also Lev. ix. 23–24 and Ps. cxxxiv.

5. The best of food here indicated; cf. Gen. xlv. 18; Ps. lxv. 11; Isa. lv. 2; Jer. xxxi. 14; (b) more lit. = "with lips uttering joyous shouts."

6. (b) as marg. Israelites divided the night into three watches.

7. "shadow . . . wings," a favourite phrase with David, xvii. 8; xxxvi. 7; cf. words of his ancestor Boaz, Ruth ii. 12; "will I shout for joy."

8. Lit. "cleaveth after Thee," s.H.w. Gen. ii. 24; here, like a timid child clings to its parent in tender affection and due reverence.

9. "But as for those who seek my life (they shall be) for sudden destruction," they shall . . ." see 2 Sam. xvi. 11; lit. fulfilled in the history, 2 Sam. xviii. 6–8 (cf. Num. xvi. 30–33) also prophetically, Rev. xix. 20–21.

10. Jackals prey upon unburied corpses.

11. "the king" was God's anointed and his foes were therefore rebels against God; "sweareth by Him (God)," *i.e.* His loyal worshippers; Deut. x. 20; Joshua xxiii. 7–8; Isa. xix. 18; xlv. 23. Jehovah and Jesus our Lord identified, Phil. ii. 9–11. Rom. xiv. 11; (c) cf. Rom. iii. 19.

PSALM LXIV. ARROWS OF THE ADVERSARIES

I. CONCERNED APPEAL (1–6). PRAYER. The Cry and the Cause. The Wicked in Power.

    1. Complaint of the Psalmist (1–2).

    2. Conspiracy of the Enemy (3–6). Their Words. "Their arrow suddenly shot."

II. CONFIDENT ASSERTION (7–10). PREDICTION. The Certainty and the Cause. The Wicked under Punishment.

    1. Confounding of the Enemy (7–8). God's Work. "His arrow suddenly smites."

    2. Consequences among Men (9–10).

        (a) Reverence and Public Acknowledgment (9). All men.

        (b) Rejoicing and Public Acclamation (10). The Upright.

SUPERSCRIPT.—A psalm of David.

SUBSCRIPT.—For the Chief Musician.

PRIMARY ASSOCIATION.—Composed by David almost certainly during the period of Absalom's insurrection, 2 Sam. xv.–xvii. The secret counsel here referred to in that case will be that of Ahithophel and those with him. It is plain that the machinations of the rebels against David recoiled upon their own heads.

PROPHETIC ANTICIPATION.—Messiah as God's anointed Head of the nation makes the cause of the godly remnant fully His in the days when Antichrist and the apostate portion of Israel attack them. Other Scriptures confirm that this attack will be secretly planned and suddenly executed. While it is the people of God who suffer, the main object of aggression is Messiah Himself, even as David was in the history.

PERSONAL APPLICATION.—Our great weapon against secret evils is prayer. Saints need guarding not only from the enemy himself, but from *fear* of the enemy and his secret plots (1). The wicked find many allies (2). "Go not with a multitude to do evil," Exod. xxiii.

2. From the secret plans of the enemy, God hides His people in a secret place (2, 10). Evil minds love secrecy (5); cf. John iii. 20. Bitter words are like poisoned shafts (3). The power of the tongue to do evil is often dwelt upon in the Scriptures, cf. James iii. Harm done by the tongue is often through thoughtlessness rather than malice. The arrows of the wicked are apt to rebound upon themselves, their own sword to be turned against them (3, 7); cf. 1 Sam. xvii. 51; Luke xix. 22. The godly man is always a mark for secret arrows (4). The voice of slander delights in veiled suggestions; God alone can fathom the depths of iniquity in the human heart (6). Cf. Jer. xvii. 9–10. When God smites, He needs but one arrow (7). Immediate catastrophe may follow immoral conduct (7). The Lord often allows men to perfect their evil scheme, then strikes unerringly (7). He is glorified even in His judgment work (9).

VERSE NOTES

2. Or, "Thou wilt hide . . . "; "tumult" = tumultuous throng: (a) indic. secret designs; (b) overt attack; cf. ii. 1–2.
3. Or, "Aimed as their arrow a deadly scheme"; probably metaphorical allusion to a poisoned shaft.
4. "perfect"; of our Lord in an absolute sense, but of the godly in a relative sense = upright.
5. (c) cf. x. 11, 13; xii. 4; lix. 7 et al; with the verse cf. Matt. xxii. 15 ff; John viii. 6.
6. Br. "They plan deeds of iniquity, 'We have perfected,' say they, 'a consummate plan' "; see Isa. xxix. 15.
7. "Therefore God . . . smitten; cf. 11 with 4; the punishment is described in terms of the crime; arrow for arrow.
8. See 3; cf. Ahithophel's fate.
9. Br. "And shall understand His operation."
10. "trust" = take refuge in.

Psalms lxv.–lxviii. all bear the double title "Psalm" and "Song." Songs were intended for singing at public worship in the Temple (Isa. xxxi. 29; Amos viii. 3) and are all in a strain of joyous celebration.

PSALM LXV.   THE BLESSER AND THE BLESSING

I. EARTH'S ACCEPTED WORSHIPPERS ASSEMBLED (1–4).

Manifestation of Divine Grace connected with the Sanctuary. Sins removed.

II. ELOHIM'S AWE-INSPIRING ACTS ACCLAIMED (5-8).

Manifestation of Divine Greatness connected with Society.

    1. Effect upon all Peoples (5). "Thou." Universal Confidence.
    2. Exhibition of Almighty Power (6-7). "He." Nature and the Nations.
    3. Effect upon all Peoples (8). "Thou." Universal Fear.

III. EARTH'S ABUNDANT HARVEST ACKNOWLEDGED (9-13).

Manifestation of Divine Goodness connected with the Soil. Curse removed.

SUPERSCRIPT.—A psalm of David. A song.

SUBSCRIPT.—For the Chief Musician.

PRIMARY ASSOCIATION.—Composed by David most probably in connection with the Spring Festival of Firstfruits (13), in a period when his kingdom was established and peaceful.

PROPHETIC ANTICIPATION.—This group of "Songs" tells of restoration and rest for Israel, following the long period of rebellion in which Messiah the King is in rejection. The usurper and his followers have been destroyed, the true King (Christ) has returned, is recognised and received after due exercise of soul on the part of the remnant (as seen in other psalms). Under Messiah enthroned in Zion, the land enjoys millennial blessedness with Israel restored and the curse removed from the earth. It is to be noted that the psalm refers to the removal of the great hindrance to the outpouring of divine blessing, namely in the purgation of sins, though we need to look elsewhere for prophetic details of this all-important event. Messiah's voice as ruler and representative of His people is here heard leading the praises. In answer to His use of the singular in 3*a*, it would seem that the people break in with the words of the rest of this verse. 4*a* reminds us of Isa. xlii. 1, and 5 of Isa. xxxii. 17. The temple referred to will be Israel's grand distinction and privilege in the Millennium.

PERSONAL APPLICATION.—Does our praise wait for God or does He wait for our praise (1)? "Hearer of Prayer" (2) is a precious title for our God. When iniquities prevailed, only One could purge them away (3). Only purged sins can be pardoned (3-4). After absolution comes access (4). Unless sin be removed there can be no approach to God (4). Saints are chosen not only to approach God, but to dwell in His presence (4). The divine habitation (Eph. ii. 22) will be satisfying both to God and to His people (4). What a glorious prospect is seen in 5. "God of our salvation" (5) is "God of *my* salvation" in xxv. 5. God alone can and will still the convulsions of the earth and of society (6–7). Verses 9–13 form a perfect "Harvest Song." There should be not only thankfulness but thanksgiving. The language may be applied to the needs of the soul. God first creates a desire then meets it (9). The divine flow leads to fertility and fruitfulness. God is not only the God of sunshine and showers, He is the God of salvation. Harvest is (*a*) the Reception of God's gifts; (*b*) the Reward of man's labour; (*c*) the Realisation of early hopes.

VERSE NOTES

1. Or, "Praise becometh Thee . . . "; "the vow," or vows.

2. (*b*) cf. Mark xi. 17 marg.; John xii. 32.

3. (*b*) The Hebrew verb here is "kaphar" to cover; "Thou" (emph.).

4. "Happy is he whom . . . "

5. *i.e.* things that inspire rare dread in God's enemies and reverent awe in His people; (*c*) cf. Isa. xxxiii. 13.

7. God controls alike the turbulent elements of nature and the tumultuous hosts of the nations they symbolise. (*b*) "peoples" = races (a less usual Hebrew word).

8. Br. "So that they who dwell . . . " (*b*) *i.e.* from farthest east to farthest west; "rejoice" = shout for joy.

9 ff. Portrays a joyous landscape rich with promise; (*b*) "river," or stream; prim. the rain, prophetically "the River," cf. Rev. xxii. 1.

10. Br. "Saturating its furrows, levelling its ridges."

11. "paths," or tracks; fig. of a richly laden cart dropping its contents in its track.

PSALM LXVI.   DIVINE DISCIPLINE DISCERNED

I. CELEBRATION OF DIVINE POWER (1–7).   Universal.
   1. The Worship (1–4).   Earth exhorted.   Selah.
   2. The Witness (5–7).   Manward.   Earth addressed.
   "Come and see."   What God did for Israel.   Selah.

II. CONFESSION OF DISCIPLINARY PROVIDENCE (8–12).   National.
   1. The Worship (8–9).   Peoples exhorted.
   2. The Witness (10–12).   Godward.   Elohim addressed.
   "Thou didst test us."   What God did to Israel.

III. CONSUMMATION OF DEVOUT PLEDGES (13-20). Personal.
    1. The Worship (13-15). King exercised. Selah.
    2. The Witness (16-20). Manward. Elect addressed.
    "Come and hear." What God did for the Psalmist.

SUPERSCRIPT.—A song; a psalm.

SUBSCRIPT.—For the Chief Musician; upon Neginoth.

PRIMARY ASSOCIATION.—This psalm is anonymous, but the language appears to connect it with the deliverance of Judah from the host of Sennacherib, Isa. xxxvi.–xxxviii. In this case, Hezekiah will be the speaker (13-20) and the psalm may well have been composed by him or by Isaiah for him. With verses 1-4 cf. Isa. xxxvii. 20; 16-20 with Isa. xxxviii. Hezekiah's restoration from sickness was both a type and a pledge of the national deliverance. For meaning of "Neginoth" see Ps. iii. notes.

PROPHETIC ANTICIPATION. In verses 1-12 we hear the voice of restored Israel; in 13-20 the voice of Messiah the King. The period is that which follows the signal defeat of Israel's powerful foes in the last days immediately preceding the millennial age. The King is in the midst of His delivered people and as their representative Head He leads the joyous praises of the nation. The terrible sufferings of the Great Tribulation are at last understood and acknowledged to have been God's disciplinary action, necessary to bring His people to a true knowledge of their sins and a proper appreciation of His marvellous grace. Note the significant marginal reading at 3. In the Millennium, multitudes will render unwilling homage to Messiah the Conqueror. Israel alone will be all holy, Isa. iv. The psalms do not go beyond the Millennium, hence they omit mention of the great revolt which immediately precedes the final judgment, Rev. xx. Utterance of national and universal praise is seen here to be in fulfilment of Messiah's vows (cf. Ps. xxii.), and God discerns in the worship of the redeemed people the sweet perfume of Messiah's work.

PERSONAL APPLICATION.—It is the privilege of Christians both to worship and to witness. If man looks (5) and listens (16) he will learn valuable lessons. Terrible in His works against the rebellious, God is tender in His ways with the righteous (5). The terror of God is not so much to intimidate as to impress us with a due sense of His majesty and might (5). Come and see His works of grandeur (5), come and hear His words of grace, cf. John i. 39, 46. Meditate much upon the multitude of His mercies. The result of seeing and hearing is praise. The praise of the saints is the fruit of the Saviour's Passion. What is true of the past is true in the present and future; God's sovereignty is eternal (7). He is the ever-wakeful Watcher of the World (7). The Lord sometimes finds it necessary deliberately to bring His people into trouble to prove and to purify, to chastise and to cleanse (10-12). The divine hand disciplines and delivers the godly (10-12). The way to true liberty often lies through fire and water (12). Always pay what you owe to God (13). Zeal for God and love to man brought the Saviour down into the world. Israel's God is the only God, and God of all the earth (1, 8). Do we tell others what God has done for our souls (16)? "Every blade of grass catches its own drop of dew" (16). Faith is ever ready to praise even while offering the petition (17). The character of all true service is to exalt God (17). Hypocrisy disqualifies a suppliant with God (18).

VERSE NOTES

1. Or, "Shout unto . . . " as xlvii. 1.

2. "Sing forth . . . " lit. = psalm; so 4 *bc*.

3. Cf. lxv. 5; (*b*) note marg., or "cringe before Thee," cf. xviii. 44; lxxxi. 15.

5. Ctr. the invitation of the Gospel, John i. 39, 46.

6. Israel's passage of the Red Sea and the crossing of Jordan are notable examples of God's "terrible works." (*c*) cf. Exod. xv.

7. "Observe" or, "keep watch upon . . .," Isa. xxxvii. 17; (*c*) cf. Isa. xxxvii. 23.

9. "Who hath set . . . not suffered . . ."; ref. to the recent deliverance.

10. "proved . . . tried," *i.e.* tested and refined as precious metal; Isa. i. 25. God used the Assyrians to this end.

12. Fig. of remorseless victors riding down the defeated forces. Such a scene is often portrayed on the ancient monuments; "men" = enosh (frail men). Fire and water are symbolic of extreme dangers. (*c*) as marg. or, "a place of liberty," *i.e.* into freedom; so LXX, etc.

16. (*b*) cf. Isa. xxxviii. 17; Hezekiah had prayed both for himself and for his people.

17. (*b*) as margin; *i.e.* even as he prayed his praise was ready to be offered, so sure was he that his petitions would be answered favourably.

18. (*b*) as margin, cf. Isa. xxxviii. 3.

PSALM LXVII.   IMMANUEL AND ISRAEL

I. APPLICATION OF THE ELECT PEOPLE (1-2). ISRAEL.
    1. The Fervent Desire (1). "God bless us." Selah.
    2. The Final Object (2). Winning of all Nations.

II. ACCLAMATION BY THE EARTH PEOPLES (3-5). GENTILES.
  1. The Prayer (3). "Let them give thanks."
  2. The Purport (4). Reign of Immanuel. The Central Message.
      i. Rejoicings (4*a*).
      ii. Reasons (4*bc*). Selah.
  3. The Prediction (5). "(They) shall give thanks."

III. ANTICIPATION OF THE ELECT PEOPLE (6-7). ISRAEL.
  1. The Fruitful Earth (6). "God shall bless us."
  2. The Fulfilled Purpose (7). Worship by all Nations.

SUPERSCRIPT.—A psalm. A song.

SUBSCRIPT.—For the Chief Musician.

PRIMARY ASSOCIATION.—Writer is anonymous, but most probably the same as preceding psalm and in connection with the same historical occasion; see Isa. x. 33 to xi. 9. A joyous song dedicated, it would seem, to temple use, either at the Feast of Pentecost (Harvest) or the Feast of Tabernacles (Ingathering) (6). A double celebration may be discerned: (*a*) Deliverance from the Assyrian invasion; (*b*) Favour of a bountiful harvest. The psalm is sometimes called Israel's Missionary Psalm, and Israel's Millennial Prayer. It is characterised by a peculiar structure and profound spirituality. The seventh of the series, it has exactly seven verses, and is obviously introversive in form with the fourth verse containing the core of the composition. This verse, moreover, has three lines, while the others all have but two each.

PROPHETIC ANTICIPATION.—A psalm of Messiah's Millennial Missionaries. Here we see God reigning upon earth in the person of His anointed King, even Immanuel. Israel is the channel of testimony and of blessing to the gentile nations. They themselves are living examples of the manifold grace of God to man. Disasters, such as defeat and drought, shamed Israel before the nations (Joshua ii. 17-19) while deliverances and domestic prosperity witnessed to the true character of Israel's God. Thus it had ever been in their history, but now is seen the greatest testimony of all in the presence of Immanuel upon the throne of Zion. Verse 6 shows the ground also delivered from the curse and the general result is summed up in (7).

PERSONAL APPLICATION.—God hath blessed, doth bless and will bless us. Those who know God should make Him known to others

(2). God's way is the highway of holiness (2). Christ is "the Way," John xiv. 6; Christianity is "this Way," Acts ix. 2; xxii. 4. The sunshine of God's favour causes the human heart to burst forth in song, like the birds on a sunny morning in springtime. Praise should be spontaneous, may be cultivated (by contemplation of God's works and meditation on His word) and should be vocal. If the redeemed cannot "shout for joy," who can? Praise is the healthy habit of happy hearts. Joy cannot be forced or even imitated. When the righteous Ruler reigns, there will be real rejoicings (4). The sceptre will be in the hand of the Shepherd (4). Draw encouragement for the future from the experiences of the past (6). "Thy kingdom come!" (6–7); cf. Matt. vi. 10.

VERSE NOTES

1. Br. "God be gracious . . . " see Num. vi. 24 ff. Echoes of the priestly blessing are frequently found in the Psalms, cf. iv. 6; xxix. 11; xxxi. 16; lxxx. 3, 7, 19; (b) note margin; the prep. "with" suggests God's favour abiding with His people.
2. Knowledge of God's way betokens a deeper knowledge than the knowledge of His work, cf. ciii. 7.
4. "nations . . . nations"; br. races (of men) . . . races (of men); "judge" = rule; (c) as margin; (b) indic. government; (c) guidance.
5. Here it seems better to read, "The peoples shall . . . "
6. "earth" or, land; cf. Lev. xxvi. 4; (b) br. "doth bless us."

PSALM LXVIII.   MARCH OF THE MIGHTY MONARCH

I. THE NATION'S CRY TO GOD (1–3). TRADITIONAL INVOCATION. ISRAEL. "Let God arise."
    1. Enemies scattered (1–2).
    2. Elect gladdened (3).

II. THE NATION'S CALL TO PRAISE (4). SPECIAL INVITATION.
    The Psalmist's Summons to Israel. "Sing ye to God."
    "Rider through the deserts" acclaimed.

III. RELATION OF PAST TRIUMPHS (5–14).
    1. The Divine Ministry (5–6). Mercy and Might.
    2. The Divine March (7–10). The "going forth" of God. Selah.
    Departure from Egypt and Entry into Canaan.
    3. The Divine Mandate (11–14). Command of Jehovah. History.
    Conquest of Canaan. Portrayal and Promise.

IV. REVELATION OF PRESENT TRIUMPH (15–18). The Saviour
seated in the Sanctuary—Dwelling-place of Jehovah-God. The Ark.
The Divine Habitation (Central thought of the psalm).
        i. The Mountain of God (15–16).
        ii. The Messengers of God (17–18).

V. REPRESENTATION OF PROSPECTIVE TRIUMPHS (19–31).
        1. The Divine Ministry (19–23). Mercy and Might. Selah.
        2. The Divine March (24–27). The "goings" of God.
        Arrival at Zion and Entry into the Sanctuary.
        3. The Divine Mandate (28–31). Command of God. Prophecy.
        Conquest of the World. Prayer and Prediction.

VI. THE NATIONS' CALL TO PRAISE (32–34). UNIVERSAL
INVITATION.
        The Psalmist's Summons to Gentiles. "Sing ye to God."
        "Rider upon the heavens" acclaimed. Selah.

VII. THE NATIONS' CRY TO GOD (35). GENERAL INVOCATION.
        "Blessed be God." Gentile Response.

SUPERSCRIPT.—A psalm of David. A song.

SUBSCRIPT.—For the Chief Musician; relating to Shoshannim (= Lilies).

PRIMARY ASSOCIATION.—Processional psalm composed by David,
no doubt for the occasion of the Ark's translation to Zion, 2 Sam.
vi.; 1 Chron. xv. Compare and see notes to Ps. xxiv. As the psalm
celebrates also the deliverance from Egypt, it seems to have been
appointed (see subscript) for public use at the spring festival of
Passover. This "Dedication Ode" has been called "one of the
masterpieces of the world's lyrics." As Israel's God-inspired
national marching song it has a unique place among the world's
national compositions. Alternative title, "The Goings of God."
    PROPHETIC ANTICIPATION.—Celebrates God's final triumph and
universal sovereignty displayed in the person and reign of Messiah.
The quotation of 18 by Paul (Eph. iv. 8) confirms the interpretation
of the psalm as typical of Christ's victory in resurrection, ascension
and coming personal return to rule over the entire earth. Christ's
present session in the heavenly sanctuary is full guarantee of blessing
yet in store for the Church, for Israel and for the gentile nations.
Verses 21–23 refer to the destruction of the "Beast" and his armies
(Rev. xix.). Restored Israel is here seen under the terms of the new
covenant, again beginning their triumphant progress with their

Divine Leader at the head; then, as entering upon their inheritance in Christ and safely dwelling in the land, sheltered by the wings of redeeming love (13). Many other prophetic details may be gathered by close study of this deeply instructive psalm.

PERSONAL APPLICATION.—The rebellious run from the presence of God (2) but the righteous rejoice in it (3). El (the Mighty One) scatters His enemies (1) whether they be kings (14) or peoples (30). In the plenitude of His power, God rides in places where all human resources fail (4). He enriches as well as emancipates those who were once enslaved (6). The presence of God spells power to deliver the saints and to destroy the sinners (8). He supplies abundant water for His people even in the arid wastes (9). Israel's history is an illustration of God's provision for the poor and His aid for the "afflicted," (10). When the Lord gives the word, His people are to publish it (11). God expresses His love for His people by dwelling among them (16). In the Millennium He purposes to be accessible to men; He has chosen the lowly hill of Zion, not the high peaks of Bashan (16). About Zion there will be abundant glory, but no fringe of fire as at Sinai (17). The joy of the crown follows the journey of the cross (18). Even now the ascended Christ has precious gifts for men, 18 with Eph. iv. 8. God Himself prepares my daily "load"; burden or blessing, either is a "benefit" (19). Our God is the Bearer of burdens (19), therefore see lv. 22; 1 Peter v. 7; Phil. iv. 6–7. Our God is the "God of deliverances" (20). Deliverance of the elect people necessarily involves destruction of their enemies (20–21). In the worship of God the human voice has the precedence of all instrumental praise (25). The spirit of praise is the spirit of power. Praise awakens praise (25). Bless God in public as well as in private (26). The nations that delight in war shall be scattered (30). The voice of the Lord is the voice of power (30); cf. John v. 25–28. The redeemed will share the Redeemer's triumph (33). Trace in 33–35: (a) the Source of Power; (b) the Voice of Power; (c) the Place of Power; and (d) the Gift of Power. Can you join in the closing benediction (35c)? God is guardian of the friendless and forlorn (5).

VERSE NOTES

1. Based upon Num. x. 35; words appropriate to the setting forward of the ark from the house of Obed-edom.

2–3. Verbs perhaps to be rendered as futures. The ark represented the presence of God.

4. "Jah," cf. 18 and Exod. xv. 3.

6. As marg. Sense is, "He brings the exiles home"; "dwell," br. have made their dwelling . . ."

7–8. Cf. Judges v. 4–5.

9. Br. ". . . rain on Thy heritage, and strengthenedst it when . . ."

10. "congregation," or community.

11. "the word," i.e. the command that results in victory; "publish," here by singing not by preaching.

12–14. Contain further allusions to Deborah's song.

13–14. The elliptical construction creates a difficulty, but the meaning is clear if we bear in mind the prophetic significance. Read, "Though ye may lie among the sheepfolds (or, hurdles) the wings of a dove (are there) covered with silver, and her pinions with green-tinted gold." The dove is a double type, (a) of the Holy Spirit (John i. 32), and (b) of Christ Himself (Lev. i. 14). The general sense of the verse, therefore, is that wherever God's people may be, they are sheltered by the wings of redeeming love. Silver speaks of redemption; green-tinted gold of divine glory seen in the revival of nature; cf. Rev. iv. 3.

14. "Almighty" = Shaddai; title occurs elsewhere in the Psalms only at xci. 1; "therein" = on her account, i.e. Israel's. (b) i.e. they were scattered like snowflakes.

15. Br. "The mountain of God, is it Bashan? A mountain of peaks is Mount Bashan"; prob. ref. to Hermon, the grandest of Palestine's mountains and at the northern boundary of Bashan, Deut. iii. 8. It has three summits of nearly equal height.

16. "askance" = enviously; (b) i.e. Zion, which among mountains is comparatively insignificant. (c) Sinai had been God's temporary abode, Exod. xxiv. 16; on Zion He will dwell perpetually. This choice of God is a parable of His methods when dealing with men, 1 Cor. i. 26–29.

17. Br. as primitive text, ". . . are twenty thousand, even myriads; Jehovah among them hath come from Sinai into the Sanctuary."

18. For a good parallel cf. 2 Cor. ii. 14 R.V.; (bc) br. as A.V.; qtd. by Paul (Eph. iv. 8) in a divinely inspired adaptation; he omits (c) which refers to Israel and will have fulfilment when Christ comes again. Verse primarily refers to the ascent of the ark to Zion (formerly Jebus), a literal "going up," cf. Ps. xlvii. 5. Jehovah is addressed as represented by the ark.

19. Or, as A.V. Many ancient versions read, ". . . beareth us," cf. Isa. xlvi. 3–4; verse may be also read, "Blessed be Jehovah (so primitive text) day by day, Who loadeth us (with blessings); God Himself is our salvation." (b) "God" = El (Mighty One); so 20a (twice) 24b and 35b.

20. "salvation," Heb. plur. = saving deeds; "issues" or, escapes.

21. (c) "Yea, God shall . . ." In ancient times warriors were accustomed to let their hair grow long in connection with a vow of consecration to their cause.

22. A.V. wrongly inserts "my people"; ref. to the enemies; cf. sim. language, Amos ix. 2–3.

23. LXX etc. have "bathe thy foot . . ."

24–27. Describes the solemn procession of thanksgiving to the tent and later the temple. The same processional order is seen in 1 Chron. xv. First the Levites (16-19), then the *alamoth* (maiden singers with timbrels) and over them the leaders named, with their psalteries (20); and, lastly, the *sheminith* (men singers with harps) and their leaders (21).

25. (*b*) *i.e.* the damsels being on either side; "timbrels" = tambourine or hand drums; used while dancing along, cf. Exod. xv. 20.

26. Jacob regarded as the fountain head of the nation; cf. Isa. xlviii. 1.

27. (*a*) "little," for Benjamin was the youngest of Jacob's sons and smallest of the tribes in numbers and territory; br. "their conqueror," *i.e.* of the enemies (23); (*b*) " . . . Judah, their close compacted band"; names of the tribes mentioned here have typical and prophetical significance.

29. "out of Thy temple," probably belongs to end of 28; then read, "Up to Jerusalem shall kings . . ."

30. (*a*) ref. to the crocodile or hippopotamus, symb. of Egypt; "bulls" ref. to the leaders, "calves" to the peoples themselves; but cf. Jer. xlvi. 20-21, = mercenaries. These are repr. in their proud defiance and comfortable security respectively.

31. "princes," *i.e.* as ambassadors; (*b*) *i.e.* in token of submission and supplication, Egypt and Ethiopia often coupled in Scripture.

34. "excellency," or majesty.

35. Br. "Terrible is God out of thy sanctuary (lit. = sanctuaries); Gentile response to Israel's summons (32-34), acknowledging the terrible power of the God (El) of Israel; "power," Heb. plur. = abundant power.

Book Two. III. Dominion of the Enthroned Redeemer: lxi.–lxxii.

2. The Restored Kingdom, lxix.–lxxii.

(i) The Foundation. The Cross, lxix.
(ii) The Faithful One, lxx.
(iii) The Faithful Ones, lxxi.
(iv) The Fruition. The Crown, lxxii.

PSALM LXIX. SORROWS OF THE SAVIOUR.

I. MESSIAH'S ACT OF RESTITUTION (1-21).   Representative Victim.
    1. Commencing Prayer and Cogent Pleas (1-4).
      "Save me . . . for . . ."
    2. Consoling Principle and Characteristic Petition (5, 6).
      "Thou knowest . . ."
    3. Cardinal Plaint (7-12). "Reproach."
    4. Concise Prayers and Cogent Pleas (13-18).
      "Answer me . . . for . . ."
    5. Consoling Principle (19). "Thou knowest . . ."
    6. Concluding Plaint (20-21). "Reproach."

II. MESSIAH'S APPEAL FOR RETRIBUTION (22-28).   Righteous
    Vengeance.
   1. Cry of Denunciation (22-25).
   2. Cause of Denunciation (26).   "For they persecute . . ."
   3. Cry of Denunciation (27-28).

III. MESSIAH'S ANSWER IN RESURRECTION (29-36).   Resultant
     Victory.
   1. Compensating Prospect (29). Psalmist Extricated.
   2. Consequent Praise (30-31).   Personal.
   3. Comforting Prospect (32-33).   Meek Encouraged.
   4. Concordant Praise (34).   Universal.
   5. Crowning Prospect (35-36).   Zion Established.

SUPERSCRIPT.—David's.

SUBSCRIPT.—For the Chief Musician.

PRIMARY ASSOCIATION.—That David is the author as stated in
superscript is confirmed by Rom. xi. 9. Arguments of the critics
to the contrary are therefore worthless. David being a prophet as
well as a poet, often wrote of matters outside his own experiences,
though these may have been the starting point of the composition.
What was the occasion we cannot tell, though the reference to
reproach suffered has suggested to some a possible connection with
2 Sam. xvi. Alternative title, "The Source of Salvation." Here is a
story of weariness (3), loneliness (8, 20) and sorrowfulness (29).
   PROPHETIC ANTICIPATION.—This aspect entirely overrules the
historical. Its Messianic bearing is generally recognised, for it is
more frequently quoted in the New Testament than any other
psalm except xxii., and always as fulfilled in relation to the Lord
Jesus Christ Himself and to the consequences of His rejection. We
hear the voice of Christ on the cross as "smitten" (26) but not
"forsaken" of God, xxii. 1, only by men (20). "Forsaking" is
associated only with the higher grades of the sin offering (Lev. iv.)
hence Ps. xxii. which presents the sin offering aspect of the cross.
Our present psalm is the trespass offering aspect of Christ's vicarious
sufferings (4), which involves the idea of reparation as well as of
expiation. The emphasis is upon the governmental side of atonement
(Lev. v. 14 ff.), therefore judgment upon the Christ-rejectors is
necessarily mentioned. Messiah's identification with His people is
obviously involved in His vicarious sufferings for them. This is

seen in verses 1–6. He becomes the object of causeless hostility on the part of countless foes. He bears in His own holy soul the trespasses of others, making restitution on their behalf. Upon His acceptance with God depends the salvation of those whom He represents (6). In verses 7–12 the Saviour sees in retrospect His life among men, suffering for righteousness' sake and, therefore, for God. 13–21 bring us back to the Cross with the last indignity He suffered before He died. The succeeding verses of solemn denunciation are much misunderstood, see Appendix IV. Divine love must affirm the doom of all who reject its operation, and here we find but the confirmation of the righteous sentence of God in its Old Testament character, which, in general, covers only earthly penalties, though eternal judgment is implied. The remaining verses show the victory side of the Cross—the blessed results of Messiah's accepted work. Christ crucified in weakness, lxix.; conquering in power, lxviii.; Christ in humiliation and Christ in honour, respectively.

PERSONAL APPLICATION.—Persecution is hardest to bear when it is at the hands of our own kinsfolk (8). The world makes even the Christian's very zeal for God a matter for insult (9–10). Our deepest concern should ever be for the honour of our God (9–10). Not every occasion of our Lord's tears is recorded in the Gospels (10). Christ became a subject for "gossip at the gate" and for the songs of the sots (12). Like Him, let us ever be subject to the will of God (13). We often find it most difficult to await God's time (13), but see Isa. lxiv. 4 R.V. It is a comfort to the saint to realise that God knows his sins and his sufferings (5, 19). When foes are present, friends may be absent (20). The failure of our friends is often harder to bear than the fury of our foes (20). Christ and His followers are often treated with calculated cruelty (21). Peace and prosperity may prove a pitfall (22). Satan too often gets even Christians so occupied with worldly things (perhaps harmless in themselves) that the things of God are shut out, 1 Tim. vi. 17–19. A full table may be as much a judgment as an empty one (22). Satan's snares are often silken (22). Woe to them who add persecution to saints who are under the chastening hand of God (26). Christians are called on to suffer with Christ for righteousness' sake (26b). The afflicted are not neglected, nor the prisoners despised by the Lord, especially if they suffer for Him (33); cf. Eph. iii. 1; Luke iv. 18–19.

VERSE NOTES

2. (*a*) *i.e.* he felt as if floundering in a quicksand or quagmire, where there is no foothold and struggling only plunges one deeper. (*b*) *i.e.* like fording a river and in imminent danger of being carried away by the strong current.

3. He complains not of tearful crying, but of prayerful crying, though he had much of the former (10).

4. LXX quoted John xv. 25; (*b*) hostility was based upon misconception and misrepresentation; (*c*) historically, may refer to the psalmist being robbed in the name of justice; forced to make good what he had not plundered.

5. "Thou" (emph.), so 19; (*b*) "sins," see margin and cf. notes previous page.

6. The cause of God's people was bound up with that of the sufferer.

8. (*b*) lit. "unto the sons of my own mother"; cf. of Christ. Mark iii. 21, 31; John vii. 3-5.

9. "zeal," *i.e.* jealousy for the honour of God's house was like a fire consuming him within; quoted John ii. 17 (LXX); (*b*) contempt for God shown by mocking His servant; qtd. Rom. xv. 3.

10. (*a*) *i.e.* because of the nation's sad condition morally and spiritually.

12. "gate" see notes at lxxxvii. 2; highest and lowest classes indicated; cf. Lam. iii. 14.

13. He now turns from human callousness to the divine compassion; lit. "a time of acceptance," or, good pleasure; this connects with "answer me" (*c*).

14, 15. He prays that despite dire circumstances (2, 4) he may not be altogether overcome; cf. Heb. v. 7 (Gk. = *out of* death); "overwhelm," s.H.w. as "overflow" (2).

17. "distress" = strait.

18. "redeem me" = set me free. The work of the "goel" (redeemer) was twofold; (*a*) first to avenge, then (*b*) to ransom. Former is the aspect here. Root idea of redemption = to demand back what had been taken away by intervening in power. Here, the restoration of the psalmist's life would be "redemption"; cf. "restore" (4*b*).

20. "broken my heart." Concerning Christ it is an interesting fact that a ruptured pericardium agrees with the details of His death; the loud cry—the rent veil—the blood and water flowing from the spear thrust. (*a*) as margin, or, "death-sick."

21. Br. "Yea, they . . ." *i.e.* they not only refused sympathy (20), but they added to his sufferings by offering poisonous food and nauseous drink; cf. Matt. xxvii. 34; John xix. 28-29; "gall," Hebrew seems to indicate the poisonous poppy which commonly grows in Palestine. To fulfil the last line Christ uttered His need aloud, and suffered their last indignity.

22. Prophetically, between this and preceding verse, Christ's death supervenes; cf. the indicated "gap," Ps. xxii. between 21 and 22. Present verse freely quoted from LXX at Rom. xi. 9-10.

23. *i.e.* in dread of the unseen.

25. Adaptation of LXX qtd. Acts i. 20.

26. At the Cross, our Lord's cry of anguish (Matt. xxvii. 46) seemingly justified the persecutors (so they thought) for it showed that God had indeed

smitten Him, Isa. liii. 4; nevertheless they had no call to add to the trials of the Sufferer. (*b*) br. "And they talk of (LXX 'add to') the suffering of Thy wounded ones." God's people are associated with Christ not in His atoning work, but in persecution by men for righteousness' sake. God had smitten Him—their Representative—but not them.

27. Br. "Impute iniquity according to their iniquity"; (*b*) *i.e.* bestowed righteousness; cf. Rom. iii.

28. "book of life," a figure borrowed from the registers of citizenship; cf. Exod. xxxii. 32; Ezek. xiii. 9; Isa. iv. 3, etc.; (*b*) "written with"= enrolled among.

29. "But as for me—poor and suffering—Thy salvation, O God, setteth me on high."

31. (*b*) Omit "Or"; "horns and hoofs" indicate a clean animal of full age, hence suitable for sacrifice.

32. "The meek (or, afflicted) see it . . ."; "live" = revive.

33. "prisoners," or captives.

34. The redemption of Zion is an event of universal significance.

PSALM LXX.   CONTRASTED CONSEQUENCES OF THE CROSS

I. IMPLORATION FOR DELIVERANCE (1).   "Make haste."

II. IMPRECATION AGAINST SEEKERS AFTER HIS LIFE (2–3).

III. INTERCESSION FOR SEEKERS AFTER HIS GOD (4).

IV. IMPLORATION FOR DELIVERANCE (5).   "Make haste."
    1. Extremity of Trouble (*a*).
    2. Entreaty (*b*).   "Make haste."
    3. Expression of Trust (*c*).
    4. Entreaty (*d*).   "Make no tarrying."

SUPERSCRIPT.—David's. To bring to remembrance.

PRIMARY ASSOCIATION.—This is a repetition of Ps. xl. 13–17 with slight intentional, not accidental, variations. Superscript, "To bring to remembrance" may have reference to this repetition, or it may be a note connected with its liturgical use, either at the offering of incense (see corresponding notes to Ps. xxxviii.; cf. Luke i. 9–10), or at the offering of the "azkara," the name given to that portion of the meal offering which is mixed with oil and burnt with incense on the brazen altar, Lev. ii. 2; the term is also used of the incense placed on the shewbread and afterwards burnt, Lev. xxiv. 7.

PROPHETIC ANTICIPATION.—This portion of the "Burnt Offering

Psalm" (xl.) is here added as an appendix to the "Trespass Offering Psalm" (lxix.)—a fact of much significance; cf. notes to Ps. xl. We hear the voice of Messiah, the Holy Sufferer, continuing in prayer, The verbs in 2-4 may all be rendered as futures, in which case, sections II and III are predictive. Anywise we see the contrasted results as affecting the rejectors of Christ and the redeemed of Christ respectively.

PERSONAL APPLICATION.—See corresponding notes to Ps. xl. God never hurries, but He does sometimes hasten, especially to the help of the needy; cf. Luke xv. 20. For the Christian's place to find help in a time of need, see Heb. iv. 16. All the enemies of Christ shall certainly be put to shame, and they who delight to do harm to God's people shall surely suffer dishonour.

VERSE NOTES

1. "Be pleased," or "Hasten . . ." to be supplied at the beginning. Omission of the first word is not due to "clumsiness or to a torn fragment of MSS.," as critics allege, but is to fix the attention upon the preceding psalm, particularly 13 ff., and to refer the mind back to its connection with Ps. xl.

2. "soul" = life; "turned backward" = driven backward.

3. Br. "Let them turn back on account of their shame . . ."

5. "But as for me, who am afflicted and needy . . ." cf. lxix. 29, 33.

PSALM LXXI. READINESS FOR REVIVAL

I. CONFIDENT PETITIONS (1-4).
    1. Profession of Trust (1a).
    2. Prayers for Deliverance (1b-3a).
    3. Profession of Trust (3b).
    4. Prayer for Deliverance (4).

II. COGENT PLEAS (5-11). Youth and Age.
    The Psalmist's consistent trust and Jehovah's constant care.
    1. Avowal of Trust (5).
    2. Acknowledgment of Care (6).
    3. Ascription of Praise (6)
    4. Astonishment of Men (7).
    5. Avowal of Trust (7).
    6. Ascription of Praise (8).
    7. Appeal for Preservation (9-11). "Forsake me not."
        (i) Request (9).
        (ii) Reason (10-11).

III. CONTINUED PRAYER (12–13).
    1. Request (12). Aid desired.
    2. Reprobation (13). Adversaries denounced. "Them that seek my hurt."

IV. CONTEMPLATED PRAISE (14–16). THEME = "Thy Righteousness."

V. COGENT PLEAS (17–18). Youth and Age.
    Jehovah's constant care and the psalmist's consistent testimony.
    1. Acknowledgment of Instruction (17).
    2. Activity in Testimony (17).
    3. Appeal for Preservation (18). "Forsake me not."
    4. Aim in Testimony (18).

VI. CONFIDENT PRONOUNCEMENTS (19–20).
    1. Attributes of God (19).
    2. Acts of God (20).

VII. CONCLUDING PRAYER (21).

VIII. CONTEMPLATED PRAISE (22–24). THEME = "Thy Righteousness."
    1. Rendition (22–24a). Aid conferred.
    2. Reason (24b). Adversaries confounded. "They that sought my hurt."

PRIMARY ASSOCIATION.—The psalm is anonymous and occasion unknown. The writer is evidently elderly (9, 18). The close connection with the two preceding psalms, the absence of title here, and the style, all suggest Davidic authorship, in which case it belongs to his later life, perhaps the time of Adonijah's revolt. The LXX attributes it to David, and the superscript in that version seems to indicate that this was a favourite psalm of the Rechabites, Jer. xxxv. The composition contains many quotations from other psalms, but the new combination has a significant individuality of its own.

PROPHETIC ANTICIPATION.—The godly remnant in Israel here anticipates the renewal of national youth. The proper exercise of heart suited to the coming revival of the nation is manifested in the psalmist's utterance as its representative. Appropriately also, this follows almost immediately upon the psalm (lxix.) which gives the necessary foundation of the national restoration. The earlier verses give the theme which is expanded and illustrated in the rest of the poem; cf. Ezek. xxxvii.; Dan. xii.; Rom. xi. 15. In 6–11 is represented what God has been to His people from their beginning as a nation, and with this retrospective view is linked a prospective one of restoration to come.

PERSONAL APPLICATION.—Every Scripture which we incorporate into our own experience possesses a new meaning and operates with a new force. Faith is the expression of self-renunciation (1). Divine righteousness is a theme upon which we, as well as the psalmist, should delight to dwell (2, 15, 16, 19, 24). Unchanging rectitude is an inalienable attribute of God. In virtue of it, He cannot desert His own (2). God's people should ever be "rock-dwellers" (3a). By reason of the Cross the sinner can now plead the righteousness of God as a ground of salvation (2a). Happy are they who have trusted God from their youth (5). The preservation of Israel as a people is the outstanding miracle of history (7). Divine providence watches over the elect, not only from birth, but before it (6); cf. Jer. i. 5; Gal. i. 15. The Christian has the assurance of Christ's own words, John vi. 37; x. 27–30; Heb. xiii. 5–6, with verse 9 of our psalm. Another instance of God's people sharing the sufferings of the Saviour is in xxx. 10–11. Praise should increase with our passing years, and hope grow stronger (14). Here is an all-day occupation (15). Enemies may take advantage of the apparent weakness of old age, but God never forsakes His saints (18). However elderly God's servant may be, there is still work for him to do (18). Grey-headed saints have a message for the rising generation (18). With the Christian, an aged body should be accompanied by a youthful spirit, 2 Cor. iv. 16. The first note of renewed Israel's song will be God's truth (= troth), i.e. His abiding faithfulness (22b). The freed soul sings aloud (23).

VERSE NOTES

1–3. cf. xxxviii. 1–3.

1. (a) Br. ". . . have I taken refuge."

3. (a) Br. "Be to me a rock-dwelling."

4. (a) ". . . wicked one."

6. Read, "On Thee have I stayed myself from birth."

7. (a) Br. "I have been . . ." cf. Isa. lii. 14; Deut. xxviii. 46.

10. "concerning," or against; "soul" = life.

13. cf. xxxv. 4.

14. "But as for me, I . . ."

15. (c) Br. "For I know not how to reckon it."

16. (a) i.e. bringing them as a theme of praise; or as margin. David did this (1 Chron. xxviii.–xxix.) doubtless to the wonder of many (7).

18. Br. "Now also . . .", lit. as margin; "arm" suggests agency of power to rescue, protect, guide, govern, chastise, etc., lxxvii. 15; Isa. liii. 1; br. ". . . (this) generation."

20. (b) Br. " .. . shalt revive us again"; lit. "turn and quicken us."

21. The prayer of R.V. is practically the prediction of A.V.

22. "praise" = give thanks unto . . ." (c) lit. "I will psalm unto thee upon the harp"; (b) "truth" = troth, i.e. in keeping the promise; (d) divine title here is freq. in Isaiah, but only twice again in the Psalms, lxxviii. 41; lxxxix. 18; also found Jer. v. 29; li. 5; modified form Ezek. xxxix. 7.

23. "sing praises, lit. "psalm," see 22; Kirkpatrick always trans. "make melody." (b) "redeemed," or set free.

24. (b) Br. " . . . that sought my hurt."

PSALM LXXII.   PROSPERITY UNDER THE PRINCE OF PEACE.   THE REDEEMER'S RESPLENDENT REIGN

   I. COMMENCING PRAYER (1).   For the King.

   II. PROPHECY CONCERNING THE KING (2–7). *Character of His Rule.*
     1. Peace by Righteousness (2–4).
     2. Permanent Result (5).   Continual Reverence for God.
     3. Prosperity with Revival (6–7). "Flourish."

   III. PROPHECY CONCERNING THE KING (8–11). *Compass of His Rule.*
     Universal Homage.   Dominion of the King.

   IV. PROPHECY CONCERNING THE KING (12–16). *Character of His Rule.*
     1. Power for Redress (12–14).
     2. Permanent Result (15).   Continual Remembrance by Messiah.
     3. Prosperity with Revival (16). "Flourish."

   V. PROPHECY CONCERNING THE KING (17). *Continuance of His Rule.*
     Universal Honour.   Duration of the Kingdom.

   VI. CONCLUDING PRAISE (18–19).   Doxology.   (Closes the Psalm and
     Book II.).
     EPILOGUE (20).

SUPERSCRIPT.—To (or, for) Solomon.

PRIMARY ASSOCIATION.—It seems better to follow the Authorised Version rather than the Revised Version in the title, reading as above, see 20. It is doubtless David's last prayer for the son whom he had set upon his own throne before he died. Nevertheless it seems clear that the poet-seer with God's promise in mind (2 Sam. vii.) looks beyond the young king to the fulfilment in a yet greater Son, Messiah the King, our Lord Jesus Christ. The name Solomon is connected with the word "shalom" = peace, 1 Chron. xxii. 9, and the character of his reign was general peace, while that of David in the main was war, 1 Chron. xxviii. 3. Both typify Christ in different aspects. Solomon was also called Jedidiah, Beloved of Jehovah, 2 Sam. xii. 24-25; cf. Luke iii. 22. The closing doxology concludes not only Book II specifically, but also Books I and II regarded as a whole; cf. 2 Sam. xxiii. 1, where David remembers his humble origin. The epilogue seems to indicate two things; (a) that with the fulfilment of the last psalm, the height of David's desires will be reached, hence he has no further prayer to offer, and (b) that psalms composed by David and found in the later Books are in quite a different relationship, the nucleus of a series of psalms of later times.

PROPHETIC ANTICIPATION.—Long recognised as Messianic, this psalm "is a lovely picture of the Golden Age so graphically described by inspired prophets and so ardently desired by pious Israelites throughout all ages." "Messiah is seen as the perfect ruler, champion of the oppressed and redresser of every wrong." With the personal reign of Christ, the theocracy will be restored to Israel. We need again to remind ourselves that the Old Testament does not reveal the full and final, eternal condition of things, except in types and "dark sayings." The kingdom of Messiah is the consummation of Israel's hopes, the limit of the national horizon, and while perfectly true is nevertheless incomplete. The New Testament reveals much more concerning the close of the Millennium, the final judgment and the eternal state.

PERSONAL APPLICATION.—Our chief exercise should be to contemplate our blessed Lord as the central figure in the glorious scene portrayed. Read the psalm again in a worshipful spirit and you will surely join in the "Amen and amen," signifying your whole-hearted identification with the utterance of the sacred writer in his closing doxology. Because our lives are precious in His sight, the Saviour shed His blood for us (14). Our Lord raised the standard of human life, placing a higher value upon it than did the nations before He came and than do the nations to-day (14); cf. the Gospels. Christ champions the cause of the crushed (4). In the time of His triumph, He will show tenderness to the troubled (12-14).

VERSE NOTES

1. David desires for Solomon the divine bestowal of gifts necessary for right exercise of the kingly office. This one petition then blossoms out into clear prediction in which "a greater than Solomon" is seen; 1 Chron. xxix. 19; 1 Kings iii. 5; Isa. xi. 3-4; xvi. 5. The king is also a king's son, hence legitimate successor to the throne. Christ is King in His own divine right and King also as Son of David; see Luke i. 32.

2. "judge," or rule; not s.H.w. as in 4; "poor" = afflicted ones. Prophetically points to those who shall have suffered in the Great Tribulation.

3. Clauses divided for sake of rhythm; two subjects, one predicate; "mountains" and "hills" are types respectively of greater and lesser established powers representing Messiah's government. With the verse cf. of Solomon, 1 Chron. xxii. 8-9 and 1 Kings v. 4; of Messiah, cf. Isa. ii. 3-4; ix. 6-7; xi. 9; xxxii. 16-18; lv. 12-13; (b) "in" = by.

4. Expands verse 2; "judge" = do justice to; (c) "And crush . . . "

5. i.e. everywhere and always..

6. Showers upon the mown grass cause it to flourish again; suitable type of the effect of Messiah's reviving ministry by the Spirit upon the recently oppressed remnant of Israel; cf. Deut. xxxii. 2; 2 Sam. xxiii. 3-4. In eastern lands, water is a veritable worker of miracles. The outcome of 6 is seen in 7.

7. "the righteous," LXX has "righteousness."

8. Contrary to the usual interpretation of universal dominion, the language of this verse seems to define the limits of Israel's land—Messiah's dominion—according to the ancient promises; of Solomon's, cf. 1 Kings iv. 20 ff.; "sea to sea" = Mediterranean to Persian Gulf; br. "the River . . . unto the ends of the land," i.e. from the Euphrates to the Nile and the Red Sea; see map. This view is confirmed by the next verse. Israel has never yet obtained such wide territory for her own kingdom, even under David and Solomon; see Gen. xv. 18-21; Exod. xxiii. 31; Deut. xi. 24; Joshua i. 2-4; Ezek. xlvii. 13-48; Dan. vii. 13-14; Zech. ix. 10.

9. (a) i.e. the nomadic tribes within these borders; (b) i.e. prostrate themselves with faces to the ground in token of abject submission; also sign of dire abasement, Gen. iii. 14; Isa. lxv. 25.

10. "Tarshish," now regarded as the coast of India or Ceylon; "isles" in Scrip. gen. = western coastlands of Europe; cf. 1 Kings x. 22; ix. 26. "Sheba" = S.E. Arabia; "Seba" also in Arabia, Gen. x. 7; Isa. xliii. 3; xlv. 14. Descendant peoples of Japheth, Shem and Ham here included.

11. (a) i.e. in worship; typified 1 Kings iv. 21, 34; x. 1-13.

12. The claim to universal homage here rests upon His just and merciful rule; (b) "And the afflicted who hath . . ."

13. "souls" prim. = lives, so next line.

14. "redeem" i.e. as the Goel (Kinsman-Redeemer); see note, Ps. lxix. 18. (b) i.e. He will not suffer it to be shed with impunity; cf. cxvi. 15.

15. Variously understood. The best interpretation seems to be that which carries on the thought from the preceding verse; read, "And he (specifically one of the delivered ones) shall live, and to him shall be given of the gold of Sheba; and

prayer shall He (Messiah) make for him continually. All the day shall he be blessed." Messiah's priestly office as the true Melchizedek is emphasised. Gifts He has received He dispenses to others, cf. lxviii. 18.

16. "earth" = land. The terraced cornfields stretch right to the hilltops, which are usually rocky and bare—a picture of extraordinary fertility; ctr. Gen. iii. 17 with Isa. xxxv. 1–2; "shake . . .," *i.e.* wave or rustle like the cedars on Lebanon; "grass" = here the symbol of abundance, freshness and beauty; cf. 1 Kings iv. 20 (of Solomon's reign); Isa. xlix. 20 ff. (Messiah's reign). The Millennium will see a superabundance, both of plant life (*a*) and human life (*b*).

17. (*b*) cf. margin; here indicates, perhaps, a spiritual seed, see Ps. xxii. 30; (*c*) refers back to Gen. xii. 3.

18–19. "Blessed . . ." cf. 1 Kings i. 48; 1 Chron. xxix. 10–11, 13, 20.

19. (*c*) The response of the congregation in the temple services; implies assent and consent.

20. Cf. "David's last words," 2 Sam. xxiii. 1–7; see 2 Cor. i. 20.

This Psalm fittingly closes Book II of the Psalter. David's prayers have reached their highest peak. With prophetic insight he looks beyond the peaceful reign of Solomon to the more glorious reign of Messiah, who is both his greater Son and sovereign Lord.

Book Three.   Israel's Return and Restoration: lxxiii.–lxxxix.

As befits this "Leviticus" Book we find the Sanctuary especially in view from its ruin to its restoration. Emphasis is laid upon God's holiness in dealing with His people; see notes, Introduction III and pp. 23–24. Prophetically, we see the godly remnant in the last days with their thoughts centring round the temple and its worship. God's holiness is active in the discipline of the righteous as well as in the destruction of the wicked.

ANALYSIS.

I. REVELATION OF THE DIVINE HOLINESS, LXXIII–LXXXIII.
    The Sanctuary in its Relation to Man. The Remnant Prominent. Asaphic Psalms.
    1. Affirmed in Israel's Heart-searchings, lxxiii.–lxxvii.
    2. Applied in Israel's History, lxxviii.–lxxxiii.

II. REALISATION OF THE DIVINE HOLINESS, LXXXIV–LXXXIX.
    The Sanctuary in its Relation to God. The Redeemer Prominent. Various Psalmists.
    1. Acclaimed in Israel's Restoration, lxxxiv.–lxxxv.
    2. Attained through Israel's Restorer, lxxxvi.–lxxxvii.
    3. Attested in Israel's Restoration, lxxxviii.–lxxxix.

Book Three.   I.   Revelation of the Divine Holiness: lxxiii.–lxxxiii.

The Remnant Prominent. Asaphic Psalms.

1. Affirmed in Israel's Heart-searchings, lxxiii.–lxxvii.

PSALM LXXIII. AN ENIGMA ELUCIDATED.

I. TESTIMONY OF THE PSALMIST (1).   Concerning God.

II. TRIAL OF FAITH (2–16).
    1. Perplexity of the Psalmist (2–3). Error Committed.
    2. Prosperity of the Perverse (4–12).
        Their   (i) Peace (4–5).
                (ii) Pride (6–7).
                (iii) Pretensions (8–9).
                (iv) Popularity (10–11).
                (v) Plenty (12).
    3. Perplexity of the Psalmist (13–16).

III. TURNING-POINT OF FAITH (17). SOLUTION IN THE SANCTUARY.

IV. TRIUMPH OF FAITH (18–26).
1. Portion of the Perverse (18–20).
2. Perplexity of the Psalmist (21–22). Error Confessed.
3. Portion of the Psalmist (23–26).

V. TESTIMONY OF THE PSALMIST (27–28).
(a) Concerning Apostates (27).
(b) Concerning Himself (28).

SUPERSCRIPT.—A Psalm of (or for) Asaph.

PRIMARY ASSOCIATION.—Second of the psalms ascribed to Asaph, see Ps. l. note. In the present group there is some difficulty in understanding all as coming from the pen of the Asaph of David's day. Nevertheless if events are referred to which seem inconsistent with David's reign, we must remember that, like David himself, Asaph was a seer as well as a poet and may have been inspired to write of what was yet purely future. We are not shut up to this explanation, however, for some may have been written by an Asaph of later days. More probably in some cases at least, we should read "for (or, to) Asaph" (the Heb. preposition admits of either rendering) as being dedicated by some anonymous writer to this famous singer-poet of earlier days or by sons of Asaph for an Asaphic collection, cf. lxxxiii. It should not be overlooked that a similarity of style pervades the whole group. Ps. l. is connected with the sanctuary and it is significant that all the rest of the Asaphic psalms are found here in the "Sanctuary Book." The historical occasion of our present psalm is unknown. It is a record of personal experience common to saints of any time. Like Pss. xxxvii. and xlix. it "treats of the perennial problem of reconciling God's moral government with observed facts." How can an Almighty God be good and yet allow the wicked to prosper and the righteous to suffer? The fact that with the full revelation of the New Testament and hopes distinctly heavenly, even Christians are sometimes thus perplexed, should make them sympathise more readily with Old Testament saints who struggled with the problem, for the hopes of the latter were centred upon the earthly inheritance. Moreover, the Law had taught them that earthly blessing followed upon obedience and punishment upon disobedience.

PROPHETIC ANTICIPATION.—As with the other Books, the first

psalm is prefatory and shows the general character of what follows. The faith of the godly remnant is here exercised amid the surrounding ungodliness of an apostate nation.

PERSONAL APPLICATION.—Faith may falter, but it never fails; it may flounder, but it still fights on. After reading this psalm who would care to change places with the wealthy wicked? The slipping foot of the saint is upheld (2); xciv. 18. Well-being is not to be judged by appearances (3). It is foolish to envy the wicked (3). The seeming inequalities of life should not embitter the soul or becloud the judgment (3). A peaceful end to a prosperous life is no proof of the divine favour (4). The perverse in their prosperity have many parasites (10). A clean heart is not without conflict, clean hands not without chastening (13); cf. Heb. xii. 9–11. Stumble not any of God's family by parading your perplexities; doubts are best kept to oneself (15). Always consider the end (17). In communion with God, problems are solved that defy the intellect of man (17). The pure light of the divine presence penetrates the most perplexing problems. God may seem to be asleep (20) but it is not so, cxxi. 4. Ignorance and irritation breed doubts (21–22). In God's grasp and by His guidance I shall safely reach the glory (22–23). Is God "the Rock of *my* heart" (26)? Distance from God is death (27). This has been called "The Sceptic's Psalm."

VERSE NOTES

1. "Surely," or only; so 13, 18; (*a*) ref. to the nation; (*b*) ref. to the remnant; cf. Matt. v. 8.

3. Ctr. lxxii., the righteous flourishing; "prosperity," lit. peace; "wicked" = lawless; so 12.

4. "firm," or well-fed.

5. Br. "They have not the travail of mortal man . . .," *i.e.* circumstances seem to justify their boastings.

6. *i.e.* the pride is ostentatious.

8. or, "They scoff and talk evil; of oppression do they talk from on high," *i.e.* they speak as if they are gods and their words, oracles.

9. *i.e.* they blaspheme God and slander men.

10. "turn" br. than "return," *i.e.* even some professed people of God are carried away by the evil example; "hither," *i.e.* to the wicked and their ways; (*b*) metaphor for enjoyment of pleasure.

11. The words of the deluded followers; "God" = El.

12. cf. II chr. xx. 11.

13. Claim is to sincerity not sinlessness; (*b*) see xxvi. 6.

14. *i.e.* he was disciplined by God: "I" (emph.).

16. Br. "And I kept thinking how to understand this . . ."

20. Br. "When Thou arousest Thyself"; "image," *i.e.* their pomp was but a phantom.

21. Note margin.

23. Br. "But as for me, I . . ."

24. Br. "And afterwards in glory thou wilt receive me," or ". . . after the glory . . .," *i.e.* prophetically of the remnant who will be delivered after Christ's manifestation (2 Thess. ii. 8) and not before.

26. Note margin.

27. Br. ". . . go far . . ."; (*b*) apostasy is often expressed in Scripture as infidelity to the marriage vow.

28. Br. "But as for me, it is . . ."

PSALM LXXIV. SACRILEGE IN THE SANCTUARY

I. PASSIONATE PRAYER (1–3). "Remember."
    1. Cry of Perplexity (1). "Why?"
    2. Claim for Protection (2–3). "Remember Thy Assembly."

II. POWERFUL PLEA (4–9). Work of the Adversaries.
    Present Profanation of God's Name. Desecration of His Meeting-place.

III. PASSIONATE PRAYER (10–11). "How long? . . . Why?"

IV. POWERFUL PLEA (12–17). Work of the Almighty.
    Past Manifestation of God's Power. Display of His Might.
    1. Intervention in History (12–15).
    2. Influence in Creation (16–17).

V. PASSIONATE PRAYER (18–23). "Remember."
    1. Request—Positive (18). "Remember the Reproach." Supplication.
    2. Request—Negative (19). "Forget not the Afflicted." (Preserve them.) Deprecation.
    3. Request—Positive (20). "Remember the Covenant." Supplication.
    4. Request—Negative (21). "Forget not the Afflicted." (Answer them.) Deprecation.
    5. Request—Positive (22). "Remember the Reproach." Supplication.
    6. Request—Negative (23). "Forget not the Adversaries." (Requite them.) Deprecation.

SUPERSCRIPT.—Maschil of (or for) Asaph.

SUBSCRIPT.—For the Chief Musician, Al-tashheth (= Destroy not.)

PRIMARY ASSOCIATION.—Writer uncertain (see notes to lxxiii.). The psalm is closely connected with lxxxix. and seems to belong to the same occasion, namely the destruction of Jerusalem by the Chaldeans, 2 Kings xxv. 9; Ps. lxxiv. emphasises the Destruction of

G

the Sanctuary; lxxix., the Destruction of the Saints. "Al-tashheth" = destroy not. This is a cry in a crisis; see Pss. lvi.–lviii. and cf. Exod. xxxii. 11–14 with Deut. ix. 25, also the spirit of David's words, 2 Sam. xxiv. 16–17. Moses and David both act upon the injunction of Deut. iv. 30–31. These "Destroy not" psalms in application may well be used in times of national troubles.

PROPHETIC ANTICIPATION.—As a "Maschil" (ninth in the series of thirteen) this psalm contains special instruction for Israel in the last days when the city (Jerusalem) is ravaged and the pre-millennial temple desolated, Matt. xxiv. 15; cf. Joel ii. 1–11; Dan. xi. 40-41. Incidentally we notice that the second psalm in each of the Books of the Psalter has to do with "the enemy."

PERSONAL APPLICATION.—Sometimes a little more passion in our prayers would not be out of place! God is asked to "remember" several things—find them. Sheep may claim the Shepherd's care (1). In our prayers relationship and redemption form a double plea (1–2). Enemies of God seek to destroy both God's "temple" (1 Cor. iii. 16–17) and God's people (3–7). Infidelity (in the form of destructive criticism) and worldliness have dared to lift hatchet and hammer in the very sanctuary of God and have succeeded in working terrible havoc in the congregation of God's professed people (3–7). He is a wise teacher who knows the signs of the times (9). God's seeming inactivity must not be interpreted as indifference or impotence; it is in the interests of His immutable purpose and of His people (10–11). God must and will vindicate His name in due time (10). The people of God should remember that the dishonour done to God's name is of greater consequence than their own distress. In the wilderness man's extremity was God's opportunity (14). God can make our very foes furnish us with "food" (14). God has ordained luminaries for the darkest night (16). Winter is just as essential for the production of crops as summer, so is it in the realm of the spirit. God controls the bleakness of winter as well as the beauty of summer, the hour of pain as well as the time of pleasure (17). Foolish are the people that scorn God's name (18).

VERSE NOTES

1. "for ever" = perpetually; so 10; cf. Lam. v. 20; iii. 31; "smoke," cf. xviii. 8; "sheep," cf. lxxix. 13; c. 3; Jer. xxiii. 1; Ezek. xxxiv. 31; also Ps. xcv. 7.

2. omit "And."

3. (a) i.e. hasten to see.

4. "assembly" = place of assembly; the courts of the Temple were filled with heathen foes instead of reverent worshippers, with roars of triumph instead of songs of praise; "ensigns," br. signs (A.V.), not military insignia, but things having a religious significance.

5. Br. "They seem as men that lift up . . .," simile probably suggested because of 1 Kings vi. 21-22, 29; 2 Chron. xxxvi. 18.

7. See 2 Kings xxv. 9-10; Jer. lii. 12-17; (b) cf. Deut. xii. 11; xvi. 2 ff.

8. " . . . make havoc of . . ." more lit. "crush"; by destroying the Temple the enemy at a stroke did away with all the "solemn assemblies" of the nation; (b) as margin; cf. Lam. i. 4; ii. 6; Jer. lii. 13, 17.

9. "signs," i.e. visible religious symbols (see 4a), e.g. sabbaths, festivals, etc.; Exod. xxxi. 13, 17; Ezek. xx. 12, 20; or, perhaps, refers to miraculous signs of God's presence and power. (b) At this time the prophets were divinely commanded to be silent, Ezek. iii. 26; xxiv. 27.

10. Cf. Lam. v. 1; Ezek. v. 15.

11. Br. "Get it ready from inside Thy bosom," Lam. ii. 3.

12. "salvation" = deliverances.

13. "Thou," emphatic; so also 14a, 15ab, 16b, 17ab (seven times in all).

14. "leviathan" prob. = crocodile, symbol of Egypt; (b) cf. Num. xiv. 9.

15. "flood" = torrent; ctr. (b) marg. or, "never-failing . . ."

16. (b) marg. i.e. prob. the moon.

17. "earth" = land, civ. 8-9.

19. Read, "Give not up Thy turtle-dove (Israel) to a community of sensual men. Forget not the community of thy afflicted ones perpetually." For "community" cf. s.H.w. lxviii. 10.

20. "covenant"; is not the Mosaic covenant of law, which only condemned, but the earlier Abrahamic covenant of promise, Gal. iii. 15-17; (b) i.e. places where violence made its home. Intense cruelty characterised the Chaldeans, Jer. l. 42; vi. 23.

21. Nouns in sing.; "return," i.e. with prayer unanswered; (b) i.e. have cause to praise by reason of answered prayer.

22. Israel's cause was really God's cause; His honour was at stake; "foolish," i.e. a member of the "foolish people" (18).

23. "ascendeth," i.e. as a challenge.

PSALM LXXV. THE GOVERNMENT OF GOD

I. ASCRIPTION OF PRAISE (1). Worship presented. National.

II. ANNOUNCEMENT OF PURPOSE (2-3). Righteous Judgment.
   The Adminstrator Revealed. Selah.

III. ADMONITION TO ADVERSARIES (4-8).
   1. The Rebuke (4-5).
   2. The Reasons (6-8).

IV. ASCRIPTION OF PRAISE (9). Worship promised. Personal.

V. ANNOUNCEMENT OF PURPOSE (10). Righteous Judgment.
The Alternatives Re-affirmed.
1. Extermination of the Godless.
2. Exaltation of the Godly.

SUPERSCRIPT.—A Psalm of (or, for) Asaph. A Song.

SUBSCRIPT.—For the Chief Musician; on Neginoth.

PRIMARY ASSOCIATION.—Writer and occasion uncertain, but there is a strong link in thought and language with the next psalm and it may belong to the same period. It follows the appeal of lxxiv. and is the answer from God. Note the dramatic form of composition. God's enemies are warned and God's people encouraged. "Neginoth," see notes Ps. iii.

PROPHETIC ANTICIPATION.—Messiah anticipates receiving the kingdom at the appointed time (2), and as God's representative Ruler He judges in holiness. He is seen too as Leader of Israel's praises. In His millennial kingdom, Christ is still the perfect Servant doing the will of God. He whom all nations will obey is still the obedient One bringing to fruition the purposes of God.

PERSONAL APPLICATION.—The enemy may surround, but all the works of God declare His nearness (1). Another argument that God is not indifferent to human affairs is found here (2). Note the time, the principle and the certainty of the judgment (2). Though the whole world may be in terror and confusion, God from the first has ordained fundamental laws which are working to adjust the disorder resulting from the sin of man. This will be fully displayed when Messiah reigns (3). Presumptuous boasters should take warning from words uttered in grace (4–5). Do not look to any quarter of the earth for help (6), look up (7). Bitter indeed will be the cup of wrath which the wicked of the earth will be forced to drink (8). Lawlessness will not go unpunished nor righteousness unrewarded (10). The world can never get completely out of hand (3). Those who lift themselves up against God (4) will be surely cast down (7).

VERSE NOTES

1-3. Thanksgiving for recent manifestation of God's presence and power among His people; "name near" = attributes (of power, etc.) displayed.

2. Br. "When I reach the appointed time, I (emph.) will judge uprightly."

3. Br. "Though the earth with all the inhabitants thereof . . . I (emph.) have established . . .," cf. Isa. xxxvii. 26.

4. Tense is prophetic past; "arrogant . . . arrogantly," br. "boasters . . . boast not," cf. lxxiii. 3.

5. Metaphor from animals tossing their heads; denotes defiant self-sufficiency; (b) LXX has "Nor speak of the Rock with arrogance."

6. "south" = Egypt, cf. Isa. xxxvi. 4–6. North not mentioned, perhaps, because the Assyrians and the Chaldeans came from that direction. Moreover, in Scripture, the north seems referred to as the place where God's judgment-throne is·set; cf. Job xxvi. 7; xxxvii. 22; Isa. xiv. 13; Ezk. i. 4; Lev. i. 11. Both ideas may be conveyed, e.g. in Jer. i. 14; iv. 6; vi. 1. There was no hope for Jerusalem from any quarter of the globe, only from above (7).

7. Cf. Isa. xxxiii. 22.

8. The figure of a cup is frequently used in Scripture as a symbol of divine judgment; "mixture"—wine is often spiced to make it more seductive, and fortified to make it more potent, cf. Rev. xiv. 10; xvi. 19.

9. "But as for me, I . . . will psalm unto . . ."

10. "lifted up"; expression five times in the psalm; cf. 1 Sam. ii. 10.

PSALM LXXVI. THE ALMIGHTY AND THE AGGRESSORS

I. THE DELIVERER (1–3). HIS PRESENCE MANIFESTED. Selah.

II. THE DELIVERANCE (4–6). THE AGGRESSORS SLAIN.

III. THE DELIVERANCE (7–9). THE AFFLICTED SAVED. Selah.

IV. THE DELIVERER (10–12). HIS PERSON MAGNIFIED.

    1. In the Wrath of the Peoples (10).
    2. In the Worship of the Preserved (11).
    3. In the Warning to the Potentates (12).

SUPERSCRIPT.—A Psalm of (or, for) Asaph. A Song.

SUBSCRIPT.—For the Chief Musician. To (or, for) Jeduthun.

PRIMARY ASSOCIATION.—Identity of writer uncertain; see notes to earlier psalms of this series. For subscript cf. xxxviii. and lxi. Accepting the hint afforded by the subscript, we must look for an important victory in David's career that has to do with Jerusalem itself. The capture of Jebus (2 Sam. v. 6–10), which became Zion, the city of David and the place where he set up a tabernacle for the Ark (2 Sam. vi.), may be the event celebrated in later years by this psalm. Note the emphatic "there" (3), which fixes the locality.

Salem is an ancient name for Jerusalem (Gen. xiv. 18). Jebus was taken by a surprise attack, which may be reflected in the words of verses 5-6. LXX and other ancient versions read (6), "The horsemen are stunned." The apparent reference to the destruction of Sennacherib's army in the reign of Hezekiah cannot be ignored (Isa. xxxvi.–xxxvii.), but it must not be forgotten that "history repeats itself," and Hezekiah does use a number of David's psalms as suitably expressing the circumstances of his time. In connection with the divine judgment, Ps. lxxv. is the Preparation, or Thanksgiving in anticipation of deliverance promised; lxxvi. is the Celebration, or Thanksgiving in satisfaction of deliverance accomplished.

PROPHETIC ANTICIPATION.—The inauguration of Messiah's reign of peace, following the destruction of the world powers that will come up against Jerusalem, is here foreseen; see Rev. xix., etc.

PERSONAL APPLICATION.—God is self-revealed by His acts (1). The Prince of Peace will make war against war (3). God shivers the swords and snaps the spears of His enemies (3). Note the awe of the earth at the manifestation of the anger of Elohim (7-9). A pertinent question is 7b for those who oppose God and His people. Man's wrath shall turn to God's praise (10). God makes the wrath of His foes serve to their own final discomfiture (10). If you have prayed in the hour of peril, be sure to praise in the day of preservation (11).

VERSE NOTES

1. "known," lit. "one who has made Himself known"; "Israel" = covenant name for the people of God's choice. Historically Judah represented the whole nation; prophetically points to reunion of the two kingdoms under Messiah.

2. If marginal readings accepted, ref. to the "Lion of Judah," under which title Messiah will appear for the deliverance of His people, cf. Isa. xxxi. 4; "Salem," old name and poetic abbreviation for Jerusalem; prophetically significant as the city of the "Prince of Peace," the antitypical Melchizedek.

3. "lightnings" or, flashings; arrows so called possibly from their swiftness in flight; prophetically significant in view of modern artillery; "there" (emph.); "battle" includes all instruments of war and equipment; moreover the whole war was and will be settled at one stroke, cf. Isa. ii. 4; Ezk. xxxix. 9; 2 Kings xix. 32.

4. or, "Thou art shining forth gloriously above the mountains of prey." Jerusalem, the city of innumerable sieges, had been a prey for many enemies. The Assyrian lion met more than his match in the Lion of Judah.

5. "They slumber their (last) sleep," 2 Kings xix. 35; Jer. li. 39, 57. (c) i.e. their strength was paralysed; cf. Isa. x. 10, 13, 14, 32.

6. "rebuke," ctr. the enemy's rebuke, 2 Kings xix. 3, 4, 16. The "slumber"

was supernaturally caused; thus the victory was manifestly due to the direct intervention of God, cf. Isa. xliii. 17.

7. "to be feared," s.H.w. as "terrible" (12).

8. Cf. Isa. xxx. 30; 1 Sam. ii. 10.

11. "bring presents"; Heb. phrase always used of bringing solemn tribute to God; historically, 2 Chron. xxxii. 22–23 (?).

12. "spirit," *i.e.* their pride and fury.

PSALM LXXVII. RELIEF IN RETROSPECTION

I. THE PSALMIST'S DEEP CONCERN (1–9). THE STRESS.
   Occupation with Self. Consequent Gloom. "I . . . I . . . I . . ."
   1. His Dejection (1–3). Complaint. Selah.
   2. His Deliberation (4–6) "I call to remembrance."
   3. His Dejection (7–9). Cogitation. Selah.

II. THE PSALMIST'S DESIRED COMFORT (10–20). THE SOLACE.
   Occupation with God. Consequent Gladness. "Thou . . . Thou . . ."
   1. His Decision (10–12). "I will remember."
   2. His Declaration (13–15). God's way in the Sanctuary.
      "Thou didst redeem Thy people." Jacob and Joseph.
   3. His Description (16–19). God's way in the Sea.
   4. His Declaration (20)
      "Thou didst lead Thy people." Moses and Aaron.

SUPERSCRIPT.—A Psalm of (or, for) Asaph.

PRIMARY ASSOCIATION.—Writer and occasion uncertain, but it may belong to the time of the Chaldean invasion of Judah, Israel's ten tribes already having been taken captive by the Assyrians. In lxxvi., then, we see, Preservation from Assyrian aggressors; in lxxvii., Humiliation by Chaldean oppressors; cf. Habakkuk's prayer, iii. This prophet uses as a model the psalm poetry and many of his utterances closely resemble the language of our psalm.

PROPHETIC ANTICIPATION.—Expresses the deep soul response of the godly remnant during the latter part of "the great tribulation" period.

PERSONAL APPLICATION.—This is a melody of memories. You are not the only one of God's children who has experienced soul conflict in which despondency and hope alternate! External pressure may be accompanied by inward perplexity. When in a "strait" we know where to go (2) Only here in God's presence are peace and happiness found (13). Stress of circumstances may leave even one of God's saints both sleepless and speechless (4). Here, once more, see the history of the past affording hope for the future (11 ff). Divine deliverance is always followed by divine guidance (20). God remains the same whether in the dark or in the light, therefore we should learn to trust Him always. Note the psalmist's three main questions: (a) Is God's purpose really immutable? (b) Is God's memory really infallible? (c) Is God's loving-kindness really inexhaustible? Note also the two comprehensive answers: (a) the answer of logic says, "Impossible! the infirmity is not in God, therefore, it must be in me"; (b) the answer of history says, "Incredible! the dealings of God with Israel in redemption prove that He does not change." The works of God may be seen in history and in nature, but the ways of God, i.e. the principles upon which He acts, can only be learned in the sanctuary. All nature owns the power of God (16 ff). Though we may not be able to trace His footsteps yet we may trust Him to lead (19-20). Choose memories that cheer. Let us be neither distracted by other folks' circumstances (lxxiii.), nor dejected by our own experiences (lxxvii.); be occupied with God in His sanctuary.

The psalmist began with a bad squint (1-9); but after an adjusted focus (10), he obtains a clear vision (11-20). (Goodman).

VERSE NOTES

1. *i.e.* he cried aloud.

2. "Stretched out," *i.e.* in prayer.

3. Sense is, "When I would fain remember God, I am disquieted, when I would fain commune (with myself) my spirit fainteth"; "commune" (or soliloquize), s.H.w. 6b, 12b.

4-9. In vigils of the night the psalmist ponders the past and anxiously wonders if it be possible that God has changed His character.

4. (a) Br. "Thou didst hold mine eyelids open"; "troubled" = agitated.

6. "Let me remember . . . let me commune . . ."; "song," Heb. = a song with musical accompaniment; (c) "And my spirit inquired (saying) . . ."

8. Br. "Is His loving-kindness come to a perpetual end? Hath His word . . .'

9. "God" = El.

11. Note marg.; the name "Jah" recalls the exodus, Exod. xv. 13-14; (b) "For," br. "Yea" . . . cf. Mark viii. 18.

13-14. Br. "Who is a mighty one so great as God? *Thou* art the Mighty One (El) that . . .," cf. Exod. xv. 11.

13. (a) see lxxiii. 17.

14. (b) "Thou didst make . . . Thou didst redeem . . ."; see Exod. xv. 13-16.

15. "Joseph," because his sons not direct sons of Jacob.

16 ff. At the time of the exodus, God manifested His sovereignty over nature; "waters," *i.e.* of the Nile and the Red Sea.

17. God came in storm and earthquake, Exod. xiv. 24–25; prophetically significant. (*b*) *i.e.* it thundered; (*c*) "arrows," *i.e.* flashes of lightning.

18. "whirlwind" or, with rumbling. The roll of thunder conceived of as a rolling of God's chariot wheels, Hab. iii. 8.

19. The Red Sea flowed back where Israel passed, leaving no visible trace of God's victorious march; a parable of His ways, Rom. xi. 33.

20. The Shepherd of Israel led forth His flock, Exod. xv. 13.

Book Three. I. Revelation of the Divine Holiness: lxxiii.–lxxxiii.

2. Applied in Israel's History, lxxviii.–lxxxiii.

PSALM LXXVIII. THE PAST A PREMONITOR OF THE PRESENT

I. PRELUDE OF THE PSALM (1–8). The Testimony.

  Prominent Fact. The Institution of the Theocracy.

  1. Summoning the People (1–2). "I."
  2. Sacred Resolve (3–4). "We."
  3. Specific Reason (5–6). "He."
  4. Stressing the Purpose (7–8) "They."

II. PROGRESS OF THE PSALM (9–64). The Testings.

  Prominent Facts. The Interpretation of National History.

  1. Prevocative Conduct (9–11).
  2. Redemptive Mercies (12–16). "Brought out."

    (*a*) Deliverance by Wonders.
    (*b*) Guidance in the Wilderness.

  3. Prevocative Conduct (17–20).
  4. Righteous Wrath (21–22). In the Wilderness. Jehovah heard.
  5. Israel's Faithlessness notwithstanding Jehovah's Indignation (23–33).

    (*a*) Provocation (23–29). Lust.
    (*b*) Punishment (30–31).
    (*c*) Provocation (32). Unbelief.
    (*d*) Punishment (33).

  6. Jehovah's Forbearance notwithstanding Israel's Insincerity (34–39).

    (*a*) Provocation (34–37). Hypocrisy.
    (*b*) Pity (38–39).

  7. Prevocative Conduct (40–42). (See 1.)

8. Redemptive Mercies (43–55). "Brought in." (See 2).
(a) Deliverance by Wonders.
(b) Guidance through the Wilderness.
9. Provocative Conduct (56–58). (See 3).
10. Righteous Wrath (59–64). In the Land. Jehovah heard. (See 4).

III. PINNACLE OF THE PSALM (65–72). The Temple.
Prominent Fact. The Institution of the Kingdom.
1. Smiting the Philistines (65–66).
2. Selection of Zion (67–69).
3. Selection of David (70–71).
4. Shepherding the People (72).

SUPERSCRIPT.—Maschil of (or, for) Asaph.

PRIMARY ASSOCIATION.—The writer may well be the Asaph of David's day, see notes to Ps. lxxiii. This is the seventh of the twelve so ascribed. It is also the first and longest of the "historical" psalms, the others being cv., cvi. and cxxxv. The psalm leads up to God's choice of a site for the Sanctuary. "Asaph here warns Ephraim not to rebel against God's transfer of their prerogative to Zion and Judah." In the outline of the national history, the order is logical rather than chronological. Note the solemn alternation of Israel's misbehaviour and Jehovah's mercy. Mark correspondences in the structure; a good example of extended alternation and introversion.

PROPHETIC ANTICIPATION.—This is the twelfth of the Maschils which all contain special instruction for Israel's faithful remnant at the time of the end. During the hour of deepest trial their faith is sustained by the Spirit of God who directs their hearts to the nation's history as supplying needful lessons of warning and encouragement.

PERSONAL APPLICATION.—A psalm of forgetfulness, ctr. lxxvii. Here are practical lessons for the people of God in all ages, see 1 Cor. x. 6, 11. We can indicate but a few. Divine precepts are powerfully enforced by illustrations from human history (2). The head of every family is under obligation to instruct his children in the things of God (3–4). Forgetfulness of God's precepts leads to failure among God's people (11, 42). Doubt and disobedience are twin evils. The unbelief which provokes divine judgment is that which arises, not from want of evidence, but from a rebellious will (20). To put God to the test is the very essence of unbelief (18, 41). "Can God?" is the language of unbelief (19); to limit God is sin (8d). Only the obedient can overcome; disobedience leads to defeat (62 ff). God expects in each of us a spirit of loyalty (8*d*). They who are divinely equipped should not turn back in the day of battle (9). Hearts not lips determine our true attitude to God (37). Remember, God is our Rock and our Redeemer (35). To be sorry for the sufferings is not the same as being sorry for the sins (34). Awful indeed is the righteous anger of the Almighty (21, 59, 62 ff). Sin is incorrigible and punishment therefore inevitable (32–33). God sometimes punishes men by answering their prayers (29–31). God tolerates no rival (58). Human nature is frail and human life transitory (39). God remembers though His people forget (39 with 11, 42). He provided food to nourish a race of mighty men (25). In light of John vi. 57–58 what spiritual heroes Christians ought to be! Note the seven occurrences of "El" (Mighty One), 7, 8, 18, 19, 34, 35 (followed by "Elyon"), 41. Divine mercy often redeems our human mistakes.

VERSE NOTES

2. It is the function of prophecy to interpret the past as well as to foretell the future. It is best to put a full stop at the end of verse and continue. "The things which . . . us . . . will not hide from . . ."

2. Qtd. Matt. xiii. 34–35.

4. "praises of Jehovah," *i.e.* His praiseworthy acts.

5. (*b*) *i.e.* the express precept indicated next lines, not the law generally.

8. (*b*) cf. Deut. xxi. 18. (*c*) cf. 37. (*d*) br. "not faithful," as in 37.

9. Ctr. Gen. xlix. 24; "Ephraim," see Appendix IX. The action of this tribe is typical of all Israel.

12. "Zoan" = Tanis, capital of the Hyksos dynasty, situated east bank of the Tanitic branch of the Nile.

16. (*a*) "rock," br. cliff; two incidents ref. to in 15–16, *viz.* Exod. xvii. 6 and Num. xx. 8 ff.

17–18. Rebelling against and tempting God sum up Israel's behaviour.

20. Climax of unbelief; mercy made an occasion of mockery.

24. " . . . gave them the corn of heaven"; the manna therefore was not the exudation of wilderness trees as some allege.

25. "Man . . ." as R.V.m.; cf. 2 Tim. ii. 13.

29. (*b*) Br. "For He brought them that for which they lusted."

32. Br. "In (or, amid) all this . . ."

33. or, " . . . consume as a breath."

34. Verb tenses denote repeated alternations of punishment and repentance; cf. Judges ii. 11 ff.

35. Title El Elyon occurring here found elsewhere only Gen. xiv. 18 ff.

36. As though God were a man to be deceived by hypocrisy!

39. Cf. ciii. 14.

40 ff. As God multiplied His acts of mercy, Israel multiplied their acts of rebellion.

43. "redeemed" = delivered as in Exod. xiii. 13.

45. Heb. word used only in connection with this plague; "of flies," omit; "Swarms" prob. mosquitoes; these and frogs are both connected with marshes.

48. (b) Br. "to fiery lightnings."

49. (c) Br. "A mission of messengers of evil."

50. (c) Ignore margin.

51. Ham was the ancestor of Mizraim = Egypt, Gen. x. 6.

52. Cf. Isa. lxiii. 11–14.

54. "this mountain" may refer to Zion; otherwise as R.V.m. = Canaan.

55. The land of the Canaanites was distributed among the Israelites by lot, Josh. xxiii. 4.

56. Note title "Elohim Elyon"; (b) "testimonies" = commandments as being witnesses to His will.

61. "strength . . . glory," i.e. the Ark of Testimony, symbol and seat of divine majesty, 1 Sam. iv.

64. (a) Prob. ref. to Hophni and Phineas and their companion priests. (b) Amid such widespread distress the customary rites of mourning went unperformed even for a husband, cf. 2 Sam. xi. 26–27.

66. "backward" or, in the rear.

67 ff. When Jehovah interposed once more, He destroyed Israel's adversaries and the sanctuary was restored, but not to Shiloh. The ark was later deposited in a special "tent" at Zion, by David.

70. Saul, the people's choice, is not mentioned here; "His servant" = a title of honour gained by a few persons only.

71–72. Metaphors peculiarly suitable in David's case.

PSALM LXXIX. THE SLAUGHTER OF THE SAINTS

I. THE PLAINT (1–3). RUIN BY ENEMY NATIONS.
1. Descent upon the Land (1a).
2. Desecration of the Temple (1b).
3. Destruction of the City (1c).
4. Decimation of the People (2–3). "Thy Servants . . . Thy Saints."

II. THE POIGNANCY (4). REPROACH OF NEIGHBOURING PEOPLES.
The Record.

III. THE PRAYER (5–9). REFUGE OF A CHASTENED REMNANT.
1. Expostulation (5). "How long?"
2. Supplication (6–7). For Vengeance upon the Nations.
3. Intercession (8–9). For Deliverance of the People. "Thy pity."
4. Expostulation (10a). "Wherefore?"
5. Supplication (10b). For Vengeance upon the Nations.
6. Intercession (11). For Deliverance of the People. "Thy power."

IV. THE POIGNANCY (12). REPROACH OF NEIGHBOURING PEOPLES. The Requital.

V. THE PRAISE (13). RENDITION BY GRATEFUL ISRAEL.
    1. Relation Claimed (13*a*). "Thy People—Thy Sheep."
    2. Resolution Formed (13*bc*).
       (*a*) Thanksgiving (13*b*).
       (*b*) Testimony (13*c*).

SUPERSCRIPT.—A Psalm of (or, for) Asaph.

SUBSCRIPT.—For the Chief Musician; upon Shoshannim Eduth (= Lilies of Testimony).

PRIMARY ASSOCIATION.—See notes to Ps. lxxiv. The subscript indicates the "testimony" as relating to the Feast of Second Passover, Num. ix. 5-14; cf. 2 Chron. xxix. 25-35, xxx. 23.

PROPHETIC ANTICIPATION.—See Ps. lxxiv. Note relation between cause and effect.

PERSONAL APPLICATION.—The psalm is simple in character and the meaning plain. When our own "world" seems to lie in ruins God is still our refuge and prayer our true resource. Sometimes the Lord has to bring His people very low before He can lift them up (8). When brought low we should look very high (8). If we fully trust God, He will keep us not only from sinning but from sinking. Sooner or later God will avenge the blood of His servants (10). All sin must be judged and the agents of chastisement are sometimes the greater sinners, cf. Hab. i.

VERSE NOTES

1. What the nation had itself defiled, God gives up to defilement, Ezk. v. 11; xxiii. 38; xxiv. 21; "heaps" = in ruins.

2. Indicates a remorseless slaughter aggravated by the disgrace of unburied bodies; "servants . . . saints," the use of these titles urges relationship not merit, cf. l. 5; "saints" = favoured ones.

5. Br. " . . . be angry perpetually?" (*b*) "(How long) shall . . . "

6. "pour out" = s.H.w. "shed," (3); verse quoted Jer. x. 25.

8. Context shows that innocence is not claimed for his own generation.

9. Lit. "for the sake of the glory of Thy Name"; (*b*) "forgive" = make atonement for; Heb. kaphar, to cover.

10. (*c*) *i.e.* do not defer it to some future generation.

11. "preserve" or, with ancient versions, "set free."

12. *i.e.* such as Ammonites, Moabites, Edomites, etc., who rejoiced in Israel's discomfiture, cf. Ezk. xxv.

13. "We" (emph.).

PSALM LXXX. VICISSITUDES OF THE VINE

I. THE PRAYER (1-2). INVOCATION. "Give ear."
   REFRAIN (3). "Turn us . . . shine." "O God."

II. THE PLAINT (4-6). EXPOSTULATION. "How long?"
   REFRAIN (7). "Turn us . . . shine." "O God of Hosts."

III. THE PRAYER (8-18). REPRESENTATION. Israel a Chosen Vine.
   1. The Vine Rooted (8-11). Transplantation. National Prosperity.
   2. The Vine Ravaged (12-13). Devastation. National Adversity.
   3. The Vine Revived (14-18). Restoration. National Recovery.
   REFRAIN (19). "Turn us . . . shine." "O Jehovah, God of Hosts."

SUPERSCRIPT.—A Psalm of (or, for) Asaph.

SUBSCRIPT.—For the Chief Musician; upon Gittith (= winepresses).

PRIMARY ASSOCIATION.—Written possibly by a poet of the southern kingdom after the northern kingdom had been deported to Assyria and before the Babylonian exile. Subscript shows that the temple was still standing. "Upon Gittith" relates to the autumn festival of Tabernacles, hence the allusion to the vine and vineyard.

PROPHETIC ANTICIPATION.—The scene is the same as in the preceding psalms. Here the suffering remnant lament the national disaster but hope for the speedy revival to be brought in by the advent of Messiah the Branch, the predicted "shoot" from the house of David. They recognise that there is no true turning to God without the operation of the Spirit of God in their hearts.

PERSONAL APPLICATION.—Repentance is an essential condition to restoration and it must be God's own work. The wrath of God is a manifestation of His holiness. In the light of God's countenance is salvation (3). Our Lord is the true Benjamin (= Son of the right hand, cf. Ps. cx.) and Son of Man (17). He is the True Vine (John xv.). God gives a gleam of glory through the gloom (19). Christians should pray for Israel, "Visit this Vine," (14).

VERSE NOTES

1. "Shepherd of Israel," alludes to Gen. xlviii. 15; xlix. 24. (c) br. "Thou that sittest enthroned upon , . . "; "shine forth," i.e. manifest Thyself in power and glory for our deliverance: blaze out as from behind a cloud.

2. These three were of common descent from Rachel, regarded in Jer. xxxi. 15 as mother of the northern kingdom. All encamped west of the tabernacle and

marched in the immediate rear of the ark, Num. ii. 17 ff.; x. 21-24. The principal Benjamite towns belonged to the northern kingdom.

4. Title used denotes universal sovereignty; (b) see margin; perhaps = the "smoke" of divine wrath interposes as a thick cloud between their prayers and God; Lam. iii. 44.

6. "strife," i.e. a contending for the spoil among the petty states round about.

8. "a vine"; cf. Isa. v. 1-7; xxvii. 2-6; Jer. ii. 21; xii. 10, etc. A vine is good for nothing else but fruit, and its trailing branches make a striking image of dependence; so Israel. The vine was the emblem of the nation on the coins of the Maccabees. A colossal sculptured cluster of golden grapes overhung the porch of the second temple, and grapes of Judah still mark tombstones of the race in certain ancient cemeteries of Europe.

11. See note at lxxii. 8.

12. The causes of such dire distress are only hinted at in 18.

13. Remorseless enemies lay waste to Israel's land. It is of prophetic interest to note that the boar was the military ensign of the Roman power.

15. (b) i.e. tended it with loving care till it grew a sturdy vine. Note the repetition of the phrase and its connection (17). The psalmist here uses an argument similar to that of Moses, Num. xiv. 13-16.

16. (b) Fig. of the vine now dropped.

17. Though its primary reference was to Israel, yet the words undoubtedly point to Messiah, the True Vine. Many Jewish scholars have so explained it.

18. Note the virtual acknowledgment of backsliding.

PSALM LXXXI. HERALDING THE HOPE

I. THE FESTIVAL OF REJOICING (1-5). Psalmist's Call to Celebration.
   1. The Request (1-3). Three Classes. People—Levites—Priests.
   2. The Reason (4-5). Three Clauses. Statute—Law—Testimony.

II. THE FACT OF REDEMPTION (6-10). Jehovah's Compassion and Covenant.
   1. Decreed Deliverance (6).
   2. Answered Appeals (7). Selah.
   3. Covenant Conditions (8-10a).
   4. Promised Provision (10b).

III. THE FAILURE OF RESPONSIBILITY (11-16). Israel's Conduct and Consequences.
   1. The Refusal (11). To Hearken.
   2. The Result (12). Bane.
   3. The Request (13). To Hearken.
   4. The Result (14-16). Blessing.
     (a) Subjugation of Foes (14-15).
     (b) Satisfaction of Soul (16).

SUPERSCRIPT.—Asaph's.

PRIMARY ASSOCIATION.—Beyond the title we have no clue to writer and occasion. The psalm seems to have been composed for the Festival of Trumpets, that is, the civil New Year. Like all Asaphic compositions it is therefore connected with sanctuary worship.

PROPHETIC ANTICIPATION.—The third verse affords the clue. The moon is Israel's own symbol. The new moon with its returning light points to the return of Jehovah's favour toward Israel and to the reflection of that light upon the world. Lunar light is derived and dependent, and that which is first received is reflected back upon an otherwise dark sphere. In the preceding psalm, Israel cries for God's face to shine upon her as of old. Here we see the beginning of the answer. The blowing of trumpets on the first of the seventh month (commencement of the civil year) is the first of the set times which speak of Israel's blessing. The earlier festivals in the sacred year, namely Passover, First-fruits and Pentecost, typifying respectively the cross, the resurrection of Christ and the coming of the Holy Spirit, are some time past. Prophetically the extended interval between Pentecost and Trumpets sees the out-calling of the Church. The seventh month brings in the completion of the divine purposes with Israel in the forefront of the scene. The Feast of Trumpets typifies the recall and regathering of Israel; the Day of Atonement, their repentance and restoration; the Feast of Tabernacles is a memorial of redemption and experience of rest; see Lev. xxiii. and xxv.

PERSONAL APPLICATION.—Let us rejoice in "God our Strength" (1). Those whom God delivers He tests (7). "God loveth a cheerful giver," and He practises what He preaches (10). His blessing is limited only by our capacity to receive (10). It is important to listen to God's voice (11). Many blessings may be missed through heedlessness (13 ff). God punishes men by leaving them to their own course of self-will, which leads to ruin (12). Great are the results of loyalty to our Redeemer; He bestows victory (14) and abundance (16). Divine actions are affected by our attitude.

VERSE NOTES

1. The whole congregation addressed.
2. The Levites as musical leaders addressed; br. "Raise a psalm and sound the timbrel."

3. The priests as the ordained trumpeters addressed; "trumpet" = Heb. shophar, *i.e.* the horn (see Appendix XII) prescribed for the year of jubilee, in practice it was used at new year also. For the Christian's light, see 2 Cor. iv. 6.

5. "Joseph," Heb. here has the extended form "Jehoseph"; (*c*) "I" = Israel. The fact that in Egypt the Israelites toiled for masters whose language they could not understand, greatly increased the misery.

6. "His hands shall go free from the basket"; ref. to the method of carrying the bricks or clay; often represented in Egyptian paintings.

7. (*b*) *i.e.* a heavy black thundercloud.

8. "testify," *i.e.* to protest as a solemn warning.

9. Absolute fidelity to Jehovah was the fundamental principle of the Sinaitic covenant, embodied in the first "word" of the decalogue.

10. "I" (emph.); (*b*) shows His claim upon Israel's allegiance.

11. The trouble was not mere failure but revolt, though inattention often leads to disobedience, as one may see in a children's schoolroom.

13. Cf. Isa. xlviii. 18.

15. (*a*) cf. xviii. 44; lxvi. 3; "time" = time of prosperity.

16. The transition from indirect to direct address is common in Heb. though it sounds harsh to our ears.

PSALM LXXXII. JEHOVAH'S JUDGMENT OF THE JUDGES

I. ANNOUNCEMENT BY THE PSALMIST (1). PROCLAMATION. First Scene.

II. ARRAIGNMENT BY THE JUDGE (2-7). PRONOUNCEMENT.
   1. Sin of the Judges (2-4).
      (*a*) The Accusation (2).   Selah.
      (*b*) The Admonition (3-4).
   2. State of the Judges (5). Self-complacency.
   3. Sentence upon the Judges (6-7).
      (*a*) The Constitution (6).
      (*b*) The Condemnation (7).

III. APPEAL BY THE PSALMIST (8). PETITION. Final Scene.

SUPERSCRIPT.—A Psalm of (or, for) Asaph.

PRIMARY ASSOCIATION.—See remarks under Ps. lxxiii. The present psalm is dramatic in form and characterised by intensity as well as brevity. It is a companion composition to Ps. l., the only Asaphic psalm in Book II. In the latter we see the assembly of Israel gathered for judgment; in lxxxii. the authorities of Israel are gathered for judgment. Cf. Ps. lviii.

PROPHETIC ANTICIPATION.—One of the first effects of returning light (Ps. lxxxi.) is the exposure of evil in the nation. This must be judged and purged. God begins with the men that have administered the government as His representatives. Man having failed, there is no other refuge for the creature than in God Himself, who, in the person of Messiah upon the throne, will be the true successor to the administrators of earth (8).

PERSONAL APPLICATION.—"A man's opportunity determines his responsibility, and his responsibility (ability to respond) measures his accountability." This applies not only to individuals, but also to cities and nations. When God holds the scales of justice the balance is even. He is no respecter of persons. The office of one who rules is not only to defend but to deliver (3-4). Even princes of this world must die (7). Our Lord shows us why men continue to walk in darkness notwithstanding the shining of the light, John iii. 19-20.

VERSE NOTES

1. Lit. "assembly of El." God solemnly takes His place as president of the court amid the assembly of the rulers of His people; "gods" = Heb. elohim, the authorities in Israel (6).

2. The judges are accused of injustice and partiality; "wicked" = lawless, so 4. "Selah" connects the accusation with the admonition.

5. Jehovah's indignant aside; "They have no knowledge, neither will they get understanding," needful qualities for a judge; (c) the illegal administration of law, and the lack of justice and mercy, principles upon which all moral order is based, endanger the moral stability of the world.

6. "I" (emph.); "gods," see 1. Administrators are so called as being invested with divine authority to execute judgment in God's name; His representatives were responsible to judge in accordance with His character of righteousness and mercy; qtd. by our Lord (John x. 34 ff.), who reasons that if such unworthy representatives were called gods, was it blasphemy for God's special representative, His life and work testifying to the fact, to call Himself the Son of God? It is not, however, a mere verbal argument but a hint of the incarnation; "ye" (emph.).

7. (b) or, "And fall like (men), O ye princes!"

8. "Thou" (emph.); Israel's only resource is in God Himself; He alone is worthy to undertake the office as Sovereign and Judge, not only of Israel but of all the nations.

PSALM LXXXIII. AN ALLIANCE OF AGGRESSION

I. THE STRONG APPEAL (1). Desired Response from Jehovah.

II. THE SINFUL ALLIANCE (2-8).
    1. Confederation of Enemies (2-3). Their Expedition. "For."
    2. Contemplation of Enemies (4). Words quoted.
    3. Confederation of Enemies (5-8). Their Enumeration. "For." Selah.

III. THE STERN AVENGEMENT (9-15).
    1. Confusion of Enemies (9-11). Comparisons with History.
    2. Contemplation of Enemies (12). Words quoted.
    3. Confusion of Enemies (13-15). Comparisons with Nature.

IV. THE SACRED AIM (16-18). Desired Recognition of Jehovah.

SUPERSCRIPT.—A Song; Psalm of (or, for) Asaph.

SUBSCRIPT.—For the Chief Musician; upon Gittith (= winepresses).

PRIMARY ASSOCIATION.—This is the last of the Asaphic psalms. We cannot be positive as to writer and occasion, but there are strong coincidences between the words of the psalm and events recorded in 2 Chron. xx., where, perhaps, the answer is seen to the prayer. It is worthy of note that Jahaziel (II Chr: xx. 14) was of the sons of Asaph. However, Asaph was a prophet, and like Isaiah and others, may have foreseen things which were fulfilled in the days of kings later than David, so that we should not hastily assume that the title is misleading, lxxiii. note. The subscript indicates that it was intended for use at the autumn Festival of Tabernacles.

PROPHETIC ANTICIPATION.—Awaits a further fulfilment in the last days. The ten-kingdom confederacy here portrayed, adumbrates a final and similar gathering against Jerusalem on the part of neighbouring states, the old enemies of Israel. This allied assault seems to be organised after the destruction of the Beast and False Prophet, leaders of more distant foes. This prayer enshrines a confident prediction.

PERSONAL APPLICATION.—God can be attacked only through His people (2). Safe is the shelter where God secretes His saints (3). God's people are ever surrounded by foes (5), cf. Eph. vi. 12. A common enmity makes close amity. A common cause collects curious company (5), cf. Luke xxiii. 12. Consent may be spoken or silent, a look may convey loyalty or disloyalty. Exaltation of God's name is ever a worthy aim (18). Enemies of God and His people have but one alternative, either conversion or confusion for ever (16–17). Repeated victories may be the experience of every one of God's people (9–11). The believer has ever fresh foes to conquer. Hatred is a potent cement (3; cf. Luke xxiii. 12), but so also is love, Eph. iv. 16.

VERSE NOTES

1. "God" = El. God has only to speak the word and all enemy plans are defeated.

2. The plot to destroy the nation is a plot to frustrate Jehovah's purposes and to end His worship.

3. "hidden ones," cf. xxvii. 5.

5 ff. Note the tenfold confederacy followed by the sevenfold (complete) destruction (10–12). A glance at the map will show Israel to be surrounded by these enemies.

7. "Gebal" does not seem to be the place mentioned Ezk. xxvii. 9, but the northern part of the mountains of Edom, east of the Dead Sea, and known anciently as Gebalene.

8. The mention of Assyria as only an auxiliary of Moab and Edom suggests a date for the psalm before Assyria became a great power; (b) cf. marg.; Isa. xxxiii. 2. Moab and Ammon (type of the flesh) are singled out as the leaders; "children of Lot" = a term of opprobrium, in light of Gen. xix. 30–38.

9. See Judges iv.–v. This was regarded as a typical triumph, cf. Isa. ix. 4; x. 26. Like Jehoshaphat's enemies, they destroyed one another, 2 Chron. xx. 20–23; "river" = torrent.

10. (b) Contemptuous expression for the fate of unburied corpses; omit "as"; "earth" = ground.

11. (a) Midianite generals; "Oreb" = raven; "Zeeb" = wolf; (b) the Midianite kings; see Judges vii. 25; viii. 12.

12. "Who have said," i.e. the present enemies of Israel not the Midianites; "habitations" see margin; "possession," = inheritance, 2 Chron. xx. 11.

13. (a) Heb. "as a rolling thing," prob. "refers to the feather-light globular heads of the wild artichoke, which in autumn break off from the parent stem and in thousands scud over the plains rolling, leaping and bounding along" (Thomson's "Land and the Book"); (b) "stubble" i.e. dry, light broken straw and husks of grain whirled away from the threshing floors.

14. (b) Peasants set light to the luxuriant growth of thorns and briers before the rains come, in order to prepare the ground for the plough. Whole mountain sides are often seen in a blaze; cf. Isa. x. 16–19; Jer. xxi. 14.

16. i.e. disgraced by defeat and disappointed by failure of plans.

18. Zeal for the honour of Jehovah; cf. 2 Chron. xx. 6.

Book Three. II. Realization of the Divine Holiness: lxxxiv.-lxxxix.

1. Acclaimed in Israel's Restoration, lxxxiv.--lxxxv.

PSALM LXXXIV. THE HOME OF HOLY HEARTS

I. THE SAINT'S ASPIRATION (1-4).
1. The Ecstatic Exclamation (1). "Thy Tabernacles."
2. The Exalted Ambition (2). The Temple Courts.
3. The Expressive Illustration (3a). The Birds.
4. The Emphatic Confession (3b). The Temple Altars.
5. The Encouraging Benediction (4). "Thy House."
   Happy the Priestly Ministrants. Selah.

II. THE SAINT'S APPROACH (5-8).
1. The Encouraging Benediction (5).
   Happy the Pilgrim Worshippers.
2. The Exiles' Progression (6-7). Pilgrims' Progress.
3. The Earnest Supplication (8). "Hear my prayer." Selah.

III. THE SAINT'S ARRIVAL (9-12).
1. The Earnest Supplication (9). "Behold our Shield."
2. The Enlightening Declaration (10). "For." (Reason for I.).
3. The Exultant Explanation (11). "For." (Reason for II.).
4. The Encouraging Benediction (12).
   Happy the Pious Man.

SUPERSCRIPT.—A Psalm of (or, for) the sons of Korah.

SUBSCRIPT.—For the Chief Musician.

PRIMARY ASSOCIATION.—Composer and occasion unknown, but that it belongs to the period of the monarchy, and while the temple was yet standing, is shown by verse 9. The psalm is a companion to xlii.-xliii., having the same structure of three stanzas, but divided by "Selah" (see Introduction V.) instead of refrains. It may have originated in the same circumstances. Pss. xlii.-xliii.—Sadness at being debarred from access to the Sanctuary; lxxxiv.—Gladness at the privilege of access to the Sanctuary; cf. also Pss. lxi., lxiii. and xxvii. For the superscript, see xliv. notes.

PROPHETIC ANTICIPATION.—Shows the godly remnant of Israel in exile in the last days, yet happy in the anticipation of reaching their national home. Note that Messiah is now the link with God not the Law, which the nation had broken.

PERSONAL APPLICATION.—God Himself is the true goal of godly souls (2). Devout Israelites associated inward communion with outward aids. The Christian does not need the latter, yet in the assemblies of the saints God's presence may be realised in a special way, cf. Matt. xviii. 20. Divine grace shelters all who seek refuge in the presence of God, though they may be worthless as sparrows (Luke xii. 6) and wandering as swallows (3). The world is no place for the saint to build his nest (3). Praise is the overflowing joy of the soul conscious of the true source of its blessing (4). Let us qualify for the threefold happiness mentioned here (4, 5, 12). As the rains transform an eastern wilderness, so the Spirit of God transforms this world-wilderness in the path of His saints (6). Sorrows are transmutable into blessings; faith finds a source of refreshment even in the deepest valley (6). God preserves His pilgrims from fainting and falling. As they journey step by step, fresh strength is given (7); cf. Isa. xl. 31. Everyone will reach his destination (7b). There is grace for every step of the way and glory at the end of it (11). It is because God looks upon the face of His Anointed that the believer finds acceptance (9); cf. Eph. i. 6. Any service that keeps us near Him should be welcome (10). The sun that scorches the stubble heals the sick (11a with Mal. iv. 1-2). The One who is our Sun and Shield affords all we need of light and protection in this life (11). Grace is connected with the shield, glory with the sun (11). Be fully persuaded of the truth stressed in 11bc. Do we love the presence of God and the fellowship of saints (10)? The saint finds security, strength and serenity in God.

VERSE NOTES

1. "How lovely (or, lovable) . . ."; "tabernacles," Heb. plur. of majesty or magnitude, or may be allusion to the many buildings that composed the whole structure.

2. "soul . . . heart . . . flesh," = intensity of the whole being; "Living God" = El Chay. He is the final object of desire. To the Israelite His presence was associated only with His place.

3. There seems little doubt that in this verse "Yea . . . young," should be in parenthesis, the words "even Thine altars . . ." following on verse 2 in expansion of the expressed desire. Otherwise an ellipsis may be understood, "Even (so have I found) Thine . . ." It is a fact of history that small birds found sanctuary in the temple precincts. The nesting expresses complete confidence of safety; even birds offer suited testimony to the Creator's care. "altars," i.e. (a) the brazen

altar, typical of Christ crucified—Expiation of sin, and (b) the golden altar, typical of Christ risen—Intercession for saints.

4. Cf. 1 Chron. ix. 33.

5-7. Note interesting structure (Introversion); 5a corresponds to 7b, 5b to 7a, 6a to 6b.

5. "Blessed" = happy, so 4 and 12; (b) i.e. those whose minds were set upon the pilgrimage to Zion and therefore prepared to surmount all obstacles to get there; "in Thee," i.e. whatever the circumstances; "ways," i.e. Jehovah's.

6. "Vale of Baca" is certainly figurative and possibly literal. Heb. is derived from a root meaning "to weep" but the word is nowhere translated "weeping"; prob. ref. to a balsam tree exuding "tears" of gum and growing in arid places, the presence of such trees giving name to a vale on the highway to Jerusalem; yet there seems to be an intentional connection with weeping. (b) R.V. correct. Graphic picture of the transformation of scene in Eastern lands after heavy showers. So faith ever finds refreshment in trials, for God always responds with showers of blessing. The path to His presence may lead through a vale of tears, but the saint's desires are fulfilled (7).

7. i.e. at every step their strength increases.

8. Note title. "God of Hosts" speaks of power; "God of Jacob" speaks of grace.

9. R.V.m. preserves the Heb. parallel; "shield" = the king as God's representative and protector of the people; cf. lxxxix. 18. The poet regards himself as leader of the pilgrim band and so prays; they seek audience upon arrival at the temple. (b) i.e. graciously accept him and in him accept us. The welfare of the nation was bound up with that of such rulers as David, Jehoshaphat, Hezekiah and Josiah.

10. "better . . . thousand," i.e. spent elsewhere; (b) note R.V.m.; cf. work of the Korhites, esp. Heman and his sons; remembering also their history. Now they are not seeking the nearness of the priesthood, but are content to perform the humblest service, satisfied at last with their divinely appointed lot. "tents of wickedness" alludes to Num. xvi. 26; prophetic of apostate Jewry; "house," a permanent dwelling; "tent," a temporary abode.

11. As the sun is this world's light and life, so is God to His people.

PSALM LXXXV. ABIDING ACCEPTANCE

I. A GRATEFUL ACKNOWLEDGMENT (1-3). The Plea.
    Mercies to the Land. "Thy land."
    1. Restoration of Prosperity (1).
    2. Remission of Sins (2).
    3. Removal of Wrath (3).

II. A GREAT APPEAL (4-7). The Prayer based upon the Plea (I).
    1. Ardent Petition (4). "Turn us." Repentance—the manward side.
    2. Anxious Pleading (5-6).
    3. Ardent Petition (7). "Show us." Rescue—the Godward side.

III. A GODLY ATTITUDE (8). The Preparation based upon the Prospect (IV).
  1. Expectant Waiting (8*ab*).
  2. Essential Warning (8*c*).

IV. A GLAD ANTICIPATION (9-13).   The Prospect.
  Mercies to the Land. "Our land."
  1. Reassurance of Deliverance (9).
  2. Reconciliation of Attributes (10-11).
  3. Restoration of Prosperity (12-13). Material and Moral.

SUPERSCRIPT.—A Psalm of (or, for) the Sons of Korah.

PRIMARY ASSOCIATION.—Writer and occasion of this psalm are not certain. There seems to be some reference to Hezekiah's time and words, 2 Chron. xxix. 9–10; xxx. 8–9, 27, and there are connections with Ps. lxxx. God's people are still in the land, yet verses 4–7 show they were suffering under God's wrathful visitation, which by faith they anticipate as wholly removed. For superscript see notes to xliv.

PROPHETIC ANTICIPATION.—Here we see the attributes of God displayed in the salvation of His people. Though Messiah is not mentioned, the work of the cross is shown as the very foundation of permanent national blessing (10). "Truth is manifested in the fulfilment of glorious promise as well as in the execution of necessary judgment." Israel's history has been one of repeated departures from God, repeated chastisements and repeated returnings. Recognising this, the psalmist pleads for a final reconciliation and abiding acceptance with Israel going astray no more. Such blessed time was revealed to Daniel (ix. 24). The curse being removed the land becomes exceedingly fruitful, and ways of righteousness are Israel's response to the righteous rule of Messiah; cf. the culminating thought in the song of Moses, Deut. xxxii. 43.

PERSONAL APPLICATION.—Note the sixfold "Thou hast" of God's blessed work (1-3). God is a God of Salvation (4). It is always important to listen to what God has to say (8). The many voices of the world only produce a chorus of chaotic counsel. The favour of forgiveness (2) should not be followed by further folly on the part of the forgiven (8). The cross of Christ saw the eternal reconciliation of the divine attributes (10). Happy the time when earth and heaven shall be in true harmony (11). Christians now are set in the way of His steps, let us wholeheartedly follow in it (13).

VERSE NOTES

1. (b) or, "Thou hast turned the fortune of," see liii. 6. The line does not point to the return from the Babylonian captivity; see for example the use of the phrase Job xlii. 10.

2. "forgiven," Heb. indicates the removal of a burden; (b) "covered" concealed, *not* Heb. "kaphar" to cover (by atonement).

3. "taken away," lit. withdrawn.

4. A foretaste received, fulness now requested.

5. "draw out" = prolong.

6. "Wilt not *Thou* turn and quicken us."

7. "Shew," lit. cause us to see.

8 ff. The psalmist listens for Jehovah's answer to the people's prayer and conveys fresh assurance of blessing; cf. Hab. ii. 1. (a) God = El. (b) br. ". . . even to His saints," = favoured ones; (c) or, "That they turn not again to folly," *i.e.* of self-confidence and rebellion.

9. This "glory" is the manifest presence of Jehovah. It was true at Christ's first advent (John i. 14); it will be true at Christ's second coming.

10. "Lovingkindness and truth" (troth, or faithfulness). Note the fourfold harmony.

11. Cf. Isa. xlv. 8; "earth" or, land, s.H.w. 1, 9, 12.

12. In the Millennium material prosperity will accompany moral progress.

13. *i.e.* go before like a herald, the people following the divine leadership.

Book Three. II. Realization of the Divine Holiness: lxxxiv.-lxxxix.

2. Attained through Israel's Restorer, lxxxvi.-lxxxvii.

PSALM LXXXVI.   SUPPLICATION OF THE SUFFERING SERVANT

I. IMPLORATION (1–6).   Prayers and Pleas.
  1. Prayer (1a). For a hearing. Double Petition.
  2. Plea (1b). *The Psalmist's Affliction.* "I" (emph.).
  3. Prayer (2a). "Preserve."
  4. Plea (2a). A Favoured One.
  5. Prayer (2b). "Save."
  6. Plea (2b). A Trusting One.
  7. Prayer (3a). "Be gracious."
  8. Plea (3b).
  9. Prayer (4a). "Rejoice."
  10. Plea (4b).
  11. Plea (5). *The Lord's Attributes.* "Thou" (emph.).
  12. Prayer (6). For a hearing. Double Petition.

II. INVOCATION (7). **Waiting upon God—Personal.**
    1. The Resolve (7a).
    2. The Reason (7b). "for."

III. INCOMPARABLENESS OF JEHOVAH (8). **Central Thought.**
    1. Peerless in Person (8a).
    2. Peerless in Performance (8b).

IV. INTIMATION (9-10). **Worship of God—Universal.**
    1. The Reverence (9).
    2. The Reason (10). "for."

V. IMPLORATION (11-17). **Prayers and Pleas.**
    1. Prayers (11).
        (i) Prayer (11a). "Teach."
        (ii) Purpose (11a). "Walk."
        (iii) Prayer (11b). "Unify."
        (iv) Purpose (11b). "Fear."
    2. Product (12). The Psalmist's Praise.
    3. Pleas (13-15).
        (i) God's Goodness (13).
        (ii) Man's Wickedness (14). Manward—Godward.
        (iii) God's Goodness (15).
    4. Prayers (16-17a). Five Petitions.
    5. Product (17bc). The Persecutors' Portion.

SUPERSCRIPT.—A Prayer of David.

PRIMARY ASSOCIATION.—This is the only psalm in Book III ascribed to David. It was written perhaps on the same occasion as xxxiv. and lvi. or, possibly, during the time of Absalom's rebellion. The poet has harmonised fragments from other psalms and earlier scriptures into one beautiful prayer. Here are words that express the suppliant's deepest emotions. Note the frequency of divine titles. It is significant that the title "Adonai" occurs exactly seven times in keeping with the theme. Note also the intense personality of the prayer. In Ps. lxxxvi. the servant owns his Lord; in Ps. lxxxvii. the Lord owns His servants.

PROPHETIC ANTICIPATION.—Messiah associates Himself once more with His suffering people in the last days. In connection with the title "Servant" it is instructive to note that in the latter half of the Book of Isaiah it refers first to Israel (xl.-xlviii.) who proved unfaithful; then to Messiah (xlix.-lx.) the perfect Servant and Sufferer for the sins of others; and finally, to the faithful remnant (lxi.-lxvi.).

PERSONAL APPLICATION.—David trusted though he was tried. At one time or another most of the brief petitions in the psalm will find an echo in our hearts. Our hearts should ever be united, not divided or distracted by various interests (11*b*); cf. Phil. iii. 13-14. If we desire to walk in the truth, we must be taught God's way (11). However rough His way, it can never lack a song (11-12). Like David let us be wholehearted in devotion (11) and in praise (12). Divine goodness calls for human gratitude. New favours demand new songs. Our praise should be from a perfect heart and that perpetually (12). In the cross of Christ God has shown us a sure token of good (17). Not signs but the Scriptures are the proper support of faith.

VERSE NOTES

1. "I" (emph.); "poor" = afflicted, or oppressed.

2. "godly" = favoured one, or, beloved; Heb. word connected with that translated "lovingkindness" (5, 13, 15); covenant relationship pleaded; "Thou" (emph.), so also in 5, 15.

3. "Be gracious unto me . . ."

8. (*b*) br. "And there is nought like Thy works." Because (*a*) is true, therefore, He is *willing* to answer prayer; because (*b*), therefore He is *able* to do so.

9. Cf. Isa. lxvi. 23.

10. "Thou . . . Thou" (emph.).

11. "fear" = revere.

12. *i.e.* when the prayer (11) is answered.

13. "lowest Sheol" or, Sheol beneath.

15. "God" = El; cf. Exod. xxxiv. 6.

16. As margin; "son of Thy handmaid," syn. with "servant" but the term expresses a closer relationship as one born in the house, Gen. xiv. 14; cf. Ps. cxvi. 16.

17. Br. " . . . That they which hate me may be ashamed when they see that Thou . . ."

PSALM LXXXVII. THE MAJESTY OF MESSIAH'S METROPOLIS

I. ELECTION OF A DWELLING PLACE (1-2).
      Other Dwellings spoken of.

II. EMINENCE OF ZION (3). Her Glory as the City of God. Selah.

III. ESTIMATE OF NATIONAL HEROES (4).
      Many Nations spoken of.

IV. EMINENCE OF ZION (5). Her Glory as the Capital of Nations.

V. ENROLMENT OF THE PEOPLES (6).
All Peoples spoken of. Selah.

VI. EMINENCE OF ZION (7). Her Glory as the Confession of Saints.

SUPERSCRIPT.—A Psalm of (or, for) the Sons of Korah; a Song.

SUBSCRIPT.—A Song; a Psalm of the Sons of Korah; for the Chief Musician; set to Mahalath Leannoth.

PRIMARY ASSOCIATION.—Writer uncertain, but occasion most probably is the translation of the Ark to Zion. It "expands the thought of lxxxvi. 9 in the style and spirit of prophecy, and is terse, abrupt and enigmatic." Note abrupt introduction of the theme (1) and abrupt conclusion (7). Repetition in superscript and subscript is for emphasis. "Mahalath Leannoth" for "mahalath" (br. vocalized "m(e)holoth") cf. Ps. lii. note; "leannoth" is from Heb. verb meaning to celebrate by responsive shouting; therefore read phrase, "Dancings with shoutings;" ref. to 2 Sam. vi. 14 and 1 Chron. xv. 28–29. The musical directions are in complete harmony with the last verse. Note how the transference of these directions from superscript of lxxxviii. to subscript of lxxxvii. according to Dr. Thirtle's suggestion (see Introduction V.) disposes of the much discussed difficulty of ascribing the former to two different authors. The designation "Song" (Heb. shir) could not be truly applied to the sorrowful tones of lxxxviii. The Song of the Procession, lviii.; the Entry into Zion, xxiv.; the Joy of the Entry, lxxxvii.; the Offering of Worship, cv. with 1 Chron. xvi.

PROPHETIC ANTICIPATION.—This is clearly indicated by the outline analysis. Zion was, and will be (a) the Sojourning-place of the divine presence; (b) the Seat of the divine government; (c) the Sanctuary of the divine worship. Following the translation of R.V. verse 4 is generally interpreted to mean that the nations mentioned will attain the rights of citizenship in Zion. Against this, however, is the inclusion of Babylon and Philistia, nations which prophecy threatened with total extinction, Isa. xiv. 22–23; Zeph. ii. 5; Amos i. 8. Moreover the names used for Egypt (Rahab = pride) and Babylon (Babel = confusion) are terms of disparagement. It seems better then to read as A.V. and understand God as drawing a contrast between these nations with their pride in national heroes and Zion with her truly great men. That Gentile peoples will be "enrolled" among the people of God, including Egypt and Ethiopia (Cush) is clear enough in the prophetic Scriptures; see Isa. xix. 23–25. Here is a foreshadowing (6) of the great truth that for entrance into the Kingdom a "new birth" is requisite, not cultural progress, not social reform, and not regulations of any "League of Nations."

PERSONAL APPLICATION.—The world needs to be reminded that God has chosen Jerusalem as His earthly "seat" and loves the city (1–2). Nations have sought to make their capitals glorious, but Zion's glorious prospect far surpasses the dreams of men (3). Blessed are they whose knowledge of God is experimental (4). The rebirth of nations is by the rebirth of individuals (6). Those who possess the franchise of the Heavenly City may sing now, "All my springs are in Thee" for Christ is there (7); see Rev. xxi. 22–23. The citizen-roll of the "Jerusalem above" is kept by God Himself, not by any official of church or state.

VERSE NOTES

1. Br. "His . . . doth Jehovah love, (He loveth) the gates . . ."

2. "gates . . ." poetic term for the city with especial reference to its activities. The gates were the places of popular concourse, for the administration of justice, for business transactions, etc. They were also the places of ingress and egress for the pilgrims attending for worship; "dwellings of Jacob," ref. esp. to the places of the ark's sojourn, viz. Shiloh, 1 Sam. i. 3ff.; Bethshemesh, vi. 13; Kirjath-jearim, vii. 1; Gibeah, 2 Sam. vi. 3–4; Obed-edom's house, vi. 10–12. "Jacob" implies divine grace there manifested.

3. May refer to the prophetic promises generally; but it is possible to translate, "Thou art gloriously bespoken" (lit. gloriously spoken) i.e. betrothed. In old Heb. (Cant. viii. 8) and modern Arabic (so also in Chinese) the word "spoken" applied to a maiden means bespoken in marriage. Intensive form of Heb. verb indic. spoken repeatedly.

4. "Rahab," i.e. Egypt, the world power of the south; "Babylon" the world power of the north; Philistia, a warrior nation; Tyre, a commercial state.

5. Psalmist again speaks. The A.V. reading is to be preferred, see notes under "Prophetic Anticipation."

6. i.e. reckon, when He registers the peoples; official confirmation of citizen rights.

7. Br. "And singing as well as dancing (shall they chant), "All my springs,"= fountains (metaphorical). True prophetically because Messiah will be there enthroned as Zion's glory; "singers," lit. "they that shout," see subscript.

Book Three. II. Realization of the Divine Holiness: lxxxiv.-lxxxix.

3. Attained in Israel's Restoration, lxxxviii.-lxxxix.

PSALM LXXXVIII.   SUPPLICATION OF A SUBMERGED
SOUL

I. THE APPEAL (1-2).
  1. Continual Prayer (1).
  2. Cogent Pleading (2).

II. THE AFFLICTION (3-8).
  1. Dissolution Expected (3-6).
  2. Divine Displeasure Exhibited (7).   Waves of Wrath.
  3. Desolation Experienced (8).

III. THE APPEAL (9-14).
  1. Continual Prayer (9).
  2. Cogent Pleading (10-12).   Questions.
  3. Continual Prayer (13).
  4. Cogent Pleading (14).   Question.

IV. THE AFFLICTION (15-18).
  1. Dissolution Expected (15).
  2. Divine Displeasure Exhibited (16-17).   Waves of Wrath.
  3. Desolation Experienced (18).

SUPERSCRIPT.—Maschil of (or, for) Heman the Ezrahite.

PRIMARY ASSOCIATION.—Heman was celebrated for wisdom, 1 Kings iv. 31; 1 Chron. vi. 33, 44; xxv. 4-5, which expressly attests he was sometimes inspired of God in his utterances. He was a Kohathite by birth, but reckoned with Zerah of Judah, because among Levites dwelling there (1 Chron. ii. 6); Ezrahite = Zerahite. For similar examples of reckoning cf. Elkanah, 1 Sam. i. 1, and the young Levite, Judges xvii. 7. For note on the double superscript (A.V.) see lxxxvii. This psalm is an elegy, the saddest song in the Psalter. The writer is in deep but not utter despair, for prayer proves the presence of a lingering hope. Note also his title for God (1). The psalm should be viewed in connection with the next, which is very opposite in sentiment.

PROPHETIC ANTICIPATION.—"Maschil" indicates the viewpoint of the psalm. It has special instruction for the "wise" at the time of the end. Here Israel is seen afflicted in soul under a deep sense of a broken law. If the physical affliction of the psalmist was a form of leprosy, which would account for the language used, this would have a typical significance concerning Israel. God has to bring the nation to a realisation of its need before He can reveal His remedy.

PERSONAL APPLICATION.—Like the psalmist, let us cling tenaciously to God in the dark. When we are afflicted there should be confession of sin, not censure of God (7, 16). "There is only one psalm like this in the Bible to intimate the rareness of the experience, but there is one to assure the most desperately afflicted that God will not forsake him." There is ever a Heart behind the Hand that applies the rod. God chastises His chosen. Acquaintances may be many, but friends are few; those who truly love us are fewer still (18).

VERSE NOTES

3. He pleads the urgency of his need; "full," lit. saturated.

4. He is regarded as a dying man; cf. Num. xvi. 31–33.

5. "slain," i.e. in battle, whose corpses were flung into a common, nameless grave.

6. (a) i.e. treated as though actually dead; "lowest pit"= nether world.

8. Acquaintance, i.e. familiar friends. Like Job, he seems to describe himself as a leper, Job xix. 21; xxxi. 34; or, as a hopeless prisoner, Job iii. 23; xiii. 27; xix. 8.

9. Sunken, lack-lustre eyes are a sure sign of suffering.

10. Br. "Wilt Thou do wonders for the dead? Shall the shades . . ."; "shades"= the dead viewed as weak and nerveless ghosts. Remember that the viewpoint is that of an Israelite whose hopes are earthly not heavenly.

11. To proclaim God's lovingkindness and faithfulness is ever the delight of God's people, xl. 10; xcii. 2. These two attributes are the keynote of the next psalm; (b) see margin; cf. Rev. ix. 11 (name of the angel of the abyss).

13. Br. "But as for me, unto Thee, Jehovah, have I cried for help." He contrasts himself with the dead—he, at least, can still pray! While there is life there is hope. (b) the first thought of each day shall be prayer.

15. "I have borne Thy terrors (till) I am distracted."

16 ff. "The fiery streams of Thy wrath have gone over me; Thine alarms have made an end of me; They have surrounded me . . . have compassed . . ."

18. In this flood of calamity there was none to hold out a helping hand; (b) "My familiar friends are darkness," cf. Job xvii. 14. Note the three circles of companionship, expressing three degrees of devotion and a ripening experience of intimacy—(a) acquaintance, (b) friend, (c) lover.

PSALM LXXXIX.   THE CHARACTER OF THE COVENANT

I. **THE INTRODUCTORY AVOWAL (1–4).** The Psalmist's Confession.
   1. Perpetual Praise (1).
   2. Proclaimed Purpose (2–4). The Theme. Retrospection. Selah.
      (a) Divine Principles (2).
      (b) Divine Promises (3–4).

II. **THE INCOMPARABLE CREATOR (5–18).**
   The Divine Character Extolled.
   1. His Praise in the Heavens (5–7). Celestial Beings.
      (a) Its Rendition (5).
      (b) Its Reason (6–7).
   2. His Power in Nature and History (8–14).
   3. His Praise in the Earth (15–18). Terrestrial Beings.
      (a) Its Rendition (15–16).
      (b) Its Reason (17–18).

III. **THE INVIOLABLE COMPACT (19–37).**
   The Davidic Covenant Elaborated.
   1. Promises concerning David's Self (19–27). (cf. 2). Faithfulness and Lovingkindness.
   2. Permanence of the Covenant (28). (see verse 3).
   3. Promise concerning David's Seed (29–32). (see verse 4).
   4. Promises concerning David's Self (33). (see verse 2).
   5. Permanance of the Covenant (34–35). (see verse 3).
   6. Promises concerning David's Seed (36–37). (see verse 4). Selah.

IV. **THE INCOMPATIBLE CIRCUMSTANCES (38–45).** The Distressful Contrast Emphasised. Protests of the Psalmist on Present Plight.
   1. Rejected by God (38–40). "*Thou*" repeated.
   2. Reproached by Men (41). "All."
   3. Rejected by God (42–45). "Thou" repeated. Selah.

V. **THE IMPASSIONED APPEAL (46–52).** The Psalmist's Cry.
   1. Powerful Pleas (46–51). The Throb. Expostulation.
      (a) Plaint (46).
      (b) Plea (47–48). "Remember" my frailty. Selah.
      (c) Plaint (49).
      (d) Plea (50–51). "Remember" my reproach.
   2. Perpetual Praise (52). Doxology to Psalm and to Book III.

SUPERSCRIPT.—Maschil of Ethan the Ezrahite.

PRIMARY ASSOCIATION.—Ethan's other name was Jeduthun, see 1 Chron. xxv. and xvi. 41–42. He was one of Solomon's wisest counsellors (1 Kings iv. 31) and must have known the divine declaration recorded 1 Kings xi. 9-13. This would come as a shock to all who had rejoiced in the covenant which God had made with David, 2 Sam. vii. With that covenant in mind Ethan here utters his impassioned acknowledgment and appeal to Jehovah. It is possible that Ethan outlived Solomon and saw the break-up of the kingdom. See also notes to Ps. lxxxviii. In light of vv. 38-45 some think the psalm must have been written at a date just prior to the Babylonian captivity by a poet of the same name. It is true that the last kings of the Davidic line were cut off or deposed in early life but this divine judgment was doubtless foreseen by the psalmist-prophet.

PROPHETIC ANTICIPATION.—The eventual restoration of Israel is seen to rest upon Jehovah's faithfulness to His covenant with David. Because of national apostasy, consistency with the divine character of absolute holiness demands chastisement upon God's people and their genuine repentance before the terms of the covenant can be fulfilled. Elsewhere we have seen that expiation of sin by Messiah was necessary before God could righteously redeem His promises. The last section anticipates the events referred to in Rom. xi. 1-2, 11-15, which culminate in the "time of Jacob's trouble" immediately preceding the coming of the Deliverer out of Zion. At that point the godly remnant will undoubtedly take up and plead with God the words which the Spirit has prepared for them in this and in other psalms. The full answer to the final appeal is given in the Fourth Book. Only in Christ is much that is here recorded fulfilled, e.g. verses 19, 26, 27, 28, 36. The covenant referred to is a covenant of grace ratified by His precious blood.

PERSONAL APPLICATION.—Note the two keywords "faithfulness" and "lovingkindness," both occurring seven times, though variously translated, the former in vv. 1, 2, 5, 8, 24, 33, 49; the latter in vv. 1, 2, 14, 24, 28, 33, 49. Loving kindness is connected with Jehovah's character, faithfulness with Jehovah's covenant. These are excellent themes for grateful and perpetual song. Both are related to performances in the past and to promise for the future. With the faithfulness of the living God contrast the futility of pagan gods, 1 Kings xviii. 27; cf. 1 Peter iv. 17. Jehovah Himself is the source and the subject of His people's joy (16). Sin brings chastisement but cannot annul the promise (30 ff). Paternal relation involves the duty of discipline, Prov. xxiii. 13 ff; Heb. xii. Men may violate God's laws, but He will never violate His covenant (34). "God works on a bigger scale than one man's lifetime (47)."

VERSE NOTES

1. (b) *i.e.* aloud and publicly.

2. Words of Ethan reminding Jehovah of His promise; note same verbs occur in 4. LXX and other ancient versions read, "For Thou hast said . . . (Thy faithfulness shalt Thou establish in the very heavens). Thou saidst, 'I have made . . .'"

3-4. Summary of the promise to David and his seed; "David" may be regarded as a dynastic name.

6. Jehovah is unique among celestial beings.

8. His power and faithfulness are pledge of performance.

9-10. Pronouns emphatic; "pride" = proud swelling. The sea represents the most turbulent and formidable powers of nature, and is emblematic of the nations. At the Red Sea, God proved His sovereignty over both. "Rahab" (pride) = Egypt.

11. "Thine . . . Thine . . . Thou" all emph.

13. Lit. "Thine (emph.) is an arm with might . . ."; arm and hand denote the exercise of power not merely its possession.

14. Righteousness is the principle of justice; judgment is the application of it, the basis of all true government; (b) br. " . . . shall attend Thy presence." These attributes are personified as attendants to do God's bidding rather than as couriers to run before.

15. Note margin; Lev. xxiii. 24; Num. xxix. 1. The trumpet sound was the signal which called Israel in the wilderness to attention, and especially on solemn occasions; perhaps a hint here of the events recorded 2 Chron. xxxv. 1, 15, 18.

18. "shield," metaphor for the king as protector of the people.

19. "Then," *i.e.* the well-known occasion referred to in 3; "have laid," *i.e.* conferred help (as a gift) = endued him with power to help his people as well as assigning him the office; "one that . . .," cf. 2 Sam. xvii. 10; "chosen" cf. 1 Kings viii. 16.

23. "And," br. But.

24. "But," br. And.

25. Cf. Pss. lxxii. 8; lxxx. 11.

26. "My Father . . . My God (El)," cf. John xx. 17, of Messiah. The Son acknowledges the Father (26); the Father honours the Son (27-28).

27. "I also" corresponds to the "He" in 26; David's posterity included in his person; points to fulfilment in Messiah; cf. Rev. i. 5; br. "appoint him as firstborn, Most high above . . ."

30 ff. "children," lit. sons; cf. 1 Kings ix. 6-7.

32. "transgression" = revolt.

33. Br. "But . . . not break off from him; neither be false to My faithfulness," 2 Sam. vii. 15.

34. S.H. verb in v. 31 = to profane.

35. "Once . . ." *i.e.* once for all.

37. "faithful witness," prim. ref. to the sun according to the Heb. parallelism, but symbolic, (a) of God, Jer. xlii. 5; Job xvi. 19. Rom. iii. 3—He attests His own oath; (b) of Christ, Rev. i. 5; Rev. iii. 14.

38 ff. The present realities seem to be in appalling contrast to the terms of the covenant. Sin came in to interrupt and delay the promised blessing, cf. 1 Kings. xi. 11–13.

38. "Thou" (emph.) . . ."; the audacity of this expostulation is the boldness of faith not of irreverence.

39. "abhorred"=disowned.

40. The king is identified with the nation whose representative he was; "hedges" = fences, lxxx. 12.

41. "neighbours," i.e. surrounding states once tributary to Israel.

42. Malignant delight of the foes aggravates the bitterness of Israel's adversity.

43. i.e. had to give way in battle.

44. "Brightness," i.e. the lustre of the kingdom.

45. "youth" = prime.

47. The psalmist desires to see the fulfilment of the promises in his own lifetime.

48. "live" = live on; "man,"=strong man, see Appendix X.

49. The prayer resumed, cf. 1; returning to the thoughts first expressed.

50. (b) br. as margin; ref. to Israel's enemies, cf. 2 Kings xxiv. 2; ellipsis br. "that of."

51. (b) i.e. like a rabble hooting and insulting him wherever he goes. It is interesting to note that the Jewish Targum interprets the words of the delay of Messiah's advent, cf. 2 Peter iii. 3-4.

Book Four. *Israel's Relapse and Recovery: xc.–cvi.*

This book shows Jehovah renewing His relationship with His ancient people. Israel is the representative nation. In her national history is mirrored the story of man in general. The future blessing of the world under Messiah's righteous rule is bound up with the restoration of Israel to her true position at the head of the nations. In this "Numbers" Book we find many references to the wilderness wanderings of Israel, and figures used (hills, floods, grass, etc.) are mostly those suggesting the earth. Four is the "earth" symbol. For further notes see Introduction.

ANALYSIS.

I. RECOGNITION OF COVENANT RELATIONSHIP. The Redeemer's Person, xc.–xciii. Rest for the Earth desired.

  1. Contrasted Characters, xc.–xci. Man and Messiah.

  2. Consequent Celebration, xcii.–xciii.

II. REVELATION OF COVENANT RELATIONSHIP. The Redeemer's Presence, xciv.–c. Rest for the Earth anticipated.

  1. Appeal for the Advent, xciv.

  2. Anthems of the Advent, xcv.–c.

III. REJOICING IN COVENANT RELATIONSHIP. The Redeemer's Praise, ci.–cvi. Rest for the Earth enjoyed.

  1. Essential Preparation, ci.–cii.

    (*a*) The King's Purpose, ci.

    (*b*) The King's Passion, cii.

  2. Ensuing Praise, ciii.–cvi. The Nation's Retrospect.

Book Four. *I. Recognition of Covenant Relationship. The Redeemer's Person: xc.–xciii.*

1. Contrasted Characters, xc.–xci. Man and Messiah.

PSALM XC. LAMENTATION OF THE LAWGIVER

I. THE IMMUTABILITY OF GOD (1–2). "Jehovah-El."

II. THE INFIRMITY OF MAN (3–11). Frailty and Failure.

  1. Declaration (3).

  2. Demonstration (4).

3. Declaration (5-6).
4. Demonstration (7).
5. Declaration (8).
6. Demonstration (9).
7. Declaration (10ac).
8. Demonstration (10d).
9. Declaration (11).

III. THE INTENSITY OF MOSES (12-17). Based upon I and II.
    1. In Appeal for Divine Comprehension (12). "Teach us."
       Computation of our days. Guidance.
    2. In Appeal for Divine Restoration (13). "Thy Servants."
    3. In Appeal for Divine Compensation (14-15). "Satisfy us."
       Consolation all our days. Gratification.
    4. In Appeal for Divine Restoration (16). "Thy Servants."
    5. In Appeal for Divine Commendation (17). "Be kindly disposed to us."
       Confirmation of our works. Graciousness.

SUPERSCRIPT.—A Prayer of Moses the man of God.

PRIMARY ASSOCIATION.—This is probably the oldest of all the Psalms and was written by Moses almost certainly during the thirty-eight years of Israel's penal wanderings in the wilderness. The psalm is properly understood only if Israel's experience at that time be kept in view. Consider, for example, verse 10. While it is true that life at best is very brief, for the people of God the closing years of life are not necessarily "labour and sorrow." On the contrary see Prov. iv. 18, Ps. xcii. 14. Israelites condemned to "fall" in the wilderness would all be from sixty to eighty years of age towards the close of the wandering period, Num. xiv. 29-35; xxvi. 63-65. At the announcement of the divine judgment, the effect upon the sinners is well described as "panic-stricken" (7b), and verse 9 has special force in the circumstances. Other significant points cannot fail to be noticed. Jehovah's connection with the nation is apparent and Moses looks to Him to renew relations so broken, and that blessing and beauty may again be upon them as a people favoured by God. "Man of God" (title); seven persons in the Old Testament are specially so designated and four are unnamed. In the New Testament Timothy is the only one thus called. It is a title given by the Spirit of God to a man raised up in a time of crisis to represent Him.

PROPHETIC ANTICIPATION.—Again we hear the voice of the godly remnant in the last days under a realisation of national sin and necessary discipline, turning to Jehovah in earnest entreaty for restoration.

PERSONAL APPLICATION.—A psalm of man and his Maker. God is an eternal habitation for the soul, but man, alas, seldom takes advantage of the open door (1). Though so lofty God is not inaccessible (1). He is a timeless Being; moments with Him can do the work of centuries (4). Death and decay result not from finite being, but from sin (7-8). The same sun that strengthens the sick can smite the strong; the same light that solaces the saint can strike the sinner (8). Secrets cannot be shut out from the searchlight of the divine gaze (8). How different (12) are the efforts of men to "kill time" in a ceaseless round of senseless amusements. Satan encourages men to banish all thought of God's righteous anger against sin (11-12). The only joyful life is one satisfied with the love of God (14). The creature can never be satisfied apart from his Creator (14). Moses prays that the divine discipline may prove effectual—a worthy example (16). To glory in the possession of things apart from God is pride (10c), cf. 1 John ii. 16. God is said to repent when, having vindicated His justice in punishing the sin, He so deals with the sinner as to restore him to gladness instead of sadness. God does not change. It is His unchanging principle to treat men according to their attitude to Him. It is the sinner who by true penitence changes his relation to God, see 13.

VERSE NOTES

1. "Lord," Heb. Adonai = a title having special ref. to the earth, see Appendix II; br. "Thou (emph.) hast been a habitation for us"; "habitation," s.H.w. only xci. 9 and Deut. xxxiii. 27. (b) i.e. in successive generations.

2. Mountains were regarded as the most ancient parts of the earth; (b) "or" = ere; "world," = the habitable earth; (c) lit. "Thou art El (Mighty One)" = God of power.

3 ff. The emphasis is not so much upon the brevity of human life as upon the fact that it is at God's absolute disposal; br. "Thou makest man (enosh = frail man) return to dust"; emphasises the dissolution of the body into its constituent elements. (b) refers to the creative fiat which replaces the old generation by a new; death and life are in continual alternation; "children of men," = lit. sons of Adam.

4. "For," i.e. though one should outlive even Methuselah it is nothing compared to eternity. For converse of this line see 2 Peter iii. 8. (c) i.e. to the unconscious sleeper. To God time has no existence; all is an eternal present.

5. (a) i.e. like a building suddenly swept away in an Eastern cloudburst.

7. "troubled" = lit. dismayed, or, panic-stricken; see notes.

9. The lives of Israel's "men of war" closed under a cloud, the sentence of death because of unbelief, Num. xiv. 29; (b) "a sigh" or, a moan.

10. See note under "Primary Association"; br. "travail and vanity."

11. (a) "anger," i.e. against sin; (b) i.e. "According to the (present) dread so is the (coming) wrath."

12. "So" = so then . . . ; "number," in the circumstances this could actually be done.

13. "Return" or, turn; "how long," i.e. shall we wait for thy "turning"; the expostulation not of impatience but of wistful yearning, cf. Deut. xxxii. 36; "repent," see note under "Personal Application."

14. Israel still in the dark night of trouble deeply desires the dawn (prophetically).

15. i.e. let the joy of restoration be proportionate to the depth of humiliation, Isa. lxi. 7. This prayer was partially answered in the great triumphs God gave the nation upon their entrance into Canaan; "afflicted us," cf. s.H.w. "humble thee," Deut. viii. 2, 3, 16.

16. "work," = working; i.e. let it be manifested in deliverance. "their children," cf. Num. xiv. 31, 33.

17. "favour" or, pleasantness, i.e. graciousness; "Lord" as 1; "work of our hands" is a phrase characteristic of Deuteronomy, where it appears seven times. While the ordinary undertakings of daily life may be included, service for God is also in view. May there not be, too, a hint of their special work in the building of the Tabernacle? Exod. xxxv.–xxxvi.

PSALM XCI. MESSIAH AS THE MODEL MAN

I. ANNOUNCEMENT THROUGH THE NATIONAL LEADER (1). Preservation Promised. The Theme. "He."

II. AVOWAL OF THE FAITHFUL ISRAELITE (2). Purpose Proclaimed. Confession. "My Refuge."

III. ANNOUNCEMENT THROUGH THE NATIONAL LEADER (3–8). Preservation Promised. "Thou . . . thy."

IV. AVOWAL OF THE FAITHFUL ISRAELITE (9a). Profession Proclaimed. Citation. "My Refuge."

V. ANNOUNCEMENT THROUGH THE NATIONAL LEADER (9b–13). Preservation Promised. "Thou . . . thy."

VI. AVOWAL OF THE FAITHFUL JEHOVAH (14–16). Purpose Proclaimed. "He." The Troth.

PRIMARY ASSOCIATION.—There seems little doubt that Moses is the writer of this psalm as well as of xc., in which case all the Scriptures quoted in Matt. iv. are from his writings. Like Ps. xc. it was most probably composed at the beginning of the thirty-eight years of the wilderness wanderings. The two psalms are in striking contrast, the former presenting primarily the condition of the faithless Israelites under divine judgment, and the latter indicating those who came under God's special protection. These would need comfort amid what their own eyes saw of the reward of the wicked (7-8). Note the significance of the word "tent" (10). This is one of the "dialogue" psalms, see analysis. The words of the psalmist in I, III and V are virtually utterances of the Spirit of God, and may be the result of a direct revelation to Moses.

PROPHETIC ANTICIPATION.—Here the perfect Pattern is portrayed. Undoubtedly a Messianic psalm in which we see Christ associating Himself with Israel. His faithfulness as the Second Man is set over against the failure of the first man (Ps. xc.). The latter lost God as his "habitation," but, Christ though Lord of all, took the place of absolute dependence and fully maintained it. Thus as the perfect Man owning the God of Israel, the promises are made His. His perfect preservation until the moment when "He was delivered up for our offences" is described and the victory of the cross followed by the exaltation is hinted at (13-14). v. 15 shows God's personal response to Christ's personal righteousness. No doubt there is an application also to the faithful remnant during the last days. Concerning Satan's quotation of v. 11 when tempting the Lord, it is significant that the tempter knew this psalm to be Messianic. He wished to imply that Moses was on his side! But God keeps His own only while they walk in the way. Satan omitted this important part and added the words, "at any time." For our Lord to put God to the test would have been to sin like the Israelites, Exod. xvii. 7; Deut. vi. 16. Satan tried to turn Him from His great purpose by accepting a present deliverance. The second attempt recorded was through Peter, Matt. xvi. 22. Note that the adversary also failed to quote verse 13 which concerns himself!

PERSONAL APPLICATION.—The solemn sadness of xc. gives place to the sunny gladness of xci. Divine protection is ever assured to those who abide in the "secret place" of the Most High (1). In the company of God are the true safeguards of life. Is "God my

Refuge" true in practice as well as profession (2)? God desires His people to remain unafraid whatever happens around (5). The godly have two "homes"—one shelters the inner life, the other shelters the outward life. Note "dwelling-place" (9b) and "tent" (10b); the former is permanent, the latter is temporary. No *evil* can befall those who trust in Jehovah (10). Angels are the protectors of the saints in connection with the outer activities of life; see Heb. i.14. They are not charged to remove stones from the way, but to lift us over difficulties. Hindrances are intended to exercise our faith (11-12). There are many moderns who change the word of God by adding to it, or omitting some important part of the context. Such are consciously or unconsciously the tools of Satan (11-12), see "Prophetic Anticipation." We are specially warned against satanic emissaries professing to be messengers of light (2 Cor. xi. 14-15)—who misapply God's word and often use such phrases as, "In the light of modern discovery," and "In the interests of progressive knowledge." Note the threefold condition of true deliverance (14-15); (a) Clinging to Jehovah; (b) Confessing His Name; (c) Calling upon Him. God's own presence is the best answer to the saint's call (15b). The crowning promise to the believer is a rapturous experience of a full salvation (16).

VERSE NOTES

1. "secret place" = covert or hiding-place. Prophetically of the Jewish remnant may be connected with Rev. xii. 13-14; "shadow" indicates shelter or protection, cf. 4.

2. Br. "I will say unto Jehovah, 'My Refuge . . . I will trust.'"

3 ff. Assurance to the Israelites excluded from the class referred to in preceding psalm, where see notes.

3. "He (emph.)"; (b) omit "And."

4. Cf. Deut. xxxii. 11; Pss. xvii. 8; lxiii. 7; power and gentleness united; "truth" = troth, or faithfulness; this rather than our trust is the true defence. Our faith grasps the shield; "buckler," Heb. only here, prob. = coat of mail.

5. *i.e.* sudden assault by night and open assault by day.

6. Plague and pestilence are here personified as destroying angels.

7. "Though a thousand . . .," emphasis on "thee."

8. "wicked" = lawless.

9. Br. "Because thou (emph.) (hast said) to Jehovah, 'My Refuge' . . . hast made . . ." The profession (2) is here taken up by the Spirit and repeated. "habitations," = place of asylum, cf. xc. 1.

11. Quoted in part by Satan, Matt. iv. 6, Luke iv. 10-11; see note under "Prophetic Anticipation"; cf. Satan's misquotation, Gen. iii. 15.

12. (b) *i.e.* lest he stumble and fall.

13. "lion," = roarer; "serpent" or, sea-monster, s.H.w. Gen. i. 21. Victory as well as preservation promised; the overcoming of all obstacles whether overt or covert; whether violence or cunning, cf. Deut. viii. 15.

14. "set...," *i.e.* in safety from foes; "known..." *i.e.* the acknowledgment of God in His revealed character; it is the knowledge of loving intimacy not mere intellectual apprehension; "set... high" means more than rescue and security, it implies a life lived nearer to God Himself.

15. "I, even I..."; "honour" or, glorify.

16. "long life" = lit. length of days; see Ps. xxi. 4; Deut. xxx. 20; ctr. 7-8 and the destiny of the Israelites in Ps. xc. "satisfy," cf. xc. 14.

Book Four. I. Recognition of Covenant Relationship: xc.-xciii.

2. Consequent Celebration, xcii.-xciii.

PSALM XCII.   A SONG IN THE SANCTUARY

I. FIRST ATTITUDE OF THE PSALMIST (1-5).   Worship of Jehovah.
    1. The Excellence of Praise (1-3).
    2. The Explanation for Praise (4).
    3. The Exclamation of Praise (5).

II. FLOURISHING OF THE GODLESS (6-8).   Passing Prosperity of the Lawless Ones.

III. FALL OF THE ENEMIES (9).   Their Perdition.   "Thine."

IV. FAVOUR TO THE PSALMIST (10).   His Restoration. (Central Thought).

V. FALL OF THE ENEMIES (11).   Their Perdition.   "Mine."

VI. FLOURISHING OF THE GODLY (12-15a).   Permanent Prosperity of the Loyal Ones.

VII. FINAL AVOWAL OF THE PSALMIST (15bc).   Witness to Jehovah.

SUPERSCRIPT.—A Psalm; Song for the Sabbath Day.

PRIMARY ASSOCIATION.—Writer and occasion unknown. Closely connected with the next psalm by use of figure "anadiplosis" (rhetorical repetition) for emphasis, cf. xcii. 9 with xciii. 3; found also in Pss. xciv. and xcvi. According to the Talmud this psalm was sung at the libation of wine accompanying the sacrifice of the first lamb of the Sabbath burnt offering, Num. xxviii. 9–10. Sabbath Rest, xcii.; Sovereign Rule, xciii.

PROPHETIC ANTICIPATION.—The coming and universal reign of Messiah anticipated by the godly remnant. The "Sabbath" typifies the millennial rest of Messiah's reign. Note Jehovah's millennial title "Most High."

PERSONAL APPLICATION.—It is "good" to give thanks to God as being (a) due to Him and (b) a salutary occupation for man (1). Morning and evening are naturally suitable times for praise and prayer (2). In the millennium all that is responsive to man's hand is made to praise God (3). In darkness as in light, God's love works for His own (2). The victory of righteousness ever gladdens the hearts of the saints (4). Men who turn their backs upon God become mere sensuous animals, unreceptive and unresponsive to spiritual things (6). The faithless flourish only to fall (7). While God's foes perish, His favoured ones prosper (9–10). They who would flourish like the palm must have root in the sanctuary (13). With the people of God, age should produce ripeness in spiritual fruit (14). Elohim is eternally elevated above evil (8). Some lives have gone dry like withered trees fit only for firewood (14). The righteous are for fruit, the wicked for fuel (14), cf. xc. 6. If God is, that which is right shall be (15). "Higgaion"—three subjects are worthy of our deep meditation, namely (a) the Judgment and the Justice of Jehovah (ix. 16); (b) the Works and the Word of Jehovah (xix. 14); (c) the Favour and the Faithfulness of Jehovah (xcii. 3).

VERSE NOTES

1. (b) lit. "to psalm," or make melody.

2. Lovingkindness and faithfulness are the attributes which move God to make and to keep His covenant with His people, lxxxix.1. The two line division in this verse, as often in the Psalms, is rhythmical not logical, yet here the distinction seems quite appropriate.

3. Br. "With decachord and with psaltery, with meditative music (lit. higgaion, see Ps. ix. 16) on the harp." Higgaion is from Heb. "hagah," to speak to oneself, to soliloquize.

4. "work," or working; "works," br. doings; i.e. in providence, so 5.

6. "this" *i.e.* the truth expressed in next verses.

7–8. The verb tenses seem to indicate a particular event rather than a general truth, denoting the rapid rise and rapid ruin of certain lawless ones. Prophetically may refer to the Beast and the Antichrist, in which case the prophetic time of this psalm is at Christ's advent in glory and the overthrow of these national enemies. This seems to be confirmed by the words "For, lo . . . " (9).

8. "But Thou (emph.), O Jehovah (art enthroned) on high for evermore."

10. (*a*) Metaphor from animals tossing their heads in consciousness of vigour and victory; (*b*) symbolic of renewed power by the Spirit. The psalmist was caused to triumph over his foes.

11. Br. "Mine eyes have gazed on (the defeat of) them that lay in wait for me. Mine ear heard of (the destruction of) them that rose up against me to do evil."

12. Note strong contrast to 7; fruitfulness of the palm and the fragrance of the cedar are famous. Both trees are stately and evergreen, noted for longevity and luxuriance. The palm is graceful, the cedar sturdy. The palm is an endogen; it is found in barren soil watered deep at the roots. The cedar is an exogen and is found amid mountain snows and storms, its roots embedded in the rocks.

13. Cf. Psalm i.; omit "they are" and replace semi-colon by a comma at end of line (*a*).

14. (*a*) Like the palm which then bears the heaviest clusters of dates; (*b*) like the olive, Judges ix. 9.

15. (*a*) *i.e.* to witness by their prosperity to the faithfulness and justice of Jehovah; "unrighteousness" = perversity.

PSALM XCIII.   SOVEREIGNTY SUBSTANTIATED

I. DECLARATION OF JEHOVAH'S SOVEREIGNTY (1–2). His Rule Proclaimed.

    1. The Present (1). "He."
    2. The Past (2). "Thy."

II. DEMONSTRATION OF JEHOVAH'S SOVEREIGNTY (3–4). His Rule Vindicated.

    1. World Powers Assailing (3).
    2. Jehovah's Power Prevailing (4).

III. DISTINCTION OF JEHOVAH'S SOVEREIGNTY (5). His Rule Constituted.

    1. His Testimonies—Sureness.
    2. His Temple—Holiness.

PRIMARY ASSOCIATION.—Writer anonymous and occasion unknown. First of a group of psalms celebrating the proclamation of

Jehovah as universal King, xciii.-c. These psalms end upon a note of "holiness." Cf. Zech. xiv. 20-21; Isa. xxiii. 18. Psalms xciii., xcvii. and xcix. all begin on the same note.

PROPHETIC ANTICIPATION.—This entirely overshadows any other interpretation. From the first Jehovah had been Israel's King (Exod. xv. 18; Deut. xxxiii. 5; 1 Sam. xii. 12), but when despite all His loving warnings His people apostatised again and again, He abandoned them to their enemies, seeming thus to abdicate His throne among the nation. This and following psalms point to the time when Jehovah in the person of Messiah will reassume His royal dignity proclaiming Himself King over a restored Israel (Isa. lii. 7) and a recovered world. This does not, of course, affect God's eternal sovereignty which is never abrogated (2). Here is foretold a new proclamation of that sovereignty—a special manifestation of it at the second advent of Messiah.

PERSONAL APPLICATION.—God's throne is prior to every period of defined time (2). Words must have the power of fulfilment behind them to be worthy of trust—such are Jehovah's (5). From wild commotion (4) we pass into welcome calm (5). God not merely reigns over men, but plans to dwell among them (5).

VERSE NOTES

1-2. Self-coronation in self-created and self-manifested power. His strength holds a reeling world steady after the great convulsions of the last days immediately preceding Messiah's advent in glory. Read, "Jehovah hath proclaimed Himself King: He hath robed Himself with majesty. Jehovah hath robed Himself, hath girded Himself with strength." Verbs are in the perfect tense denoting not merely a fact but an act; "world" = habitable world; "moved" = shaken. The consequence of His re-established sovereignty is a restored moral order in the world. Though the proclamation is new, the fact is not. His being and sovereignty are eternal (2a).

3. "floods," these are rivers out of control, destructive, devastating. Emblematic of world powers threatening to overspread the world; "waves" Heb. only here; denotes the thud of the waves against obstacles or against one another, a vivid prophetic figure.

4. "mighty," the word suggests grandeur as well as power.

5. "testimonies," i.e. the law regarded as bearing witness to Jehovah's will and man's duty; "very sure," or, "strongly confirmed," cf. xix. 7; (b) Jehovah having returned to dwell, the "house" shall be no more defiled by Israel (Jer. vii. 30), nor desecrated by Gentiles, Joel iii. 17; Isa. lii. 1; "for evermore," lit. for length of days.

Book Four. II. Revelation of Covenant Relationship. The Redeemer's Presence: xciv.–c.

1. Appeal for the Advent, xciv.

PSALM XCIV. APPEAL FOR THE ADVENT OF THE AVENGER

I. ENTREATY FOR AVENGEMENT (1-7). God addressed.
1. The Invocation (1-2).
2. The Interrogation (3). Question = Earnest Appeal.
3. The Indictment (4-7). Words (4), Works (5-6), Words (7), of the wicked.

II. EXPOSTULATION WITH ADVERSARIES (8-11). Man addressed.
1. The Admonition (8).
2. The Argument (9-10). Question = Effective Answer.
3. The Affirmation (11).

III. ENCOURAGEMENT IN AFFLICTION (12-13). God addressed.
Confident Pronouncement. "Happy."

IV. EXPLANATION IN ACKNOWLEDGMENT (14-17). Man addressed.
1. The Conviction (14-15).
2. The Contention (16). Question = Emphatic Assertion.
3. The Confession (17).

V. EXPERIENCE OF AID (18-21). God addressed.
1. The Illustration (18-19).
2. The Interrogation (20). Question = Eloquent Advocacy.
3. The Indictment (21). Works of the wicked.

VI. EXPECTATION OF ANSWER (22-23). Man addressed.
Confident Prediction. "shall . . . shall."
1. The Deliverance (22). Preservation of the godly.
2. The Doom (23). Perdition of the godless.

PRIMARY ASSOCIATION.—Authorship and occasion unknown. See notes to preceding psalm. This seems to interrupt the unity of the subject in this group of psalms celebrating Jehovah as King, but not really so, for kingly power is manifested in the subjugation of rebels against the throne. Jehovah is King, xciii., Jehovah is Judge, xciv. The wicked here are not foreign oppressors but national rulers.

PROPHETIC ANTICIPATION.—The faithful remnant's passionate cry for, and confident trust in the righteous retribution of God, cf. Luke xviii. 7–8; Rev. viii. 3–5. The lawless ones mentioned point to Antichrist and his ready followers, who persecute the godly in the nation especially during the "Tribulation" days.

PERSONAL APPLICATION.—Pride is the very essence of sin; it exalts the creature and dethrones the Creator (2). God cannot be indifferent to the welfare of His people, His heritage (5). Crimes are often committed under legal forms (4–6), cf. Ps. lxxiii. It is arrogant folly to assume that God is either ignorant of, or indifferent to His people's sufferings (7). He hears the scoffs of the enemy and the sighs of His elect (7). Men do not want to be seen, then hope they will not be seen, and finally make themselves believe they are not seen (7). In spite of the temporary triumph of the wicked, God still rules (8 ff.). Modern denials are based upon the same delusion refuted here (7 ff.). Can a universe full of purpose come from a purposeless source (8–10)? The Creator of the organs of sense must Himself possess faculties corresponding to them (9). God is the great educator of mankind (10). His is not the "higher education" but the highest. God not only sees men's works, but knows their thoughts; He has insight and foresight as well as oversight (11). The wise welcome divine instruction, fools rebel against it (12). Righteousness is the eternal principle of all judicial action (15). In the world, judgment is too often divorced from righteousness; but under Messiah's rule the administration will be again conducted upon principles of equity (15). God is the mighty champion of His people (16). We may give ourselves up for lost, but the Hand of Love has hold of us all the time (18). When distracting thoughts disturb the mind of the believer, the comforts of God soothe (lit. caress) the soul (19). God will not allow rapacious judges to shelter under His authority though they may be temporarily tolerated (20). Verse 12 is worth another thought! Study the pronoun "my" in the latter part of the psalm.

VERSE NOTES

1. Br. "God of vengeance, Jehovah, God of vengeance, shine forth." Note fig. anadiplosis, the reiteration of intense feeling and pressing need; "God" = El. 2*b*. Cf. Isa, ii. 12–17.

3. "How long?" cf. Rev. vi. 10; "wicked" = lawless ones, cf. Hab. i. 2.

4. Br. "(How long) shall all workers of iniquity belch out, talk arrogantly, act haughtily?" This indicates behaviour typical of Eastern princes.

6. "sojourner," *i.e.* a guest, who in the East is deemed inviolable; to harm him would bring indelible shame upon the perpetrator. Typical forms of defencelessness are named here.

7. Thus declaring themselves to be apostates from God as well as oppressors of His people; guilty of impiety as well as injustice.

8. "be wise" = understand.

10. A noteworthy truth found in first line; positive answer in 11.

11. Cited 1 Cor. iii. 20; br. "for they are (but) a breath."

12. Cf. Heb. xii. 5 ff.; Job v. 17; "law" here = all divine revelation as the guide of life.

13. "adversity" = evil, *i.e.* times when wrongdoers seem to hold undisputed sway; (*b*) metaphor from pitfalls used by animal hunters. The words indicate a day of retribution.

14. Cf. Rom. xi. 1-2.

17. (*b*) indicates the stillness of the grave.

18. Br. "when I said, 'My foot hath slipped,' Thy lovingkindness, O Jehovah, was supporting me." Note significance of tenses.

19. "thoughts," or as marg. = distracting thoughts which "divide" (lit.) and perplex the mind; hesitations between hope and fear, etc.

21. (*b*) *i.e.* condemn the innocent to death.

22. Br. "But Jehovah will surely prove a high tower for me; And my God shall be . . ."

23. Br. "And He shall bring . . ."; "cut off" = root out . . . root out."

Book Four. II. Revelation of Covenant Relationship: xciv.–c.

2 Anthems of the Advent, xcv.–c.

PSALM XCV. REACHING REDEMPTION REST

I. THE GLAD WORSHIP OF THE PEOPLE (1–7*b*). THE SUMMONS.
   1. The Exhortation (1–2).
   2. The Foundation (3–5). Jehovah's Relation to the Earth. Sovereign Control. "For."
   3. The Exhortation (6).
   4. The Foundation (7*ab*). Jehovah's Relation to Israel. Shepherd Care. "For."

II. THE GREAT WISH FOR THE PEOPLE (7*c*). THE SOLICITUDE.
    An Invitation of Grace.

III. THE GRAVE WARNING TO THE PEOPLE (8-11). THE SERMON.
  1. The Exhortation (8). Time = To-day (implied from 7).
  2. The Foundation (9). Place "Where." Sin Perpetrated.
  3. The Explanation (10). Time = Forty years.
  4. The Frustration (11). Place "Where." Sin Punished.

PRIMARY ASSOCIATION.—The psalm is first of a group marked by common characteristics and apparently for liturgical use. The key-note was struck in xciii. According to strong tradition supported by LXX titles to xcvi.–xcvii., these psalms were used at the dedication of the second temple. They are probably inspired adaptations of earlier psalms, especially this one, which is attributed to David in Heb. iv. 7.

PROPHETIC ANTICIPATION.—At the very beginning of Israel's restoration under Messiah the King, the new generation is earnestly warned not to repeat the sins of the fathers, while celebrating the glorious advent.

PERSONAL APPLICATION.—True worship requires prepared hearts. Jubilation is a conspicuous element in worship (1–2). "To-day" is ever the critical time as it presents a passing opportunity (7). To doubt God's goodness and demand proofs of His power is tempting Him (9). They who know not God's ways choose their own (10). Israel's desert wanderings were at once a symbol and a consequence of heart wanderings (10). They who would reach God's rest must walk in God's way (11). The same power that created and sustains the physical universe, guides and guards the people of God (7). The trouble is not that God does not speak, but that men will not listen (7c). Despite abundant evidence of God's working, men still harden their hearts (8–9).

VERSE NOTES

1–2. A striking picture of the joyous tumult of the temple worship. Shrill cries of joy, loud shouts of praise and songs with musical accompaniment to western ears spell exuberance rather than reverence; "thanksgiving" = lit. confession (*i.e.* of what God is and what He has done), cf. Heb. xiii. 15.

3. It is wrong to suppose that the psalmist attributes any real existence to the gods of the nations; "God" = El; see Appendix II.

5. "He" (emph.), so "*He . . . we*" verse 7.

6. "Maker," *i.e.* God was the Creator of Israel as a nation.

7. Figure and fact here poetically blended. (*c*) The psalmist is still speaking (note "His" = the voice of Jehovah's Messenger, *i.e.* Messiah), "Oh, that *to-day*

ye would hearken to His voice," cf. Deut. v. 29. This leads naturally to the warning that follows. 7c–11 are quoted Heb. iii. 7–11 from the LXX with slight variations. The division there of the subject does not affect the apostle's purpose.

8. "Meribah (= strife) . . . Massah" (= temptation). The former occasion, namely at Rephidim, was at the beginning of the "wandering;" the latter at the close, at Kadesh, also called Meribah, Num. xx. 1–13.

9. "When" Heb. = where, so "wherefore," (11); (b) br. "Though they had seen My work," i.e. acts of judgment, His "strange work," Isa. xxviii. 21.

10. Heb. lit. ". . . did I loathe . . ."; (b) "And I said, 'They are a people whose heart goeth astray, And they (emph.) know not My ways.'"

11. "My rest," i.e. the land of promise. The quotations in Heb. iii.–iv. have a wider application.

PSALM XCVI.   REJOICING IN THE REDEEMER'S REIGN

I. EXHORTATION TO UNIVERSAL PRAISE (1–3).   The Summons.
Rendition of the "New Song."
1. Ascription (1–2a).   "Sing" three times.
2. Annunciation (2b–3).   Jehovah's Marvellous Works.

II. EXPLANATION OF UNIVERSAL PRAISE (4–6).   The Stimulus.
Jehovah's Recognised Greatness.

III. EXHORTATION TO UNIVERSAL PRAISE (7–13a).   The Summons.
1. Ascription (7–9).   "Ascribe" three times.
2. Annunciation (10).   Jehovah's Millennial Reign.
3. Acclamation (11–13a).   "Let , . ." three times.

IV. EXPLANATION OF UNIVERSAL PRAISE (13bd).   The Stimulus.
Jehovah's Righteous Government.   Reason for the "New Song."

PRIMARY ASSOCIATION.—See notes to the two preceding psalms. Compare 1 Chron. xvi. 8 ff., especially 23–33. David's psalm delivered to Asaph on that occasion is here appropriated and expanded. This psalm may be coupled with the next, the Request, xcvi.; the Response, xcvii.

PROPHETIC ANTICIPATION.—Sufficiently indicated by the contents. Yurchi observes that whenever a "new song" is mentioned, it refers to Messianic times. The language of 12b has also a symbolic significance as indicating the universal establishment of the divine kingdom, cf. Isa. lv. 12; xliv. 23; Rom. viii. 21, 23. The coronation anthem extends to all nations and embraces the renovated earth.

PERSONAL APPLICATION.—This has been called, "A Missionary Melody." The nation (Israel), the "nothings" (idols), the nations (Gentiles) and nature are all seen here witnessing to the ♦ supremacy of Jehovah. Fresh mercies demand fresh thanks (1). Our praises should be renewed with each returning day (2). We may appeal to the works of creation as proof of Jehovah's reality and power (5). Worshippers of God must be arrayed in holy garments (9), that is marked by conduct befitting His Presence. The result of the Redeemer's ruling presence will be a world established physically and morally (10). Inanimate nature will share the joy of the "regeneration" (11-12). The arousing message, "He is coming" will be changed to the world-wide proclamation, "He is come" (13a).

VERSE NOTES

2. (b) Br. "Proclaim the good tidings of His salvation from day to day."

5. "gods . . . idols"; there is a play on words here which expresses a profound truth; lit. "elohim . . . elilim," = gods . . . nuilities, cf. 1 Cor. viii. 4.

6. As often in psalms the attributes of God are personified as attendants in His presence; "strength . . . beauty," are terms applied in lxxviii. 61 to the ark, symbol of His presence; "sanctuary," i.e. not heaven but the earthly counterpart.

7 ff. Appeal to the nations to acknowledge Jehovah; "kindreds" = families.

9. The priests in the temple ministered in holy attire.

10. Br. "Jehovah hath proclaimed Himself King"; (c) "He shall minister judgment unto the peoples in equity."

11. The initials of the four Heb. words in line (a) form an acrostic of the name Jehovah. "fulness thereof," i.e. all that is in them.

13. "judge;" the predominant idea here is not punishment but government, though the former is included in the latter. The accession is a single act, the judging a continual process; (d) as margin.

PSALM XCVII.   COMING IN THE CLOUDS

I. EXHORTATION TO REJOICE (1-2). The Earth.
    1. Proclamation of the Kingdom (1a).
    2. Prompting to Rejoice (1bc).
    3. Pillars of the Kingdom (2).

II. EFFECTS OF THE REVELATION (3-9).
    1. The Coming Described (3-6).
    2. The Consequences Declared (7-9).
      (i) Idolators Judged (7). "Gods" (= rulers) addressed.
      (ii) Israel Jubilant (8-9). God addressed.

III. EXHORTATION TO RESPOND (10–12). The Elect.
  1. Repudiation of Evil (10a).
  2. Reasons for Joy (10b–11).
  3. Rendering of Thanks (12).

PRIMARY ASSOCIATION.—See notes to preceding psalms of this group. Here is an extension of xcvi. 13, a condensed epitome of Messiah's advent in glory; the event and the effect.

PROPHETIC ANTICIPATION.—Indicated by the analysis. "By the harmonious combination of passages from earlier psalms, this one indicates that in the consummation to come at Messiah's second appearing, all the scattered rays of inspired prophecy, psalmody and history, shall all be brought into one focus in the person of the coming King of Righteousness."

PERSONAL APPLICATION.—The power of the "Presence." The godly exult because their Lord is exalted (12). Earnest exhortation should always be based upon firm faith. God is light, but there are holy mysteries of His person and purposes that are hidden from mortal eyes (2). Faith enters the cloud and is not afraid; it apprehends what is known to be within (2). God desires to be known and remembered by His acts (12). His name is that which brings to remembrance all that He is and does (12). World thrones are seldom founded upon righteousness and justice (2). Yes! every eye shall see Him (6). They that love God cannot love evil (10). If light and gladness be but the seed, what must the following harvest be (11)? The Old Testament message, "Be glad in Jehovah;" the New Testament, "Rejoice in the Lord," (Phil. iv. 4).

VERSE NOTES

1. Br. "Jehovah hath proclaimed Himself King;" (b) lit. "many isles," or, coastlands, i.e. of the Mediterranean = the gentile world. In Scripture prophecy "isles" seems to refer to western lands even beyond the Mediterranean.

2. The theophany of Sinai seems to supply the symbolism.

3. "fire," fig. of destructive and purifying power.

4 ff. Graphic word picture expressing the measure and terror of His power; cf. Hab. iii. 6. Title in 5b first found significantly at Josh. iii. 11, 13; "Lord" = Adon, is specially connected with earth rule.

6. Br. "have declared," i.e. because they had witnessed His great act of delivering the chosen nation. The heavens are mainly the scene of His appearance, the earth the theatre of His working.

7. "graven images," lit. an image (sing.) whether graven or molten; "idols" lit. nullities.

8. "daughters of Judah" = daughter cities.

9. Br. "For *Thou* art the Most High . . ."

10. "souls" = lives; "saints" = beloved or favoured ones; "wicked" = lawless ones.

11. An interesting figure. Light is scattered in rich profusion even as the sun sows abroad its beams; or refers to the diffusion of light at the dawn giving promise of increasing light until the full blaze of day. Such indeed (metaphorically) will be the fulfilment of the promise inherent in Messiah's Coming.

12. Lit. " . . . the memorial of His holiness." Only they who have experienced the divine redemption can do this. The remembrance of God's holiness would instil only terror into the heart of the unrepentant sinner.

PSALM XCVIII. THE REDEEMER'S RETURN

I. RENDITION OF PRAISE (1*a*).   The Exhortation.

II. REASONS FOR PRAISE (1*b*-3).   The Explanation.   "For."
   The Salvation of God—Revealed.

III. RENDITION OF PRAISE (4-9*a*).   The Exhortation.
   1. Summons to the Nation (4-6).
   (*a*) The People (4).
   (*b*) The Levites (5).
   (*c*) The Priests (6).
   2. Summons to all Nature (7-9*a*).
      (Sea—World—Rivers—Mountains.)

IV. REASONS FOR PRAISE (9*bd*).   The Explanation.   "For."
   The Administration of God—Righteous.

SUPERSCRIPT.—A Psalm.

PRIMARY ASSOCIATION.—See notes to preceding psalms of the group. Another anthem of praise for the deliverance of Israel. Pss. xcviii. and xcix. form a pair similar to xcvi. and xcvii., xcviii. being an echo of xcvi. and xcix. an echo of xcvii. This is the only psalm bearing the simple title without addition.

PROPHETIC ANTICIPATION.—This is clear from the contents, which point to the period following the second advent. The salvation of Israel is principally in view, the visible manifestation of Jehovah's faithfulness to His covenant. In contrast with preceding psalms, here the heavens are not summoned to join the harmony of praise, but all nature is called upon to swell the chorus of rejoicing since the curse is removed.

PERSONAL APPLICATION.—A song of salvation. Jehovah's working speaks even more loudly than Israel's witness thereto (2). Salvation in all its manifold aspects is the work of God alone (1). It is a good thing that God's memory is better than man's (3). Note three forms of worship in this group of psalms: (a) material presents; (b) vocal and instrumental praise, and (c) silent prostration; with xcvi. 8, cf. Rev. iv. 10; with xcviii. 4-6, cf. Rev. v. 9; with xcix. 5, cf. Rev. v. 14.

VERSE NOTES

1. "new song," cf. the old song, Exod. xv. 2, 6, 11-12. (c) Br. "His own right hand . . . His own . . ."

3. (b) Cf. Isa. lii. 10.

4. Br. "Shout unto Jehovah all the land . . . yea, psalm (or, make melody);" shouts, music, trumpet-blast and hand-clapping (8) are appropriate upon a king's accession. Note fig. anadiplosis (4-5 ff.).

5. "Make melody (psalm) unto Jehovah with the harp; with the harp and the sound of melody."

6. "trumpets," Heb. "khatzotzerah," see Appendix XII; "sound of cornet" = blast of horn, Heb. "shophar,"; originally a ram's horn, later a metal instrument of the same shape, see Appendix XII; (b) br. "shout aloud . . ."

8. "Floods" = rivers; "hills" = mountains; "clap hands" = fig. of waves striking against one another with a sound as of applauding palms. Rivers symbolise kinds of refreshment and channels of blessing from a source known or unknown.

PSALM XCIX.   A MILLENNIAL MELODY

I. FIRST MOVEMENT (1-3). (Single).
     EXPRESSION OF PRAISE (1-3). Potentate and Peoples.
        (i) The Proclamation (1). "Let them tremble."
        (ii) The Predication (2). "He"—Jehovah.
        (iii) The Precept (3). "Let them praise."
     REFRAIN. "Holy is He."

II. FURTHER MOVEMENT (4-5). (Double).
     1. EXHIBITION OF JEHOVAH'S CHARACTER (4). In the Present.
     Power and Justice wedded. Might and Right.
     2. EXHORTATION TO WORSHIP (5). "Exalt and worship."
     REFRAIN. "Holy is He."

III. FINAL MOVEMENT (6–9). (Triple).
    1. EXEMPLIFICATION FROM HISTORY (6–7).
      (i) Specified Persons (6).
      (ii) Sanctified People (7).
    2. EXHIBITION OF JEHOVAH'S CHARACTER (8). In the Past.
      Lovingkindness and Holiness wedded.   Love and Light.
    3. EXHORTATION TO WORSHIP (9).   "Exalt and worship."
      REFRAIN.   "Holy is Jehovah our God."

PRIMARY ASSOCIATION.—Writer and occasion unknown; see notes to preceding psalms of this group. The predominant thought here is the King's holiness as the central and eternal principle of His rule. The refrain was possibly responsive in the liturgical use of the psalm.

PROPHETIC ANTICIPATION.—Sufficiently indicated above and in notes under earlier psalms of the group. Messiah's reign is an active rule.

PERSONAL APPLICATION.—The holiness of the Highest. Note the thrice pronounced, "Holy" (3, 5, 9) and cf. Isa. vi.; Rev. iv. 8. Divine holiness is not merely moral purity; it is "separation" by elevation above all that is finite and imperfect (2). This presents a claim to adoration (3). God's attributes are translated into acts (4–5). Obedience to the revealed will of God is the virtually expressed condition of prevailing prayer (7). History, especially in the Scriptures, teaches many lessons concerning the character of God (6–8). When God pardons sin, He still must vindicate His holiness by chastising the sinner, lest men imagine He makes light of sin. Earthly penalties as the natural results of sin, in constitution or in memory, in habit or in circumstances, are not removed by pardon, but their character is changed to loving chastisement for our profit (8); cf. Heb. xii. The holiness of God is exhibited in (a) Remission of sins; (b) Retribution upon evil (8). Grace reigns in holiness as well as in righteousness. Contemplative awe is reconcilable with confident approach (2). Forgiveness and chastisement express grace and government respectively (8).

VERSE NOTES

    1. "Jehovah hath proclaimed Himself King . . . Sitting enthroned upon the cherubim . . ."
    2. Zion is the seat of His visible glory and universal sovereignty on earth."
    4. "the King"=Jehovah-Messiah, cf. Isa. lxi. 8; "*Thou . . . Thou . . .*

5. "footstool," in 1 Chron. xxviii. 2 refers to the ark. Jehovah conceived as sitting upon the cherubim with His feet, as it were, touching the ark, *i.e.* at His sanctuary in Zion.

6. It was the office of priests to intercede and mediate between God and man. Moses, grandson of Levi, exercised priestly functions before Aaron. Samuel, though not officially a priest (he was a Levite) practically stood in that place when the Aaronic priesthood had apostatised. (*c*) omit "they."

7. "them" refers to the people of Israel, not to the persons mentioned in 6.

8. "Jehovah our God, *Thou* didst answer them, A pardoning God didst Thou prove Thyself to them, yet withal an avenger of their doings"; "God" = El; Exod. xxiv. 6–7.

9. The extension in the refrain shows that there is access to the "Inaccessible."

PSALM C.   WORLD-WIDE WORSHIP

I. RENDITION OF PRAISE (1–2).   THE THANKSGIVING.
   1. The Injunction (1–2*a*).   "Shout and serve."
   2. The Invitation (2*b*).   "Come before His presence."

II. REASONS FOR PRAISE (3).   THE THEME.   Triple Declaration.
   Jehovah's relation to Israel.   "He is God."

III. RENDITION OF PRAISE (4).   THE THANKSGIVING.
   1. The Invitation (4*ab*).   "Enter into His gates."
   2. The Injunction (4*c*).   "Thank and bless."

IV. REASONS FOR PRAISE (5).   THE THEME.   Triple Declaration.
   Jehovah's revelation as Immanuel.   "He is good."

SUPERSCRIPT.—A Psalm of thanksgiving (or, for the thank-offering).

PRIMARY ASSOCIATION.—Writer anonymous and occasion unknown. This is the end of the series of anthems beginning with xcv. From ancient times this psalm has been used in the daily service of the synagogue except on certain festivals. In the metrical version of the Psalms it is set to the well-known tune, "The Old Hundredth." Superscript, cf. Lev. vii.

PROPHETIC ANTICIPATION.—See notes to preceding psalms. Israel here calls upon the gentiles to share her holy joy in the presence of the enthroned Redeemer. All are welcomed to His sanctuary to join the concluding chorus of praise.

PERSONAL APPLICATION.—It might be well if Christians knew more of the abandonment to holy joy expressed in these psalms.

Such worship must be spontaneous and not imitated, cf. Eph. v. 19. Perfection and rest are both found in God. All service should be joyous (2). It is by His dealings with Israel as a nation that God's exaltation will be made known in the earth (3). God is good (5) and He is great, xcv. 3. Note the fourfold call to praise (4). Thanksgiving to God here means simply confessing (so the word in Heb., cf. Heb. xiii. 15) what God is and how worthy of all praise are His excellencies (4). The knowledge referred to (3a) will characterise the millennium. None must appear before God empty (4), cf. Deut. xxvi. with Heb. xiii. 15–16.

VERSE NOTES

1. "Shout unto Jehovah, all the earth." What may have primarily referred to "the land," is prophetically to be understood of the earth. The shout of acclamation upon His accession as King is heard.

2. "serve," i.e. the homage of worship now replaces the homage of mere submission (Ps. ii. 11), so that men draw near with gladness instead of with fear.

3. Israel is created and cared for. "Know that Jehovah is God, He it is that made us, and we are His, His people and the . . ." God made Israel a people, xcv. 6.

5. This is Israel's old motto sung at the dedication of the temple and at its rebuilding in Ezra's day. It will again resound in the sanctuary courts; (b) lit. "unto generation after generation."

Book Four. III. Rejoicing in Covenant Relationship. The Redeemer's Praise: ci.–cvi.

1. Essential Preparation.   The King's Purpose, ci.
The King's Passion, cii.

PSALM CI.   A RULER'S RESOLVE

I. THE MAINTENANCE OF PERSONAL INTEGRITY (1–4). THE MONARCH.
  1. By Emphasising Worship (1).
  2. By Exercising Wisdom (2a). "The Perfect Way."
  3. By Establishing Walk (2bc). "Within my House."
  4. By Eschewing Wickedness (3–4). "Before mine eyes."

II. THE MAINTENANCE OF PUBLIC INTEGRITY (5–8). THE MINISTERS.
  1. By Eradicating Evil-doers (5). His Retinue. "Rooted out."

2. By Encouraging Faithful Ministers (6). "A Perfect Way."
3. By Excluding False-hearted Ministers (7). "Within my House . . ."
4. By Eradicating Evil-doers (8).   His Realm.   "Rooted out."

SUPERSCRIPT.—A Psalm of David.

PRIMARY ASSOCIATION.—David wrote this psalm in the early period of his reign. Primarily it is his vow to rule in righteousness, banishing baseness from his own heart and expelling all evil-doers from his presence, that he may be worthy to receive Jehovah in the visible symbol of the ark.   Written therefore in connection with and after 2 Sam. vi. 9, when the fear then engendered had changed into yearning for Jehovah's presence in the city of His choice. The evils here mentioned had no doubt characterised the last troubled years of Saul's reign.   Such evil-doers are too often found in court circles especially in the East where royal palaces are notorious as abodes of lust and extravagance. This royal proclamation against vice and immorality was sadly falsified in David's own history, 2 Sam. xi. ff.

PROPHETIC ANTICIPATION.—Here is the voice of David's "Son" and David's Lord.   Messiah states governing principles especially "within the House."   Note the twin characteristics of the divine rule in 1a. It is significant that this description of what a king should be immediately follows a series of psalms telling unmistakably who the King is.   One cleansing at the beginning of a reign is insufficient (8); there must be a continual process, cf. Matt. xiii. 41. Messiah's judgments will be daily and carried out immediately.   Thus no prisons will be needed and the land will be kept clean.

PERSONAL APPLICATION.—Here are principles for a potentate. Whether king or subject the first responsibility is to worship God (1). We should put away evil from our own hearts before we begin to deal with those around us (2c, 7a).   God's representatives should eschew the path of self-indulgence (2 ff.).   A "perfect" heart expels a "perverse" heart (2, 4).   Private integrity and public integrity go together (2, 7).   We should shake off "worthless" (3a) and wicked (3b) things that take hold of us unawares (3c) like Paul did the viper, Acts xxviii. 3-6. High looks are a visible sign of a haughty heart (5). Pride like a "puffed up" (so Heb. word) child's balloon is liable to sudden collapse (5b).   Faithfulness to God guarantees fidelity to man (6).   Ill weeds grow apace, even under just rule (8).

VERSE NOTES

1. (a) "lovingkindness" is love in action; (b) " . . . will I make melody."

2. or as margin; "perfect" = blameless; (b) David feels that his resolves require the presence of God Himself to carry them out; (c) cf. margin and David's earlier resolutions, 1 Sam. xviii. 5, 14–15, 30; and see 1 Chron. xxviii. 9; xxix. 19.

3. "base thing," lit. = matter of Belial (= worthlessness). (b) or, "I hate the practice of depravities."

4. Psalmist is still speaking of himself; (b) "Evil I will not know," i.e. by experience and love of it.

5. "destroy," Heb. = root out, so 8a; "him . . . him" (emph.).

6. (c) "He shall minister . . ." In Messiah's kingdom office will go not to mere ability or servility, or birth, but to moral and spiritual qualities. God's city will be pure, cf. Rev. xxii. 15.

7. (b) "before mine eyes" = in my presence.

8. (b) Br. "That I may cut off . . ." The king holds his court of justice each morning (2 Sam. xv. 2; Jer. xxi. 12) that he may purge Jerusalem of evil and make it a "holy city" worthy of its title "City of Jehovah," cf. Pss. xlvi. 4; xlviii. 1, 8; Isa. i. 26.

PSALM CII.   AFFLICTION OF THE ANOINTED

I. PRESSING APPEAL (1–2).   The Prayer.

II. PROFOUND AFFLICTION (3–11).   The Plea.   "For."
    1. Distressed in Body (3–5).   Days shortened.
    2. Desolated in Soul (6–7).
    3. Derided by Men (8).
    4. Disciplined by God (9–11).   Days shortened.

III. PERFECT ASSURANCE (12–22).   The Persuasion.
    1. Concerning Jehovah's Permanence (12).
    2. Concerning Jehovah's Pity (13–22).
        (i) Restoration of Zion (13–14).
        (ii) Result among the Nations (15-17).   "When."   "Name feared."
            (a) Reverence (15).
            (b) Reasons (16-17).
        (iii) Regeneration of Israel (18–20).
            (a) Celebration (18).
            (b) Causes (19-20).
        (iv) Result among the Nations (21–22).   "When."   "Name declared."

IV. PROFOUND AFFLICTION (23).   Days shortened.

V. PRESSING APPEAL (24a).

VI. PERFECT ASSURANCE (24b-28).
   1. Concerning Jehovah's Permanence (24b-27). Immanuel.
   2. Concerning Israel's Preservation (28).

SUPERSCRIPT.—A Prayer of the afflicted, when he is about to faint, and poureth out his complaint before Jehovah.

PRIMARY ASSOCIATION.—Verses 13–14 seem to suggest that this psalm was written when Zion was in ruins and the time of restoration at hand, but this is not conclusive as the prophetic aspect overshadows the historical. The superscript is unique in the Psalter. This is one of the seven so-called "Penitential Psalms." Note the deep contrast to preceding psalms and the explanation suggested by the analysis of this section of the Book.

PROPHETIC ANTICIPATION.—A psalm of sorrow and solace. Long recognised as Messianic, this psalm shows something of the depth of Messiah's humiliation—the Deathless One as death-stricken. Verses 24b–27 are the key to the understanding of the whole composition, so that while the writer primarily refers to Jehovah, contrasting the fulfilment of the promises to Zion with his own brief days, Heb. i. clearly shows the passage to refer to Christ. We realise afresh the mystery form in which some of the most glorious intimations in the Psalms are clothed. 24a gives Messiah's appeal and the remainder of the psalm Jehovah's answer. What is emphasised here is not so much the *atoning* sufferings of Christ as His personal sense of rejection in connection with the remnant. These sufferings, however, led to His vicarious death and are inseparably associated therewith. By reason of the latter, the Second Man shall restore to the world more than the first man ever lost through the Fall.

PERSONAL APPLICATION.—The Creator and the creature are in Christ for ever linked. The suffering saint often finds solace by reiterating familiar petitions. They are none the less his own, because they have been the cry of others. Here is another example of shadows shot with sunbeams. No mercy was shown to Him who delighted in mercy. Sadness and solitude usually go together (5–6). Zion cannot perish while Zion's God lives (12, 13). The assurance that God will restore Zion is here seen to rest upon (a) the Stability of the Troth ("for," 13 b); (b) the Signs of the Times ("for" 13c); (c) the Solicitude of the True-hearted ("for" 14). True servants of God are always in sympathy with

His purposes (14). The restoration of Zion is prelude to the conversion of the nations (15 ff.). God hears the sighs of His prisoners (20). "God desires that we should know Him since that knowledge is life eternal. He is not greedy of adulation nor dependent upon recognition, but He loves men too well not to rejoice in being understood and loved by them. Love ever hungers for return." Jehovah's praise shall be universal and unceasing (21). Not only man, but even heaven and earth are transitory contrasted with the eternity of God (26). God's personality in its essential nature is unchanging (27) and Christ is God. He is the unchanging Author of all change. His eternity is pledge of the permanence of His people (28).

VERSE NOTES

3. He feels like a sick man whose strength is consumed by a burning fever; "as a firebrand" = as charred wood.

4. "for," br. Yea. (a) like a sunstroke; (b) sorrow and sickness deprive Him of all appetite.

5. i.e. groaned himself into emaciation.

6. Comparison with solitude-loving birds which haunt desolate places and ruins. Pelican and owl are both "unclean" according to Mosaic law.

7. "I keep vigil . . ."i.e. his nights are sleepless and he spends them like some solitary bird. The sparrow is a gregarious bird; when one has lost its mate it will sit on the housetop alone and lament by the hour in melancholy chirps.

8. Sufferings aggravated by mockery of foes; (b) i.e. His foes felt they could utter no blacker curse against others than to wish them in circumstances like him; some read, " . . . are sworn (together) against me."

10. The suffering is on account of sin; viewed prophetically of Christ the sin is not His own but His people's; (b) i.e. caught up only to be flung away with greater impetus.

11. (a) i.e. lengthening shadows of evening soon disappear; (b) "I am withering away . . ."

12. "But Thou, O Jehovah, shalt sit enthroned for ever; And Thy memorial shall be for generation after generation." He is comforted by the thought not merely of Jehovah's eternity, but of His eternal sovereignty. The memorial Name (Exod. iii. 15) is pledge and proclamation of that sovereign rule.

13. "Thou (emph.); "set time," i.e. (a) end of the seventy years, Dan. ix. etc.; (b) the still future "set time" in God's counsels.

15. The Spirit of God always mentions future glory in connection with Messiah's sufferings.

16 ff. "When Jehovah . . . Zion, hath appeared . . . hath regarded, etc."

20. Comparison to a condemned prisoner languishing in a dungeon.

23. "the way," i.e. of his humiliation.

24. "O my God," Heb. Eli = my El (Mighty One).

27. Br. "Thou art He" = emphatic assertion of immutable personality; or, regard as a title, "the Same," cf. Deut. xxxii. 39; Neh. ix. 6.

28. Lit. "The sons . . . shall dwell," *i.e.* in the land once more; "established in Thy presence."

Book Four. III. Rejoicing in Covenant Relationship: ci.-cvi.

2. Ensuing Praise, ciii.-cvi. The Nation's Retrospect.

PSALM CIII. PRAISE OF A PARDONED PEOPLE

I. SUMMONS TO PRAISE (1-5). PERSONAL.
    First Note, "Bless Jehovah, O my soul."

II. SUBJECT OF PRAISE (6-19). JEHOVAH'S CHARACTER MANI-FESTED IN REDEMPTION. Grace and Government.
    1. Joyful Confession (6-12).
        (i) Divine Righteousness Exhibited to Israel (6-7).
        (ii) Divine Lovingkindness Exemplified in Experience (8-12).
            Its Proof—Sins Pardoned.
    2. Instructive Comparisons (13-16).
        (i) Compassion of God—Like a Father (13-14).
        (ii) Course of Man—Like a Flower (15-16).
    3. Joyful Confession (17-19).
        (i) Divine Lovingkindness Enduring in Character (17-18).
            Its Permanence—Saints Preserved.
        (ii) Divine Rule Established in General (19).

III. SUMMONS TO PRAISE (20-22). UNIVERSAL.
    Final Note, "Bless Jehovah, O my soul."

SUPERSCRIPT.—David's.

PRIMARY ASSOCIATION.—The psalm seems to belong to David's later life (5). He identifies himself with the destinies of the nation, which in his character as king he represented before God. There is no note of sadness in the music of this psalm despite 15-16. Here is the praise promised in ci. 1.

PROPHETIC ANTICIPATION.—Pss. ciii. to cvi. show the blessed consequence of Messiah being "cut off" as in cii. Here Messiah Himself leads the praises of a restored Israel. It is a song of millennial saints on earth. With her national life redeemed from destruction and strength renewed Israel will call for universal praise and see the glad response. In the day contemplated, Israel's blessed experience will include in the fullest way bodily healing (3), a pledge of which was seen in Messiah's ministry at His first Advent.

PERSONAL APPLICATION.—This world will one day hear praise flowing like one unbroken stream ever broadening as it runs. God's gifts are all benefits whether pleasurable or otherwise (2). Note the fivefold activity of our God: (a) Remission, (b) Restoration, (c) Preservation, (d) Coronation, (e) Satisfaction (3-5). This catalogue of blessings begins with forgiveness and ends with immortal youth (3-5). The divine lovingkindness and compassion make a beautiful garland for the brow of the redeemed (4b). David's God is not a God of imagination but of revelation (7 ff.). Jehovah's lovingkindness is constant like the sunshine; His anger transitory like the lightning (8). God's blessings are universal, but man is not hindered from self-exclusion. Note the threefold condition, "them that fear (revere) Him" (11, 13, 17). Though slow to anger, the time comes when God must convict His people of their sin and show His indignation by chastising them; but even then His anger does not last for ever (9). He chastises less than iniquities deserve (10). Man's weakness appeals to God's compassion (14). Man is like a fragile earthen vessel, therefore God handles us tenderly (14). God remembers what man forgets (our infirmities) and forgets what man remembers (our sins) (14); cf. Isa. xliii. 25; xliv. 42. Man soon passes away, but God's compassion endures for ever (17). They who fear God may safely leave their posterity to His care (17). The universe praises the mighty Maker and Ruler; man alone praises the merciful Mediator and Redeemer (20-22). Worship links the individual with the Infinite (20-22).

VERSE NOTES

1. "soul," word here evidently ref. to the complete personality, the sum totality of being, cf. Gen. ii. 7. Next line views the unity of personality in its diversity of powers.

2. "all," i.e. any of; "benefits," i.e. gracious dealings.

3. "healeth," cf. Exod. xv. 26, where the divine title is Jehovah-Ropheca.

4. "tender mercies," = compassions.

5. Br. "Who adorneth thee to the full with goodliness"; (b) no reference here to fable, but to fact. Moulting and renewal of a bird's feathers result in continued accuracy and strength in flight. The eagle's wings never seem to tire.

6. He not only makes laws, He applies them.

7. "ways . . . doings," *i.e.* principles and performances respectively. To Moses were revealed the former; Israel only saw the latter.

8. "Jehovah is full of compassion and gracious, longsuffering . . ."

9. "chide" or, contend.

8–9. Cf. Exod. xxxiv. 6–7.

11. (*b*) br. " . . . so mighty hath prevailed . . . upon them . . ." The perfect tenses in 10–12 suggest a recent experience; prophetically significant.

13. "pitieth" = hath compassion on; connects with 8.

14. "He" (emph.); "our frame," = our formation; alludes to Gen. ii. 7; iii. 19; Ps. lxxviii. 39.

15. "man" = enosh (frail man); for fig. see Ps. xc. 5–6, etc.

16. Br. " . . . over him and he is not, And his place shall know him no more."

17. "righteousness" here = His covenant faithfulness. The new covenant (not the Mosaic) is a re-statement in fuller blessing of the Abrahamic covenant in its precise application to Israel.

18. But His mercy is above all human merit.

21. Perhaps ref. to all the powers of nature that subserve God's purpose.

22. All nature, inanimate and animate, called upon; (*b*) this completes the circle of praise, cf. 1.

PSALM CIV.   THE CREATOR AND THE CREATURE

I. SUMMONS TO PRAISE (1*a*). PERSONAL. "Bless Jehovah, O my soul."

II. SUBJECT OF PRAISE (1*b*–32). JEHOVAH'S CHARACTER MANI-
FESTED IN CREATION.   Greatness and Goodness.

   1. Days One and Two Recalled (1*b*–5).

   2. Day Three Recalled (6–18).   Earth and Waters.

   3. Day Four Recalled (19–23).   The Luminaries.

   4. Day Five Recalled (24–26).   Earth and Sea.

   5. Days Six and Seven Recalled (27–32).

III. SUMMONS TO PRAISE (33–35). PERSONAL. "Bless thou Jehovah,
   O my soul."

   1. Purpose (33–34).   Celebration (33); Meditation (34*a*); Exultation (34*b*).

   2. Prayer (35*ab*).

   3. Prompting (35*cd*).

PRIMARY ASSOCIATION.—Writer is anonymous and the occasion unknown, but with high probability David is the author. The psalm pairs beautifully with ciii. (compare analyses). The latter is the testimony of history to the graciousness of Jehovah—His beneficent rule among men; civ., the testimony of creation to the greatness of

Jehovah—His beneficent rule in nature. In ciii. He is seen as the Redeemer; in civ. He is seen as Creator. Both begin and end similarly. Our, present psalm is conspicuous for its poetic beauty. Its general arrangement is suggested by the record of creation in Gen. i., but the treatment is "free." The maintenance of the universal order rather than the process of creation is emphasised, *i.e.* God's providential care; cf. Job xxxviii.-xli. for similar pictures. Keynote here is 24.

PROPHETIC ANTICIPATION.—Messiah as the last Adam and Head of the new race leads creation's praise to the Creator. Another millennial song. *Redemption is the key to all the mysteries of Creation.* "Death seems to have been wrought into the constitution of things from the beginning, even before Adam's moral ruin introduced it into the human race. This is evidenced by geological strata stretching long ages before Adam. "Forms of life died and disappeared before the earth was prepared as a home for the Adamic race, and Scripture more than hints at sin in the universe as the cause of the great cataclysm, the effects of which are so briefly stated in Gen. i. 2." The fruits of the redemptive work of the Cross will be found beyond the immediate interests of the human race. God will be glorified in *all* His works. The psalm ends with the divine Sabbath.

PERSONAL APPLICATION.—The rejoicing of the redeemed. Jehovah-Saviour written in brief is "Jesus." Man is the only real spokesman of creation. "Scientist and artist must rise to the psalmist's point of view if they are to learn the deepest lessons of nature." The universe is the garment of God (2); the visible is the robe of the Invisible. "The Uncreated Light arrays Himself in created light which reveals while it veils Him." Physical facts illustrate spiritual truths. Look for the typical significance throughout the psalm, which is full of deeply instructive matter along this line. All natural phenomena are issues of God's present will. It is well to remember that God controls all the elemental forces (3 ff.) and a "look," a "touch" from Him is sufficient (32). Matter and motion alone do not explain heavenly phenomena (2-3). Water is one of God's greatest gifts and like all His great gifts to man is free (10 ff.). Living water is typical of the Holy Spirit. "By His marvellous alchemy God produces manifold gifts from the ground by the agency of water. The element which desolated the world when guided and restrained by divine power effects a beneficent ministry." Throughout the

I

passage the psalmist is thinking of utility rather than beauty. Note that earth is ever dependent upon heaven, man upon God. God provides for man's enjoyment as well as his sustenance (15). It is God who makes the soil respond to man's tillage (15). The sun is a punctual servant (19). Who can repress such an exclamation of wonder and admiration when contemplating the variety and wisdom of God's works (24)? Life not death prevails in the world that God rules (30). In nature, preservation is a continual creation (30). Creation is in deep sympathy with its Creator (32). Universal Providence meets universal dependence.

VERSE NOTES

1. Heb. verbs express an act rather than a state; (c) "Thou hast clothed Thyself . . ." In the creative act God has made visible these inherent attributes.

2. Light, the first created element, is universally diffused, a necessary condition of life and emblem of purity; (b) canopy of the sky compared to a tent curtain stretched out over the earth. In next verse this "tent" roof pictured as His "floor." The verbs are particles, "covering . . . stretching . . . to end of 4, i.e. the original act is regarded as continued in present maintenance.

3. "chambers" lit. upper chambers, so 13; "waters," i.e. above the firmament; (bc) symbolic of His advent; "clouds" = thick clouds.

4. May be translated as R.V. or as the quotation at Heb. i. 7. Both contain profound truth, for God is Creator and Controller of physical and spiritual forces.

5. As R.V.m.

6. Primitive state of the earth; br. "The waters were standing . . ." The graphic imperfect tense denoting process is continued to 8a; "they flee . . . haste away . . . rise . . . sink down . . ."

8. (b) Br. ". . . which Thou didst prepare . . ."

9. This decree confirmed after the Flood, Gen. ix. 9.

10. "Who sendeth forth . . ."

11. (a) Wild animals as distinct from domesticated.

12. "Beside them . . ."

13. "Who giveth the mountains drink from . . ." i.e. the rains.

14. "herb," includes all vegetable products; line as marg.

15. "And that wine may gladden . . . That He may make his face to shine with oil and that bread may sustain . . .;" corn, wine and oil were the chief products of Palestine.

16. Points to the natural growth of the primeval forest in contra-distinction from that planted by man; "are filled", i.e. satisfied with the rain from heaven.

18. "conies," i.e. the Hyrax syriacus, Prov. xxx. 26; not the rabbit.

19. Note that night precedes day as usual in Scripture.

21. Beasts of prey are also part of God's creation and dependent on His bounty. All life is fitted to its environment; "God" = El.

24. "riches" = possessions.

25. The sea was probably in the poet's sight when he wrote; "creeping" or, moving; (c) br. "Living creatures both great and small."

26. "leviathan," = a term here for sea monsters in general; "play" = sport.

27. "All of them wait for Thee," *i.e.* not the marine animals only, but all the living creatures.

28 ff. Swift clauses without connecting particles vividly represent divine acts as immediately followed by providential consequences.

29. All are dependent upon God for life as well as for food; "troubled," = dismayed or, panic-stricken.

30. Life not death rules nature; a new generation replaces the old. God perpetually sends forth His Spirit in continued creative acts.

31. Br. "The glory . . . shall be for ever, Jehovah rejoiceth in His own works," Job xiv. 15.

34. "But as for me, my meditation shall be sweet unto Him"; "sweet," or, acceptable, a word used of sacrifices.

35. The last prayer is that the only blot upon the scene may be removed. Not an imprecation but a desire for restoration of perfect harmony in creation by the banishment of sin, which is a personal thing and cannot be separated from its agent, the sinner. The intensitive form of the Heb. word for sinner implies incorrigible habit.

There is strong reason to believe that the final "Hallelujah" really belongs to the beginning of next psalm. It is a phrase never found in the purely Davidic psalms; so the LXX.

PSALM CV.   A MEMORIAL OF MANIFOLD MERCIES

I. RENDERING OF PRAISE (1–6).   Hallelujah.   (From civ. 35*d*).

II. REASONS FOR PRAISE (7–12).   The Remembered Covenant.   Promise.

III. REVIEW OF HISTORY.   *The Patriarchs* (13–22).
      Divine Foresight demonstrated.
    1. Their Destined Migration (13).
    2. The Divine Protection (14–15).
    3. Their Dire Affliction (16).
    4. The Delivering Mission. JOSEPH (17–22).
      (i) The Sending (17).
      (ii) The Suffering (18–19). Joseph's Prison. The Word of Jehovah.
      (iii) The Saving (20–22).

IV. REVIEW OF HISTORY.   *The People* (23–41).
      Divine Faithfulness demonstrated.
    1. Their Destined Migration (23).
    2. The Divine Protection (24).

    3. Their Dire Affliction (25).
    4. The Delivering Mission (26-41). MOSES and AARON.
      (i) The Sending (26).
      (ii) The Smiting (27-36). Egypt's Punishment. The "Words of His Signs."
      (iii) The Saving (37-41).
V. REASONS FOR PRAISE. (42-45b). The Remembered Covenant. Performance.
VI. RENDERING OF PRAISE (45.). Hallelujah.

PRIMARY ASSOCIATION.—The psalm is anonymous and the occasion unknown, but the poet incorporates (verses 1-15) a large section of the psalm of thanksgiving written by David for the translation of the ark of God to Zion (1 Chron. xvi.). Closely related to the next psalm with which it forms a pair in designed contrast. Both are retrospective and didactic. Keynote to cv., Jehovah's mighty deeds remembered; keynote to cvi., Jehovah's mighty deeds forgotten. Jehovah's constant faithfulness; His lovingkindness celebrated; the obverse of the national history; God's ways with Israel, cv. Israel's continual faithfulness; their lawlessness confessed; the reverse of the national history; Israel's ways with God, cvi. Note that the closing "Hallelujah" of Ps. civ. probably belongs to the beginning of our present psalm (so the LXX etc.) in which case cv. and cvi. begin and end alike, as also do ciii. and civ.

PROPHETIC ANTICIPATION.—These words will be upon the lips of the faithful remnant in the last days and doubtless of the restored nation in millennial celebrations. Verse 8 points to what will then have been a recent experience. It is very significant that the first "Hallelujah" psalm immediately follows the announcement of the destruction of the "lawless ones" (civ. 35); cf. the first "Hallelujah" in the New Testament (Rev. xix. 1-2).

PERSONAL APPLICATION.—What we know of God we should make known (1). While singing, meditate; while meditating, sing (2). Seek strength from its Source (4). Present-day believers are also of the "seed" of Abraham (6 with Gal. iii. 29). Because God in faithfulness remembers us, we should in gratitude remember Him (5, 8). He may use a famine to fulfil His loving purpose (10). Many of His devoted servants have been in prison (17-18). God's promise tests all His children sooner or later (19). In Joseph's case patience had its perfect work (19), cf. Jas. i. 4. All trials are only "until the time" appointed. The world ever hates those whom God favours (25). When God delivers, He does so with abundance of blessing and great joy (37). Those whom He delivers He also cares for (39). The object of His delivering grace is to have an obedient people (45). Obedience was the condition of Israel's retaining these blessings (45). What God has done is the best revelation of what God is (1). Without a clear and close knowledge of God our witness will be cold and cheerless (4).

VERSE NOTES

1. Transfer "Hallelujah" from civ. end. It is significant that the first "Hallelujah" in the Psalms immediately follows upon the announcement of the destruction of the wicked, cf. Rev. xix. 3ff. (a) Rather " . . . proclaim His Name," as in Exod. xxxiii. 19, etc.; (b) indicates Israel's mission. Jehovah's works and wonders are Israel's witness to the world.

2. "sing praises" = make melody, lit. psalm (as a verb.)

4. (a) "Seek" indicates attitude; (b) "Seek" indicates act; not s.H.w.

5. (b) i.e. the sentences pronounced and executed upon the Egyptians.

7. "He, Jehovah, is our God." Though He has a special relation to Israel, yet He exercises universal rule.

8. Obligations under which God has placed Himself with regard to Israel, represented as (a) a covenant, implying mutual responsibilities; (b) a word, i.e. His will expressed in an articulate utterance; (c) an oath, i.e. a solemn sanction and pledge given.

9 ff. The promise made to Abraham was renewed to Isaac and Jacob because in their persons it was limited to a particular branch of Abraham's descendants.

11. (b) = for your appointed inheritance.

12. A.V. and A.R.V. punctuation correct here; "sojourners" i.e. without rights of citizenship.

13. (a) "And (when) they . . ."

15. "anointed," because set apart and endowed for appointed tasks; "prophets" as receiving divine communications.

16 ff. Note divine agency.

17. "He had sent . . . a slave."

18. The Genesis narrative does not give these details. Here are further particulars divinely revealed; (b) "He was put in irons."

19. (a) Omit comma at the end of the line; (b) "word," or promise.

22. Ctr. 18.

23. "So Israel came . . .," i.e. Jacob and his family.

24. "stronger," i.e. in number.

25. (b) i.e. by their crafty plans to destroy the nation. The psalmist sees but one hand at work—Jehovah's.

27. Most ancient versions read, "He set . . ."

28. Plagues mentioned out of chronological order. Ninth first probably because

it seems to have wrought conviction in the minds of the Egyptian people. Of the plagues recorded here the first two attack the elements; the next three concern animal life, the following two concern vegetable life; the last destroys human and animal life; (b) refers to the Egyptians. For a time they were appalled into perfect stillness and obedience. Egyptians were worshippers of the sun-god.

29. First plague.

30. Second plague.

31. (a) Fourth plague, = "gadflies"; (b) Third plague, = sandflies, or more probably mosquitoes.

32-33. Seventh plague.

34-35. Eighth plague.

34. (b) Ref. to locust larvæ.

35. (a) "herb," Heb. word includes all vegetable growth except trees.

36. Tenth and last plague; (b) br. " . . . the firstlings of their strength."

37. "So He . . . not one that stumbled." Israel marched out like a victorious army with spoils which were virtually the reward of their long compulsory service; " . . . His (Jehovah's) tribes."

38. "fear" = dread.

39. The Cloud here regarded as a canopy to shelter them from the burning rays of the desert sun; cf. Isa. iv. 5-6.

40 ff. Israel's murmuring not mentioned for it is the psalmist's purpose to emphasise God's goodness not Israel's unbelief.

41. (b) "They flowed through the deserts—a river."

42. The psalmist returns to his theme, cf. 8.

43. (b) "(And)" br. Even . . .

44. (b) "labour," metonym for what is produced by labour. These two verses show the completion of that which began in Egypt.

45. Br. "To the end that . . .," shows the object of God's favour; the practical effect He desired.

PSALM CVI. A RECORD OF REPEATED REBELLION

I. RENDERING OF PRAISE (1-3). "Hallelujah."
    1. Commencing Exhortation (1). Summons and Stimulus.
    2. Challenging Exclamation (2).
    3. Confident Expression (3). "Happy." Beatitude.

II. REQUEST FOR DELIVERANCE (4-5). Personal.

III. REVIEW OF HISTORY, PERSONAL (6). "We have sinned."

IV. REVIEW OF HISTORY, PATERNAL (7-46). "Our fathers (sinned)."
    1. Rebellion and Recovery (7-12). Provocation. Exodus from Egypt.
      (i) The Sin (7).
      (ii) The Salvation (8-12). "Nevertheless."

2. Rebellion and Recovery (13-23).
   (i) The Sin (13-16).
   (ii) The Searching (17-18).
   (iii) The Sin (19-22).
   (iv) The Searching (23a).
   (v) The Salvation (23bc). Intercession of Moses.
3. Rebellion and Recovery (24-31).
   (i) The Sin (24-25).
   (ii) The Searching (26-27).
   (iii) The Sin (28-29a).
   (iv) The Searching (29b).
   (v) The Salvation (30-31). Interposition of Phinehas.
4. Rebellion and Recovery (32-43a).
   (i) The Sin (32a).
   (ii) The Searching (32b-33).
   (iii) The Sin (34-39).
   (iv) The Searching (40-42).
   (v) The Salvation (43a). Intervention of Jehovah.
5. Rebellion and Recovery (43b-46). Provocation. Experience in Canaan.
   (i) The Sin (43bc).
   (ii) The Salvation (44-46). "Nevertheless."

V. REQUEST FOR DELIVERANCE (47). National.

VI. RENDERING OF PRAISE (48). "Hallelujah."
   1. Crowning Expression (48ab). "Blessed." Benediction.
   2. Closing Exhortation (48c).

PRIMARY ASSOCIATION.—Writer and occasion unknown, but 47 might seem to indicate the period of the Exile. Yet it is not necessary to assume such a late date for the psalmist may have been speaking prophetically. The Dispersion was well known as a prophetic event, Deut. xxviii. 64. Solomon himself prays this prayer, 1 Kings viii. 46-50. See notes to cv. "Never but in Israel has patriotism chosen a nation's sins as a theme of song, or in celebrating its victories written but one name, the name of Jehovah, upon its trophies." (Maclaren). Compare other hymns of national confession, 1 Kings viii.; Neh. ix.; Dan. ix.; Deut. xxvi. With verses 47-48 cf. 1 Chron. xvi. 34-36; also Isa. lxiii.; Ezk. xx. This psalm closes Book IV. The chronological order of Israel's relapses is not preserved.

PROPHETIC ANTICIPATION.—Notes to cv. apply equally to the present psalm though the prayer (47), which is the climax of the composition, points more especially to the end time immediately before the national deliverance effected by Messiah's advent.

PERSONAL APPLICATION.—The history of God's past is a record of continuous mercies; the record of man's past is one of continual sin. Man's wickedness cannot alter God's character (1). Israel's relapses did not exhaust Jehovah's lovingkindness (1). No human voice can adequately celebrate His works or worthily proclaim His praises (2). God's mercy and might are sure ground for His people's hope (1–2). "Is it right?" (3) is a higher law than, "Is it profitable?" or "Is it popular?" or "Is it pleasant?" God expects His people to have and to exercise spiritual insight (7). Forgetfulness often leads to sin (7). The sin of rebellion is obstinate resistance to the revealed will of God (7c). God is tempted when unbelief demands proof of His power (14). We should never try to force the hand of God (13–15). Full-fed flesh often makes starved souls (15). Many Christians suffer from a spiritual "wasting sickness" (15). Our hearts are often slow to recognise the divine mark in His saints (16). Jehovah is the glory of Israel (20). For God's people to follow their own counsel is rebellion (43). An act of judgment may be an act of faith (31). Even a strong leader may be dragged down by the prevailing tone (33). Divine discipline takes account of all alike (32). If we do not overcome our spiritual foes they will overcome us (34). Envy often masquerades as the champion of common rights (16). Envy of God-given leaders is not confined, alas, to Israel (16). "It took forty hours to get Israel out of Egypt, but forty years to get Egypt out of Israel." In the world's history human lawlessness and divine long-suffering have appeared in constantly repeated cycles. The long recital of Israel's lapses and failure ends upon the note of Jehovah's lovingkindness and forgiveness (44 ff.).

VERSE NOTES

1. "good," *i.e.* not God's essential goodness, but His kindness to Israel.

3. Br. "O how happy . . ."; (b) in experience true only of Christ.

4. Cf. Nehemiah's interposed prayers, Neh. v. 19; vi. 14; xiii. 14, 22, 31. Psalmist prays that he personally may share in the nation's restoration to the divine favour; lit. " . . . with (or, in) the favour (or, acceptance) of Thy people."

5. Note the three names for Jehovah's people; "glory," or triumph.

6. Main theme of the psalm; confession of recurrent sin; "with" expresses not merely "like (our fathers)" but identification in a sense of national solidarity. Note threefold description of the sin.

9. (b) *i.e.* on dry ground.

10. "redeemed them," *i.e.* as a kinsman-redeemer.

12. This allusion to their momentary faith and gratitude serves only to emphasise the later relapses.

13. They were only three days on their journey when they murmured; six weeks later they murmured again.

14. (*b*) *i.e.* by questioning His will and ability to provide.

15. Cf. their complaint, "Our soul is dried away" (Num. xi. 6); *i.e.* vitality exhausted.

16. (*b*) as marg. Aaron was specially set apart for Jehovah and consecrated to His service, Num. xvi. 3 ff.

17. Korah's family did not perish.

19. "Horeb," the name always given to Sinai in Deut. except at xxxiii. 2.

20. "their glory," ancient reading was "My glory." Note the instructive moral order in Israel's doings from 16 on.

23. (*b*) Moses was like a warrior standing in the breach of a city wall to repel the enemy at risk of his life.

24. They despised the "delightsome" land and disbelieved God's promise to give it them.

25. (*a*) Graphic picture of Israelites sulking in their tents instead of boldly preparing themselves for the march.

26. Br. "So He lifted up His hand unto them; That He would make them (emph.) fall in the wilderness," *i.e.* He swore solemnly; fig. anthropopatheia.

27. "overthrow," br. disperse.

28. They attached themselves as devotees to Baal-peor, *i.e.* the particular Baal worshipped at Peor by the Moabites, Num. xxv. 3. (*b*) This either pertains to necromancy or else refers to "dead" gods in ctr. with the Living God.

29. "provoked," = grieved or irritated; not same Heb. word as in 7, 33, 43.

31. This zeal of Phinehas was for God, not for a party, and he acted upon the impulse of faith.

32-33. 33*a* parallels 32*a*, 33*b* parallels 32*b*; "His Spirit," *i.e.* God's; "he (Moses) spake rashly . . ."; but Rotherham renders 33*a*, "For they embittered his spirit," still ref. to Moses.

34. They did not destroy the Canaanites, so the Canaanites destroyed them.

35. *i.e.* by matrimonial alliances and intercouse generally.

37. "demons," Heb. word only here and Deut. xxxii. 17. Israel failed to take warning from the fate of the Canaanites.

38. The climax of Canaanitish abominations; (*c*) = profaned by bloodshed; see also of Israel, Ezk. xvi. 20–21; xx. 31.

39. Br. " . . . their own works, and prostituted themselves with their own doings." Relation of Israel to Jehovah is often expressed by the figure of the marriage vow.

43. (*b*) Br. "But as for them, they . . ." Note the old story: (*a*) Rebellion; (*b*) Retribution; (*c*) Repentance; (*d*) Restoration, in recurrent cycles.

46. "them" (emph.). In answer to Solomon's prayer, 1 Kings viii. 50.

47. This prayer is the climax of the psalm.

48. A liturgical direction (cf. 1 Chron. xvi. 36); a doxology forming part of the psalm as well as marking the close of the Fourth Book.

Book Five. *Israel's Regathering and Retrospect: cvii.–cl.*

This "Deuteronomy" Book shows Israel regathered and ready to take full possession of their land. The nation is represented as taking a retrospective view of Jehovah's dealings with His people, bringing them to a recognition of what their Covenant-God is to them and proving them that He might fully bless them "at the latter end." See Deut. viii. 2–3, where Jehovah Himself gives the reason for the trials of Israel's pilgrimage. Israel strikes the keynote of praise in cvii. which is taken up by the gentiles (cxvii.) and the sound increases in volume until the grand climax is reached in cl. See further notes at Introduction, p. 24.

Pss. cvii.–cx. introduce a series of nine psalms (cxi.–cxix.) almost certainly sung at the laying of the foundation of the second temple. Ps. cxix. may be regarded as the preaching after the praise. It was doubtless composed by Ezra himself. Pss. cxxxv.–cxlv. celebrate the happy completion of the work. The remaining psalms (cxlvi.–cl.) were sung most probably at the consecration of the city walls under Nehemiah.

ANALYSIS.

I. THE WAYS OF GOD RETRACED IN THE NATIONAL HISTORY, CVII–CXII.
1. Divine Dealings with Israel, cvii.–cviii. National. The Gathered People.
2. Divine Dealings with Messiah, cix.–cx. Special.
3. Divine Dealings with Israel, cxi.–cxii. Individual. The God-fearing Persons.

II. THE WAYS OF GOD RECALLED IN THE NATIONAL HOMAGE, CXIII–CXVIII.
SONGS FOR PASSOVER. THE "HALLEL."
1. The Commencement. Praise, cxiii. The Theme introduced.
2. The Celebration. cxiv.–cxvii. The Testimony and Tribute.
3. The Conclusion. Praise, cxviii. The Thanksgiving inspired.

III. THE WORD OF GOD REVERED BY THE LOYAL HEART, CXIX. (CENTRAL).

IV. THE WAYS OF GOD RECALLED IN THE NATIONAL HOME-COMING, CXX–CXXXIV.
SONGS OF PILGRIMAGE. THE ASCENTS (DEGREES).
Cycle 1. *Human Stress and Divine Sufficiency: cxx.–cxxii.*
Jehovah the National Refuge. The Keeper of Israel.
Cycle 2. *Human Stress and Divine Sufficiency: cxxiii.–cxxv.*
Jehovah the National Rescuer. The Helper of Israel.
Delivered from Foes.

Cycle 3. *Human Stress and Divine Sufficiency: cxxvi.–cxxviii.*
  Jehovah the National Rebuilder. The Establisher of Israel.
Cycle 4. *Human Stress and Divine Sufficiency: cxxix.–cxxxi.*
  Jehovah the National Redeemer. The Saviour of Israel.
  Delivered from Sins.
Cycle 5. *Human Stress and Divine Sufficiency: cxxxii.–cxxxiv.*
  Jehovah the National Reconciler. The Uniter of Israel.

V. THE WAYS OF GOD RETRACED IN THE NATIONAL HISTORY,
   CXXXV–CXLV.
   1. Witness in Praise, cxxxv.–cxxxvi. Israel.
   2. Workings of Providence, cxxxvii.–cxxxix.
   3. Waiting in Prayer, cxl.–cxliv.
   4. Witness in Praise, cxlv. Messiah.

CHORAL APPENDIX:—

VI. THE WORSHIP OF GOD RENDERED IN UNIVERSAL HARMONY,
   CXLVI–CL.
   1. Praise Universal, cxlvi. The Initial Descant.
   2. Praise National, cxlvii.
   3. Praise Universal, cxlviii.
   4. Praise National, cxlix.
   5. Praise Universal, cl. The Final Doxology.

Book Five. I. The Ways of God Retraced in the National History:
cvii.–cxii.

1. Divine Dealings with Israel, cvii.–cviii. National. The
   Gathered People.
   (i) Restoration of the People, cvii.
   (ii) Repossession of the Land, cviii.

PSALM CVII. THE PRINCIPLES OF PROVIDENCE

I. EXHORTATION TO PRAISE (1–3). Jehovah's Lovingkindness.
   1. The Invitation (1).
   2. The Incentives (1). "for . . . for."
   3. The Individuals (2–3). The Redeemed.

II. EXHIBITION OF JEHOVAH'S PRESERVING GOODNESS (4–32).
   Distress and Deliverance. Extremity and Extrication.
   FIRST ILLUSTRATION (4–9). Lost in the Desert.
   1. The Plight (4–5).
   2. The Prayer (6a). Cry of the Scattered.

     3. The Preservation (6b–7). Jehovah the Leader.
     4. The Praise (8–9).
       (a) Request (8).
       (b) Reason (9). "For."

  SECOND ILLUSTRATION (10–16). Languishing in the Dungeon.
     1. The Plight (10–12).
     2. The Prayer (13a). Cry of the Shackled.
     3. The Preservation (13b–14). Jehovah the Liberator.
     4. The Praise (15–16).
       (a) Request (15).
       (b) Reason (16). "For."

  THIRD ILLUSTRATION (17-22). Languishing in a Disease.
     1. The Plight (17–18).
     2. The Prayer (19a). Cry of the Sick.
     3. The Preservation (19b–20). Jehovah the Life-giver.
     4. The Praise (21–22).
       (a) Appeal (21).
       (b) Amplification (22).

  FOURTH ILLUSTRATION (23–32). Lost on the Deep.
     1. The Plight (23–27).
     2. The Prayer (28a). Cry of the Storm-tossed.
     3. The Preservation (28b–30). Jehovah the Lord.
     4. The Praise (31–32).
       (a) Appeal (31).
       (b) Amplification (32).

III. EXHIBITION OF JEHOVAH'S PROVIDENTIAL GOVERNMENT
    (33–42).
     Bane and Blessing. Punishment and Pity. Cf. verses 4–5.
     1. Penalty (33–34).
     2. Prosperity (35–38).
     3. Penalty (39–40).
     4. Prosperity (41–42).

IV. EXHORTATION TO PONDER (43). Jehovah's Lovingkindness.
     "Observe . . . consider."

PRIMARY ASSOCIATION.—This psalm almost certainly belongs to the early post-exilic period, although the authorship is unknown. There is no mention of the temple, but 22, 32 suggest a national feast as the occasion; cf. Ezra iii. 1–8. See Analysis Book V. notes. Here is a most fitting preface to the Book celebrating Israel's restoration and return. It illustrates the divine ways with Israel and with men in general. Observe the keynote appearing here, *the healing word sent* (20). Notwithstanding the division of the Books, this psalm is closely related to the preceding ones, cv.–cvii. forming a kind of trilogy. Celebration of Israel's Redemption from Egypt, cv. Confession of Israel's Rebellion against El, cvi. Celebration of Israel's Restoration from Exile, cvii. Note the three successive periods indicated; "He gave them the lands of the nations," cv. 44; "He would scatter them in the lands of the nations," cvi. 27; "He gathered them out of the lands," cvii. 3.

PROPHETIC ANTICIPATION.—The unfailing faithfulness of Jehovah is the theme of song for restored Israel. The psalm gives not only facts but figures of the national condition. The deliverances mentioned are combined with a present redemption. Israel's return from the Babylonian exile prefigures a full and final return of "the dispersion" yet to come. The furnace of affliction was provided for in the original Abrahamic covenant, and that as a means of bringing back to Himself a rebellious people. Of such a furnace the Egyptian bondage was one example, even as the wilderness journeyings were prototype of their many wanderings. In their typical aspect the four strophes illustrating the nation's experiences are very expressive and instructive. The "city of habitation" (7) speaks of the abiding rest to which Israel is at last brought in millennial days.

PERSONAL APPLICATION.—In spite of their rebellious behaviour God does not abandon His people, but finds a way of restoring and blessing them, acting always in power, love and holiness. The obligation of praise lies upon all God's redeemed ones (1–2). Israel's well-known song is not out of place for a Christian (1). An old motto may bring a new message (1). Hymns of former days are often the best vehicles for praise to-day (1). Verses 4–32 give vivid representations of a life apart from God. Trouble, trust, triumph and tribute is a common order in Christian experience (4–32). A crooked way is necessarily a long way (7). God's way is ever the straight (right) way (7). The lovingkindness of God is expressed in His works (8). Divine provision exactly meets our needs (5 with 9, 10 with 14), etc. There is no hope or help for the sinner except in the very One against whom he has rebelled (12). Sometimes God has to use trouble to subdue our hearts (12). All sin is folly (12). A fool is one who is slow to learn lessons from his own experience (17). Inveterate sin ruins physical health (17 ff.). Sin brings sickness to the soul (17 ff.). Sickness is not necessarily a proof of sin (cf. Job) but may be a pointer to it (17). God's word is His messenger to perform His will (20). God is a sure guide on land (7) and on sea (30). All mockery of God's people and blasphemy against our God will one day be silenced (42). Wise are they who observe and consider the ways of God (43).

VERSE NOTES

2. Br. "clutch of the oppressor."

3. The returning exiles stream from every quarter—"gathered" is a prominent thought in Book V.

4. "desert way" = trackless waste, so 40.

6. "trouble" = strait.

7. "And He guided them in the straight (right) way," cf. Ezra viii. 21.

8. Br. "Let them (= the delivered ones) give thanks to Jehovah for . . ."; "children" = sons; "men" or, Adam.

9. "Because He satisfied . . . filled."

10. "shadow of death" or, deathly gloom, so 14; cf. xxiii. 4; xliv. 19; "affliction" = oppression.

11. "words" = sayings, or utterances.

12. i.e. "so that He subdued their heart with travail—"fell down" = lit. stumbled.

15. Trans. as 8 and so at 21, 31.

16. This hints at the manner of the attack by Cyrus (conqueror of Babylon) as Jehovah's unconscious instrument.

17. "Fools," the word denotes moral perversity not mere weakness of intellect or ignorance. Such folly leads to ruin; cf. Deut. xxxii. 6; "transgression" = revolt. Note margin; this implies persistence in evil courses.

17. (b) More lit. = "bring affliction on themselves."

20. The peculiar expression "sent His word" prepares the way for the fuller revelation of the Divine Logos, John i; "destructions," see margin, or, pitfalls; perhaps = graves into which they had almost fallen.

24. Br. "These (men) have seen . . ."

25. "For He spake and raised . . ."

26. "they" (the sailors); "Their soul melteth in evil plight;" cf. Deut. xxviii. 65.

27. (b) i.e. skill in navigation fails them.

30. "they (the waves) are calmed;" "bringeth" = guideth.

32. Br. "Yea, let them extol Him in . . . session of the elders;" i.e. publicly declare His praises.

33. Note change in the style of the "He hath turned, etc." The verbs should be translated in the past tense as ref. to facts of experience not merely to general truths. This applies to verses 33–41; 33–34 probably refer to Babylon; 35 to Palestine as reinhabited by the returned exiles.

34. Like Sodom and Gomorrah.

36. "prepare" or, found.

39. "And when they were diminished . . ." Should be comma, not full stop at the end of 39. "And He set the needy . . . and made . . ."

41. (*b*) *i.e.* makes them numerous.

42. "The upright see and are glad . . . stoppeth her mouth."

43. "Whoso is wise let him observe . . . and let them consider . . ." cf. Hosea xiv. 9.

PSALM CVIII.　　FIXITY OF FAITH

I. ASCRIPTION OF PRAISE (1-4).

1. Expression of Purpose (1).
2. Exhortation to Praise (2*a*).
3. Expression of Purpose (2*b*-3).
4. Explanation of Praise (4).

II. APPEAL IN PRAYER (5-6). Looking for the Liberator.

1. Plea (5).
2. Purpose (6*a*).
3. Petition (6*b*).

III. ANSWER OF PROMISE (7-9). Jehovah speaks.

1. Declaration concerning the Land (7-8*a*). Palestine.
   Three representative territories mentioned.
2. Declaration concerning Israel (8). The People. "Mine" = Central Thought.
   Three representative tribes mentioned.
3. Declaration concerning Enemies (9). The Peoples.
   Three representative nations mentioned.

IV. APPEAL IN PRAYER (10-12). Looking for the Leader.

1. Pleading (10-11).
2. Petition (12*a*).
3. Principle (12*b*).

V. ASSURANCE OF PROSPERITY (13).

1. The Faith (13*a*).
2. The Foundation (13*b*). "*He.*"

SUPERSCRIPT.—A Song, a Psalm of David.

PRIMARY ASSOCIATION.—First of the fifteen Davidic psalms in Book V. It consists of parts of two psalms, namely lvii. and lx. Revived in this new form probably on the return from Babylon to suit the new circumstances. The psalm shows the end of God's ways with men, hence "the ends of two previous psalms are cut off from the exercise and trials connected therewith and joined together into a complete whole." Slight word changes are found to accord with the new purpose.

PROPHETIC ANTICIPATION.—Points to the same period as preceding psalm. At the manifestation of Messiah's "Presence" (Parousia) the Beast and the False Prophet with their armies are destroyed at Armageddon, II Thes. ii. 8; Rev. xix. 19-21. Between this event and the full setting up of the millennial kingdom, however, other enemies of God and of Israel, including the "Assyrian," remain to be dealt with as indicated in many prophetic Scriptures. Hence Israel's thanksgiving for recent rescue is coupled here and elsewhere with appeals for complete deliverance from all national foes.

PERSONAL APPLICATION.—Old strains often suit new joys. Fixed hearts are never flurried by passing events (1). True worship must be "in spirit and in truth" (1b), cf. John iv. It is good to awaken the dawn with praise and prayer (2b). Thanksgiving should be public as well as private (3). Note again as so often in the psalms the coupling of grace (lovingkindness) and truth (troth, or faithfulness) (4). All God's people long for Him to exalt Himself by the manifestation of His supremacy on earth (5). Divine victory has as its object the deliverance of God's people from their oppressors not, as so often in human history, for the selfish exploitation of the defeated (6). God exults in the people of His possession (7–8). Many a citadel of the Evil One remains yet to be conquered in this and in other lands (10). God has *not* cast off Israel for ever (11 cf. Rom. xi. 2, 26) as some erroneously believe. Israel had to learn the lesson of 12b in the school of bitter experience. The victory is ever His, though we may be the instruments of it (13).

VERSE NOTES

In general, compare corresponding notes at Pss. lvii. and lx.

2. Here a pathetic summons to these instruments long silent in Babylon, cf. cxxxvii.

3. Jehovah having wrought salvation for them in the sight of the nations (xcviii.), His praise therefore should be published among them.

5. Or, "Exalt Thyself . . ." *i.e.* by the manifestation of supreme authority.

6. Br. "answer me" as A.V.

7 ff. Jehovah regards Ephraim as the chief defence of His kingdom and Judah as the seat of His government, while neighbouring nations are treated as His vassals,

10. "fortified," not same word as in lx. 9; anciently = "fenced", now = "fortified"; change of word may have prophetic significance.

11. Br. "Wilt not Thou, O God, Who didst cast us off . . . and didst not . . ."

13. "He" (emph.).

Book Five. I. The Ways of God Retraced in the National History:
cvii.-cxii.

2. Divine Dealings with Messiah, cix.-cx..

(i) Hated of Man, cix.
(ii) Honoured of God, cx.

PSALM CIX. HOSTILITY OF HUMANITY

I. INVOCATION OF DIVINE AID (1-5).
    1. Request (1).
    2. Reasons (2-5). Causeless Enmity.

II. IMPRECATION UPON THE DECEITFUL ADVERSARY (6-15).

III. INVOCATION OF DIVINE AID (16-27).
    1. Against the Adversary (16-20).
    2. About the Adversaries (21-27).
        (i) Prayers and Pleas (21). The Cry.
        (ii) Plaint (22). The Cause.
        (iii) Parables (23). The Comparison.
        (iv) Plaint (24-25). The Cause.
        (v) Prayers and Pleas (26-27). The Cry.

IV. INFLICTION UPON THE DECEITFUL ADVERSARY (28-29).

V. INTIMATION OF DIVINE AID (30-31).
    1. Ascription of Praise (30). Rendition of Thanks.
    2. Assurance of Preservation (31). Reason for Thanks.

SUPERSCRIPT.—A Psalm of David.

PRIMARY ASSOCIATION.—Written by David during the period of Absalom's rebellion; cf. 4-5 with 2 Sam. xviii. 5. The psalm has then much in common with xxxv. and lxix. In a commonly accepted view this is the last and most strongly-worded of the imprecatory psalms, on which see Appendix IV. David's one weapon against Ahithophel the traitor was prayer, 2 Sam. xv. 31; Ps. lxiv. 2. It is quite possible, however, that verses 6–15, or even as far as verse 19, are not David's own words at all, but the imprecation of his enemies. Note that the pronouns change from the plural to the singular at verse 6 and back again to the plural at verse 20. Scripture structure is frequently elliptical, leaving the word "saying" to be understood at the beginning of a quotation. See, for instance, 1 Kings xx. 34; Ps. ii. 2–3; Isa. xiv. 8; xviii. 2; xxiv. 14–15; Jer. xi. 19; l. 5; Acts x. 15, etc. So here the construction may be, "(Saying), Set Thou . . ." This then would be the substance of Shimei's cursing, 2 Sam. xvi. 5–14. The word "This" (20) is emphatic, and in the view just given, would mean, "*This* (cursing) is . . ." connecting with the history, 2 Sam. xvi. 10, and adding force to certain verses of our psalm, especially 28. Contrast the assurance of David (31) with the desire of his enemy (6). The fact that 8*b* is applied to Judas seems to argue against this interpretation but is not conclusive. Because of the difficulty the analysis is given with some hesitancy.

PROPHETIC ANTICIPATION.—This overrides the primary interpretation. The application to Judas, the betrayer of our Lord, gives the clue to the Messianic import. Here is the voice of the Prince of Martyrs identifying Himself with God's witnesses who have suffered at the hand of man from Abel on throughout the world's history. Messiah's atoning sufferings at the hand of God are not found in this psalm. The prophetic aspect also looks beyond Judas to apostate Israel persecuting the godly remnant and especially to Antichrist in whom treachery finds its climax.

PERSONAL APPLICATION.—All the people of God earnestly desire the eradication of evil and the triumph of truth. Grace has its limit; if its offers are refused, man's condemnation is increased. There is no contradiction between God's character and His acts. God finds it necessary at times to eradicate an evil seed lest the evil harvest overwhelm the good. Causeless enmity has its origin in the condition of heart from which it springs (3). There is One whose love was answered by loathing (5). "The sun that invigorates the living breeds corruption in the dead." The silence of God may be contrasted with the clamour of our foes (1). God is the sole object of the believer's praise (1). Ancestors and posterity often partake of a common sin (13). Man's choice of evil is frequently followed by self-retributive action. "The world is a mirror which usually gives back the smile or frown which we present to it" (17–18). It is far better to have the Almighty at our right hand (31) than the adversary (6). The mouth may be used in wickedness or in worship, but not the same mouth (2, 30); cf. Jas. iii. 9 ff. Many of God's saints have been hurried out of life by evil men (23*a*). Contrast the justified man (31) with the condemned man (6).

VERSE NOTES

1. Or, "Be not silent . . ."
2. Br. "For a lawless man's mouth, yea, a mouth . . ." This points to the leader of the psalmist's enemies.
3. "Yea, with words of hatred have they . . ."
4. "(In return) for my love . . . but *I* (am all) prayer." Heb. word for "adversaries" here is characteristic of this psalm (20, 29 and cf. 6); elsewhere in Psalms only xxxviii. 20; lxxi. 13 = accusers, opponents in a court of law. (*b*) A forceful idiom; parallel passage (xxxv. 13) suggests that his prayers were for these adversaries—a proof of the love for which they requited evil.
6 ff. Represents a trial and condemnation before a tribunal.
6. "Set (in office)" or, appoint. The culprit is himself in office (8); let him be brought before superior authority—"adversary" or, accuser; cf. Zech. iii. 1.
7. *i.e.* shown up to be what he really is and so condemned; (*b*) *i.e.* a prayer only wrung from his heart in extremity and not prompted by true repentance; last despairing cry for mercy after the day of grace is past; plea for clemency rejected.
8. Denotes a premature end; (*b*) with Ps. lxix. 25 is quoted (Acts i. 20) of Judas but is not the ultimate fulfilment; judicial office is implied, trans. "overseership.
9 ff. It seems well to point out here the important addition at Exod. xx. 5; "of them that hate Me." This should prevent misconstruing the divine principle, yet Israel were guilty of it, see Ezek. xviii. where God Himself reprobates such misunderstanding. Nevertheless the character of the father may have much to do with the condition of his children. The consequences of sin are often far-reaching in family history.
10. *i.e.* they seek their bread far from their ruined home.
13. The extinction of the family is regarded in the East as the most terrible of calamities.
14-15. Cf. 9 note.
15. "Let them . . .;" *i.e.* the iniquity and the sin, 14; (*b*) "them" = the ancestors.
18. Indicates a deliberately chosen policy.
19. "(So) let it . . . and as the belt . . ." *i.e.* let the judgment suit the sin.
20. "reward," *i.e.* wages earned, not s.H.w. as in 5.
21. "But *Thou*, Jehovah, Lord, work Thou for (lit. with) me." The combined title, "Jehovah Adonai" occurs in the Psalms only four times, and elsewhere only once.
22. "I" (emph.).
23. Form of the Heb. verb indicates compulsion from without; (*b*) *i.e.* as a locust swept along helplessly by the wind; cf. Exod. x. 19.

24. "My knees give out . . ." (*b*) " . . . is shrunken from (its) fatness."

25. "And I (emph.) am become a . . ." *i.e.* regarded with abhorrence as if he were the object of divine wrath.

27. *i.e.* personal deliverance desired not merely for personal ends, but in order that Jehovah's power may be manifested to His praise.

28. " . . . them (emph.) . . . Thou" (emph.).

31. "stand," *i.e.* as advocate and champion.

PSALM CX.   POTENTATE AND PRIEST

I. THE DIVINE ORACLE DELIVERED (1). Messiah's Present Position Prophesied. Messiah at Jehovah's Right Hand—Waiting. The King in His Throne Room.*

II. THE DIVINE ORACLE DEVELOPED (2-3). Messiah's Royal Dignity and Ready People. Manifestation of Power on Earth.

III. THE DIVINE ORACLE DELIVERED (4). Messiah's Perpetual Priest-hood Prophesied.

IV. THE DIVINE ORACLE DEVELOPED (5-7). Messiah's Radical Victory and Refreshment Place. Manifestation of Power on Earth. Jehovah at Messiah's Right Hand—Warring. The King on the Battlefield.

SUPERSCRIPT.—A Psalm of David.

PRIMARY ASSOCIATION.—Authorship confirmed by our Lord (Matt. xxii.), but the occasion of the divine oracle of the psalm is unknown. It is probably connected with some such event as the translation of the ark to Zion. No psalm is more frequently quoted and alluded to in the New Testament. It seems to stand alone in having no primary historical reference, that is, it is not typical, but directly prophetic. As for the double office of king-priest, besides Melchizedek, we may note that at 2 Sam. vi. 14 David typifies this union (Zech. vi. 13), though not actually king-priest.

PROPHETIC ANTICIPATION.—In this psalm we see Messiah's exaltation following His humiliation (Ps. cix.). It is Jehovah's answer to that prayer establishing Him as King-Priest, with which is associated the promise of Israel's revival under Him. During the present time of His rejection, He sits enthroned at Jehovah's right hand in heaven (cf. Mark xvi. 19). David's experience is in contrast. In Rev. iii. 21 our Lord distinguishes between His heavenly and His earthly thrones, indicating that the latter will be occupied by and by and shared with others. The interval between the two advents is thus only hinted at in this psalm. Enthroned in heaven the Lord Jesus is still Jehovah's Servant and perfect Man, waiting in entire dependence upon God for the appointed day of His return (1). Here it is clearly shown that for Israel also the predicted blessing could not come through the Aaronic priesthood and Levitical ritual of the Law. As the rod of power is seen going forth out of Zion (2) the enemy "head" referred to (6) would seem to be Gog (Ezek. xxxviii.) or "the Assyrian," not "the Beast" who is destroyed by "the manifestation of His (Christ's) Parousia," 2 Thess. ii. 8.

PERSONAL APPLICATION.—This consists in the adoring contemplation of the glories of Christ. It is better to be a sharer of Christ's throne (Rev. iii. 21) than to be made a footstool for His feet (1). They who follow the Priest-King are at once priests and warriors (3); cf. Rev. i. 6; xix. 14. God's people should regard themselves as "free-will offerings" (3, margin), cf. Rom. xii. 1. Where Christ found refreshment, His people may find it too (7). God provides wayside streams for war-weary souls (7).

VERSE NOTES

1. "said," Heb. verb commonly used of direct divine utterances; occurs elsewhere in the Psalter only at xxxvi. 1. The psalmist claims to be the mouthpiece of Jehovah. Verse quoted Matt. xxii. 41-46; Acts ii. 34-35; Heb. i. 13. (b) i.e. the place of honour; but more is implied, for sharing the throne means association in rule. The expression is quoted or referred to seven times in the New Testament. The Lord is set forth as both in repose and in activity. (c) Metaphor for complete subjugation derived from the practice described Josh. x. 24 etc.

2. Br. "The sceptre of thy might shall Jehovah stretch forth out of Zion." see I Cor. xv. 24-28. The sceptre is the symbol of authority. The Heb. word also = strong staff, the symbol of power (for chastisement, etc.). "Zion" is capital of the new kingdom. (b) Br. "(saying) rule . . . " Jehovah speaks, the command being virtually a promise. It should be noted here that David speaks in the Spirit in the rest of the psalm, no less than He did in recording the oracle.

3. Note marginal readings. The promised victory is not to be won without human agency. The king's subjects will be inspired with a spirit of loyal devotion. There will be no conscripts, no mercenaries and no pressed men in Christ's army, only whole-hearted volunteers. Even with David there were elements in Israel that gave him only grudging allegiance, apparent in the rebellions of Absalom and Bichre. 3cd is further description of the mustering army; "youth" = youthful warriors flocking with eagerness to the standard, clad in holy adornment—an army of priests following their Leader the Priest-King; cf. Ps. cxlix. 6-9. They are compared to the dew so abundant and so precious in hot lands of the East. The morning is "mother" of the dew.

4. Melchizedek was a representative of the true faith in a primitive world, Gen. xiv. 18ff.; cf. Heb. vii.; (b) "Thou," (emph.).

5. The scene changes to the battlefield. The King is still addressed. Form of the Heb. verbs indicates that while the victory is still future, it is regarded as already won.

6. "He shall fill (the battlefield) with corpses . . .;" (c) ref. to the arch-enemy as head over a wide territory.

7. "He," ref. to the King. David portrays Him as in hot pursuit of the enemy and halting a moment to refresh Himself from the mountain stream before proceeding to complete His victory. The interpretation seems clear as pointing to the secret of Messiah's success. He Himself as perfect Man drinks deep of the living water (the Spirit) in whose power He conquers every foe. (b) i.e. be triumphant.

Book Five. I. The Ways of God Retraced in the National History: cvii.–cxii.

3. Divine Dealings with Israel, cxi.–cxii. Individual.

(i) God—His Works, cxi. Character Displayed.
(ii) God-fearing Ones—Their Works, cxii. Character Displayed.

PSALM CXI. GOD—HIS GRACE AND GOODNESS

I. THE CONTRIBUTION OF PRAISE (1). "Hallelujah"

II. THE CAUSES FOR PRAISE (2-10). THEMES OF THANKSGIVING.
   1. The Works and the Worker (2-4. Jehovah's Righteousness steadfast for ever.
   2. The Blessings and the Blessed (5-6). Jehovah's Covenant remembered for ever.
   3. The Works and the Worker (7-8). Jehovah's Precepts established for ever.
   4. The Blessings and the Blessed (9-10b). Jehovah's Covenant commanded for ever.

III. THE CONTINUANCE OF PRAISE (10c). It "stands fast" for ever.

PRIMARY ASSOCIATION.—Anonymous and undated but probably belongs to the early post-exilic period. See Analysis Book V notes. Closely connected with cxii. in its structure, language and contents. Each consists of twenty-two lines with an alphabetic acrostic in regular order. Note verse to verse correspondence. The prefixed "Hallelujah" seems to indicate liturgical use of the psalm.

PROPHETIC ANTICIPATION.—Israel's millennial praise. The theme is the character of Jehovah displayed in His works for, and ways with the nation.

PERSONAL APPLICATION.—Jehovah's actions ever manifest His eternal attributes. He is constantly true to His promise and unfailingly just in His moral government (7–8). God has spoken as well as wrought. His words and His work carry the same message of truth (7). Thanksgiving should be wholehearted in private and in public (1). The study of God's works is always worth while (2). Note the four things that are said to be "for ever." To-day is as full of God as yesterday; still He provides for us and gives us our heritage (5–6). The fear (reverence) of Jehovah is the principal part of wisdom (10); cf. Prov. iv. 7; i. 7; ix. 10.

VERSE NOTES

1. "council" = conclave or secret assembly.

2. "sought out" = inquired into, studied.

3. Br. "His work is majesty and splendour, And . . . standeth fast for ever."

4. (b) These fundamental attributes of Jehovah are illustrated in the exodus and all later dealings with Israel.

5. God made provision for Israel's needs in the wilderness; "fear" = revere. (b) The deliverance from Egypt was both proof and pledge of this.

7. The gift of Canaan to Israel proved His troth, the expulsion of the Canaanites proved His justice; (b) i.e. they are not mutable or arbitrary; Sinai follows the exodus. The word for "precepts" is peculiar to the Psalter, xix. 8; ciii. 18; cxix. (21 times) = appointments; "sure" = trustworthy.

8. This verse further characterises the precepts; "done" = appointed, or made. The reference here is to the moral "core" of the Law, not the ceremonial portion.

9. Quoted Luke i. 68; primary ref. to the exodus. Redemption here involves (a) Jehovah's people ; (b) His covenant; (c) His name; "reverend" = to be feared; the Heb. word is elsewhere rendered "fearful," "terrible," etc.

10. Jehovah has revealed Himself as One to be feared; to fear Him therefore is the starting-point of all true wisdom; (b) lit. "that do them," i.e. His "precepts" = all that is implied in the fear of Jehovah; (c) "His praise standeth fast for ever."

PSALM CXII. THE GOD-FEARING—GRACIOUS AND GOOD

"Hallelujah."

I. DECLARATION (1–2). The God-fearing Man. "Happy is he."

II. DESCRIPTION (3-4). Character, Conduct and Circumstances.
"His righteousness standeth fast for ever."

III. DECLARATION (5-6a). The Gracious Man. "Good is he." (Heb. order.)

IV. DESCRIPTION (6b-9). Character, Conduct and Circumstances.
"His righteousness standeth fast for ever."

V. DECLARATION (10). The Godless Man. (Unhappy is he.)

PRIMARY ASSOCIATION.—See notes to preceding psalm. This also anonymous and undated but probably belongs to early post-exilic period. Keynote of this psalm is found in the last verse of cxi. Praise for the blessing of them who fear Jehovah. Most of the composition describes the blessed consequences rather than the essential characteristics of godliness. Note the parallelisms between God (cxi.) and the godly (cxii.); cf. Matt. v. 48. Note also that the Old Testament blessing, a prosperous posterity, is the first consequence of righteousness (2).

PROPHETIC ANTICIPATION.—As cxi. it looks on to millennial praise. The earthly view of millennial blessing is here described.

PERSONAL APPLICATION.—The aspect of the promised blessing being clearly Jewish not Christian, due allowance must be made in present application. Note that like Ps. i. the present psalm touches two poles of human experience in its first and last words, "Happy ... shall perish." Godliness is God-like-ness. Here is the fruit of the "study" referred to in cxi. 2. The secret and source of all true happiness is that fear of Jehovah which leads to a cheerful obedience to His word (1). The fear of Jehovah is a fountain of joy as well as of wisdom (1). Inward delight in God's word must precede the outward doing of it (1). To be able to reflect divine light in the darkness of others is a blessed work (4). He who receives grace should exercise grace (4); cf. Luke vi. 36. "Freely ye have received, freely give." Benevolence is poor if it be not translated into beneficence (5). Godliness imparts stability (6 ff.). Lives rooted in God are never uprooted (6 ff.). He who deals graciously and acts compassionately manages his affairs with discretion (5). Like God the godly man is ever remembered for his acts of mercy (6b with cxi. 4). Contrast the "desire" of the lawless (10) and the "desire" of the righteous (8); (cf. Prov. x. 24, 28) and contrast what they both "see."

VERSE NOTES

1. Br. "Happy is . . ." (c) shows the "fear" is not slavish but spontaneous.

2. Br. " . . . in the land." This is the sphere of Israel's blessing; (b) "A generation of upright ones . . .;" i.e. the "seed" of line (a).

3. "righteousness" here may include the idea of the reward of righteousness, suiting the parallelism.

4. Terms applied to God in cxi. are here applied to the godly man. Line (a) may be rendered, "He ariseth a light in the darkness for the upright (the godly poor whom he befriends, 5, 9). Being gracious . . ." He thus reflects the attributes of God in dealing with his fellows.

5. Or, "Good is the man . . . . . . lendeth"; typical of compassionate acts generally. "He manages (or shall manage) his affairs with judgment," not as R.V. rendering.

7. A clear conscience and a quiet trust militate against presentiments of evil; "fixed" = steadfast; "trusting," more lit. "led to trust," so Isa. xxvi. 3.

8. Cf. cxi. 8a.

9. First line quoted 2 Cor. ix. 9; "needy" or, helpless ones.

10. "desire," or, craving; "wicked" = lawless one.

Book Five. II. The Ways of God Recalled in the National Homage: cxiii.–cxviii.

Songs for Passover. THE HALLEL.

1. The Commencement. Praise. Theme introduced, cxiii.

Note.—Pss. cxiii.–cxviii. form the "Hallel," or Hymn of Praise, which according to Jewish liturgical usage is sung at the three great festivals of Passover, Pentecost and Tabernacles, also at the festival of Dedication and at the new moons (except new year). At the domestic celebration of Passover, Pss. cxiii.–cxiv. are sung before the meal, ere the emptying of the second festal cup; cxv.–cxviii. are sung at the close of the meal when the fourth cup has been filled. These psalms were probably sung by our Lord and His disciples at the last Passover, Matt. xxvi. 30; Mark xiv. 26. The group is sometimes called the Egyptian Hallel (cxiv. 1). The term "Great Hallel" is also used, but ancient Jewish authorities are not agreed as to its meaning. Some limit it to Ps. cxxxvi., some to cxx.–cxxxvi., and others to cxxxv.–cxxxvi. only.

PSALM CXIII. CONDESCENSION OF THE CREATOR

"Hallelujah"

I. JEHOVAH'S PRAISE, THE COMMAND (1).

II. JEHOVAH'S PRAISE, THE COMPLIANCE (2-3).

III. JEHOVAH'S PRAISE, THE CAUSES (4-9).
     1. His Glorious Exaltation over the Creation (4-5).
     2. His Great Condescension toward the Earth (6).
     3. His Gracious Exaltation of the Needy (7-9).

"Hallelujah"

PRIMARY ASSOCIATION.—Anonymous and undated, but seems to belong to the period of the second temple. The occurrence of the term "Hallelujah" indicates liturgical use. It is not found in Davidic and Asaphic psalms, but we must not overlook the possibility that it may have been appended to psalms compiled by earlier writers.

PROPHETIC ANTICIPATION.—These psalms undoubtedly look forward to the celebrations of God's millennial people. They are all more or less retrospective and point to significant deliverances and characteristic displays of the divine attributes.

PERSONAL APPLICATION.—The revelation of God's character must precede the rendition of man's praise. Jehovah's praise will be unceasing (2) and universal (3); that of Christians is a kind of first-fruits. God is not only cognisant of earthly affairs, He cares for earth's peoples (6). When God stoops it is in order to lift up (7). For the greatest stoop which raised us up out of the dust, see Phil. ii. Jehovah's infinite exaltation is wedded to infinite condescension (4 ff.)

VERSE NOTES

1-3. Note the triple repetition of "name."

3. (b) Or, "Praised be Jehovah's name."

5. (b) Lit. "Who exalteth Himself to sit, Who humbleth Himself to see, in the heavens and in the earth." Peculiar structure prob. = to sit (in heaven) . . . to see (in earth); or, "Who sits enthroned on high, Who looks far below on the heavens and on the earth."

7 ff. Examples of this condescension. There seems to be a reference to Hannah and her song in these verses; cf. 1 Sam. ii. 8.

7. To sit in the dust (Isa. xlvii. 1) or on the dunghill (Lam. iv. 5) is an oriental metaphor for extreme degradation and poverty. The dung and rubbish of an Eastern town or village are collected outside in a heap called "mezbele." Outcast beggars such as are afflicted with loathsome diseases, lay themselves down among the warm ashes by night and by day beg alms of the passers-by; "the poor" = an impoverished one; "the needy" = a needy one.

8. Br. "To seat him with nobles, with the nobles of . . ." cf. 1 Sam. ii. 8.

9. "Who seats the barren (woman) in a house, A glad mother . . ." Prophetic allusion to Israel with her restored children secure once more in her own home, Isa. liv. 1; lxvi. 8.

Book Five. II. The Ways of God Recalled in the National Homage: cxiii.–cxviii.

2. The Celebration. Testimony and Tribute, cxiv.–cxvii.

1. Acknowledgment, cxiv.   2. Acclamation, cxv.   Israel.
3. Acknowledgment, cxvi.   4. Acclamation, cxvii.   The Nations.

PSALM CXIV. THE POWER OF THE PRESENCE

I. COMMENCEMENT OF THE NATION (1-2). ISRAEL'S BIRTHDAY.

II. CONVULSIONS OF NATURE (3-4). Psalmist speaks as Narrator.
   1. The Waters (3).
   2. The Land (4).

III. CHALLENGES TO NATURE (5-6). Psalmist speaks as Spectator.
   1. The Waters (5).
   2. The Land (6).

IV. CARE FOR THE NATION (7-8). ISRAEL'S BLESSING.

PRIMARY ASSOCIATION.—Almost certainly post-exilic, but writer anonymous. Restored from Babylon, the former exiles recall with exultation the most signal example of Jehovah's condescending love referred to in cxiii., to which psalm this is companion. It is perfect in form, vividly dramatic, and emphatic by its very brevity.

PROPHETIC ANTICIPATION.—As preceding psalm. Israel's deliverance from Egypt resulting in their establishment as a nation is celebrated again and again in Scripture as typical of Jehovah's love and care for the nation. There will be a fulfilment of 7 at Messiah's future coming.

PERSONAL APPLICATION.—Only with redeemed ones can God ever dwell, and when He dwells He reigns (2). Those whom God delivers He cares for (8). The Lord (Adon) of Nature is the God of Jacob (7). He who made the water flow at Rephidim can still provide refreshing streams for His people (8). The needs of the desert way

give opportunity for the display of God's gracious provision (8).
Note (a) Double Name (1); (b) Double Deliverance (3, 5); (c)
Double Gift (8).

VERSE NOTES

1. "Israel" = princely title of the nation; "Jacob" = natural tendencies of the
nation; The destiny and the disposition of this people contrasted; (b) more lit.
a stammering people; *i.e.* barely articulate; expression conveys a similar contempt
to that of the Greek "barbarian," which imitates the unmeaning babble of a
foreign tongue.

2. The division of the lines seems rhythmical rather than logical. The whole
nation became Jehovah's sanctuary and dominion. No contrast between Judah
and Israel is intended though the difference is appropriate.

3ff. Summarises the wonders of the exodus from Egypt to the entry into
Canaan. "The Sea saw and fled; the Jordan turned backwards." Indicates the
whole spectacle of the triumphant exodus. The two miracles began and closed the
exodus period.

4. Poetic description of the earthquake which accompanied the giving of the
Law at Sinai, Exod. xix. 18. It was a theophany accompanied by great natural
phenomena.

5 ff. The past becomes present to the poet's mind. He challenges nature to
explain its behaviour.

7. The poet answers his own question, taking in a wider range; "Lord" = Heb.
Adon; "God' = Eloah; for the two titles see Appendix II; "tremble" = lit.
writhe in pangs.

8. Lit. "Turning the rock . . . ;" Heb. participle is independent of time; God
still so provides.

PSALM CXV.   IMPEACHMENT OF IDOLATERS

I. ASCRIPTION TO JEHOVAH (1).
   Negative Aspect—Positive Aspect.

II. ARGUMENT FROM EXPERIENCE (2).

III. ACKNOWLEDGMENT OF SOVEREIGNTY (3).

IV. ABSURDITY OF IDOLATRY (4-8). TRUST OF THE HEATHEN
    NATIONS.
       The Psalmist's Expostulation.
    1. The Fetishes (4a).
    2. Their Fabrication (4b).
    3. Their Futility (5-7).
    4. Their Fabricators (8a).
    5. The Followers (8b).

V. ASSURANCE OF ISRAEL (9-11). TRUST OF THE HOLY NATION.

The Psalmist's Exhortation.

1. The Appeal (9a).
2. The Answer (9b).
3. The Appeal (10a).
4. The Answer (10b).
5. The Appeal (11a).
6. The Answer (11b).

VI. ACKNOWLEDGMENT OF BLESSING (12-13).

VII. ARGUMENT FROM EXPERIENCE (14-16).

VIII. ASCRIPTION TO JEHOVAH (17-18).

Negative Aspect—Positive Aspect.

PRIMARY ASSOCIATION.—Author and date unknown, but the psalm seems to belong to the early post-exilic period. It is suited to antiphonal singing, a reference to which is found in Ezra iii. 11; also at Neh. xii. 40. The Babylonian captivity cured the nation of idolatry and Israel here answers the taunt of the heathen nations.

PROPHETIC ANTICIPATION.—The unclean spirit in Israel (Matt. xii. 43-45) went out, it is true, but it was not *cast* out nor the house occupied by the stronger One; the time, therefore, is coming when the spirit of idolatry will return in greater virulence and an image be set up in the very temple of God in the midst of those who have returned (mostly in unbelief) to their own land. The desolating judgment that follows is often alluded to in the psalms. This background helps us to understand the mention of idolatry in our present psalm in its prophetic significance. In the millennial celebrations this old controversy between God and man will be remembered and in pre-millennial days the faithful remnant will contrast the object of their trust with that of the nations.

PERSONAL APPLICATION.—Man manufactures the gods he worships (4). Gods of silver and gold often take the form of sovereigns and dollars. Anything that displaces God in the human heart is a false god, cf. 1 Jno. v. 21. Idol deities are idle deities (5-7). Idolatry degrades its devotees (8). The Infinite is neither impotent nor impassive (9 ff.). Idolatry assimilates the worshipper to his god (8). A cruel god has cruel devotees. God first made man in His own image; then (after the fall) men began to make gods after their own image; finally the gods make men after their image (8). Men win their pleas with God when they sue *in formâ pauperis* (1). If God's people suffer it is because He wills it, not because He lacks power, whatever may be the taunts of men (2). God is known by His works; man is known by his (8). "Small and great" are seen in mercy (13) and in judgment (Rev. xx. 12). God is no respecter of persons.

VERSE NOTES

1 ff. Appeal to God to vindicate His honour in succouring His people.

2. Br. "Where, then, is their God?"

4 ff. As much as to say, "Do they taunt us with the impotence of our God? What of their own deities?" The psalmist identifies the god with the image—it has no separate existence.

5. The idols cannot teach their devotees or see their needs, hear their prayers or smell the incense of the sacrifices.

8. "Like unto them shall their makers become, Even everyone . . ."

9–11. First lines probably sung by the precentor, second lines by the choir. The "He" is emphatic in each case. The threefold division recurs cxviii. 2–4; cxxxv. (with "house of Levi" added).

12. Br. "Jehovah, who hath remembered us, will bless us."

13. (*b*) *I.e.* one and all without distinction of rank or condition.

14. This is a specially appropriate promise to the small community of returned exiles.

15. "ye" (emph.).

16. Expands thought in 15; (*b*) contrast the Christian heritage, Eph. i. 3; "children of men" = sons of Adam.

18. "But *we*, we (the living) will bless Jah . . ." The LXX transfers the closing "Hallelujah" to the beginning of Ps. cxvi.

PSALM CXVI. THE RETURN TO REST

I. EXPRESSION OF PRAISE (1–2).

1. The Regard (1*a*).
2. The Reasons (1*b*–2*a*).
3. The Resolve (2*b*).   "I will call upon."

II. EXPERIENCE OF PERIL (3–6).

1. The Affliction (3).
2. The Appeal (4).   "I beseech Thee."
3. The Answer (5–6).   God's Attributes—God's Actions.

III. EXPRESSION OF PRAISE (7-9).
    1. The Rest (7a).
    2. The Reason (7b-8).
    3. The Resolve (9). "I will walk."

IV. EXPERIENCE OF PERIL (10-11).
    1. The Assurance (10a).
    2. The Affliction (10b).
    3. The Agitation (11).

V. EXPRESSION OF PRAISE (12-14).
    1. The Reflection (12a).
    2. The Reason (12b).
    3. The Resolve (13-14). "I will take . . ." (Triple).

VI. EXPERIENCE OF PERIL (15-16).
    1. The Affliction (implied) (15).
    2. The Appeal (16ab). Lit. "I beseech Thee."
    3. The Answer (16c).

VII. EXPRESSION OF PRAISE (17-19).
    1. The Resolve (17-19b). "I will offer . . ." (Triple).
    2. The Response (19c). "Hallelujah."

PRIMARY ASSOCIATION.—Anonymous. An individual thanksgiving belonging to the post-exilic period. Late grammatical forms and allusions to former psalms seem to indicate this. Note alternation of petition and praise. The psalmist had experienced a recent deliverance from deadly peril, the nature of which is uncertain.

PROPHETIC ANTICIPATION.—Israel's early millennial praise. Under her legal vow she utterly failed, but will fulfil her thanksgiving vows in the day of coming blessing, lvi. 12; Isa. xix. 21. The nation will offer these in full realisation that her salvation is solely due to the work of Another in her behalf.

PERSONAL APPLICATION.—In the psalmist's story do we all recognise our own (1 ff.)? His own name is a plea which God will certainly honour (4). It is in our personal experience that we realise the character of God (5). God's answer surpasses our appeal (4 with 8). Our Redeemer (8a); our Comforter (8b); our Keeper (8c). God ever delights to give to the maximum of our capacity, not the minimum consistent with our safety (8). "Ripples of doubt and fear do not prove the absence of a deeper trust" (10). Experience teaches that all confidence in man (lit. the adam) is in vain (11). Human help is delusive (11). Verse 8 shows abundant reasons for the "rest" of verse 7. The best way to requite God is to receive and own His grace with thanksgiving (12-13). The way to render thanks is to receive more grace (13). Blessings received in private should be acknowledged in public (14). Public expression of gratitude to God is often stressed in the Psalter. The "blood" of His people is no trivial thing in God's eyes—their death not lightly permitted (15).

VERSE NOTES

1. Lit. "I love, because Jehovah heareth my voice even my . . ." The unusual form of expression, verb without expressed object, is found again, 2, 10; cf. 1 John v. 19 R.V.

2. Br. "For He . . . and I will call as long as I live."

3. (b) "And the straits of Sheol . . ."

5. "merciful" = compassionate.

6. "simple" i.e. sincere or guileless, or those whose lack of experience exposes them to danger; "saved," see 13.

7. "rest," Heb. plur. indicating full and complete rest.

10. Br. "I believed when I (thus) spake . . ." i.e. even when he was saying, "I am afflicted and all men deceive me," he yet retained his faith in God.

11. "I (emph.) said in my agitation . . ." cf. xxxi. 22.

13. "salvation" lit. salvations; cf. "rests" (7); ref. may be to the cup drunk as a part of the sacrifice of thanksgiving (14), cf. "cup of blessing" 1 Cor. x. 16; "call upon" = rather, proclaim, i.e. acknowledging that to God alone is gratitude due; so 17.

15. Under the bitter persecution of the last days the question of life or death for the godly remnant of Israel will have great significance, for their hopes of blessing are centred upon the earthly inheritance. Death would seem to cut off participation in the promise, but here is the precious assurance confirmed by Rev. xiv. 13, that those who will suffer death during that period will not be the losers. Although the verse has this special reference, yet it contains comfort for saints of all ages; "saints" = beloved, or, favoured ones.

16. Lit. "I beseech Thee, Jehovah, for I am Thy servant . . ."; "son of Thy handmaid," syn. for "thy servant" but denoting a closer relationship, as servants born in the house (Gen. xiv. 14) were the most trusted dependents; (c) for he had been like a prisoner condemned to death, cf. 3.

17. Cf. Lev. vii. 11 ff.

PSALM CXVII.   THE PRAISE OF THE PEOPLES

I. THE RENDERING OF PRAISE (1).   ACCLAMATION OF JEHOVAH.
    Cordial Invitation to the Peoples.

II. THE REASON FOR PRAISE (2ab).   ATTRIBUTES OF JEHOVAH.
    Concise Explanation.   Lovingkindness and Truth.

III. THE RENDERING OF PRAISE (2c). ACCLAMATION OF JEHOVAH.
Closing Injunction to the Peoples. "Hallelujah."

PRIMARY ASSOCIATION.—Anonymous; probably early post-exilic. The shortest of all the psalms it is nevertheless one of the grandest.

PROPHETIC ANTICIPATION.—A recognised Messianic psalm it is quoted by Paul the Apostle (Rom. xv. 11) to show that God always had in store blessing for the Gentiles. Israel was endowed with blessing that the nation might diffuse blessing, cf. Ps. lxvii. In millennial days Israel will joyfully summon the nations to the worship of Jehovah, who has displayed in His dealings with the nation His two great twin attributes of lovingkindness and truth (faithfulness).

PERSONAL APPLICATION.—Christians delight to trace out in Israel's past history the displayed character of God. In worship we gladly anticipate the day of universal praise. How often do we come into God's presence with all praise and no prayer? "Lovingkindness and truth (troth) are twin stars which shine out in all God's dealings with His people." "These two fair messengers appeared in yet fairer form in the person of Christ Himself," John i. 14. God is not miserly in measuring His mercies.

VERSE NOTES

1. Note two different words for praise.

2. "For mighty hath been His lovingkindness toward (or, over) us." These fundamental attributes of God's character are often mentioned together in the Psalms. His grace "overcame" or prevailed over us notwithstanding all our sins. Paul unites truth with mercy, Rom. xv. 8-9. Again "Hallelujah!"

Book Five. II. The Ways of God Recalled in the National Homage:
cxii.–cxviii.

3. The Conclusion. Praise: cxviii. The Thanksgiving Inspired.

PSALM CXVIII. DELIVERANCE FROM DEATH

I. RENDERING OF THANKS (1–4).
    1. Exhortation—General (1). "Give thanks."
    2. Exhortation—Particular (2–4).
        (i) People's Assembly (2).
        (ii) Priestly Family (3).
        (iii) Pious Adherents (4).

K

II. REASON FOR THANKSGIVING (5).

III. REALIZATION OF HELP (6–7). "Jehovah is for me."

IV. REFLECTION FOLLOWING EXPERIENCE (8–9).

V. REVIEW OF CIRCUMSTANCES (10–18).
   1. Acknowledgment (Triple) (10–12). The Name of the Lord.
   2. Apostrophe (13). The Enemy thrust sore. (fig. Polyptoton).
   3. Affirmation (14). Jah—my Strength—my Song—my Salvation.
   4. Acknowledgment (Triple) (15–16). The Right Hand of the Lord.
   5. Assurance (17). "I shall live."
   6. Admission (18). The Lord chastened sore (fig. Polyptoton).

VI. RELATION TO MESSIAH (19–28).
   1. Approach of Messiah (19–20).
      (i) Request (19).
      (ii) Response (20).
   2. Ascription of Praise (21). (Sing.) "I will praise."
   3. Acknowledgment of Messiah (22–24). National.
   4. Appeal in Prayer (25). (Sing.) "I beseech Thee."
   5. Acclamation of Messiah (26–27). National.
   6. Ascription of Praise (28). (Sing.) "I will praise."

VII. RENDERING OF THANKS (29).
   Exhortation—General. "Give thanks."

PRIMARY ASSOCIATION.—David probably composed this psalm upon some special occasion of national rejoicing. The note of praise characterising the composition was first used by him (1–4, 25, 29); cf. 1 Chron. xvi. 34–35. That it was used later on occasions referred to by commentators is very likely (see Ezra iii. 10–11; Neh. viii. 14–18) especially the great celebration of the Feast of Tabernacles recorded Neh. viii. Intended as a processional hymn and antiphonal, but it is difficult to separate the parts with absolute certainty. 1–18 seems to have been sung while approaching the sanctuary; 19–29 at the "temple" gates and after entry, including responses by the priests within (20, 26). The psalm fittingly closes the "Hallel" in a spirit of jubilant thanksgiving for rest given Israel in Canaan and, secondly, after the Captivity. This was a favourite psalm of Luther.

PROPHETIC ANTICIPATION.—The voice of a representative of restored Israel in millennial days, reviewing the recent mighty deliverance of the nation by the advent of Messiah. Points on to the great millennial Feast of Tabernacles, Zech. xiv. 16–19 with Israel fully returned in heart to their God and fulfilling the prophecy uttered by our Lord in the days of His rejection, Matt. xxiii. 39; Isa. xxv. 9. For many centuries God's ancient people have remained without that which was their distinctive glory—the Temple of God, but they are seen here again in possession, and in full realization that Messiah is the sole foundation upon which the dwelling of God among them securely rests (cf. the Tabernacle types). To Christ they owe their spiritual and temporal deliverance, and the worshippers stand at last on a righteousness not their own. It is that of their once despised and rejected, but now risen and glorified Messiah.

PERSONAL APPLICATION.—A song of the saved. Israel's Deliverer is *our* Redeemer. All the redeemed people of God should be magnifiers and messengers of His Name. Christians, too, may join in the oft-repeated refrain of Israel's anthem (1). Faith in God makes us independent of human helpers, even as it makes us superior to mortal foes (6). Terror of man is removed by trust in God (6). Let me hold fast this truth—God is for me, cf. Rom. viii. 31; Heb. xiii. 6. Verse 8, the central verse of the Bible, conveys a vital truth (8). God my Helper, the profession (7a); the proof (13b). We are not only objects of divine protection (5-7), but also organs of divine power (10-12). God gives the victories; let us acknowledge it in thanksgiving (12). Salvation and song ever go together (15a). Christ is not only *at* God's right hand, He *is* God's Right Hand (15-16). Divine chastening is unto life not unto death (17-18). The righteous are the saved and the saved are righteous (20-21). What man despises and tosses aside, God takes up and uses (22); cf. 1 Cor. ii. God gives us light as well as life (27) because He is love (29b). The people of God should ever begin (1) and end (29) on a note of thanksgiving. Put no trust in earthly authorities whether emperors (9) or experts (22).

VERSE NOTES

1. Cf. cxxxvi.; Deut. v. 10.

2 ff. For sim. threefold division, cf. cxv. 9-13.

5. "distress" = strait. Massoretic text reads " . . . answered me with deliverance." The title "Jah" (occurs six times here) recalls the exodus.

7. Lit. "Therefore do I look . . ." = either, fearlessly face the foe, or look upon their defeat.

8. Br. "It is good . . . and not to put trust in . . . man . . . in nobles."

10. Br. "I did cut them off;" so 11b and 12b; verses 5 and 13 make it clear that the crisis was past.

11. Note fig. epizeuxis for emphasis, and elsewhere in this psalm. Verses 10-12 prophetically refer to the great antichristian confederacy against God's people in the last days, Isa. xxix. 2-7; Zech. xii., xiv.

12. "quenched;" LXX etc. have "blazed up." In the East a fire from thorns blazes up rapidly and fiercely, but as rapidly dies down.

13. The enemy is addressed as an individual (prophetically = Antichrist); Israel and their foes like two warriors matched in single combat; lit. "thrusting thou didst thrust;" = fig. polyptoton, see 18.

14. This verse is repeated in the "habhdalah" by the Jews every Sabbath night; cf. Exod. xv. 2; Isa. xii. 2. See 21.

15. i.e. the festival rejoicings; "righteous," i.e. Israel regarded in the light of their calling and contrasted with the lawless nations who sought to frustrate God's purpose by destroying Israel; "tents," Heb. ohel; or, dwellings; 15b and 16 give the joyous shout of the righteous after victory; based on Exod. xv. 6, 12.

18. Lit. "chastening He chastened," fig. polyptoton.

19. "gates of righteousness," because the temple was the abode of the righteous God and righteousness the condition of entrance for God's people; Jer. xxxi. 23; Ps. xx. 2; Isa. xxvi. 2, cf. Ps. xxiv.; (b) "I will go in by them . . ."

20. Response from within. "This is the gate (belonging) to Jehovah." The righteous may (or, Let the righteous) go in by it." The emphasis is on the word "righteous."

22. Metaphor from building. Combined ideas are found here. A corner-stone bonds the walls, hence is the most important part of the structure. A large and strong stone needed, Jer. li. 26; Job xxxviii. 6. It formed part of the foundation. Here ref. to topstone or headstone (Zech. iii. 9; iv. 7-9) which not only bonds the walls, but completes the building. Primarily may refer to Israel as a nation; figuratively of the "house" that God promised to build for David, of which Christ is both founder and finisher; prophetically of Christ as foundation stone and chief corner-stone of all God's "buildings." Verse quoted several times in New Testament.

23. Lit. "From Jehovah did this come to pass . . ." That the despised and rejected One should turn out to be their Deliverer and Redeemer, the chosen One of God now risen and glorified, will be a wonder to Israel.

24. i.e. To Jehovah alone we owe this day of national rejoicing; " . . . in it" or, in Him.

25. Br. as A.V. in the singular. A prayer that Jehovah will continue the blessed work He has begun; "now" is not an adverb of time but a Heb. particle of supplication. "Hosanna" was a "God save the King," and is so understood by the disciples, Luke xix. 38, etc. In later times this verse was the festal cry (used in the plural) raised while the altar of burnt offering was solemnly compassed once on each of the first six days of the Feast of Tabernacles and seven times on the seventh. This seventh day was called the "Great Hosanna," and not only the prayers, but even the branches of osiers and myrtles which are bound to the palm branch were called Hosannas (Delitsch).

26. Shows the millennial temple will be completed (prophetically seen). The priests utter a blessing upon the entering procession with its Leader. "Blessed in the Name of Jehovah be the Coming One" (lit.); (*b*) "you" = plural.

27. "El (a Mighty One) is Jehovah . . ." (*b*) A difficult line, but is evidently the worshippers' response to the divine blessing received (*a*). The Heb. cannot mean, "Bind . . . *to* the horns . . ." It seems better to render with an ellipsis, ". . . until (it is consummated at) the horns . . ." The whole ritual of sacrifice is viewed, *viz.* a sin offering (Lev. iv.), similar perhaps to that of Ezra's day (Ezra, vi. 17). If the psalm was sung at the last Passover (see *Note*, p. 277) very significantly this verse immediately preceded our Lord's journey to Gethsemane.

28. "*Thou* art my El . . . (Thou art) my Elohim." Prophetically seems to point to Israel's acknowledgment of Christ's deity.

Book Five. III. *The Word of God Revered by the Loyal Heart: cxix.*

PRIMARY ASSOCIATION.—Author and date of this unique psalm are uncertain. It has been variously ascribed by expositors to David, Hezekiah, Jeremiah and Ezra. Many coincidences between the language of the text and the history of Ezra's time seem to point to the last-named. Ezra is sometimes known as "the second Moses." He was clearly one who resolved to make God's Law the governing principle of his life, Ezra vii. 6, 10, 11. The composition is in the form of a perfect and regular alphabetic acrostic, in an eightfold repetition, through twenty-two sections corresponding to the letters of the Hebrew alphabet. The writer's theme is the surpassing excellence of the divine law. In its apparent monotony there is developed sweetest music because of many subtle variations in the great theme. To quote Maclaren again, "There are but few pieces in the psalmist's kaleidoscope, but they fall into many shapes of beauty." Several characteristic features may be mentioned. The first is the use of certain words as synonyms of the Law. For explanation of these see Appendix XI. The psalm is the third commencing with a beatitude; cf. Pss. i. and xxxii. It is an appropriate sermon on Ps. i. 1-2. Jehovah is addressed by name exactly twenty-two times. All the verses except two (90, 122) refer to the revealed word under one or other of the synonyms. One should carefully distinguish *attributes* of the Law from these synonyms, which are terms for the Law in its manifold aspects. After the first three introductory verses, in every verse but one (115) God is addressed. Despite the impression of tautology conveyed by a cursory glance, an emphatic unity appears upon a closer study. The links are found to be moral and experimental and to be discerned only as taught of the Spirit.

PROPHETIC ANTICIPATION.—Shows the effect of the Law written upon the hearts of restored Israel under the terms of the new covenant, Jer. xxxi. 31-34; cf. Heb. viii. 10. The nation is viewed as not yet in enjoyment of full deliverance, which comes only after the judgments of Messiah upon Israel's enemies at and following His advent in glory. In the obedience of faith which works by love renewed Israel will delight to carry out the will of God as revealed in His word. The excellencies of that word will be their continual praise. Note that eight—the new covenant number—is stamped upon the whole psalm.

PERSONAL APPLICATION.—For notes under this aspect see after each section.

GENERAL ANALYSIS.—The twenty-two sections seem to fall into three groups of seven, followed by the last section as a kind of appendix. The corresponding members of each group bear a certain relation to each other although the connection may not be immediately apparent to the casual reader; see "Numerical Bible" (Grant).

PSALM CXIX.   THE LAW AND THE LIFE.   WALKING IN THE WAY

I. THE WORD.   SUBJECTIVE RELATIONSHIPS EMPHASISED. SELFWARD ASPECT.   Sections Aleph to Zayin (1-56).

II. THE WORD.   SOCIAL RELATIONSHIPS EMPHASISED. MANWARD ASPECT.   Sections Cheth to Nun (57-112).

III. THE WORD.   SANCTUARY RELATIONSHIPS EMPHASISED. GODWARD ASPECT.   Sections Samech to Shin (113-168).

IV. THE WORD, THE WORSHIP AND THE WITNESS.   SHEPHERD RELATIONSHIP EMPHASISED.   Section Tau (169-176).

I.   1.   ALEPH.   ADVANTAGE AND AIM

The Word—Its Power for Blessing.

I. PREFATORY AFFIRMATION (1-4).   Third and Second Person (General). Felicity in the Law.

1. Double Beatitude (1–3). (Third Person). Six-fold Description—Five positive, one negative.
2. Divine Behests (4). (Second Person).
    (a) The Author (4a).
    (b) The Aim (4b).

II. PROFOUND ASPIRATION (5–8). First Person (Individual). Fulfilment of the Law.
    1. Prayer (5–6).
    2. Promise (7–8a).
        (a) Of Praise (7).
        (b) Of Performance (8a).
    3. Prayer (8b).

PERSONAL APPLICATION.—Happiness and holiness. The holy will of God is the only happy way for man. The word is witness to the way in which we should walk (2a). The way of self-will is the way of sin, Isa. liii. 6. "Seeking" involves not merely approach in heart, but application of mind to understand (2b). Desire must be followed by determination and devotion (5 ff.). No real disgrace or disappointment befalls those who are obedient to God (6). Without God's presence with us our best resolves prove abortive (8).

VERSE NOTES

1. "Blessed" = Happy; "perfect" i.e. those whose whole course of life is governed by a single-hearted devotion to God.
2. "keep" = guard. (b) cf. 10.
3. Connects with 2. "Yea, have done no unrighteousness, (But) have walked in His ways."
4. "Thou (emph.) hast commanded Thy precepts, That (men) should observe them diligently."
5. Prayer evoked by the thought in 4.
8. "not utterly" = not in any wise, cf. 43.

I. 2. BETH.   BASIS OF BLESSING

The Word—Its Power for Sanctification.

I. PURPOSE OF THE WORD (9). Ministration.

II. PROTESTATIONS AND PRAYERS (10–14).
    1. Protestation (10a). "I have." The Heart.
    2. Prayer (10b).

3. Protestation (11). "I have." The Heart.
4. Prayer (12).
5. Protestation (13-14). "I have." The Lips.

III. PURPOSE CONCERNING THE WORD (15-16).   Meditation.
"I will" (thrice).

PERSONAL APPLICATION.—Purification and preservation. Sanctification by ablution (9-11); Sanctification by attraction (12-16). Careful study of the word is to be accompanied by a careful study of self (9). God is best found by doing His will (10). The word that is hidden within (11) is to be told out (13). Employment follows enjoyment (13). God's testimonies are true treasure (14). The miser loves to count his gold, the saint to ponder his wealth in God (14). While pondering the precepts, we must pursue the path (15). Intention may be good, but knowledge is imperfect and strength small, hence the need of prayer (10b).

VERSE NOTES

9. "young man," i.e. a test case; "by taking heed" = s.H.w. "observe"(4, 5); "way" = path.
11. "word" = saying, or utterance, Heb. "imrah," see Appendix XI.
13. "declared" or, rehearsed. Not only treasure them but talk of them.
14. (b) or, "As over all (kinds of) wealth."
15. "ways" or, paths; a different word from that in 1, 3, 5, but used again (9, 101, 104, 128).
16. "word." s.H.w. 9 = "dabar," see Appendix XI.

I. 3. GIMEL.   COMFORT AND COUNSEL

The Word—Its Power for Knowledge.

I. PRAYERS AND PLEAS (17-19).
    1. Prayer (17a).
    2. Plea (17b).
    3. Prayer (18).
    4. Plea (19a).
    5. Prayer (19b).

II. PSALMIST AND PERSECUTORS (20-21). THE PROUD. Contrast.

III. PRAYER AND PLEA (22).

IV. PSALMIST AND PERSECUTORS (23-24). THE PRINCES. Contrast.

PERSONAL APPLICATION.—Opened eyes and an open word are both essential (cf. Luke xxiv.)—a subjective illumination and an objective revelation (18–19). A traveller is helped by signposts that point the way. The proud are they who exalt themselves out of their place. Every saint of God possesses a privy council (24).

VERSE NOTES

18. "open," lit. unveil, uncover; "behold" = discern, see clearly.

19. An alien needs instruction as to conduct in the land where he sojourns. Moreover, in the Law God made provision for the stranger guest, though he were but a fugitive slave, Deut. xxiii. 15–16; x. 18–19. See also Lev. xxv. 23. This entire dependence upon God is a significant reference to the recently returned exiles. Jehovah's commands stand ready to meet their material and spiritual needs.

20. "breaks," lit. is crushed, s.H.w. only Lam. iii. 16; "ordinances" = just decisions.

21. "the proud" here refers to apostate Israelites, those who sin wilfully and presumptuously.

24. Though enemies take counsel against him, he too has counsellors (lit. "men of my counsel") to direct him; "also" = nevertheless.

I. 4. DALETH. DISTRESS AND DESIRE

The Word—Its Power for Reviving.

I. THE PLAINT (25a). The Psalmist's Depression.

II. THE PRAYER (25b). "Revive me."

III. THE PLEA (26a). His Confession.

IV. THE PRAYERS (26b–27a). "Teach me—make me understand."

V. THE PURPOSE (27b). MEDITATION.

VI. THE PLAINT (28a). The Psalmist's Depression.

VII. THE PRAYERS (28b–29). "Strengthen me, etc."

VIII. THE PLEAS (30–31a). His Choice.

IX. THE PRAYER (31b). "Shame not."

X. THE PURPOSE (32). MINISTRATION.

PERSONAL APPLICATION.—Though our soul may "cleave to the dust" (in grief), let us "cleave to the word" (in trust) (25, 31). Tell God thy ways and He will teach thee His will (26). With confession of my ways let there be confidence in God's way (26, 30). Note the contrast of the two ways (29–30). The Law though holy is not harsh (29*b*).

VERSE NOTES

25. *i.e.* is bowed with grief. "Quicken," first of nine prayers in this psalm for "quickening;" see 25, 37, 40, 88, 107, 149, 154, 156 and 159; Heb. verb may be variously understood according to context, "to give life to, preserve alive, revive the heart, impart fresh courage to, etc." Life is repeatedly promised as a reward of obedience to the Word of God, Deut. viii. 3; xxx. 6, 15, 19-20; xxxii. 47.

26. Br. " . . . have rehearsed . . . hast answered."

27. Prayer for deeper insight recurs 34, 73, 125, 144 and 169. (*b*) "That I may meditate . . ." as in 15, 23. "wonders," *i.e.* the mysteries of God's will as revealed in His word (18).

28. Br. "weepeth itself away . . ."

29. (*b*) br. "And (with) Thy law (here = instruction) be gracious unto me."

31. (*b*) *i.e.* disappoint me not of the promised blessing.

32. When the heart is freed from restraint of trouble and anxiety, his liberty will be used for more energetic obedience. Some read, "For Thou dost enlarge . . ."

I. 5. HE.   HEART AND HEAD

The Word—Its Power for Establishing.

I. REQUESTS AND REASONS (33-36).
1. Request (33*a*).
2. Reason (33*b*). "That."
3. Request (34*a*).
4. Reason (34*ab*). "That."
5. Request (35*a*).
6. Reason (35*b*). "For."
7. Request (36).

II. REQUESTS AND REMINDERS (37-40).
1. Requests (37–38*a*).
2. Reminder (38*b*).
3. Request (39*b*).
4. Reason (39*b*).
5. Reminder (40*a*).
6. Request (40*b*).

PERSONAL APPLICATION.—Obedience should be unlimited (33) and unreserved (34). To translate desires into deeds means a struggle, hence the need of divine aid (35). Our profession (35*b*) should be made petition (36). Attachment to God means detachment from the world (36). This world is ever a rival to His word (36). We must understand the will of the Lord if we are to observe it aright (34). The life which pleases God is its own reward (33*b*) (alternative translation). The heart is often led astray by the eyes (36–37).

VERSE NOTES

33. Lit. "Make me see . . ." (*b*) Br. "That I may . . ."; "unto the end," Heb. gen. means reward, so here thought may be " . . . as a reward."

34. "Make me understand . . . (*b*) "That I may . . ."

35. "to go" = walk.

37. Lit. "Make my eyes turn from . . ." ; "vanity" includes all that is worthless, unreal and false; "quicken" = revive; see note verse 25.

38. "word" *i.e.* utterance (of promise); (*b*) *i.e.* which leads to reverence of Thee; or may be trans., "Confirm Thy promise to Thy servant, who is (inclined) to Thy fear."

39. "Make my reproach pass away . . .;" *i.e.* the scorn which he has to bear because of his loyalty to the word of God.

40. The heart is willing, but he needs reviving in strength.

I. 6. VAU.   WITNESS AND WALK.

The Word—Its Power for Testimony.

I. PRAYERS AND PLEAS (41–44).   "Let . . . lovingkindness."
    1. Petition (41).   Positive.
    2. Pleas (42).   "So shall . . . for."
    3. Petition (43*a*).   Negative.
    4. Pleas (43*b*–44).   "For . . . so shall."

II. PRAYER AND PROMISE (45–48).   "Let . . . liberty."
    1. Prayer (45*a*).
    2. Plea (45*b*).
    3. Promise (46–48).   Fourfold "I will."

PERSONAL APPLICATION.—Every Christian should have the double testimony of lip and life. One who is constrained by his affections walks in true liberty (45). Restraints that are loved are not bonds (45, 47). Israel waits for a salvation already enjoyed by the Christian (41).

VERSE NOTES

In Hebrew each verse begins with "And."

42. "answer" = lit. a word.

43. Br. "And pluck not ..." *i.e.* be deprived of the power for testimony.

45. Br. "Let me walk ..." "at liberty" = lit. a broad place, cf. 32; (*b*) or, "For I have studied ..." *i.e.* have given diligent heed to.

46. Compare the experiences of Daniel, Nehemiah, etc.

48. "which I have loved" should probably be omitted in this verse; "lift ... hands" indicates (*a*) the attitude of prayer, and (*b*) as here, the swearing of an oath.

I. 7. ZAYIN.   ZEST AND ZEALOUSNESS

The Word—Its Power for Comfort.

I. REMEMBRANCE AND REST   (49–50). "Remember Thou Thy promise."

II. REACTION TO RIDICULE (51).   Increased Loyalty.

III. REMEMBRANCE AND REST (52).   "I have remembered Thy judgments."

IV. REACTION TO REBELS (53).   Indignant Lament.

V. REASON FOR REJOICING (54).

VI. REMEMBRANCE AND REST (55–56). "I have remembered Thy Name."

PERSONAL APPLICATION.—History, both personal and national, should be read in the light of the divine purpose. True hope is based upon the word of God (49); cf. Heb. xi. 1 with Rom. x. 17. "To be laughed out of one's faith is worse than to be terrified out of it" (51). Cling to God's name in the dark (55). Indignation against the forsaking of God's word is not inconsistent with sorrow for those who thus forsake it (53, 136). Let God's word (the written word and the living word) be the theme of our songs (54). It ever brings joyful satisfaction to the saint to keep God's precepts (55). It is the word of God that revives us (preserves us alive) in affliction (50).

VERSE NOTES

49. (*b*) Br. "On which ...'

50. See note verse 25.

52. Br. " ... ordinances (which have been) from ancient times."

53. "wicked" = lawless, *i.e.* careless or apostate Israelites.

54. "songs" lit. psalms; "pilgrimage" = sojournings.

55. All that God has revealed Himself to be, is the most powerful motive for observing His laws.

56. "This . . . because . . .," *i.e.* all this comfort and joy in the midst of trials; or, render, "This (happy lot) has been mine, That I have kept Thy precepts."

II. 1. CHETH.   PORTION AND PURPOSE

The Word—Its Power of Satisfaction.

I. PRECIOUS PORTION (57).   Jehovah's Person.

II. PURPOSEFUL PRAYER (58).   "Be gracious."

III. PONDERING PURSUIT (59–60).

IV. PROFANE PERSECUTORS (61).

V. PROMISED PRAISE (62).   Jehovah's Precepts.

VI. PIOUS PARTNERS (63).

VII. PERSISTENT PETITION (64).   "Teach me."

PERSONAL APPLICATION.—God Himself is the precious possession of all His saints (57). Let us acknowledge it before the world. God has promised to be gracious (58*b*). Careful consideration of our ways should turn our feet into the way of God's word (59). Let there be no hesitation or procrastination in our obedience (60). Jehovah's lovingkindness universally manifested should make us long to know more of His will (64). The true ground of hope is not our prayers but God's promise (58). Men are often ruined from lack of thought (59). Never let resolve have time to cool (60). Saints always gravitate towards like-minded people (63). Solitude has its temptations no less than society (63). Can all our associations be approved of God (63)? A man becomes known by the company he keeps.

VERSE NOTES

57. As margin or, "My portion, I have said, O Jehovah, is to keep Thy words."

58. "favour" lit. face; br. "Be gracious unto me according to Thy saying (= promise)."

61. Br. ". . . have entangled me"; the metaphor is from the hunter's snare.

62. This is the reverse of forgetting (61).

63. "I" (emph.); "fear" = reverent fear.

II. 2. TETH.   TAUGHT BY TRIALS

The Word—Its Power for Good.

I. ACKNOWLEDGMENT CONCERNING JEHOVAH (65–66). Dealings Good.
  1. Avowal (65).
  2. Appeal (66).

II. ADMISSION CONCERNING HIMSELF (67). Discipline Good.

III. AFFIRMATION CONCERNING JEHOVAH (68). Attributes and Acts Good.
  1. Avowal (68a).
  2. Appeal (68b).

IV. ARRAIGNMENT OF PERSECUTORS (69–70). Acts and Attitude Evil.
  1. Accusation against the Proud (69a).
  2. Attitude despite the Proud (69b).
  3. Accusation against the Proud (70a).
  4. Attitude despite the Proud (70b).

V. ADMISSION CONCERNING HIMSELF (71). Discipline Good.

VI. ACKNOWLEDGMENT CONCERNING JEHOVAH (72). Decrees Good.

PERSONAL APPLICATION.—We need the power of prompt discernment between right and wrong (66). The psalmist suffered from the mud-slinging of the wicked (69 = lit. plastered falsehood over me). The preciousness of the word of God (72) is a lesson learned in the school of affliction. The instincts of faith are swift and sure (66). "Teach me Thy statutes" is an oft-recurring prayer reached by many paths (68b). Every view of man and every thought of God brought the psalmist to the same desire. The revelation of God's character and conduct prompts the prayer for further knowledge (68b). Both the lash (71) and the Law (72) are good for me! In God's school there is the rod as well as the lesson-book (71). The presence of evil is permitted that the saint may have his spiritual faculties exercised (66), cf. Heb. vi. 15. God desires His children to learn love of the good and hatred of the evil. God's acts are in full accord with His attributes (68). The "proud" ever rebel against the restraint of the divine precepts (69). The whole section is a reminder to the believer of Rom. viii. 28.

VERSE NOTES

If we begin 67 with "Till" and 71 with " 'Tis . . ." each verse of this stanza will correspond to the Hebrew acrostic. Five of the eight verses in the Heb. begin with the word "Good."

65. "word" = promise.

66. (a) Lit. " . . . goodness of taste."

67. " . . . I (emph.) did err . . ."

68. "Thou" (emph.).

69. (b) Br. "As for me, with . . ."

70. Or, "Gross is their heart as fat, As for me, I . . ." i.e. their heart is utterly insensible to divine things. He opens his heart, they close theirs.

71. "Good for me . . ." = right, fitting. 72 also begins thus.

II. 3. YOD.   YEARNINGS AND YIELDING

The Word—Its Power for Accomplishment.

I. APPEAL FOR COMPLETENESS (73). "Give me."

II. APPEAL CONCERNING ASSOCIATES (74). The God-fearing Ones.

III. ASSURANCE IN AFFLICTION (75).

IV. APPEAL FOR CONSOLATION (76–77). "Let . . . let."

V. ACCUSATION AGAINST ADVERSARIES (78).

VI. APPEAL CONCERNING ASSOCIATES (79). The God-fearing Ones.

VII. APPEAL FOR COMPLETENESS (80).

PERSONAL APPLICATION.—O Lord, complete the gracious work Thou hast begun in me (73)! Sorrows are still grievous although sent in love, hence we need sustaining and solace (76). Chastisement without comfort would overwhelm us (75–76). Have we the same assurance as the psalmist concerning affliction (75)?

VERSE NOTES

73. i.e. he desires to be perfected in spirit.

74. Br. "Let them that fear (= revere) Thee see . . . " i.e. fulfil Thy promise to me so that other God-fearing ones may be encouraged.

75. "righteous" = lit. righteousness; "afflicted" or, humbled; "judgments" here = providential acts.
76. "word" = promise.
77. "tender mercies" = compassions; (b) the ground of his appeal.
78. " . . . for they have subverted me by falsehood."
79. Or, "That they may know . . ."
80. "perfect" cf. 1, *i.e.* thorough, or fully devoted to.

II. 4. CAPH.   CRY OF THE CRUSHED

The Word—Its Power under Testing.

I. ACUTE AFFLICTION (81–84).   Integrity under Trial.
    1. Plaint (81a).
    2. Plea (81b).
    3. Plaint (82a).
    4. Problem (82b).   Consolation—when?
    5. Plaint (83a).
    6. Plea (83b).
    7. Plaint (84a).
    8. Problem (84b).   Vindication—when?

II. ARROGANT ADVERSARIES (85–88).   Insolence against Truth.
    1. Accusation (85).
    2. Assurance (86a).
    3. Accusation (86b).
    4. Appeal (86c).
    5. Accusation (87a).
    6. Avowal (87b).
    7. Appeal (88a).
    8. Avowal (88b).

PERSONAL APPLICATION.—It is not doubt but delay that often tries the soul of the saint (82). However intense the trial, let us maintain our integrity like the psalmist and Job. Wrongly persecuted saints have a sanctuary refuge in God (86). The prophecies of God may be pleaded as promises (86). The "word" for which Christians wait (81b) is indicated, 1 Thess. iv. 16; it also is a word of deliverance, Rom. viii. 23-25.

VERSE NOTES

81. "fainteth," s.H.w. "fail."
82. His soul grows faint and his eyes ache with the strain of watching for the word (= promise) of deliverance. (b) "Saying, when . . ."

83. *i.e.* like a wine-skin shrivelled and blackened in the smoke of the room until it loses its former appearance. So the writer as the result of his sufferings is disfigured almost beyond recognition.

84. Brevity of his own life made a plea for the speedy judgment of his persecutors. Prophetically significant as the cry of the godly remnant to whom the "times and seasons" mentioned Acts i. 6–7 will be opening up.

85. *i.e.* like the pitfalls of the hunter of wild animals. The hostility of his enemies was active not passive. (*b*) "They who."

86. "faithful" = lit. faithfulness. Note the antithesis between this faithfulness and the falsehood of the persecutors; both afford ground for the prayer, "Oh, help me!"

87. Or, " . . . in the land;" "almost" = soon; "consumed" = made an end of; "But as for me, I . . ."

88. "quicken;" here = keep alive, or preserve; see note verse 25.

II. 5. LAMED. LIVING AND LASTING

The Word—Its Power of Stability.

I. STABILITY OF THE WORD (89–91). ETERNAL.

II. SUPPORT BY THE WORD IN AFFLICTION (92).

III. STATEMENTS ABOUT THE WORD (93–94).

    1. Remembrance and Reason (93).

    2. Request and Reason (94).

IV. STUDY OF THE WORD NOTWITHSTANDING ADVERSARIES (95).

V. SCOPE OF THE WORD (96). ENDLESS.

PERSONAL APPLICATION.—The stability of nature witnesses to the steadfastness of God's word which sustains it. Jehovah is Sustainer as well as Creator of the universe. He sustains by a continual putting forth of His will. Ownership has its obligations; God cannot but take care of His possessions (94). "How sure a foundation, ye saints of the Lord, is laid for your faith in His excellent word."

VERSE NOTES

89. "is settled" or, standeth fast. The permanence of the earth which God created is symbol and sign of the permanence of His faithfulness.

90. "abideth" = stands firm.

91. "They" = the heavens (89) and the earth (90). May be rendered "For Thy ordinances they (heaven and earth) stand ready this day," *i.e.* ready to subserve God's will.

92. "then" = in that case.
94. "sought" or studied.
96. "end" = limit. Earthly perfection has its limit, but God's law is all embracing.

II. 6. MEM.   MEDITATION AND MATURITY

The Word—Its Power of Enlightenment.

I. WELCOME FOR THE WORD (97).

II. WISDOM FROM THE WORD (98–100).
    Threefold Result—Three Reasons.

III. WALK ACCORDING TO THE WORD (101–102).

IV. WELCOME FOR THE WORD (103).

V. WISDOM FROM THE WORD (104).

PERSONAL APPLICATION.—The word is a well of wisdom, whose waters never waste. Pondering the precepts (99) should be followed by practice (100 ff.). Note the moral order for the attainment of true wisdom: (a) the word with me; (b) my meditation; (c) I have kept (98–100). Abstinence from evil must be accompanied by obedience to the word—a positive attitude as well as a negative (101). A study of the word gives the power of discernment to "prove the spirits," 104 with Jno. iv. 1–4; 1 Cor. xii. 10. With the detection of mere sophistries there should be detestation of forbidden paths (104). Love for the light is a mark of God's children (97). The Bible is the true educator of the human race. Countries possessing "an open Bible" may be traced by their comparative intellectual gain in other directions.

VERSE NOTES

This stanza and that of "Shin" contain no petition.

98. Lit. "For it is mine for ever." The use of the singular in this line implies the unity of God's law.

99. "teachers," i.e. the appointed "traditional" teachers, or, those who derive their learning from other sources.

100. "I have more discernment . . ." The aged have learned from experience.

101. "way" includes religious ways.

102. Br. "For Thou Thyself hast instructed me."

103. "sweet" = smooth, agreeable, not s.H.w. in xix. 10.

II. 7. NUN.   NEED IN THE NIGHT

The Word—Its Power for Guidance.

I. PILGRIM PATH (105). The Word a Light. Illumination.

II. PROCLAIMED PURPOSE (106). The Word obeyed. Intention.

III. PRAYER IN PERSECUTION (107-108).

IV. PROTESTATIONS AMID PERIL (109-110).

V. PERPETUAL PORTION (111). The Word a Legacy. Inheritance.

VI. PURSUED PURPOSE (112). The Word obeyed. Intention.

PERSONAL APPLICATION.—They who obey the word will suffer persecution (107). Without divine instruction and grace our vows will be vain (108). A lamp is for the night; light is for the day (105) —night and day the word illumines the way. Though the world is dark, God's wayfarers walk with lantern in hand along a lighted way (105). Like the psalmist let us perform what we promise (106). A snare may be in the way, but we must keep right on (110).

VERSE NOTES

105. "lamp" or, lantern.

106. "confirmed" or, fulfilled.

107. "Quicken me," *i.e.* preserve me alive.

108. Cf. Heb. xiii. 15.

109. "soul"=life; explained next verse.

111. Israel had forfeited the land through sin, but the godly could still claim an eternal inheritance in God's word.

112. "unto the end," s.H.w. 33.

III. 1. SAMECH. SEPARATION FROM SINNERS

The Word—Its Power for Holiness.

I. PROTESTATIONS OF SINCERITY (113-114). Shelter and Shield.

II. PUTTING AWAY OF EVILDOERS (115). Excluded by the Loyal One.

III. PRAYERS FOR SECURITY (116-117). Support and Safety.

IV. PUTTING AWAY OF EVILDOERS (118-119). Expelled by the Lord.

V. PROTESTATIONS WITH SHUDDERING (120).

PERSONAL APPLICATION.—In these days of weak compromise, it is refreshing to read of the devotion and determination of saints of old. The godless life is a blunder as well as a sin (118b). Wholesome dread is not incompatible with whole-hearted devotion (119b and 120). Separation is the portion of impenitent sinners, both now and in the world to come. If the believer keeps company with evildoers, he will find it most difficult to obey the word of his God (115). God's people are as silver to be purified from dross; the lawless are regarded as all dross (119). To live aright needs sustaining grace (116).

VERSE NOTES

114. "Thou "(emph.). (b) or, "I have waited for Thy promise."

116. "ashamed," i.e. disappointed.

118. Or, "Thou hast rejected." (b) i.e. the principles upon which they act are false and baseless; or, they are self-deceived by false hopes. Laxity and lawlessness are twins.

119. "Therefore," i.e. because in this judgment he sees God's righteousness manifested.

120. "My flesh shudders (or, creeps) for awe of Thee;" Heb. lit. "hair stands on end (gooseflesh)," i.e. at the judgment executed upon the wicked.

113. i.e. the waverers, who one moment are for God and the next for Baal. They have no real conviction.

117. " . . . so shall I be saved."

III. 2. AYIN.   APPEAL FOR AID

The Word—Its Power in Prayer.

I. APPEAL FOR DELIVERANCE (121-124).   Oppression of Men.
   1. Prayer (121-122). "Thy Servant."
   2. Pining (123).
   3. Prayer (124). "Thy Servant."

II. APPEAL FOR DISCERNMENT (125-128).   Obliquity of Men.
   1. Prayer (125). "Thy Servant."
   2. Portent (126).
   3. Protestations (127-128).

PERSONAL APPLICATION.—The saint's conduct should correspond to the character of God (121). To urge our relationship to God as His servants is a sound plea, for the righteous God will not fail to

fulfil His obligations as Master (125). If we fail in *our* obligations
we can plead His lovingkindness (124). The more men depart from
the word of God, the more we should cling to it (126 ff.). God will
act in due time and deal with those who rebel against His will (126).

VERSE NOTES

122. *i.e.* guarantee Thy servant's welfare.
123. Cf. 81-82, note; "righteous word," *i.e.* the promise of deliverance which
God in righteousness is pledged to fulfil.
126. "It is time for Jehovah to act, They have broken (or, frustrated) Thy law."

III. 3. PE.   PRAYER FOR PRESERVATION

The Word—Its Power unto Wisdom.

I. PRONOUNCEMENT CONCERNING THE WORD (129-131).
    Desired by the Psalmist.
    1. Admiration for the Word (129).
    2. Action of the Word (130).   Illumination.
    3. Aspiration for the Word (131).

II. PRAYER BASED UPON PRIVILEGE (132-135).
    1. Petitions (Two) (132*a*).   For Return of Divine Favour.
    2. Plea (132*b*).   The Privilege.
    3. Petition (133*a*).
    4. Purpose (133*b*).   "so."
    5. Petition (134*a*).
    6. Purpose (134*b*).   "so."
    7. Petitions (Two) (135).   For Return of Divine Favour.

III. PLAINT CONCERNING THE WORD (136).   Disregarded by Men.

PERSONAL APPLICATION.—Compare the psalmist's longing for the
word (131) with his lament (136). Our longings may be either
lawful (131) or lustful (133*b*). The depths and difficulties of God's
word do not stumble devout souls. It is the "simple" heart, not the
sharpened intellect that penetrates the deepest (130). Steps established
in the word will preserve us from the tyranny of sin (133). To look
upon forsakers of the word aroused various emotions in the
psalmist's heart: (*a*) indignation (53); (*b*) grief (136), cf. Mark iii. 5;
(*c*) zeal (139); find others. God's works are wonderful (lxxvii.

11–14) and His word is wonderful (129). The word is the "doorway" to wisdom (130). Intense longing for the word is rare to-day (131). Here is an example of coming *boldly* to the throne of grace (132).

VERSE NOTES

129. "wonderful," lit. wonders; "keep them," more exactly, "keep them safely."

130. "opening" = doorway. In the East a doorway is the open way for light in the absence of windows; "simple," *i.e.* single-minded not weak-minded.

131. He is like a wild creature panting open-mouthed for water.

132. " . . . and be gracious unto me." (*b*) Lit. "According to the ordinance unto . . ." See Appendix XI. Here = "as is the right (or, privilege) of those that . . ." —a bold plea;

133. "And (so) let no iniquity . . ."

134. "Redeem," = Heb. padah = deliver by power; (*b*) or, "That I may . . ."

136. Cf. English idiom "floods of tears."

III.   4. TZADDI.   ZENITH OF ZEAL

The Word—Its Power unto Righteousness.

I. ATTRIBUTES OF THE WORD (137–138).   Righteousness.

II. ADVERSARIES OF THE WRITER (139).   His Zeal for the Word.

III. ATTRIBUTE OF THE WORD (140).   Purity.

IV. AFFRONT TO THE WRITER (141).   His Zeal for the Word.

V. ATTRIBUTE OF THE WORD (142).   Truth.

VI. AFFLICTION OF THE WRITER (143).   His Zeal for the Word.

VII. ATTRIBUTE OF THE WORD (144*a*).   Righteousness.

VIII. APPEAL OF THE WRITER (144*b*).   His Zeal for Wisdom.

PERSONAL APPLICATION.—Nothing should move us from allegiance to the Word of God (141, 143). The Law is a true transcript of the righteous character of God (137). God recognises and fully discharges His obligations (138*b*). The moral essentials of the Law are everlasting, though certain elements (the ceremonial) are transient (142, 144). The same fire of affliction tried both the loyalty of the psalmist and the faithfulness of the word (140, 143). Let us magnify the promise that enables us to stand.

137. "Thou" (emph.); "And upright . . ." br. "And faithfulness to the uttermost."

140. Br. " . . . well tried by fire, And Thy . . ."

144. "righteous," lit. righteousness.

III. 5. QOPH.   QUEST FOR QUIET

The Word—Its Power unto Hope.

I. CALLING IN PRAYER (145-149). Promise in the Word.
    1. Appeal (145-146). "Answer . . . save."
    2. Anticipation (147-148). Morning and Evening.
    3. Appeal (149). "Hear . . . revive."

II. CIRCUMSTANCES OF PERIL (150). The Presence of Danger. Foes nigh.

III. COMFORT IN PERIL (151). The Presence of the Defender. Jehovah nigh.

IV. CONFIDENCE IN PROPHECY (152). Permanency of the Word.

PERSONAL APPLICATION.—Mischief-makers may gather, but with God near we need not fear (150-151). Waves that ruffle the surface do not reach the depths; the passing storm that sways the branches does not disturb the roots (152). Let us, like the psalmist, resist the temptation to join the ranks of them that abandon the word of God (151). God's word is eternally valid, whatever its enemies may say (152). Persecutors may be near, but our Protector is nearer (151).

146. Or, "That I may observe . . ."

147. Br. "In the early twilight did I cry for help, (While) I waited with hope for Thy words."

148. He compares himself to a sentinel who wakes before time to go on duty; or, perhaps, to a Levite rising for his watch in the temple, and while waiting, meditates upon God's law.

149. "Hear" (emph.) = Oh, do hear! "ordinances," here and frequently = rules or principles of action. (b) "Quicken," see note verse 25.

150. " . . . that maliciously persecute me, that have gone far . . ."

III. 6. RESH.   REQUESTS FOR REVIVAL

The Word—Its Power for Overcoming.

I. PRAYER FOR REVIVAL (153-154). Lit. "See my affliction."
   "Revive me according to Thy Promise."
   1. Petitions (Two) (153*a*).
   2. Plea (153*b*).   The Psalmist's Practice.
   3. Petitions (Three) (154).
   4. Plea (154).   Jehovah's Promise.

II. PRONOUNCEMENT CONCERNING THE WICKED (155).
   Remark and Reason.

III. PRAYER FOR REVIVAL (156).
   "Revive me according to Thy Pronouncements."

IV. PLEAS BASED UPON PERSONAL RECTITUDE (157-158).
   1. Loyalty despite the Adversaries (157).
   2. Lamentation because of the Adversaries (158).

V. PRAYER FOR REVIVAL (159). Lit. "See my ardour."
   "Revive me according to Thy Pity."

VI. PRONOUNCEMENT CONCERNING THE WORD (160).

PERSONAL APPLICATION.—Note the threefold cry for revival. (This is prophetically of great significance as the utterance of the godly remnant in the last days. What Israel needs as a nation is spiritual "quickening," and this she will experience when the Spirit of God is outpoured upon her according to the promises.) The word often denotes the removal of adversity so that new life and liberty may be enjoyed. It is well to preserve the double sense of personal need and of divine fulness. Those who love God's precepts cannot but loathe apostasy from them (158). When God becomes our Advocate, victory is assured (154).

VERSE NOTES

153. "deliver" = rescue (as with a gentle hand).
154. "redeem," *i.e.* as from bondage.
155. "Seek not," *i.e.* study not, as 45, 94. They have no desire to know the will of God.
156. Or, "Many are Thy compassions."

158. Br. "I have seen . . . and felt loathing, Because they have not . . ."
160. "sum," lit. head; includes sum and substance—the word and the words;
all is truth; cf. Jno. xvii. 8, 14; xiv. 6.

III. 7. SHIN.   SUFFICIENCY AND SATISFACTION

The Word—Its Power unto Rest.

I. SUPREMACY OF THE WORD (161-165).   The Psalmist's Observations.
  1. Persecution because of the Word (161).
  2. Pleasure in the Word (162).
  3. Probity because of the Word (163).
  4. Praise on account of the Word (164).
  5. Peace through the Word (165).

II. SUBMISSION TO THE WORD (166-168).   The Psalmist's Obedience.
  1. Obedience with Longing (166).   Aspiration.
  2. Obedience with Love (167).   Admiration.
  3. Obedience with Life (168).   Action.

PERSONAL APPLICATION.—Note that this stanza contains no petition,
see "Mem." Reverential awe and rapturous appreciation are
concurrent effects of listening to God's word (161-162). They who
love the Law must necessarily loathe lying (163). Submission to the
will of God always brings peace (165). If we pray three times a day
(Ps. lv. 17) we should praise seven times (164). Waiting for the
fulfilment of the promised salvation is not idle anticipation but a
strenuous obedience and watchful observance (166). It is well
to recount our happy experiences in the ears of our God (166 ff.).
Righteousness is illustrated and confirmed in the government of
God (164). The word of God should be wrought into our
practical life (166b). *Praise* without ceasing (164), cf. 1 Thess. v. 17.

VERSE NOTES

161. "Princes" = rulers.
162. "word" or, promise.
163. Br. "I hate falsehood and will abhor it."
165. " . . . no stumbling block."
166 ff. The psalmist speaks in no spirit of self-righteousness, but delights to
recount his glad experience to God's glory.

APPENDIX.   TAV.   TROUBLE AND TRUST.
Repentance of the Remnant.

This stanza seems to point to Israel's regeneration day—their spiritual re-birth as a nation. It is the sigh for salvation addressed to the Shepherd of Israel by His "sheep," fully conscious of their sin. "Threads that have run through the psalm are here knotted firmly together" and the unique pattern of the composition stands out in all its exquisite beauty.

I. PRAYER (169–170).
   1. Petitions (Two)
   2. Plea. Jehovah's Promise (169).
   3. Petitions (Two).
   4. Plea. Jehovah's Promise (170).

II. PRAISE (171–172).
   1. Promise.
   2. Prompting (171).   "Because."
   3. Promise.
   4. Prompting (172).   "Because."

III. PRAYER (173).
   1. Petition.
   2. Plea. The Psalmist's Purpose.

IV. PLEAS (174).
   1. Desire for Divine Deliverance.
   2. Delight in Divine Decrees.

V. PRAYER (175).
   Petitions and Plea.   The Psalmist's Praise.

VI. PLAINT (176a). Expression of Penitence.

VII. PRAYER (176bc). The Psalmist's Piety.

PERSONAL APPLICATION.—Manifold petitions of the psalm are condensed here into two (a) for understanding and (b) for deliverance. These meet the twin needs of man for inward illumination and outward salvation (169–170). Note how petition now passes into praise (171–172). Our devotion to the Lord should not consist of grudging service but of constant delight (174). Our hope lies not in our docility as sheep, but in the active seeking of the Shepherd (176). Profession of present devotion is not inconsistent with confession of past defection (176).

VERSE NOTES

169. "cry" Heb. indicates an outward expression of urgent entreaty.

170. "supplication" here refers to the substance of his prayer; "deliver" = rescue; "word" = promise.

171. Br. "My lips shall pour forth (or, bubble over with) praise."

172. Br. "My tongue shall . . ."

173. Cf. Deut. xxx. 1-3.

174. Closely connected with preceding verse. Three reasons pleaded for answer to prayers: (a) his deliberate resolve; (b) his long and eager waiting; (c) his delight in the will of God.

175. Br. " . . . live, that it may praise Thee." (b) "ordinances" here probably rf. to acts of divine judgment by which the enemy is punished (Isa. xxxvii. 33-36); or, just decisions.

176. "lost" = strayed and in danger of perishing, cf. Matt. xviii. 11; Luke xix. 10.

Book Five. IV. The Ways of God Recalled in the National Homecoming: cxx.–cxxxiv.

Songs of Pilgrimage.   The Pathway to the Presence.

Much has been conjectured concerning the origin of this group of psalms distinguished by the title over each composition, "A Song of Degrees." The Hebrew word for "degrees" is variously rendered in the Old Testament, e.g. "going up," "ascents," "steps," "stairs." It is certainly used of making pilgrimage to Jerusalem for the great annual festivals (1 Sam. i. 3; Ps. cxxii. 4) and we know from Isa. xxx. 29 and Ps. xlii. 4 that it was customary for the pilgrim bands to sing *en route*. Many therefore have concluded that these songs were then used. In the majority, however, the subject-matter seems to have nothing whatever to do with pilgrimage. A second view associates the group with the steps (traditionally fifteen) which led from the great court of the temple to the inner court, and it is suggested that these songs were sung upon the steps at festival times. The third and most acceptable view is that suggested by Dr. John Lightfoot some three hundred years ago and more recently put forward by Dr. Thirtle who connects these psalms with King Hezekiah and the "degrees" on the "sundial" of Ahaz. For the double record, see 2 Kings xx.; Isa. xxxviii. Briefly stated the reasons are (a) Hezekiah's reference to "my songs" which were to form part of the temple liturgy at least during the rest of the king's lifetime; (b) Hezekiah himself was a poet as his composition recorded Isa. xxxviii. shows; (c) there are just fifteen songs corresponding to the number of years added to his life; (d) apparently the king himself wrote the ten anonymous songs, corresponding to the number of the degrees, the remaining five being chosen from a royal collection of poems as suitably expressing his feelings; (e) the contents of these songs are in close keeping with the circumstances of the triple crisis in Hezekiah's days—the Assyrian invasion, the king's desperate sickness and the lack of an heir to the throne. The Hebrew word for "degrees" has the article, "of (or relating to) the .degrees," and the only degrees Scripture actually records are those mentioned 2 Kings xx. 8–11. To our finite understanding the miracle then worked by the Creator seems even more remarkable than the miracle of Joshua's day (Josh. x. 12–14). That it made a profound impression upon the surrounding nations is clear from 2 Chron. xxxii. 31. There are strong reasons for believing also that Hezekiah was the author of other psalms relating to his life and times. He employed a company of men as copyists to transcribe and transmit the sacred text, Prov. xxv. 1. This formed part of the service he rendered in his zeal for God, 2 Chron. xxxi. 21. The work of these copyists no doubt included transcriptions of the Law and of the words of David and of Asaph the Seer, Deut. xvii. 18–19; 2 Chron. xxix. 30. Note that this last view does not rule out the possibility of the later use of the songs by pilgrims going up to Jerusalem and the exiles returning from Babylon.

The fifteen "Songs" group into five triads (see Analysis), each triad covering the threefold experience of Trouble, Trust and Triumph, or Distress, Dependence and Deliverance. The central psalm is by Solomon and each of the two sevens thus separated contains two by David and five are anonymous. The last psalm of each group has blessing and peace for its theme, reminding of Hezekiah's last recorded words, 2 Kings xx. 19. Psalms cxx.–cxxxiv. are sometimes called the "Pilgrims' Song-book"; "A Psalter within a Psalter"; "A Pentateuch of Song" corresponding to the larger pentateuch of the Psalms as a whole.

Cycle 1. *Human Stress and Divine Sufficiency: cxx.–cxxii.*

Jehovah the National Refuge.   The Keeper of Israel.

PSALM CXX.   A DAY OF DISTRESS.   SOJOURNING IN SOLITUDE

I. ENCOURAGING ACKNOWLEDGMENT (1). Past Deliverance. Plea.

II. EARNEST APPEAL (2). Jehovah Addressed. Prayer.

III. ENERGETIC APOSTROPHE (3–4). Adversary Addressed. Prediction. Question (3). Answer (4).

IV. EXCEPTIONAL AFFLICTION (5–7). Present Distress. Plaint.

SUPERSCRIPT.—A Song of the Degrees.

PRIMARY ASSOCIATION.—See previous page. The anonymous writer is probably Hezekiah, in which case the fulminations of Rabshakeh may be referred to in 2–3. 2 Kings xviii. 19–35; xix. 8ff.

PROPHETIC ANTICIPATION.—Seems to portray the experiences of

the godly remnant.in the last days opposed and oppressed by their great adversary Antichrist. Quite possibly the view is retrospective, Israel recapitulating in the happier times to follow, their past experiences preceding the advent of Messiah. The reference to Meshech and Kedar are very significant from this prophetic standpoint (see verse notes).

PERSONAL APPLICATION.—Past answers encourage further appeals (1-2). "God does not always cash His notes at sight, but if not He pays large interest upon them." Many men and nations are lovers of war, but God's people should always be lovers of peace. Saints of God are sometimes found in most unlikely dwelling-places. False tongues may be more dangerous than armed foes. God often makes the punishment fit the crime.

VERSE NOTES

1. "distress" = straits; "cried" = called; cf. 2 Kings xiv. 3-4, 14-19.

3. Br. " . . . He give . . . what shall He add . . ."

4. Answer to 3. Retribution suits the offence. "juniper," see marg. Arabs still prepare the finest charcoal from the broom. Glowing coals symbolise divine judgments, cxl. 10; cf. Rev. viii. 5; "mighty" = Mighty One.

5. "Meschech," name of barbarous tribes which then inhabited the highlands to the east of Cilicia and in later days retreated northwards to the neighbourhood of the Black Sea and beyond. In prophecy = Muscovy i.e. Russia; see Gen. x. 2. "Kedar," one of the great Bedouin tribes of the Arabian desert; cf. Gen. xxv. 13 with xvi. 12. Kedar is a general rabbinic name for Arabia. Primarily, the psalmist does not mean that he was actually living among these widely separated peoples, but applies the names typically as we do "Huns" and "Vandals," to indicate a cruel and merciless character. It is quite possible however that among the armies besieging Jerusalem there were numbers of these barbarous foes. For long centuries the Jews have suffered at the hands of Arabs and Muscovite peoples more perhaps than from any others, hence the prophetic significance.

6. "My soul hath," i.e. I have.

7. Lit. "I am peace," i.e. one characterised by peaceableness. For similar verbal construction, see cix. 4; "peace," cf. Hezekiah's desire, Isa. xxxviii. 17; "war," cf. 2 Chron. xxxii. 2 margin.

PSALM CXXI. THE GUARDIANSHIP OF GOD

I. PERSONAL PROFESSION (1-2). First Person.
   1. The Pondered Creation (1a). The Mountains.
   2. The Pressing Challenge (1b). The Question.

3. The Proclaimed Confidence (2a). The Answer.
4. The Peerless Creator (2b). The Maker.

II. PROMISED PRESERVATION (3-8). Second Person.
   1. The Constant Protection (3-4). Negative—not suffer.
   2. The Competent Protector (5). Positive. Jehovah the Keeper.
   3. The Constant Protection (6). Negative—not smite.
   4. The Competent Protector (7-8). Positive. Jehovah the Keeper.

SUPERSCRIPT.—A Song of the Degrees.

PRIMARY ASSOCIATION.—See introduction to cxx. If Hezekiah be the anonymous author, how appropriate to the circumstances of the siege of Jerusalem by the Assyrians! In that case, too, the first two verses would be an expression of personal trust and the rest of the psalm very possibly an oracular response granted through a prophet of God (Isaiah?) and calculated to assure his heart. The psalm seems adapted for antiphonal song.

PROPHETIC ANTICIPATION.—Belongs to same period as cxx. Not yet can Israel look to Zion for help. This must first come direct from heaven (2) in the person of a manifested Messiah, before the throne is established in Zion. Note the national aspect (4) and the individual (5).

PERSONAL APPLICATION.—Note the soul (1-2) and its Saviour (3-8). Jehovah as the Keeper is mentioned three times; the keeping (cognate verb) also three times. Consider what He keeps from. "When dwelling upon the lower levels lift your eyes higher than the heights" (1-2). Keep your eyes on your Keeper. We must distrust self if ever we are fully to trust God. The Keeper of the Assembly is the Keeper of the individual (4-5). God takes account of units. He loves all because He loves each. Here are many precious promises for God's pilgrims. God keeps the soul entrusted to Him by faith as a very precious deposit (7b); cf. John x. 28-29. Verse 8 covers all our circumstances and all our future.

VERSE NOTES

1. The poet considers Jehovah's power as displayed in creation, cf. cxxv. 2; "Lift up mine eyes," cf. cxxiii. 1-2.

2. For Jehovah's promised help see 2 Kings xix. 12-34; xx. 6. His trust rests upon the divine promise. (b) An expression common in the later psalms. It contrasts Jehovah's omnipotence with the impotence of the heathen deities, such as the Assyrian invaders of Judah worshipped; see 2 Kings xxi. 15; 2 Chron. xxxii. 19.

3. The negative particle is usually employed in commands or wishes; may render, "May He not . . . feet to stumble." So with next line.

4. An unslumbering and unwearied Watchman; not like some human sentinel liable to fall asleep at his post, nor like the heathen gods, 1 Kings xviii. 27.

6. Cf. Ps. xci.

7. "thy soul" = thy life; for fulfilment of the promise see 2 Chron. xxxii. 22.

PSALM CXXII. THE JOYS OF JERUSALEM

I. THE CITY'S PRE-EMINENCE (1–5). Object of Praise.

    1. Indicated Purpose (1–2).
        (a) Anticipation (1).
        (b) Realisation (2).

    2. Imposing Prospect (3).

    3. Illustrious Privileges (4–5).
        (i) The Temple—Religious Centre.
        (ii) The Throne—Civic Centre.

II. THE CITY'S PEACE (6–9). Object of Prayer.

    1. Invited Prayer (6).
    2. Invoked Prosperity (7).
    3. Indicated Purpose (8–9).
        (i) Benediction Pronounced (8).
        (ii) Benefit Pursued (9).

SUPERSCRIPT.—A Song of the Degrees; David's.

PRIMARY ASSOCIATION.—David first published his composition probably soon after the removal of the ark to Zion and God's immediately subsequent promise of a seed, a house and a throne for ever to David. In the Psalms he often recurs to this God-given promise (2 Sam. vii.). He evidently designed to draw the affections of all Israel round Jerusalem and its sanctuary as the sacred bond of national unity. The psalm is chosen by Hezekiah as being eminently suited to his own purpose. He loved the house of Jehovah even as did his ancestor David; see 2 Chron. xxix–xxxi.

PROPHETIC ANTICIPATION.—Here we see the millennial metropolis with its restored temple as the dwelling-place of Jehovah, and the city as the uniting centre of the new Israel, the tribes going up on their pilgrimages with songs expressive of their unalloyed joy. With verse 5 cf. Ezek. xlvi.

PERSONAL APPLICATION.—The peace of Jerusalem will spell the

universal welfare of men and the universal worship of God. Our Lord loved Jerusalem (Luke xix. 41) and His followers should do the same. Christians are characterised by love of the saints and love of the sanctuary (8-9).

VERSE NOTES

1. Or, "We will go . . ." cf. Isa. ii. 3, where Isaiah appropriates the words in a new relation.

2. As R.V.—a rapturous realization of the anticipation in 1.

3. Br. "Jerusalem! built up as a city compacted together"; cf. 1 Chron. xi. 7-8; 2 Sam. v. 9-11. The city had existed for centuries, but David made it a well-built metropolis, joining the lower city with the fortress by the "walls" and adorning the whole with "palaces" such as described in 7; cf. li. 18.

4. Line (b) is in parenthesis, = "according to the testimony (or, ordinance) appointed for Israel." See Exod. xxiii. 17; xxxiv. 23; Deut. xvi. 16.

5. The king was evidently assisted in his judicial functions by members of the royal family. Note prophetic significance.

6. Doubtless an allusion to the name. Jerusalem = city (or, possession) of peace. In Heb. "peace" and prosperity" have a similar sound. May the "nomen" become the "omen," so to speak. Cf. cxxv. 5; cxxviii. 6.

8. *i.e.* those dwelling in Jerusalem.

9. In the Psalms, David often calls the tabernacle of the ark, "the house, or the temple of Jehovah."

Cycle 2. *Human Stress and Divine Sufficiency: cxxiii.–cxxv.*

Jehovah the National Rescuer. The Helper of Israel. Deliverance from Foes.

PSALM CXXIII. CRY OF THE CONTEMNED

I. PATIENT SUBMISSION (1-2).
    1. Dependent Attitude (1).
    2. Double Analogy (2). Master and Man; Mistress and Maid.

II. POIGNANT SUPPLICATION (3-4).
    1. Distressed Appeal (3a). Prayer.
    2. Deep Affliction (3b-4). Plea.

SUPERSCRIPT.—A Song of the Degrees

PRIMARY ASSOCIATION.—Anonymous writer probably Hezekiah, who here appeals to Jehovah on account of the contemptuous challenge of Rabshakeh; see Isa. xxxvi.

PROPHETIC ANTICIPATION.—Israel in the hour of her deepest distress (yet to come) in the new spirit of obedience looks to Jehovah in the heavens for deliverance. The nation is brought at last to realise that He is the only resource. The answer will be in the manifestation of Messiah in glory to the discomfiture of Israel's powerful enemies.

PERSONAL APPLICATION.—The servant's attitude is not only one of willing service, but of waiting trust. It is humbling to the pride of the natural man to acknowledge his utter dependence upon God. For Jew and Gentile alike, divine deliverance is dependent upon divine grace. God's people in all ages are contemned because of their trust in God.

VERSE NOTES

1. Cf. cxxi. 1. He lifts his eyes higher than the hills, even to the heavens; " . . . sittest (enthroned) . . ." 2 Kings xix. 15.

2. Servants and slaves are dependent upon master and mistress of the household for all needed supplies. "Until He be gracious unto us."

3. "Be gracious unto us, O Jehovah, be gracious unto us."

4. " . . . scorn of the careless . . ." They were satiated, so to speak, with the contumely cast upon them by the enemy. See refs. above, and note use of s.H.w. Isa. xxxvii. 29, R.V.m.

PSALM CXXIV. SNATCHED FROM THE SNARE

I. ACKNOWLEDGMENT OF PLIGHT (1–5). The Extremity.
    1. Noteworthy Confession (1–2). Jehovah our Help.
    2. Neat Comparisons (3–5).
        (i) Ferocious Beasts (3).
        (ii) Flood Waters (4–5).
II. ASCRIPTION OF PRAISE (6–8). The Escape.
    1. Neat Comparisons (6–7).
        (i) Ferocious Beasts (6).
        (ii) Fowler's Snare (7).
    2. Noteworthy Confession (8). Jehovah our Help.

SUPERSCRIPT.—A Song of the Degrees; David's.

PRIMARY ASSOCIATION.—Evidently points to a sudden national danger providentially averted. Only such period recorded in David's history was that of the Syrian and Edomite wars, cf. Pss. xliv., lx. This is the thanksgiving for deliverance. Language and style confirm David's authorship. Note the step-like structure; before the next

L

forward move, the writer goes back half a step. It is not so much poetic art as a passionate heart. The repetition is for emphasis. Patient Resignation, cxxiii.; Jubilant Celebration, cxxiv. Hezekiah uses David's composition as eminently suited to the new crisis in the nation in his day. Three hundred and fifty years earlier David had been in similar danger, especially when pursued by Saul, 1 Sam. xxiii.–xxvi.

PROPHETIC ANTICIPATION.—Jehovah has intervened for the deliverance of His people in answer to the appeal of Ps. cxxiii.; cf. notes to Ps. lxxxiii. See Joel ii. 32.

PERSONAL APPLICATION.—Thanksgiving for answered prayers should be as persistent as the prayers. Shallow gratitude is poured out in one gush; deep gratitude flows on like a river. God changes our notes of alarm into songs of joy. Sin both snares and swallows up its victims. What Jehovah's name declares Him to be that He is to our souls.

VERSE NOTES

1. "on our side," br. "for us," so 2a. For the construction of verse cf. cxxix.
1–2. The repetition may indicate more than one divine intervention; e.g. first over Hadadrezer and then over Edom.
4. "our soul" = us (emph.) so 5 and 7; "stream" = torrent. Cf. xviii. 16.
5. "proud," Heb. from root "to boil over." 4–5 show the imminence of the danger; 6–7 the completeness of the deliverance.
7. "we" (emph.). Note the beautiful comparison of the fluttering feebleness of the bird snatched from the snare by the delivering hand. It is interesting to note that on Sennacherib's cylinder (now in the British Museum) the Assyrian king refers to Hezekiah as a bird in a cage.
8. Cf. cxxi. 2, cxxxiv. 3.

PSALM CXXV. SECURITY OF THE SAINTS

I. REALISED REST (1–3).
   1. Safe Position (1–2).
      (i) The Faithful Established (1). Stability.
      (ii) The Faithful Encompassed (2). Security.
   2. Sure Promise (3).

II. RIGHTEOUS RECOMPENSE (4–5).
   1. Simple Prayer (4). Sincerity.
   2. Solemn Pronouncement (5). Subtlety. Benediction (5c).

SUPERSCRIPT.—A Song of the Degrees.

PRIMARY ASSOCIATION.—See notes introductory to the group. Ps. cxxiv. views Israel Escaped; Ps. cxxv. Israel Established. Suitable to the circumstances following the discomfiture of the Assyrians in Hezekiah's days. Verse 3 doubtless refers to deliverance from their invasion.

PROPHETIC ANTICIPATION.—Plainly points to the days when Israel shall be in full enjoyment of deliverance from her future great adversaries. Millennial blessing.

PERSONAL APPLICATION.—They that trust Jehovah shall not totter on their foundation. Remember that steadiness is not stubbornness (1). They who keep company with workers of iniquity will be led away to share the same fate. Loyalty and lawlessness both meet a suited recompense. They who trust Jehovah (1) are called righteous —Godward aspect (3); good—manward aspect (4); and upright in heart—selfward aspect (4). Have you noted the beautiful Pauline benediction (Gal. vi. 16)? Peace spells harmony, security, liberty and felicity. It is the end of all hostility, tyranny, instability and anxiety (5c).

VERSE NOTES

1. For Hezekiah's trust cf. 2 Kings xviii. 5; Isa. xxxvii. 10. Br. " . . . which shall not be shaken, but is set fast for ever."

3. *i.e.* no alien world power shall remain permanently upon the soil of Israel's inheritance, the land of Palestine, lest the nation in deep discouragement turn away permanently from God, or by mingling with the heathen learn their evil ways. " wickedness," LXX reads "the lawless one." Wickedness in Scripture is nearly always associated with spiritual evil rather than social evil. "righteous" = righteous ones. "For" at beginning of the verse shows that the confidence expressed in 2 is justified; "sceptre" = symbol of rule.

4-5. The true-hearted and the treacherous are here contrasted. The latter are those who temporise instead of trust (5). "their" = the enemies'; "forth" or, away.

Cycle 3. *Human Stress and Divine Sufficiency: cxxvi.-cxxviii.*

Jehovah the National Rebuilder. The Establisher of Israel.

PSALM CXXVI. CONFIDENCE IN COMPLETION

I. PRAISE FOR PRESERVATION (1–3). Past Experience.
"Captivity turned."
1. Comparison (1). Like dreamers. Parallel drawn.

2. Celebration (2-3). Joy expressed. "Shouts of Joy."
   (i) Israel's Triumph (2a).
   (ii) Gentiles' Testimony (2b).
   (iii) Israel's Tribute (3).

II. PRAYER FOR PROSPERITY (4-6). Present Entreaty.
   "Captivity—turn."

   1. Comparison (4). Like streams. Parallel drawn.
   2. Celebration (5-6). Joy expected. "Shouts of Joy."

SUPERSCRIPT.—A Song of the Degrees.

PRIMARY ASSOCIATION.—Anonymous writer probably Hezekiah, see notes to preceding psalms. The reference to the "captivity" may be connected with those taken away by Sennacherib (2 Kings xviii. 9-13). Hezekiah had the welfare of all Israel ever on his heart, 2 Chron. xxx. 6-11. However, the Hebrew words commonly bear another construction, see verse notes.

PROPHETIC ANTICIPATION.—Points to the time of the partial restoration of the Jews to their land. With renewed hearts and hopes they appeal to Jehovah for the full accomplishment of the promised blessing in restoring also the ten tribes, that Israel may once more be a united nation enjoying the full favour of Jehovah their God.

PERSONAL APPLICATION.—Partial fulfilment of divine promises should encourage us to continue praying for the complete blessing. Realities are sometimes like pleasant dreams substantiated. Every saint of God in every age can echo the words of 3. Precious promises for pioneer workers are found in 5-6. Between sowing and reaping there is much patient toil. Earnest Christian workers know what it is to shed tears; cf. Acts xx. 19, 31.

VERSE NOTES

1. Cf. 4. "turn . . . captivity," the Heb. idiom may be rendered "restore the prosperity of," or as R.V. See Job. xlii. 10. This very ambiguity seems designed by the Holy Spirit to suit both the historical circumstances and the prophetic outlook; "dream," i.e. they could hardly believe the reality. Cf. the record, 2 Kings xix. 35
2. "laughter," cf. Job. viii. 31; "singing" = shouts, or cries of joy. Last line is an exclamation of wonder and envy. Cf. A.V.m. with 2 Chron. xxxii. 22-23.
3. Omit "Whereof"; the very terseness is expressive.
4. Or, "Restore our prosperity . . ." see notes 1. (b) "Like watercourses in the Southland," i.e. the arid Negeb whose wadies run out into the Arabian desert.

These dried up watercourses become raging torrents in the rainy season. So the psalmist desires to see Israel returning not as a mere trickle, but as a surging flood.

5. Br. "... reap with shouts," or cries of joy. The scene is not that of exiles in Babylon, but of agriculturalists in the land.

6. The Hebrew implies persevering work despite tearful disappointment; see Jehovah's sign to Hezekiah, 2 Kings xix. 29. There may be a reference also to the king's own faithful efforts to reunite all Israel by recalling the remnant of the northern tribes to the true worship of Jehovah, 2 Chron. xxx. "doubtless" = surely; "... with joyful cries when he bringeth (home) his sheaves." Prophetically of those who "shall turn many to righteousness," Dan. xii. 3.

PSALM CXXVII. TRUST TRANSCENDS TOIL

I. VANITY OF HUMAN EFFORT (1-2). Futility Betokened.
    1. Necessary Reminder of Man's Insufficiency. His "Busyness." Building—Defending—Sustaining.
    2. Necessary Reminder of God's All-sufficiency. His Bounty.

II. VALUE OF DIVINE ENDOWMENT (3-5). Felicity Bestowed. His Blessing. Gift of Sons to Build—Defend—Sustain the "House."

SUPERSCRIPT.—A Song of the Degrees; Solomon's.

PRIMARY ASSOCIATION.—This psalm is significant in view of Solomon's many labours in building (a) the temple, and (b) his palace. The former took seven years to complete, the latter thirteen, 1 Kings vi.–viii. The connection between the first part of the psalm and the remainder is better understood if it be remembered that the Hebrew word for "children" is from a root meaning to build. This is the middle psalm of the group and seems to have been chosen by Hezekiah as suited to his own childless condition during the siege of Jerusalem by Sennacherib the Assyrian. He remembers the Lord's promise to David (2 Sam. vii. 12) and longs for the fulfilment of it in his case by the granting of an heir; cf. 2 Chron. vi. 16; vii. 18. Manasseh was born in Hezekiah's seventeenth year on the throne, that is, the third of the added fifteen, 2 Kings xx. 18; xxi. 1.

PROPHETIC ANTICIPATION.—A reminder to the newly restored nation of Israel in early millennial days. Note that the blessing here is strictly Jewish in character; communal life (1), domestic life (2).

PERSONAL APPLICATION.—Without God both working and watching are in vain, cf. Neh. iv. 13–23. Long hours do not necessarily mean a prosperous work (2). The world struggles and snatches, the believer quietly works and waits on God. God does not encourage laziness, but He does rebuke anxious drudgery, cf. Matt. vi. 25-34. He gives to His own what the godless strive for in vain; cf. Phil. iv. 6.

VERSE NOTES

2. All that godless ones seek with much toil and in vain, God bestows upon His beloved ones while they sleep. The passage is addressed to toilers who, by reason of constant anxiety and unremitting labour, lose the enjoyment that is the portion of those who trust God. God gave to Solomon in sleep, 1 Kings iii. 5-13; so Adam, Gen. ii. 21-22; Abraham, Gen. xv. 12-16; cf. the growth of Messiah's kingdom, Mark iv. 26; Luke xvii. 20. "Beloved," Heb. *yedid*, a reminder of the name given to Solomon, 2 Sam. xii. 25.

3. "children" = sons, so also (4); br. "from Jehovah"; omit italicised words.

4. ". . . of (a father's) youth;" or, "sons, the young men," taking the Heb. as genitive of apposition.

5. "the gate," = chief place of city concourse for commerce, courts, etc. A stalwart family conveys a sense of influence and power, enough, *e.g.* to make an unjust adversary hesitate to lodge unfounded complaints.

PSALM CXXVIII.   THE GAIN OF THE GODFEARING

I. BLESSEDNESS PROCLAIMED (1). 3rd person. He that revereth Jehovah.

II. BLESSINGS PROMISED (2-3). 2nd person—"thou."
    1. Upon thy Work.
    2. Upon thy Wife.
    3. Upon thy Weans.

III. BLESSEDNESS PROCLAIMED (4). 3rd person. He that revereth Jehovah.

IV. BLESSINGS PROMISED (5-6). 2nd person—"thou."
    1. Public Prosperity. Welfare of Jerusalem seen.
    2. Private Prosperity. Welfare of Posterity seen.
    3. Public Prosperity. Welfare of Israel seen. Benediction.
SUPERSCRIPT.—A Song of the Degrees.

PRIMARY ASSOCIATION.—Probably one of Hezekiah's "songs" see notes to preceding psalms. Here he declares his sense of blessing received in the promise and gift of a son as heir to the throne of David. Hezekiah trusted in Jehovah for (*a*) Victory over the Assyrians, (*b*) Recovery from his sickness, and (*c*) Bestowal of an heir. One of the "Beatitude" group.

PROPHETIC ANTICIPATION.—Clearly points to millennial times. The promised blessings are distinctly Jewish—earthly prosperity and domestic felicity.

PERSONAL APPLICATION.—Family felicity is for the faithful. Happy homes make a happy nation. The welfare of the state is dependent upon the wholesomeness of its family life. Godliness in the home ever leads to domestic happiness.

VERSE NOTES

1. "Blessed" = happy, as in 2.

2 ff. Ctr. the lot of those who turn from Jehovah, Lev. xxvi. 16; Deut. xxviii. 30-33; Amos v. 11; Mic. vi. 15.

3. The vine is characterised by gracefulness, fruitfulness, preciousness and dependency. (*b*) the usual arrangement in the East for the women's apartments. "children" = sons. The evergreen olive symbolises vitality and vigour. It sends out young saplings which grow round the decaying parent tree sheltering it from storms that would otherwise destroy it.

4. Br. "Lo, surely thus . . . "

5. (*a*) *i.e.* where He sits enthroned as King. (*b*) or, "That thou mayest see . . . "

6. "Yea, see Thy son's sons . . . "

Cycle 4. *Human Stress and Divine Sufficiency: cxxix.–cxxxi.*

Jehovah the National Redeemer.   The Saviour of Israel.
Deliverance from Sins.

PSALM CXXIX.   OMNIPOTENCE OVERRULING

I. EXPERIENCE OF JEHOVAH'S FAITHFULNESS (1-4).
   1. Oft-recurring Distress (1-2*a*).
   2. Oft-repeated Deliverance (2*b*).
   3. Oft-recurring Distress (3).
   4. Oft-repeated Deliverance (4).

II. EXPRESSIONS OF ISRAEL'S FAITH (5-8).   Verbs as futures.
   1. Confusion of the Godless (5).
   2. Comparison with the Grass (6-8).
   Fate of the Foe—contrasted with the Felicity of the Faithful.

SUPERSCRIPT.—A Song of the Degrees.

PRIMARY ASSOCIATION.—Probably by Hezekiah; see notes introductory to the group.

PROPHETIC ANTICIPATION.—The godly remnant takes a retrospective view of the national history showing it to be one of repeated suffering (on account of sin) but repeated deliverance in the overruling mercy of Jehovah. The purpose is to emphasise what will then have been a recent great manifestation of divine power for the salvation of Israel.

PERSONAL APPLICATION.—No enemy can prevail against those who are the Lord's (2) whether an individual, or Israel, or the Church (Matt. xvi. 18). Jehovah Himself is the great Emancipator (4). The ban not the blessing shall be the portion of all that hate Zion. Ploughing is necessary preparation for an eventual harvest. Gashed trees exude precious gum; endured sorrows yield hallowed joy. The survival of the saints is sure.

VERSE NOTES

1. *i.e.* from the beginning of the national history—the bondage in Egypt. (*b*) Probably a liturgical direction.

2. The existence of the Jews to-day proves the truth of second line.

3. Metaphor for cruel maltreatment (Isa. l. 6); the figures of a slave under the lash and a field under tillage are blended.

4. "cords," cf. Job xxxix. 10. The figure is probably of a draught ox harnessed to the plough rescued after suffering harsh treatment and enduring hard toil (two aspects of bondage). Points to Israel's rescue from successive oppressions and particularly to a recent great deliverance such as Hezekiah experienced. May be rendered "Jehovah the righteous has cut . . ."

5. Br. "Put to shame . . . shall be all that . . ." Cf. 2 Chron. xxxii. 21.

6. Br. "They shall be as . . ." On the flat roofs of oriental houses plants quickly spring up, but as quickly wither away for lack of moisture (cf. Matt. xiii. 8) before reaching maturity. There is a reference doubtless to Isa. xxxvii. 27. There is neither seed nor crop (7); fig. of short-lived success.

7. "bosom" = the loose fold of the eastern garment at the bosom often used as a receptacle; even children are sometimes carried in it.

8. Cf. Ruth ii. 4. Last line is perhaps the reapers' response.

PSALM CXXX. PENITENCE AND PARDON

I. EXPRESSION OF ISRAEL'S REPENTANCE (1-4). CONFESSION.

1. Woeful Request (1-2).
2. Wise Remark (3).
3. Weighty Reason (4). "For."

II. EXPECTATION OF ISRAEL'S REDEMPTION (5-8). **CONFIDENCE.**

    1. Watchful Regard (5-6).

    2. Wise Recommendation (7a).

    3. Weighty Reason (7b-8). "For."

SUPERSCRIPT.—A Song of the Degrees.

PRIMARY ASSOCIATION.—Written probably by **Hezekiah who** alludes to Solomon's prayer (2 Chron. vi. 40–42). Lying at the gates of death his prayer is heard and he is raised up. Last of the seven "Penitential Psalms," so-called by the early Christian Church.

PROPHETIC ANTICIPATION.—Points to the fulfilment of Israel's Day of Atonement. We see here the effect of the "ploughing"— the disciplinary process mentioned in the preceding psalm. The nation longs for the end of the long night of trouble and the dawn of the promised millennial day.

PERSONAL APPLICATION.—Wistful waiting and watching. Experience rises from the depths of sinfulness (1) to the heights of salvation (8) by four steps. All are guilty before the bar of divine justice, cf. Rom. iii. The realisation of personal sin casts the soul upon the mercy of God alone. Forgiveness is a "cutting off" (so Heb. word)—a spiritual "surgery," the significance of which is worth pondering.

VERSE NOTES

    1. Deep waters symbolise distress and danger; "cried" = called.

    2. "Lord" = Adonai, so 3b.

    3. "mark" s.H.w. (6) watch; here = to take account of; "stand," i.e. before God in judgment and maintain innocence.

    4. Heb. is "the forgiveness," i.e. not only that pledged to the nation upon repentance, but that for which Hezekiah himself gives thanks, Isa. xxxviii. 17. "feared" = devoutly reverenced; cf. 1 Pet. i. 17.

    5. Patient hope consequent upon a sense of Jehovah's readiness to forgive; "word," rf. doubtless to the message sent by Jehovah to Hezekiah through Isaiah, 2 Kings xix. 6.

    6. Lit. "My soul is towards Jehovah," signifies a complete turning of the whole being to God; a fundamental attitude in all true repentance. (b) "More than watchers for . . ."

    7. "plentious redemption." Hezekiah was delivered not only from the king of Assyria (Isa. xxxvii.), but also from the King of Terrors—death (Isa. xxxviii).

    8. i.e. from both the penalty and the power of them; "iniquities"=perversities; "He" (emph.).

PSALM CXXXI.   CALM AND CONTENT

I. EXPRESSION OF HUMILITY (1–2).   Addressed to Jehovah.
    1. Simple Submissiveness (1).   Lowliness.
    2. Striking Similitude (2).   Likeness.

II. EXHORTATION TO HOPE (3).   Addressed to Israel.

SUPERSCRIPT.— A Song of the Degrees; David's.

PRIMARY ASSOCIATION.—It is probably King Hezekiah who takes up this beautiful psalm of David's as eminently suitable to set forth his own soul exercise at the time of his serious illness. If so, it belongs to the latter part of that period.

PROPHETIC ANTICIPATION.—Clearly points to the state of soul to be reached by Israel as a result of Jehovah's disciplinary dealings with the nation in the last days. They learn to look solely to the lovingkindness of God in hope of (a) Perfect Redemption, cxxx. 7; (b) Permanent Rest, cxxxi. 3.

PERSONAL APPLICATION.—Stillness after storm. A spirit of childlike humility as an essential attitude of all the people of God is taught in Old Testament and New Testament alike; cf. Matt. xviii. 3. Man learns this lesson only in the school of suffering. Pardon (cxxx.) is followed by peace (cxxxi.). The believer learns to rest in the Saviour's love rather than for ever craving something from Him. It is difficult for the human heart to give up its treasured ambitions and rest entirely content in the will of God.

VERSE NOTES

1. Refers to the renunciation of ambitious schemes rather than to refraining from probing the higher mysteries of God, though this also may be implied.

2. More exactly " . . . upon (the breast of) its mother, . . . my soul upon me." Ellipsis may be supplied thus, "Yea, as the weaned child (so) upon (Jehovah) my soul (rests)." The psalmist here likens himself to a child during the weaning process. At first it sobs and struggles, but at last learns to lie satisfied upon the mother's bosom without further cravings. The point of comparison is the child's contentment, not its helplessness.

3. To introduce Israel here may seem forced, but the verse links the three psalms of the group, cxxix. 1; cxxx. 8; cxxxi. 3.

Cycle 5. *Human Stress and Divine Sufficiency: cxxxii.–cxxxiv.*

Jehovah the National Reconciler. The Uniter of Israel.

PSALM CXXXII.   ZEAL FOR ZION

I. DEVOUT APPEAL (1-10). The King's Prayer.
>   Plea based upon David's sincere devotion (1).
>   1. Solemn Affirmation (1-5). David's Resolution. "Sware." Human
>   Covenant.
>   2. Sacred Habitation (6-7). Ark at Kirjath-jearim.
>   3. Spontaneous Invocation (8-10). Israel's Co-operation. Supplications.
>   (i) The Ark (8).
>   (ii) The Priests (9).
>   (iii) The Pious Ones (9). "Shout for Joy."
>   (iv) The Anointed (10).

II. DIVINE ANSWER (11-18). The Lord's Promise.
>   Plea based upon Jehovah's sure declaration (11).
>   1. Solemn Affirmation (11-12). Jehovah's Stipulation. "Hath sworn."
>   Divine Covenant.
>   2. Sacred Habitation (13). Sanctuary at Zion.
>   3. Sovereign Declaration (14-18). Israel's Portion. Statements.
>   (i) The Ark (14).
>   (ii) The Poor (15).
>   (iii) The Priests (16).
>   (iv) The Pious Ones (16). "Shout aloud for joy."
>   (v) The Anointed (17-18).

SUPERSCRIPT.—A Song of the Degrees.

PRIMARY ASSOCIATION.—Differs in rhythm from the other Songs of the Degrees and seems Davidic in style, notwithstanding which we still incline to the view that Hezekiah is the anonymous writer. There seem to be clear references to Solomon's prayer (2 Chron. vi. 40–42) in 1, 8, 9, 10*b*. Promises to the House of David rested upon the choice of Zion as Jehovah's earthly abode. Deliverance from Sennacherib's host proved that God had not abandoned Jerusalem and the king leads the rescued nation into joyful retrospect of the divine promises. In this last triad note (*a*) Blessing sought for Jehovah's House, cxxxii.; (*b*) Blessing seen in Jehovah's House, cxxxiii.; (*c*) Blessing sent from Jehovah's House, cxxxiv.

PROPHETIC ANTICIPATION.—The Davidic promises are to be fully realised only in Messiah, the antitypical and true Son of David. We hear His vow of service in holy zeal for the house of Jehovah—established as His dwelling-place among men. Thus is accomplished at His own tremendous cost (mentioned elsewhere) the loving purpose of the Eternal God. David's "afflictions" (1) point to those of the great Sufferer Himself.

PERSONAL APPLICATION.—God takes the will for the deed (2); cf. 1 Kings viii. 18–19. Saints' petitions should be based upon sound pleas. God's answer ever exceeds our asking; His promise always surpasses our prayers. Cf. (a) First request (8) with response (14); (b) Second request (9) with response (16); (c) Third request (10) with response (17–18). Note the added promise for the "poor" (15) and the added word "aloud" (9b with 16b). Without the divine presence any arrangement is incomplete and futile (8). Christians can surely rejoice in the glorious promises of God yet to be fulfilled to His ancient people Israel, for the Lord Jesus is intimately concerned therein.

VERSE NOTES

1. "Remember," *i.e.* so as to fulfil the promises made to David, 1 Kings, viii. 15–21; Isa. lv. 3; "for" or, to; "afflictions," *i.e.* the trouble he took, his solicitous exertions in preparation for the building of Jehovah's sanctuary; cf. 1 Chron. xxii. 14.

2. No record of this oath in the history; see 2 Sam. vi.–vii.

5. Lit. as margin, here = a dwelling-place. Heb. plur. of amplification expresses dignity, majesty.

6. The psalmist now introduces the people of David's time as speakers. The translation of the ark to Zion was a national movement; "it" = the ark, anticipatory allusion, see 8. "Ephratah" probably = Caleb-ephratah (1 Chron. ii. 24), the district in which Kirjath-jearim was situated. This latter name = "City of woods." The line implies that the ark was in obscurity and retirement, a sign of Israel's estrangement from God.

7. When the ark was "found," David's first thought is worship. He intelligently placed it in Zion and invited Jehovah to take possession. Jehovah's rest broken by the nation's apostasy and recovered by grace, was finally reached in the place of divine choice—a blessed portent of a coming day. May be rendered "Let us go . . . let us worship . . ."

8. Compare and contrast Num. x. 33, 35. There, "enemies" present; here "enemies" gone; see also 2 Chron. vi. 41–42. (b) cf. lxxviii. 61 notes.

9. Linen garments of the priests were symbol of purity of character; cf. Rev. xix. 8; "saints" = beloved, or godly, or pious ones. Here may refer specially to the Levites, cf. s.H.w. Deut. xxxiii. 8.

10. "David's sake," cf. 2 Kings. xix. 34; xx. 5-6.

11. Cf. 2 Sam. vii. 8-17. The promise, like that to Abraham, has two different applications, *viz.* (*a*) the nation, (*b*) the Messiah. Hezekiah, then childless, grounds his hope of an heir upon this promise.

12. "children" = sons; so 12*c*. This condition is implied in 2 Sam. vii. 14 and stated 1 Kings viii. 25, but note Ps. lxxxix. 30 ff. Distinguish from 11 and 13 ff., all of which is unconditional.

13. The choice of Zion is regarded as antecedent to the choice of David, the reason for the establishment of the Davidic monarchy. Temple and throne are indissolubly connected. The verse is the interjected utterance of Israel. In the divine answer note the parallel form of response determined by the form of the earlier requests, but the answers surpass the appeals.

14. Jehovah again speaks; cf. 1 Chron. xxviii. 2.

17. Ref. to Messiah, Jer. xxiii. 5; xxxiii. 15; Zech. iii. 8; vi. 12; "horn," symbol for king, cf. Luke i. 69. "There" = Jerusalem. (*b*) as margin; a burning lamp is a natural metaphor for the preservation of the dynasty, cf. 2 Sam. xxi. 17; 1 Kings xi. 36; xv. 4.

18. Ctr. 16. (*b*) cf. Ezek. xxxiv. 23-24. Expression suggests combination of priestly with royal dignity. Verse speaks of the final triumph—plans of the foe frustrated.

PSALM CXXXIII. THE FRATERNITY OF FAITH

I. (DAVID'S) COMMENDATION (1). The Blessedness—Unity in Love.

II. DELIGHTFUL COMPARISON (2). The Anointing Oil.
Descends—Resulting in Fragrance.

III. DELIGHTFUL COMPARISON (3*a*). The Abundant Dew.
Descends—Resulting in Fruitfulness.

IV. DIVINE COMMAND (3*b*). The Blessing—Eternity of Life.

SUPERSCRIPT.—A Song of the Degrees; David's.

PRIMARY ASSOCIATION.—Probably celebrates the reunion of the whole nation after the civil discords of David's early reign. Hezekiah adopts this, no doubt, as one of his "songs" because it suitably expresses his own sentiments, particularly when celebrating the Passover for "all Israel," 2 Chron. xxx.

PROPHETIC ANTICIPATION.—Looks on to millennial days when Israel's ten tribes will again be reunited with Judah in the land, Ezek. xxxvii. 16-28. The tribes will constantly assemble at Jerusalem for the worship of Jehovah and dwell in a blessed spiritual unity, Isa. xxxii. 15. In the midst of the scene Messiah as Great Priest is viewed. As King He builds and establishes the House of God (cxxxii.), as Priest He alone furnishes it. The new covenant will be the abiding security of the redeemed people.

PERSONAL APPLICATION.—Spiritual unity characterises the Church of God. This unity is to be maintained, Eph. iv. 3, but, alas, Christians have sadly failed. Ponder the grace of brotherliness—its beauty and its blessedness.

VERSE NOTES

2. The oil refers to the sacred perfumed oil used for anointing the high priest (Exod. xxx. 23 ff.). It was poured upon Aaron's head (Lev. viii. 12; xxi. 10) when consecrated to office. The ordinary priests were only sprinkled with it (Exod. xxix. 21). Oil is type of the Holy Spirit in His sanctifying power, the fruit being "love, joy, peace," etc. (Gal. v. 22); "skirt," br. as margin. Note that the true point of comparison is not the fragrance of the oil, though this beautiful thought is not to be ruled out, but its abundance. It did not remain upon the head but flowed downward, thus sanctifying the whole body. All the members shared the blessing. The application to Christ and His people is clear.

3. The dew is also type of the Holy Spirit in His reviving power. Heavy dews in the East are vital to the well-being of all nature. Here "dew" seems to refer rather to the copious mist resembling recent rain sometimes seen in Palestine. Again the point of comparison is not the refreshing qualities of the "dew" or its all-pervading properties, but rather that it falls alike upon both the mountains mentioned. Lofty Hermon in the north represents Israel, while the lowlier Zion in the south represents Judah. "There," i.e. Jerusalem; cf. Deut. xii. 5-21. Israel's unity (1) is a corporate one, as the Hebrew word indicates, having Jerusalem as the one place of worship and all blessing commanded "there." Note the threefold "flowing down" 2 (twice), 3; "life for evermore,"—first mention of eternal life in Old Testament; only other place, Dan. xii. 2; both are in connection with the millennium.

PSALM CXXXIV. SALUTATIONS IN THE SANCTUARY

I. JEHOVAH'S SERVANTS ADDRESSED (1-2). THE VALEDICTION.
    Request to the Ministrants remaining in the Temple. The Watching
        Priests. Blessing Jehovah enjoined.
    1. Their "Style," (1a) (title.)
    2. Their Station (1b).
    3. Their Service (2).

II. JEHOVAH'S SAINTS ADDRESSED (3). THE BENEDICTION.
    Response to the Multitude returning from the Temple. The Worshipping
        People. Jehovah's blessing enjoyed.

SUPERSCRIPT.—A Song of the Degrees.

PRIMARY ASSOCIATION.—Probably Hezekiah's "Song." Its scope is best understood in light of 2 Chron. xxix.–xxxi. He pictures the departing congregation of happy worshippers saluting the priests and Levites who are to remain watching in the temple. In 3 we hear the voice of the priestly leader responding with the usual blessing. This interchange of salutation and exhortation suitably ends a notable group of psalms.

PROPHETIC ANTICIPATION.—Clearly millennial, with Israel seen in the new sanctuary. Night brings no cessation to the constant flow of praise from the happy redeemed people of God.

PERSONAL APPLICATION.—The scene is distinctly Jewish. Christians *now* enjoy the privilege of entering the true sanctuary (the heavenly) by faith, and with full assurance of heart by the "newly-slain and living way" to worship in spirit and in truth. Blessed as Israel's portion will be, that of the Christian is immeasurably superior, but God and the Lamb are the objects of worship of the redeemed people in all ages. Make a habit of worship.

VERSE NOTES

1. Cf. 1 Chron. ix. 33. These ministers are exhorted to pray and praise while watching and waiting upon God. Cf. 2 Chron. xxix. 11; xxxi. 2.

2. The gesture of prayer; lit. " . . . to the sanctuary," *i.e.* the holy of holies; cf. 2 Chron. xxxi. 8.

3. Cf. cxxxiii. 3*b*, also Num. vi. 24; "thee," *i.e.* the people are regarded individually. See 2 Chron. xxx. 27; xxxi. 10.

Book Five. V. The Ways of God Retraced in the National History:
cxxxv.–cxlv.

1. Witness in Praise, cxxxv.–cxxxvi.

PSALM CXXXV. SOVEREIGNTY OF THE SUPREME

"Hallelujah"

I. EXHORTATION TO PRAISE (1-3). God's Servants.
   Summons to Worship,

II. EXPLANATION FOR PRAISE (4). The Subjects of Worship.
   1. Choice of Jehovah (4). Israel's Election.

2. Comparison with Idols (5-12). Omnipotence of Jehovah.
    (i) Proved in Nature (5-7).
    (ii) Proved in History (8-12).
3. Continuance of Jehovah's Name (13). Eternal.
4. Compassion of Jehovah (14). Israel's Vindication.
5. Comparison with Idols (15-18). Impotence of Idols.
    (i) Their Fabrication (15).
    (ii) Their Futility (16-17).
    (iii) Their Fabricators (18a).
    (iv) Their Followers (18b).

III. EXHORTATION TO PRAISE (19-21). God's Saints.
        Summons to Worship.
        Hallelujah.

PRIMARY ASSOCIATION.—Pss. cxxxv.-cxxxvi. form a pair apparently composed for worship in the second temple. In this case they were probably written by Ezra, see Analysis Book V, notes. In contents they combine Exod. iii. and Deut. xxxii. The term "Great Hallel" is sometimes applied to these two psalms alone. The former is a summons to celebrate, the latter is the response. cxxxv. contains many allusions to other psalms. "Fragments of familiar songs are rearranged by the inspired writer like fragrant flowers into a fresh bouquet."

PROPHETIC ANTICIPATION.—A song of restored Israel celebrating Jehovah their God as the grand Deliverer and Disposer of the nation. He has once more taken up the cause of His people. Israel at last acknowledges His faithfulness and wisdom in all His dealings with them throughout their history. The old Egyptian deliverance will be paralleled by a more striking deliverance in Israel's future. It is to be noted that judgment must precede the nation's future blessing (14).

PERSONAL APPLICATION.—"True worship is as spontaneous as the singing of birds, expressing a gladness which unuttered loads the heart. Conquests of the past furnish confidence and courage in present conflict. It is cheering to know that all the 'apparatus of storm' is in God's hand and made to serve His beneficent purposes."

VERSE NOTES

1 ff. Cf. cxxxiv. 1; but note addition of "courts."
3. "Praise Jah, for . . ."; "Sing praises," or make melody; lit. "psalm to . . ."
4. As margin; cf. Exod. xix. 5; Mal. iii. 17.

5. "I" (emph.).

6. This covers all space.

8. Last plague mentioned as being the culminating point of judgment which led to Israel's release.

13. "memorial," syn. with "name," as bringing to mind all that Jehovah is and does.

14. (a) " . . . will right (vindicate or, do justice to) . . . and will relent . . ." cf. Deut. xxxii. 36.

15. For the vanity of idols, cf. cxv.; here a slight abbreviation and one notable difference (17b). The variation emphasises the fact of the lifelessness of the idols. There seems a reference to the national sin before the Babylonian captivity and the yet future idolatrous apostasy of the nation.

19 ff. Cf. cxv. 9-11 (where word "trust" is repeated); cxviii. 2-4.

21. Cf. cxxxiv. 3—the blessing comes out of Zion from Jehovah; cxxxv. 21— the blessing returns from Zion to Jehovah.

PSALM CXXXVI. GREATNESS AND GOODNESS OF GOD

I. EXHORTATION TO THANKSGIVING (1-3). First Summons.

II. EXPLANATION FOR THANKSGIVING (4-23). Fruitful Subjects.
   God's Goodness and Greatness.
   1. Manifested in Creation (4-9).
   2. Manifested in History (10-24).
      (i) Remote Events (10-22).
         (a) Deliverance from Egypt (10-15).
         (b) Direction through the Wilderness (16).
         (c) Donation of Canaan (17-22).
      (ii) Recent Events (23-24). New Deliverance.
   3. Manifested in Providence (25).

III. EXHORTATION TO THANKSGIVING (26). Final Summons.

PRIMARY ASSOCIATION.—Almost certainly intended for liturgical use in the second temple. This psalm is based on cxxxv. and is antiphonal, the first part of the verse being the recital by the precentor and the second part—the refrain—the response by the people; or, the arrangement may have been for a leading chanter and a Levitical choir, cf. Ezra iii. 11; see 2 Chron. vii. 3, 6. The psalm concludes the "Great Hallel." If Ezra was not the actual composer, it is probable he was responsible under divine guidance for including the psalm in this Book.

PROPHETIC ANTICIPATION.—See notes to preceding psalm. No

doubt the older history of Israel will be recounted with new light shed upon the many events by latter-day experiences. At any rate the nation is at last brought to acknowledge that all the divine activities and dealings with them, even in judgment, have had as a prime motive the lovingkindness of God.

PERSONAL APPLICATION.—In His judgments as well as in His deliverances God acts in lovingkindness. Let us ponder the fact that the Creation was an act of divine love. God *is* good, therefore everything He does must be good.

VERSE NOTES

Compare notes to preceding psalm.

2. "gods" Heb. sometimes = rulers, see Appendix II 6.

5 ff. Creation here seen from a new viewpoint, the divine motive—God's eternal lovingkindness. Verse 5 views the second day of Creation; verse 6 the third day; verse 7 the fourth day, expanded in verses 8 and 9.

6. "above" = upon; "spread" s.H. root in "firmament," Gen. i.

13. "divided in sunder," s.H.w. Gen. xv. 17. God clave the Red Sea in two as with a sword, His people passing between the "parts."

23. Probably alludes primarily to the exile; prophetically, to the deliverance of the last days.

26. "God of Heaven," = a late title occurring only here in the Psalter, but found in the Books of Ezra, Nehemiah, Jonah, and Daniel. See also 2 Chron. xxxvi. 23.

Book Five. V. The Ways of God Retraced in the National History: cxxxv.–cxlv.

2. Workings of Providence: cxxxvii.–cxxxix.

PSALM CXXXVII.   HEAVY HEARTS AND HANGING HARPS

I. PLAINTIVE RECOLLECTION (1-4).
    1. Desolation of the Exiles (1). Zion remembered.
    2. Demand of the Enemy (2-4). Babylon requiring.

II. PREDICTED REAFFIRMATION (5-6).
    Declaration of the Singer. Jerusalem remembered.

III. PREDICTED RETRIBUTION (7-9).
    1. Denunciation of the Edomites (7). Edom remembered.
    2. Destruction of the Enemy (8-9). Babylon requited.

PRIMARY ASSOCIATION.—Evidently written in the early days of the return from the Babylonian captivity, but the writer is anonymous. He was probably a temple singer. His composition is characterised by intense fervour. Many Jewish exiles made a home in captivity; not so this writer. He thought it better to remember Zion and weep than to settle down in the enjoyment of Babylonian amenities.

PROPHETIC ANTICIPATION.—We are here carried back to the pre-millennial period with many Jewish exiles returning to the land, among whom are some of Jehovah's loyal ones. The long foretold sentence upon Edom and upon Babylon is not yet carried out, though obviously soon due. Contrast the scene in the next psalm.

PERSONAL APPLICATION.—It is better to weep with the saints than to revel with sinners. Remember the New Jerusalem—our beautiful mother city. Destruction of evil is the complement of the preservation of the good. There is a divine surgery which is necessary for the safety of society (8); e.g. the extinction of the Canaanites. Verse 8 is not the christian attitude though it is the attitude of many Christians.

VERSE NOTES

2. "willows" *i.e.* rather, a species of poplar abundant along the banks of the numerous canals that traversed Babylonia. The Jews often resorted to the river-side for prayer (Acts xvi. 13) because of convenience for ceremonial ablutions. Babylonia consisted of flat, fertile plains, while Palestine is a country of hills.

4. They would not profane these sacred songs used only in the temple worship at Jerusalem, though Belshazzar profaned the sacred vessels of the temple, Dan. v.

6. Or, "If I set not Jerusalem above the summit of my joy."

7. (b) *i.e.* the day of its overthrow. The inveterate hatred of the elder brother referred to; cf. Obad. 12–14, 4. It was perpetuated by the grandson Amalek. The psalmist prays for the fulfilment of that which God had already fore-announced, Ezek. xxv. 12; xxxv. 5; Jer. xlix. 7–22; Lam. iv. 21–22.

8–9. This singer is also a seer; he anticipates the fall of Babylon. Verse 9 is based upon Isa. xiii. 16–18, and was lit. fulfilled, see Appendix IV. Evil seed must be destroyed lest the whole world be corrupted.

Pss. cxxxviii.–cxlv.

This group of psalms by David, an octave closing his contribution to the Psalter, was apparently a late "find" among the documentary records of the Kingdom of Judah. They were then suitably incorporated here by the compiler of Book V acting, of course, under the direct guidance of the Holy Spirit of God.

He was led to modify the original words of David, even as New Testament writers often modify when quoting from the Old Testament. This accounts for the fact that Aramaic words are introduced.

PSALM CXXXVIII.   HAPPY HEARTS WITH HARP IN HAND

I. ACKNOWLEDGMENT IN PRAISE (1-3). Personal—the King. VOW OF PRAISE. Divine promises have been abundantly fulfilled.

II. ANTICIPATION OF PRAISE (4-6). Universal—all kings. VISION OF PRAISES.

III. ASSURANCE OF PRESERVATION (7-8). Personal—the King. VOICE OF PRAYER. Divine purposes will be assuredly fulfilled.

SUPERSCRIPT.—David's.

SUBSCRIPT.—For the Chief Musician.

PRIMARY ASSOCIATION.—Writer is David; historical occasion probably 2 Sam. vii. One of the many psalms called forth by this divine promise through Nathan of the perpetuity of his house and throne; cf. Pss. xviii., xxi., lxxi., ci., ciii., and cxvi.

PROPHETIC ANTICIPATION.—Voices the praise of restored Israel in a coming day. Brought out of their low estate and delivered from the wrath of their enemies the nation confesses what God has done and what He will yet do.

PERSONAL APPLICATION.—Thanksgiving should be wholehearted (1). In fulfilling His promises God also reveals Himself (2). A cry in the hour of distress may not meet immediate deliverance, but always shall strength be given. God is always within earshot (3). Scripture oft reiterates in one form or another the truth that God regards the humble and resists the proud, cf. Jas. iv. 6. Though we may walk in the midst of trouble, God will "preserve us alive" (7). What He commences He always completes (8).

VERSE NOTES

1. "gods," i.e. the judges who represent God in the place of authority, see Appendix II 6. Lit. " . . . will I psalm" or, make melody.
2. "give thanks," or, confess Thy name; " . . . Thy saying in accordance with all Thy name;" i.e. God had fulfilled His promise in such a manner as to bring out all

that His Name implies; or, in the abundant fulfilment of His promise (to David) God had surpassed all previous revelation of Himself. "Word" here may have special reference to the incarnate Word, cf. John i.

3. "encourage" or, embolden.

4. Or, " . . . shall confess . . ." cf. 2. "words," *i.e.* the promises they had seen fulfilled.

5. "glory," *i.e.* manifested in Israel's deliverance (prophetically).

6. Contrast the lowly and the lofty, see 1 Chron. xvii. 16–17. (*b*) *i.e.* no distance hides from His eyes or protects from His judgments.

7. "revive," or, "preserve me alive," cf. Ps. cxix. freq. (*b*) frequent figure for the exertion of divine power to help or to punish, cf. 2 Sam. viii.

8. *i.e.* carry to completion His promises and purposes, cf. Phil. i. 6; see Gen. xxviii. 15.

PSALM CXXXIX. OMNISCIENCE AND OMNIPRESENCE

I. RECOGNITION OF JEHOVAH'S OMNISCIENCE (1–5).
"Thou hast searched."

II. REACTION OF DAVID'S OWN SOUL (6). REVERENT AWE.

III. RELATION OF JEHOVAH'S OMNIPRESENCE AND OMNI-POTENCE (7–16).
1. Recognition of His Omnipresence (7–12).
2. Recognition of His Omnipotence (13–16).

IV. REACTION OF DAVID'S OWN SOUL (17–18). REJOICING ACKNOWLEDGMENT.

V. REPROBATION OF JEHOVAH'S OPPONENTS (19–22).

VI. REACTION OF DAVID'S OWN SOUL (23–24). RESPONSIVE APPEAL. "Search me."

SUPERSCRIPT.—A Psalm of David.

SUBSCRIPT.—For the Chief Musician.

PRIMARY ASSOCIATION.—Closely linked with preceding psalm. The same divine promise is in David's mind, cf. 2 with 2 Sam. vii. 18, 1 Chron. xvii. 16. Note also 17–18 as referring to the divine purposes. 18*b* suggests that the precious promise was the one thought which occupied him the night after Nathan had announced it and it is not unlikely that the main outline at least of this meditation was sketched out then under the guidance of the Spirit of God. Regarding the so-called "Chaldaisms" found here, see notes at head of this group.

PROPHETIC ANTICIPATION.—This is viewed by many as a Messianic meditation upon the mystery of His manhood. Verses 15–16 may be *applied* to Christ's mystic "Body" the Church as well as to His physical body which God had "prepared" Him.

PERSONAL APPLICATION.—Notable instances of God's omniscience and omnipresence in Scripture are Hagar (Gen. xvi.), Jacob at Bethel, Achan and Jonah; cf. 2 Cor. v. 10–11. "Thou God seest me" may be a dread or a delight, it may paralyse action or prompt it. We are hemmed in and held fast by the Lord (5). Do not forget that the One who knows all about us, loves us. During our prenatal period God prepares and plans (16). God is our guide and guard (13). Man is the masterpiece of God's creation (14). The problem of the existence of evil has perplexed saints of all ages (19); cf. Job xxi. 7 ff. Evil is not a mere abstract idea, it is embodied in evil men (19). People who keep the key of their heart do not pray as 23. Many secret sins hide under a cloak of zeal for God (23–24). Christians should not take too much for granted lest they fall into a habit of carelessness; we should ponder our ways and examine our hearts, submitting ourselves entirely to the scrutinising gaze of our God (24), 1 Cor. xi. 30–31. Contrast the way of sorrow with the way of life (24).

VERSE NOTES

1. "searched" describes a process of minute investigation; "known," *i.e.* the result in a knowledge that embraces the whole man in action and in repose—inner as well as outer life.

2. "Thou" (emph.).

3. As margin; "my path," lit. my walking.

4. *i.e.* before the thought is framed in words, He knows it.

6. (b) "(So) exalted (that) I . . .''; refers to its inaccessibility.

7. Question does not express desire to escape, but the impossibility of it.

8. "If I should ascend . . . If I should make Sheol my couch."

9. "If I should take . . ." *i.e.* fly with the swiftness of light from east to west; "the sea," *i.e.* the Mediterranean = the west.

10. There is no place in the universe where one can escape the control and authority of God, or His protection.

11–12. "If I say, 'Only let darkness cover me and the light about me be (as) night,' Even . . .'' (b) "But," render "And." Darkness is the friend of fugitives.

13. "For it was *Thou* that didst acquire my reins" (lit. kidneys). As important excretory organs the kidneys symbolise retention of good and rejection of evil, hence corresponds to later idea of conscience; "For" indicates the reason of God's intimate knowledge; "cover," as margin.

15. "frame," *i.e.* bony framework; "curiously wrought" indicates fashioning with great skill and care; s.H.w. Exod. xxviii. 8; "in the lowest," or "in under parts of earth," for the body is "formed . . . of the dust" (Gen. ii. 7).

16. First line ref. to the undeveloped embryo. Third line may be perhaps, "And for it (the birth) there was one among them," *i.e.* predestined for the birthday.

19. Br. "Wilt Thou not slay the wicked, O Eloah?" cf. 2 Sam. iii. 28–29; iv. 10–12; 1 Kings ii. 5–6. Previously David had not felt himself strong enough to execute righteous vengeance (2 Sam. iii. 39). With the one exception of Uriah (a sin now forgiven) all David's bloodshedding had been forced upon him, hence Shimei's charge (2 Sam. xvi. 7) could not debar David from the promised blessing.

20. "Who speak of Thee mischievously, They lift themselves up in vain as Thine enemies."

21. "hate" *i.e.* loathe.

23. David could welcome continued scrutiny, cf. verse 1 and xxvi. 2.

Book Five. V. The Ways of God Retraced in the National History: cxxxv.–cxlv.

3. Waiting in Prayer: cxl.–cxliv.

PSALM CXL. THE RESOURCE OF THE RIGHTEOUS

I. PETITIONS FOR DELIVERANCE (1–8). The Lawless—His Violence.
    1. Prayer of the Psalmist (1).
    2. Plotting of the Enemy (2–3). The Slanders. Selah.
    3. Prayer of the Psalmist (4*ab*).
    4. Plotting of the Enemy (4*c*–5). The Snares. Selah.
    5. Prayer of the Psalmist (6–7).
    6. Plotting of the Enemy (8). The Schemes. Selah.

II. PREDICTIONS OF DESTINY (9–13). The Loyal—His Vehemence.
    1. Punishment of the Wicked Announced (9–11).
        (Render the verbs as futures).
    2. Preservation of the Righteous Assured (12–13).
        (i) Goodness of Jehovah (12).
        (ii) Gratitude of the Righteous (13).

SUPERSCRIPT.—A Psalm of David.

PRIMARY ASSOCIATION.—Written by David but the period is uncertain; it seems to belong to the time of the Sauline persecutions. Companion psalm to the next.

PROPHETIC ANTICIPATION.—Carries us forward again to the premillennial persecution of the godly Jewish remnant in the last days. We see them compassed by evil men and driven to Jehovah as their sole resource. "Men of violence" points to the "Beasts" of Rev.

xiii. and their ruin is shown in 10, cf. Rev. viii. 5, xix. 20. Has also been applied messianically; 1-8 to His first advent; 9-13 to His second. It should be remembered that the Spirit of Messiah speaks in the soul exercises of the remnant in the last days.

PERSONAL APPLICATION.—Preservation from the plots of the perverse. The path of God's people in all ages is ever beset by the enemy with traps and snares. Satan delights to turn aside the steps of the saints (4). God Himself is our "stronghold" of salvation (7). He provides the "helmet" for our equipment (7), cf. Eph. vi. 17. Notwithstanding all they may have suffered, God's people will have abundant reasons for giving thanks to His Name when they at last dwell in His presence (13). Wounds by words may be worse than wounds by weapons (3).

VERSE NOTES

1. "man of violence," cf. 4, 11, 2 Sam. xxii. 49.
2. (b) "Every day do they stir up strife."
3. This shows them to be instruments on earth of Satan's malignant power specially characteristic of the last days; second line quoted Rom. iii. 13, from LXX.
5. "gins," i.e. baits or lures.
6. "I have said unto Jehovah, 'Thou art my El.'" See Appendix II.
7. "day of arming," cf. 1 Sam. xvii. 38; cf. also term used for the king's bodyguard, 1 Sam. xxviii. 2. Jehovah Himself would be such to David.
8b-9. Maclaren renders, "... evil plan, They who compass me about lift up the head ..."
10. Fire falls from above and fire yawns below; see references above.
11. "A slanderer shall not ... in the land." (b) Render "A man of violence (and) evil, He (Jehovah) shall hunt him with blow on blow." This answers to 1; the hunters become the hunted.
13. "Surely," Heb. word implies "notwithstanding all."

PSALM CXLI. PRAYER FOR PATIENCE UNDER PROVOCATION

I. PRAYER (1-5).
    1. The plea (1-2). "I call upon Thee." Invocation in Trouble.
    2. The Prayer (3-4). Supplication for Preservation from Moral Danger. "Workers of iniquity"—their Works.
    3. The Protestation (5). Correction by the righteous invited.

II. PREDICTION (6). Destruction of the Godless Rulers.

III. PLAINT (7). Distress of the Godly Remnant.

IV. PRAYER (8-10).
    1. The Plea (8*ab*). "I look unto Thee." Indication of Trust.
    2. The Prayer (8*ac*-9). Supplication for Preservation from Moral Danger. "Workers of iniquity—their Wiles."
    3. The Petition (10). Retribution upon the wicked invoked.

SUPERSCRIPT.—A Psalm of David.

PRIMARY ASSOCIATION.—The circumstances under which David wrote this psalm are unknown, but it seems to belong to the period of the Sauline persecution. Many commentators find the psalm an enigma. There are difficulties, but most of these disappear when we bear in mind that the writer was a seer as well as a poet, a fact which destructive critics so persistently overlook.

PROPHETIC ANTICIPATION.—The oppressed godly remnant seek grace to resist temptation during the period of prosperity of the world powers. This temptation is a double one, retaliation and recantation. These loyal ones at the close of the times of the gentiles would be like Daniel and his friends at the beginning of those times, and keep themselves unspotted from the world, cf. Dan. i.

PERSONAL APPLICATION.—Provocation may easily lead the saint into sin. Be on your guard. Christians should avoid corrupt associations, cf. 2 Cor. vi. Plain living goes with high thinking and noble doing (4). The eye of faith has a fixed focus (8). The wise welcome just reproof, only a fool resents it (5). *Lex talionis* was a fundamental article of faith with all the psalmists (10). God renders the enemy powerless while His people pass on unharmed (10).

VERSE NOTES

2. "set forth," br. "set in order," s.H.w. 2 Chron. xxix. 35, xxxv. 10-16; "incense," cf. Exod. xxx. 7-8; elsewhere in Psalter only lxvi. 15; "lifting . . ."—the attitude of prayer; "sacrifice" br. as margin. Heb. word strictly refers to the meal offering, which accompanied the burnt offering. Time of evening sacrifice a recognised time of prayer, cf. Luke i. 10. Acts iii. 1.

3. "Set . . ." or, "Keep guard over . . .," cf. xxxix. 1; xxxvii. 1. He desired to be guarded from (*a*) adopting the profane language of the ungodly surrounding him; (*b*) from retaliating with unwise retorts.

4. "men," Heb. = ish, *i.e.* men of rank and position; "dainties," cf. Prov. iv. 17; Dan. i.

5. Cf. Prov. x. 17; xii. 1; xiii. 18; xv. 5, 31-32; xxvii. 6; Lev. xix. 17; " . . . such oil for the head, my head shall not refuse." Last line somewhat difficult; if taken

as R.V. = he will use no weapon but prayer against his enemies' wickedness (connecting with 3), if taken as margin the connection is with 4*b*.

6. "judges" = rulers among the enemy; cf. 2 Chron. xxv. 12; "sweet" s.H.w. as "dainties," (4); prophetically of the antitype Messiah. Taught by the calamities, those that are left alive will heed His words.

7. " . . . plougheth and maketh furrows upon the earth," graphic picture of widespread slaughter: unburied bones lie scattered like clods behind the ploughman. This prophetically hints at the resurrection of the nation, for ploughing ever has in view a coming harvest. (*b*) For connected idea further developed, see Isa. xxvi. 19, Ezek. xxxvii.

8. As margin: for Heb. expression cf. Isa. liii. 12. The life is identified with the blood.

9. Cf. cxl. 5.

10. "Whilst *I* pass by (unharmed)." Ensnaring of the enemy and the escape of the psalmist are simultaneous.

PSALM CXLII.   SURE SANCTUARY OF THE SOLITARY SOUL

I. ANNOUNCEMENT OF FAITH (1-2). "I cry."

II. ASSURANCE AMID DISTRESS (3).
    1. In Despondency (3*ab*).
    2. In Danger (3*cd*).

III. ASSERTION OF FORLORNNESS (4).   Abandonment by Friends.

IV. AVOWAL OF FAITH (5). "I have cried."

V. APPEAL FOR DELIVERANCE (6-7*b*).
    1. From Despondency (6*ab*).
    2. From Danger (6*c*-7*b*).

VI. ANTICIPATION OF FAVOUR (7*cd*).   Association of Friends.

SUPERSCRIPT.—Maschil of David, when he was in the cave; a Prayer.

PRIMARY ASSOCIATION.—The cave referred to in the superscript is probably that of Adullam to which David retired when obliged to leave his retreat among the Philistines, cf. Ps. lvii., 1 Sam. xxii. Last of the thirteen "Maschil" psalms, it worthily closes the series by showing that God alone is man's sure refuge.

PROPHETIC ANTICIPATION.—As we have seen, the title "Maschil" indicates the psalm as one specially intended to instruct—to make wise—in the last days, days of deep perplexity and distress for all who remain loyal to God. He will be found the only safe refuge in that dark hour of trial.

PERSONAL APPLICATION.—Though deserted by every human helper, go on praying. In praying, the voice often helps the thoughts (1). The outpouring of complaint is not to tell God something He does not already know, but to afford the soul necessary relief. It also expresses the suppliant's faith in God and His power to help. Every Christian has experienced a conflict between his fears and his faith. David's faith triumphed over his fears (cf. lvi. 3; 1 Sam. xxx. 6). What about yours? Those who cannot protect us in our trouble may yet participate in our triumph. Prayer opens the prison doors of the soul, and sometimes opens the doors of the cell. Christians should be able to sing even in prison; see Acts xvi. 25.

VERSE NOTES

1. "Aloud to Jehovah do I cry, Aloud to Jehovah do I . . . ."
2. (*b*) "I declare . . . my strait."
3. Cf. cxliii. 4; or, " . . . wraps itself in gloom;" "Thou" (emph.); "snare," cf. cxl. 5; cxli. 9.
4. "right hand" = place of the champion or protector in battle; "knoweth" = acknowledgeth; (*c*) "No refuge is left me."
5. "I have cried . . . I have said . . ."; "refuge" not s.H.w. as in 4.
7. This may have a double significance: (*a*) to the cave, (*b*) figurative of his soul distress. "Compass . . ." or, gather round about me. Then he was not so isolated as he seemed, cf. Elijah in similar circumstances; he would be surrounded by those who would both congratulate him and share in the thanksgivings.

PSALM CXLIII.   A CRY IN A CRISIS

I. PENITENT PLAINT (1-6).   "Hear me—Thy servant."   Trouble overwhelms.

    1. Preliminary Invocation (1-2). Petitions and Pleas.
    2. Perilous Situation (3-4). Cause and Consequence.
    3. Poignant Recollection (5).
    4. Pious Aspiration (6).   Selah.

II. POWERFUL PLEADING (7–12). "Answer me—Thy servant." Trouble
   overcome.
   1. Persevering Supplication (7–10). Petitions and Pleas.
      (i) For Delivering Grace (7).
      (ii) For Directing Grace (8).
      (iii) For Delivering Grace (9).
      (iv) For Directing Grace (10).
   2. Positive Anticipation (11–12). (Render verbs as futures).
      (i) Deliverance of the Afflicted (11).
         The grace and the ground of it.
      (ii) Destruction of the Adversaries (12).
         The government and the ground of it.

SUPERSCRIPT.—A Psalm of David.

PRIMARY ASSOCIATION.—Written by David in all probability
during the flight from Absalom (so the LXX). Last of the
"Penitential Psalms," so styled by the early church. Note the
sequence of petitions and pleas throughout.

PROPHETIC ANTICIPATION.—The cry of the godly remnant of
Israel brought at last to realise the impossibility of self-justification
before God. This knowledge is reached through the experience of
unparalleled sufferings. Note graphic description of the nation's
condition (3).

PERSONAL APPLICATION.—It sometimes takes physical peril to
produce penitence. Remission of the sin precedes rescue from the
suffering. In our prayers we cannot plead merit; we may plead our
need; we may even plead our trust, but it is best to plead the attributes
of God Himself. "God is our refuge from God. When a child
has done wrong it hides its face in the mother's bosom." In verse 2
David anticipates Rom. iii. It is ever the great enemy's plan to keep
men in the dark (3), cf. 2 Cor. iv. 4. Few believers are free from
what Spurgeon called "fainting fits" (4); if one is imminent tell
the Lord your trouble, cf. cxlii. 2–3. The psalmists ever look for
"the morning" (8). 10*ab* affords a splendid motto for saints of all
ages.

VERSE NOTES

1. "faithfulness" presupposes a promise, doubtless the Davidic covenant of
2 Sam. vii. 12; "righteousness," *i.e.* God regards it as necessary to His honour to
save those who put their trust in Him; cf. 1 Jno. i. 9.
   2. "Thy servant" see 12; cf. 2 Sam. vii. 5, 19–21, 25–29. It was Jehovah Himself

who first applied this term to David, so David fastens on to it as a plea, magnifying not his own service but God's electing grace; "Enter not . . ." *i.e.* with the present enemy as a divine agent.

3. "persecuted" = pursued; "smitten" = crushed; (c) " . . . like the dead of long ago" = and so forgotten.

4. "overwhelmed" = "wraps itself in gloom"; "desolate" = appalled or benumbed.

6. Cf. lxiii. 1 and 2 Sam. xvi. 2, 14; xvii. 2; "weary" = thirsty, *i.e.* as a parched land in time of drought longs for the refreshing rain.

8. He longs for speedy and seasonable help; "the way," *i.e.* the way to deliverance.

10. Marginal readings better; lit. "a level land," *i.e.* a life free from the ups and downs of his recent experience.

11. Br. "Thou wilt preserve me alive . . . wilt bring . . . strait"; "name's sake," no greater plea than this, for God supremely desires to maintain the honour of His name.

12. "Thou wilt cut off." Rebels against God's anointed deserve no quarter.

PSALM CXLIV.   HELP AND HAPPINESS

I. ASCRIPTION OF PRAISE (1-4).   Present Thanksgiving.
  1. Divine Conferment of Skill recognised (1-2).
  2. Divine Condescension to Man recognised (3-4).

II. APPEAL IN PRAYER (5-8).   "Rescue me."
  1. Destruction of Foes requested (5-6).
  2. Deliverance of Himself requested (7-8).
    (i) Out of Great Waters.
    (ii) Out of Alien Hands—the hands of those whose words are vain and false.

III. ASCRIPTION OF PRAISE (9-10).   Prospective Thanksgiving.
  1. Divinely-given Success recognised (9-10a).
  2. Divinely-given Succour recognised (10b).

IV. APPEAL IN PRAYER (11-14).   "Rescue me."
  1. Deliverance of Himself requested (11).   Out of Alien Hands—the hands of those whose words are vain and false.
  2. Destiny of Israel resulting (12-14).

V. AFFIRMATION OF PRINCIPLE (15).   Concluding Benediction.

SUPERSCRIPT.—A Psalm of David.

PRIMARY ASSOCIATION.—The occasion of this psalm is not known, but it probably belongs to David's later life.   He seems to be recounting past experiences and past mercies for the benefit of his posterity. Ps. xviii. is more his own personal thanksgiving at the time. There are also reminders of Pss. xxxiii., xxxix. and civ. This psalm contains the concluding prayers of the Psalter. The use of the title "God" absolutely is peculiar to David in Books IV and V, the only exception being Ps. c. 3, which however may be of Davidic authorship.

PROPHETIC ANTICIPATION.—Here is the godly remnant's last appeal for full and final deliverance from the national foes.

PERSONAL APPLICATION.—God is the source and sum of lovingkindness (2) and the source and sum of all happiness (15). Note the seven titles expressing what God was to David (1-2).

VERSE NOTES

1. "teacheth . . . to" = trains . . . for; cf. xviii. 34.

2. "My lovingkindness" = poetic abbreviation for "God of my lovingkindness," cf. lix. 10; br. ". . . in whom I have taken refuge"; "my people," many MSS. and versions read "the peoples" here and at the parallel passages, xviii. 47; 2 Sam. xxii. 48. Not only the tribes of Israel and Judah referred to, but the surrounding nations which finally submitted to David. The line is of prophetic significance.

3. Cf. viii. 4; 2 Sam. vii. 18-19. Connected with 2, this verse emphasises the divine condescension in strengthening such a creature for conflict and conquest; connected with 5-8 it exposes the presumption of such a creature in defying God.

6. "arrows" syn. with lightning flashes, 2 Sam. xxii. 15.

7. "great waters," prophetically of the great world powers seeking to overwhelm Israel in the last days. Last line more exactly, "From the hands of the sons of the alien," i.e. those who are alien to God and His people (cf. xviii. 44-45), finally to be either won or crushed under Messiah's rule.

8. "right hand," i.e. lifted in swearing a solemn compact is a lying hand, points to treachery of Israel's foes.

9. "new" because of the fresh manifestation of divine grace in the promise to his seed and because of recent victories granted; "sing praises" = make melody.

10. "His servant," the ground of the deliverance, cf. cxliii. 2, 12.

11. This and similar passages may prophetically ref. to "the prince," Ezk. xliv.-xlvi. (a) More exactly as 7c.

12 ff. The construction of A.V. preferable here as expressing the purpose of the desired deliverance. 12. "That our sons in their youth may be as well-grown saplings and our daughters as sculptured columns fashioned for a palace, i.e. stately, tall and graceful. Note the threefold description of national prosperity: (a) racial fecundity (12); (b) agricultural productivity (13); (c) territorial integrity (14). It is possible however that verses 12-15a are the quoted words of the "aliens"— a false estimate of happiness which the world thinks consists in material prosperity

only. To this the psalmist replies as 15b "(Yea, rather) Happy the people whose God is Jehovah." So reads the LXX which often represents an older Heb. text, cf. xxxiii. 12.

14. Or, " our kine heavy with young. No breach—no sally and no (battle) cry in our open spaces," i.e. no hostile invasion of the land.

Book Five. V. The Ways of God Retraced in the National History: cxxxv.–cxlv.

4. Witness in Praise: cxlv. Messiah.

PSALM CXLV. PLENITUDE AND PURITY OF PRAISE

COMMENCING SECTION (1–9).

I. ANTICIPATION OF PRAISE (1–2).   Precentor's Recital.   Personal Worship.

II. ANTIPHON OF PRAISE (3). People's Response. "Jehovah is great" (a).

III. ANTICIPATION OF PRAISE (4–7).   Precentor's Recital.
1. General (4).
2. Personal (5).
3. General (6a).
4. Personal (6b).
5. General (7).

IV. ANTIPHON OF PRAISE (8–9).   People's Response.   "Jehovah is gracious" (b).   "Jehovah is good " (c).

CENTRAL SECTION.   THE KINGDOM (10–13).
Manifestation of Might and Majesty.

V. ANTICIPATION OF PRAISE (10–11).   Precentor's Recital.

VI. ANTIPHON OF PRAISE (12).   People's Response.

VII. ASCRIPTION OF PRAISE (13).   Precentor's Recital.
Permanence of the Power.

CONCLUDING SECTION (14–21).

VIII. ANTIPHON OF PRAISE (14).   People's Response.   "Jehovah is upholder" (d).

IX. ASCRIPTION OF PRAISE (15–16).   Precentor's Recital.
Plenitude of the Provision.

X. ANTIPHON OF PRAISE (17-20). People's Response. "Jehovah is righteous" (e). "Jehovah is nigh" (f). "Jehovah is preserver" (g).

XI. ANTICIPATION OF PRAISE (21). Precentor's Recital. Universal Worship.

SUPERSCRIPT.—David's Praise.

PRIMARY ASSOCIATION.—This psalm of David's is pure worship and fittingly closes the Psalter proper, the remaining psalms being in the nature of a supplement. The superscript is unique; it is reserved for David's last psalm to indicate that all his many utterances find their consummation in praise, cf. ciii. This is also the last of the alphabetic psalms. The letters appear in regular order except that "Nun" is omitted. The last verse anticipates the final anthem of cl. and carries the praise into eternity. Note alternation between words spoken to God and words spoken of Him.

PROPHETIC ANTICIPATION.—The voice of Messiah leads the praises of men according to xxii. 25. Zion's days of mourning now ended, anthems of the coming kingdom continue to the end of the Psalter. To speak of the glory of that kingdom shall be Israel's office as a nation of priests among the nations in the millennial age. They will be living witnesses to God's ways with men in general. The alphabetic arrangement suggests "all men's language restored from Babel strife of tongues to unity of mind and purpose" in the worship of God. The omission of "Nun" here is a reminder that the fulness of praise is not yet reached until the voices of the heavenly saints, including the Church, join in.

PERSONAL APPLICATION.—Prayer occupies us with our needs, thanksgiving with our blessings, worship with God Himself. To praise is to speak well of—to tell out the excellent qualities of a person. The person is more precious than his gifts. Blessings are forgotten in the joy of the Blesser's presence. "Worship is the overflow of love." Note the title "Jehovah" nine times (3×3), seven times in relation to His attributes and acts (see analysis). Seven times David declares his purpose of praise; ten times (number of universality) that the righteous shall praise. In the concluding section note the repetition of "all" eleven times. Other remarkable features characterise this psalm. The worship of the saints is for all time (2a) and all eternity (2b). Recipients of divine grace should be messengers of that grace (11-13). Ponder the phrase "the splendour of the glory" in relation to Jehovah's majesty (5) and Jehovah's kingdom (12). Jehovah saves and satisfies (14 ff.). Goodness without righteousness would display weakness (17). The hypocrite is always out of favour with God (18*b*). In our attitude to God, reverence (godly fear) and love go together. The former keeps our love from degenerating into presumptuous familiarity; love prevents reverence from becoming mere servile dread (19). Jehovah manifests Himself not only in "mighty acts" of deliverance for His people (4), but in "terrible acts" of judgment against His adversaries (6).

VERSE NOTES

1. David's full heart heaps word upon word in the attempt to express his exuberant gratitude. "My God the King" strikes the keynote.

3. " . . . and exceeding worthy to be praised."

4. "deeds," *i.e.* of deliverance.

5. Br. "The glorious splendour of Thy majesty, and all Thy marvellous works, shall be my theme," lit. I will occupy myself with.

6. "terrible" or, dread; "greatness" or, great deeds.

7. "utter" lit. well forth; s.H.w. xix. 2; "sing" = sing joyfully, or shout aloud.

8. Cf. Exod. xxxiv. 6; the antithesis is between "slow" and "great," not "anger" and "lovingkindness."

9. "tender mercies" = compassions.

10. "works" here = works of creation; "saints" = beloved, or favoured ones.

11. "power" = might.

13. Lit. " . . . a kingdom of all the ages," cf. Dan. iv. 3; 1 Tim. i. 17; "saints" as in 10.

14. "raiseth," s.H.w. elsewhere only cxlvi. 8.

15. Pictures God as the great Householder, Matt. vi. 26; cf. civ. 27; "wait" = look expectantly. "Thou" (emph.).

16. Cf. civ. 28. First line indicates free, effortless process.

17. "gracious" or, loving; Heb. is cognate with the noun "lovingkindness".

Book Five. VI. The Worship of God Rendered in Universal Harmony: cxlvi.–cl.

1. Praise Universal: cxlvi. Initial Descant.

"The psalter closes with five 'Hallelujah' psalms in which with constantly swelling diapason all themes of praise are pealed forth until the melodious thunder of the final psalm, which calls upon everything that has breath to praise Jehovah"

350 ANALYTICAL STUDIES IN THE PSALMS

(Maclaren). The group most probably commemorates the completion of Jerusalem's religious and civil polity in the dedication of the city walls under Nehemiah; see Neh. vi. 15–16; xii. 27–43. All are undoubtedly prepared for liturgical use in the second temple about Ezra's time, a summary of praise without a note of prayer. Prophetically they point to the time of Israel's restoration in the millennium, when Jehovah in the person of Messiah will be enthroned amid the praises of His creatures.

PSALM CXLVI. PREREQUISITE POWER

"Hallelujah"

I. VOW OF PRAISE TO JEHOVAH (1–2).
    1. Present Praise (1).
    2. Prospective Praise (2).

II. VANITY OF TRUST IN MAN (3–4). Human Insufficiency.
    1. His Impotence (3).
    2. His Impermanence (4).

III. VALUE OF TRUST IN JEHOVAH (5–10). Divine All-sufficiency.
    1. Pronouncement concerning the godly (5). "Happy."
    2. Particulars concerning Jehovah (6–10).
        (i) Power and Providence in Holy Activity (6–9).
        (ii) Presence and Perpetuity of His Kingdom (10).

"Hallelujah"

PRIMARY ASSOCIATION.—Introductory to the group. The LXX attributes authorship of this psalm and the next to Haggai and Zechariah, as also do certain other versions. See introductory notes above.

PROPHETIC ANTICIPATION.—See above. Power is recognised as the basic requirement of all government, and it will not be lacking in the millennium.

PERSONAL APPLICATION.—The first requisite for trust is the assurance of power in the one trusted, but power needs unchanging faithfulness in its exercise, and is still unworthy of trust unless it works in righteousness with beneficence. Grace makes a prince (Israel) out of a prevaricator (Jacob), a saint out of a supplanter (5). Contrast the faithlessness and impotence of man with the faithfulness and omnipotence of God (6 ff.). Ponder the eleven activities of God (four participles and seven brief sentences) in grace and government (6–9). Note title "Jehovah" emphasised five times (number of grace) in these same verses. A man must be not merely afflicted but reckoned among the "righteous" to secure the promised help of Jehovah (8c). Note the seven afflictions which God alleviates (7–9).

VERSE NOTES

2. "sing praises," more lit. "I will psalm . . ." or, make melody.

3. See Ezra iv. for the change of mind in the Medo-Persian kings owing to Samaritan slanders; cf. Ps. cxviii. 8–9; lit. " . . . son of adam, he has no salvation (to give)." Man as son of Adam the earth-born inherits the feebleness and fleetingness which deprive him of the power to help.

4. "earth," Heb. "adamah" connects with "adam" (3b); "thoughts" = what he thinks to do; see R.V. marg.

5. This last of the twenty-five "beatitudes" in the Psalter presents a beautiful and comprehensive ideal of the godly life.

6. Cf. Neh. ix. 6; "truth" = troth.

7 ff. May be taken both literally and spiritually. Note that these divine works were manifested also in Christ's miracles at His first advent; (c) "prisoners" or, captives.

8. Blindness is a frequent figure for moral and spiritual ignorance, and of helplessness in general.

9. These are typical cases of need; br. " . . . He turneth aside," i.e. so that it leads elsewhere than the wicked (lit. lawless) intend, namely to destruction; or, " . . . He thwarts."

Book Five. VI. The Worship of God Rendered in Universal Harmony: cxlvi.–cl.

2. Praise National: cxlvii.

PSALM CXLVII. AN INSPIRATION TO ISRAEL

"Hallelujah"

I. SUMMONS TO PRAISE (1). (See LXX rendering).
    1. The Call.
    2. The Comeliness.

II. SUBJECTS FOR PRAISE (2–6). Jehovah's Acts and Attributes.
    1. His Work in the Restoration of the Nation (2–3).
    2. His Wisdom in the Regulation of Nature (4–5). The Sidereal Sphere.
    3. His Way in the Recognition of Natures (6). The Lowly and the Lawless.

III. SUMMONS TO PRAISE (7).

IV. SUBJECTS FOR PRAISE (8–11). Jehovah's Acts and Attributes.
    1. His Work in the Regulation of Nature (8–9). The Rainy Season.
    2. His Way in the Recognition of Natures (10–11). The Physical and the Spiritual.

V. SUMMONS TO PRAISE (12).

VI. SUBJECTS FOR PRAISE (13–20). Jehovah's Acts and Attributes.
    1. His Work in the Restoration of the Nation (13–14).
    2. His Word in the Regulation of Nature (15–18). The Winter Season.
    3. His Will in the Recognition of Nations (19–20). Israel and the Gentiles.

"Hallelujah."

PRIMARY ASSOCIATION.—See notes introductory to the group. Some of the thoughts and language here seem to be borrowed from earlier psalms and other Scriptures, but they are recast into a new and vigorous song. Maclaren remarks that in this psalm there is room for all that meteorology has to tell us.

PROPHETIC ANTICIPATION.—A hymn of the restored people Israel. It tells what God is to them and mentions special tokens of God's renewed favour. Again we see Israel as an object lesson to the world of God's ways with men.

PERSONAL APPLICATION.—Note the mingling of divine majesty, divine might and divine mercy. The renewal of nature and the renewal of the nation are both instances of God's restoring grace (see also Ps. xxiii. 3). All the magnificence of power and minuteness of knowledge here mentioned guarantees the uplifting of the needy. He who knows each separate star of the countless hosts of heaven will not forget any one of His people. Jehovah's understanding and power are manifested in the moral government of the world (5–6). His power and providence are in operation even where man's cultivation and care are absent (8c). He delights not in a man's physical strength but in his reverent trustfulness (10–11). The utterance of the divine word in nature is noble (15), but its utterance in the oracles delivered to Israel is nobler still (19), Rom. iii. 2.

VERSE NOTES

    1. The LXX probably represents a better text, "Hallelujah, Praise ye Jehovah for it is good, psalm to our God for it is pleasant, praise is comely."
    2. "Jehovah is the builder of Jerusalem." Ref. to both the rebuilding and the

repopulating of the city. The use of the Heb. participle beginning this verse (so also at 3, 4, 6) implies a work still in progress; cf. Neh. ii. 5, iii. vi. 15.

4. (a) i.e. each has its own "number"; cf. Isa. xl. 26–29; "calleth," i.e. He summons each to its appointed task.

6. (b) i.e. He abases them.

7. (a) "Respond to . . ." (b) "Psalm (or, make melody) unto God upon . . ."

8. Verbs in 8, 9, and 11 again are participles expressing continuous action.

10. Cf. xxxiii. 16–18; horse and man here ref. to the warhorse and the warrior. Israel was strong, not by reason of her military power and prowess, but because of her reliance upon Jehovah.

11. "hope" or, wait for.

12. (a) Br. "Celebrate" or, extol; not s.H.w. as next line.

13. (a) s.H. verb Neh. iii. 4 ff.; (b) Zion regarded as mother of its inhabitants.

14. "peace" or, prosperity; "filleth" = satisfieth; and as margin, cf. lxxxi. 16; Deut. xxxii. 14.

15. "commandment," lit. saying. The word of God is personified as an active messenger.

17. "morsels" = crumbs of bread.

19. More exactly, "Declaring His word . . ." For Israel's peculiar privileges, cf. Rom. iii. 2, Jno. iv. 22, cf. Neh. ix. 13–14, x. 28.

20. LXX, etc. have "And His ordinances (= regulations) He hath not made known to them."

Book Five. VI. The Worship of God Rendered in Universal Harmony:
cxlvi.–cl.

3. Praise Universal: cxlviii.

PSALM CXLVIII.   CREATION CELEBRATES

"Hallelujah"

I. PRAISE CELESTIAL (1–6).

    1. Injunction to Praise (1–4).   The Place and the Participants.
    2. Incentives to Praise (5–6).   "Let them . . . for . . ."

II. PRAISE TERRESTRIAL (7–14).

    1. Injunction to Praise (7–12).   The Place and the Participants.
    2. Incentives to Praise (13–14).   "Let them . . . for . . ."

"Hallelujah"

PRIMARY ASSOCIATION.—See notes introductory to the group. Another psalm without a single petition.

PROPHETIC ANTICIPATION.—Israel invokes heaven and earth to join in the chorus of praise celebrating the restored relationship between Jehovah and the nation, a relationship clearly indicated in the last verse. In the coming kingdom age, Israel will be a nation of priests having the privilege of access to His presence as well as the responsibility (as we have seen in cxlv.) of testifying Jehovah's excellencies to the Gentile nations; cf. the privilege of the Church now, 1 Pet. ii. 5 (Godward); ii. 9 (manward). Note that the anthem of praise ringing out from the heavens above will find an answer of praise re-echoing from the earth below.

PERSONAL APPLICATION.—The praise of inanimate objects may be inaudible, but it is by no means imperceptible to the thoughtful student of nature, Rom. i. 20. Remember the myriad beautiful things in creation were first *thought* by God before He gave them being. Obedience reigns in the starry heavens, cf. Matt. vi. 10. Note God's (*a*) Creating Power (5*b*); (*b*) Sustaining Power (6*a*); (*c*) Restraining Power (6*b*); see Heb. i. 2–3—"made . . . upholding." All mankind without distinction of rank or age or sex have the same obligation and privilege of praise (11–12). Note that Scripture recognises a plurality of heavens: (*a*) the first or lowest heaven, *i.e.* the atmosphere—the cloudy heaven; (*b*) the second or middle heaven, *i.e.* space—the stellar heaven; (*c*) the third or highest heaven, *i.e.* the immediate presence-chamber of God—the unseen heaven, 2 Cor. xii. 2.

VERSE NOTES

1 ff. Cf. Rev. iv., v. 13. This is not mere poetic rapture but clear prophetic truth; "heights," *i.e.* of heaven—a reminder of the Church's place in that day, Eph. ii. 3, 7.

2. "host" = hosts, may refer to both heavenly beings and heavenly bodies.

4. (*a*) " . . . ye highest heavens," cf. Neh. ix. 6, see note above; (*b*) cf. Gen. i. 6–7; Ps. civ. 3. It is possible that unknown to present science there are immense reserves of water lying beyond the expanse. To such Scripture seems to make frequent reference. However in Gen. i. the reference may be better explained of waters stored up in clouds divided from the waters upon the earth.

5. "He" (emph.).

6. "And he hath made them stand fast . . ."; *i.e.* He not only created but sustains them; (*b*) as margin.

7. Cf. Gen. i. 21. Note that the summons to earth begins with the deeps, whereas the summons to heaven began with the heights (1). Note also the rising scale (7 ff.).

8. "Fire and hail," *i.e.* the summer storm; "snow and mist," *i.e.* the winter storm, cf. cxlvii. 16–18.

10. *i.e.* all kinds of living creatures.
11. "peoples" = races (of men).
12 Br. "old men with youths."
13. "glory" = majesty.
14. As margin, *i.e.* "horn (of salvation)," refers to Messiah the King in whose glorious person God once more dwells in the midst of His people; "saints" beloved, or favoured ones.

Book Five. VI. The Worship of God Rendered in Universal Harmony:
cxlvi.–cl.

4. Praise National: cxlix.

PSALM CXLIX. A SONG AND A SWORD

"Hallelujah"

I. ISRAEL'S WORSHIP (1–4).   A Song in the Mouth.
   The Nation as an Instrument of Praise.
  1. Exhortation to Praise (1–2).   Israel rejoices in Jehovah.
  2. Expression of Praise (3).
  3. Explanation for Praise (4).   Jehovah rejoices in Israel.

II. ISRAEL'S WARFARE (5–9).   A Sword in the Hand.
  The Nation as an Instrument of Punishment.
  1. Exultation in Victory (5).
  2. Exaltation of God (6a).
  3. Execution of Judgment (6b–9).

"Hallelujah"

PRIMARY ASSOCIATION.—See notes introductory to the group.

PROPHETIC ANTICIPATION.—This is a "new song" of the new redemption upon the lips of restored Israel, cf. the "old song" Exod. xv. The nation rejoices in One who is their Maker (2a), their King (2b) and their Saviour (4). The salvation here referred to includes more than simply rescue from national distress and victory over national foes. It points to a spiritual awakening and full recognition of the renewed relationship with God on the terms of the new covenant— a covenant of pure grace. Synonyms expressive of rapturous joy are heaped together and limbs, instruments and voices are called upon to unite in rendering this jubilant anthem. Israel is seen also as the executor of judgments upon those who refuse to submit to Messiah's rule and will not join in the universal praise of cxlviii.

PERSONAL APPLICATION.—The Christian, too, is acquainted with songs of the Spirit and the sword of the Spirit, cf. Eph. v. 18–19 with vi. 17. Rejoice in the Lord always (2), cf. Phil. iv. 4. Abandonment to joy must not degenerate into mere noisy excitement. One has said, "It takes much grace to shout 'Hallelujah' properly." Truth is always two-edged—the sword of the Spirit cuts both ways, 6b with Heb. iv. 12. Those who call down judgment upon others must submit to be judged themselves. The silent tears by night of the troubled saint shall be exchanged for shouts of triumph, 5b with vi. 6. The bride needs not to tell what makes her glad (4).

VERSE NOTES

1. Denotes the newly restored Israel as the redeemed of Jehovah; "saints"= beloved, or favoured ones; so 5a and 9b.

2. (a) " . . . in their Maker"—Israel owes its existence as a nation and its restoration to Jehovah.

3. "sing praises," lit. " . . . psalm to . . ."; "timbrel" = hand drum; cf. lxviii. 25, and see Appendix XII (8).

4. The reason for the outburst of praise is touched on only here in the psalm; "He beautifieth" or, adorneth; "salvation," note margin and see prophetic notes.

5 ff. See Isa. lx. 12; "glory," i.e. as adorned with divine salvation; or, "exult with (ascriptions of) 'Glory!'" (b) "sing for joy" or, shout aloud.

6 ff. Cf. Dan. vii. 22.

6. (a) That is, praise with voices raised high; "God" = El (Mighty One). (b) cf. Neh. iv. 9, 16 ff.; Rev. i. 16; xix. 15.

7. "peoples" lit. races (of men).

9. "them," i.e. the nations; "judgments," i.e. those recorded in the prophetic Scriptures, cf. Dan. vii. 22; "honour," i.e. the holy crusade.

Book Five. VI. The Worship of God Rendered in Universal Harmony: cxlvi.–cl.

5. Praise Universal: cl. The Final Doxology.

PSALM CL. THE WORSHIPPING WORLD

"Hallelujah"

I. SPHERE OF PRAISE (1). Terrestrial and Celestial.

II. SUBJECTS OF PRAISE (2).
    1. God's Acts (2a). "Mighty deeds." The Work of God.
    2. God's Attributes (2b). "Excellent greatness." The Wonder of God.

III. SYMPHONY OF PRAISE (3-5).
    (Eight instruments named, and the dance.)

IV. SINGERS OF PRAISE (6). Universal.

"Hallelujah"

PRIMARY ASSOCIATION.—See notes introductory to the group. The Book of Psalms fitly closes with this full-toned call to universal praise with every accompaniment of jubilant rejoicing. It is the great climax to which the "tears, groans and wailings for sin, meditations on the dark mysteries of providence, falterings of faith and foiled aspirations lead up." The grand finale of the universal choir.

PROPHETIC ANTICIPATION.—A final foregleam of the future. In millennial days not only the human voice but all instruments of music, secular as well as sacred, will unite in the one theme of universal song—the worthiness of God and the Lamb upon the throne. While Messiah will be enthroned in Zion where shall stand the millennial temple, in another sense the whole universe is God's temple and all its inhabitants shall be His worshippers.

PERSONAL APPLICATION.—Note the tenfold (= universality) "Praise Him." In this marvellous "Hallelujah Chorus" every voice and every instrument has something to contribute according to the individual capacity. So is it now in the worship of God's assembly the Church. Each instrument here suggests in figure the various abilities of believers. When the Spirit of God conducts the choir there is no dissonance. Note use of lungs, lips and limbs. "Praise Him" (a) worthily (2b); (b) distinctly (3a) cf. 1 Cor. xiv. 8; (c) melodiously (3b); (d) joyously (4a); (e) harmoniously (4b); (f) discriminately (5); (g) vocally (6).

VERSE NOTES

1. "God" = El; "sanctuary" prophetically may refer to the millennial temple (Ezek. xl. ff.). Both centre and circumference seem to be suggested in this verse.
2. (a) Cf. cxlv. 4, 11, 12 notes; (b) ". . . to the abundance of His greatness."

3 ff. As far as the sacred records go, these musical instruments were not all used originally in the temple service, but may have been introduced later.

3. (a) " . . . with blast of horn," see Appendix XII (1); "psaltery and harp," see Appendix XII (3-4).

4. "timbrel and dance," see Appendix XII (8); "pipe" = pipes, see Appendix XII (7).

5. "cymbals," see Appendix XII (9).

6. Primarily refers to the people as distinct from the instrument players. This invocation carries with it the prophecy of its own fulfilment.

HALLELUJAH !

APPENDIX I

THE MESSIANIC PSALMS

Messiah is the true hope of the world and Israel is the medium of the divine revelation and mission. "The Old Testament not only contains prophecies, it is in itself one vast prophecy." Christ is the key to all Scripture. He must be, and ever is, the real centre and the pre-eminent One wherever He appears, Luke xxiv. 27-44. The Messianic reference in some of the Psalms is obvious. Far more allusions are not so obvious, which the New Testament nevertheless warrants us in regarding as Messianic. It is computed that out of some two hundred and eighty-three direct citations from the Old Testament in the New, one hundred and sixteen are from the Psalms. Note that the New Testament epistles show the *efficacy* of Messiah's work, while the Psalms present His *emotions* in accomplishing it.

We may distinguish at least seven distinct lines of prophecy pointing forward to Messiah as (*a*) Sovereign Ruler; (*b*) Suffering Redeemer; (*c*) Faithful Witness (Prophet); (*d*) Royal Priest; (*e*) Divine Son; (*f*) Perfect Man; and (*g*) Coming Judge (identified with Jehovah Himself). Some of these lines are seen to converge and meet in one blessed Person, even in the Old Testament, but others harmonise only in the fulfilment. Christians reading the Old Testament in the light of the New should realise how vague and incomplete was the Messianic hope until Christ's coming revealed the divine purpose.

In the attitude of the Jews, including even our Lord's own disciples, we see how the nation failed to apprehend fully the prophecies relating to Messiah. They viewed Him mainly as One who as sovereign ruler would restore the lost power and prestige of the nation and extend His sway over all the gentile nations. That it behoved Messiah to suffer before entering upon His glory was not understood. Even their conception of Messiah as Redeemer was that of a deliverer of the nation from gentile oppressors and human foes, rather than a deliverer from sin's penalty and power, and from spiritual foes. Restoration of the kingdom rather than regeneration of the people was the great hope of the nation.

Messiah (Heb.) and Christ (Gk.) both mean "the Anointed One." He is (1) Anointed as *Prophet*, (2) Anointed as *Priest*, and (3) Anointed as *Potentate*. As Prophet, He is the *Conveyor of God's Word*; as Priest, He is the *Conductor of God's Worship*; as Potentate, He is the *Controller of God's World*.

In His connection with the remnant we often hear the Spirit of Messiah (1 Pet. i. 11) speaking either in His people or for His people. A reminder is here given of the warning uttered in the Introduction (VII 2). It is a very important principle of interpretation that unless Christ be the direct subject of the entire psalm (*e.g.* Pss. xxii. and cii.), any psalm in which the godly remnant has part must not be applied as a whole to Christ even though certain portions of it may be quoted of Him in the New Testament. J. N. Darby points out that certain moral traits and qualities which characterise the remnant will be found to be a description of Christ

Himself. This is displayed also in Matt. v. 3 ff., hence we find Him and the remnant so intermingled in numerous psalms.

I. Messiah as the Sovereign Ruler.—Kirkpatrick is worthy of quotation here. He writes:—

"To understand the typical application of the Messianic Psalms it is necessary to realise the peculiar position of the Israelite king. Israel was called Jehovah's 'son,' His 'firstborn' (Exod. iv. 22; Deut. xxxii. 6); and the king, as the ruler and representative of the people, was adopted by Jehovah as His 'son,' His 'firstborn' (2 Sam. vii. 13 ff.; Ps. lxxxix. 26-27). This was a moral relationship sharply distinguished from the supposed descent of kings in the heathen world. . . . It involved on the one side fatherly care and protection, on the other filial obedience and devotion. The king moreover was not an absolute monarch in his own right. He was the anointed of Jehovah, His viceroy and earthly representative. To him therefore was given not only sovereignty over Israel, but sovereignty over the nations. Rebellion against him was rebellion against Jehovah. Thus, as the adopted son of Jehovah and His anointed king, he was the type of the eternal Son of God, the 'Lord's Christ.' Then, as successive kings of David's line failed to realise their high destiny, men were taught to look for the coming of One who should fulfil the divine words of promise, giving them a meaning and a reality beyond hope and imagination."

II. Messiah as the Suffering One.—The sufferings of David and other saints of the Old Testament were in measure typical and anticipatory of the afflictions of Christ, even as the sufferings of Christians are regarded in the New Testament as supplementary to them. We have already mentioned that this aspect came to be passed over and not at all understood by the Jews, who began to apply the prophecies concerned with Messiah's sufferings to the distresses endured by the nation at the hands of foreign oppressors. It was our Lord Himself who showed the true interpretation to His disciples, particularly after His resurrection and during the forty days' interval before His ascension. Many psalms relate to these sufferings and are given not historically but subjectively, "expressing as by His own lips just what He felt at the moment He endured them." In psalms, however, which speak properly of atonement, Messiah is seen alone, though salvation is thereby secured for the saints. Psalms which present sufferings not atoning in their nature, even though they may lead on to death, may contain references personally applicable to Messiah, but in other portions the saints are brought in because they will have a share in those sufferings.

Sources of Messiah's Sufferings

These may be summed up as:—

(a) *Sufferings from Man*: because of righteousness.
   This brings judgment upon man. It calls for vengeance.

(b) *Sufferings from God*: because of sin.
   This brings grace to man. It concluded in victory. These sufferings were vicarious. In them He stood absolutely alone.

(c) *Sufferings from Satan*: because of testimony.
   This brings fellowship with man. It concluded in vindication. Under the government of God, Christ at the close of His life on earth was the special

object of attack by the powers of darkness and apostate Israel, Luke xxii. 53. He suffered that He might fully identify Himself with the persecuted godly remnant of Israel.

(*d*) *Sufferings in Himself*: because of His own true humanity.

This brings sympathy for man. It calls for veneration. What Christ, the Sinless One, suffered in His soul by reason of His contact with the ravages of sin is hinted at in several passages. Moreover He endured physical discomforts such as weariness, hunger and thirst, also sorrows in anticipation of the cross, the betrayal of Judas, the forsaking of friends, and the like. See Heb. ii. 10, 17-18; iv. 15-16.

All these sufferings seem to unite in the crowning sorrows of our Lord's last hours.

III. Messiah as the Perfect Man.—A few psalms describe the true destiny of man—the ideal of complete obedience, the issue of perfect fellowship with God. The last Adam triumphs where the first Adam failed. The Lord Jesus as Son of Man is the prototype of man, and in His blessed person alone fulfils the perfect type of manhood.

IV. Messiah as the Coming Judge.—Many psalms prepared men's minds for the direct intervention of God in the affairs of men. This was realised first in the incarnation of the Son of God and will be fulfilled in the glorious appearing, His second advent.

Some Messianic References.—Our Lord's first advent and its purpose, xl. 6-8; Sonship, ii. 7; cx. 1 with Mark xii. 35-37; Kingship, ii. 6; lxxxix.; Deity and humanity, xlv.; Creatorship and eternity, cii. 25-28; Human descent, viii.; lxxxix.; Witness for God, xxii. 22; xl. 9-10; Holiness, xlv. 7; Obedience, xl. 6-8; Zeal, lxix. 9; Rejection, ii. 1; xxii. 6-7; Betrayal, xli. 9; Crucifixion, xxii.; Resurrection, ii. 7; xvi. 8-10; Ascension, lxviii. 18; Session, cx. 1; Priesthood, cx. 4; Second advent, l. 3-6; xcvi.-xcviii.; Universal rule, lxxii. 8; ciii. 19; Welcome by Israel, cxviii. 22-26.

APPENDIX II

DIVINE TITLES

There are several titles used of God in the Book of Psalms, but unfortunately neither the A.V. nor the R.V. clearly distinguishes between them. The A.R.V. gives the titles "Jehovah" and "Jah," but even this does not fully meet the case, for the other titles, too, are deeply instructive in their use by the inspired writers. It was not poetic fancy, nor was it to avoid the frequent repetition that led the psalmists to choose different names for the Divine Being. Each title is found to be full of significance in connection with its immediate context or with the general scope of the psalm where it occurs, and to the devout student there appears one more proof that the various writers were indeed led by the Spirit of God to pen the very words of Scripture. It has been pointed out already that the predominating titles used in each of the Five Books are in wonderful accord with the character of each. Within the scope of our present studies, it may not be always possible to indicate the occurrence of the various terms. Readers are advised to mark them in their bibles with the aid of a "Young's" or similar concordance.

God's "Name" stands for His nature as revealed to men. No one name can fully tell out what He is in Himself, and all the names used of Him in Scripture must fall short of the blessed reality. The Word of God, the incarnate Word, alone can fully express the character of God, Ps. cxxxviii. 2; Jno. i. 18.

(1) ADON = Lord, a term often used also of men. Of God it denotes "Lord in power" or "SOVEREIGN LORD."

(2) ADONIM = plural form of above: also used of men = "lords." Of God it indicates "Lord in ownership."

(3) ADONAI = emphatic form of (1). A plural of excellence; not a noun with a pronominal affix as understood by the translators of the A.V. As used it seems to mean "Sovereign Lord" in blessing or in bane.

(4) EL. Has been traced to a root meaning "power." Its use points to God as the Mighty One; God in victorious power; the STRONG ONE. Often associated with a descriptive term, e.g. "El-chay," the living God, and so on.

(5) ELOAH. As used it denotes God as the true God in contrast with false gods. Its meaning then will be GOD, the SOLE DEITY.

(6) ELOHIM = plural form of (5) expressing the One "who combines in Himself all the fullness of divine perfections in their manifold powers and operations," the God who is reverenced and worshipped, the CREATOR. The plural form *hints* at the plurality of Persons in the One God, the singular verb used with it implies the unity of the Godhead. In the Old Testament "reserve was maintained whilst the tendency to polytheism prevailed, and as yet the redeeming and sanctifying work of the Son and the blessed Spirit was unaccomplished; when once these had been manifested the doctrine of the Trinity in Unity was fully revealed in the New Testament." The word is used also of heathen deities (= gods) because they are worshipped; of angels and human rulers, the former as "excelling in strength," the latter in their rulership on earth, and both in their capacity as representatives of God. It is also used of those "to whom the word of God came," Jno. x. 34–36, perhaps for the same reason.

(7) ELYON = The Lofty One, the Most High. The SUPREME ONE. As used in the Psalter it is commonly associated with millennial glories.

(8) JAH = abbreviated and poetic form of the following.

(9) JEHOVAH. God's personal name which distinguishes Him from all other beings in heaven and on earth, Isa. xlii. 8. Root meaning expresses eternal being, essential existence, "He Who is," ever-present and omnipresent. "Jehovah" is the name God uses in connection with covenant relationships. The COVENANT GOD and the SELF-EXISTENT ONE.

(10) SHADDAI. God as almighty in sustaining resources: prob. from root "shad" = the breast. THE SUFFICIENT ONE.

Several of the above titles will be found in combination or in close context.

Thus we find in the Psalms God's personality, unity and eternity are prominent truths: also His omnipresence, omniscience and omnipotence, His essential holiness and perfect righteousness, His infinite lovingkindness and great long-suffering.

APPENDIX III

POETIC FIGURES OF SPEECH

Scholars have discovered a very large number of these of which we may mention the following as being of most importance:—

(1) *Simile.*—A comparison of two different things which have some strong point of resemblance. The word "like" is usually introduced, *e.g.* Ps. i. 3–4.

(2) *Metaphor.*—In this the comparison is implied, though not directly expressed, by transferring a word from one object to another, *e.g.* Ps. lxxxiv. 11. "God is a sun—a shield."

(3) *Allegory.*—A form of extended metaphor; a description of one thing under the image of another; *e.g.* Israel as a vine, Ps. lxxx.

(4) *Metonymy.*—One word is put for another on account of actual relation between the things signified; *e.g.* Ps. cxxviii. 2, where "labour" stands for what labour has produced.

(5) *Synecdoche.*—A figure in which the whole is put for the part or the part for the whole; *e.g.* Ps. lii. 4. Here "tongue" = the man who uses it.

(6) *Hyperbole.*—Where more is said than is literally meant in order to increase the emphasis; *e.g.* Ps. vi. 6.

(7) *Apostrophe.*—In this, absent persons or inanimate things are directly addressed.

(8) *Personification*, in which an inanimate object or an abstract idea is represented as having the attributes of a living being; *e.g.* Ps. xxxv. 10. Here there are two figures of speech used; "bones" (fig. synecdoche) stands for the whole person; "shall say" (fig. personification) bones represented as speaking.

(9) *Anthropopathy.*—A figure of speech in which human language is used of God in order to make His attitude and actions intelligible to man's finite understanding. Thus He is represented as having "hands," "feet," mouth," etc. He is said to "laugh," "shout," "walk" and perform other actions properly belonging only to beings having material bodies.

APPENDIX IV

THE "IMPRECATORY" PSALMS

Many profess to find a "moral difficulty" in those psalms which call down vengeance upon foes in language sounding inordinately harsh to the ears of

Christians. They are surprised to find with what poetry and passion enemies are execrated. Two classes are mainly concerned with this question. Destructive critics of the Bible, ever ready to disparage the Old Testament Scriptures, maintain that such language befits only the barbarous age to which Israel belonged, and that added proof is thus afforded of the inadmissibility of these writings as part of the divine revelation. On the other hand there are many devout students of God's word who find real difficulty in reconciling such cries for vengeance with our Lord's clear teaching (Matt. v. 43-48; Luke vi. 27-28), His own blessed example (Luke xxiii. 34) with that of His faithful witness, Stephen (Acts vii. 60), and such scriptures as Rom. xii. 14 and Jas. iii. 10.

Attention should be paid to the following considerations:—

(a) *Personal Temperament.*—The denunciations of the psalmists were not dictated by a spirit of personal revenge, as some suppose. The historical records abundantly prove that David himself was not vindictive by nature. 1 Chron. xx. 3, which seems to contradict this, should be read, according to ancient MSS., "put them under" as at 2 Sam. xii. 31; that is, he made the captives work for Israel as Joshua did the Gibeonites, Jos. ix. 23.

(b) *National Zeal.*—David and other psalmists made God's cause their own, cf. Ps. v. 10-11. That cause was closely bound up with Israel's history. Antagonism against God was centred upon the people of God. It was recognised that, not merely the existence of the nation, but the principles of divine truth and righteousness were at stake. Even within the nation itself the same conflict was waged between the godly part and ungodly elements. The prayers of the psalmists are in perfect harmony with the legal dispensation to which they belonged, for the Mosaic law announced in unmistakable terms promises of national reward for obedience and threats of temporal punishment for disobedience, Lev. xxvi.; Deut. xxvii.-xxviii.; Isa. v. 24-25; viii. 14-15, *et al.* If such denunciations are found against the Israelites themselves, those who attack God through His people cannot hope to escape condemnation.

(c) *New Testament Comparisons.*—Principles of righteousness do not change with the times, though the circumstances that govern them are not always the same. Thus even in the New Testament we find the severest denunciations of evil-doers. Who could be more tender with the erring than our Lord Himself? Yet He sternly rebuked and strongly condemned the hypocritical scribes and Pharisees, Matt. xxiii.; see also Gal. i. 8-9; Jas. v. 1-6; Jude 8-15. Moreover, saints of all ages have rightly expressed in unequivocal terms their abhorrence of the flagrant evils of their day.

(d) *Victory Prayers.*—Some of the psalms are prayers for victory in warfare, and success here necessarily involves defeat for the enemy. The only possible means of Israel's deliverance from their inveterate foes lay in the destruction of all who assailed them.

(e) *Divine Government.*—This is related to paragraph (b). Old Testament writers continually express their faith in God's moral government of the world. They possessed a keen sense of the age-long conflict between good and evil, between God and His enemies. They realised, what so many forget to-day, that sin and its punishment are organically related, that retribution is a necessary part of the divine order. This important principle is also recognised among the nations of the world, each having its own code of punishment for wrongdoers, in order to the well-being and security of society in general. In the absence of a specific revelation regarding a final judgment in the next world, punishment in the present life was looked for, premature death being the sign of God's displeasure and the penal doom of the wicked, while to be childless or bereft of children was regarded, as in the East to-day, as little better than extinction. The faith of the psalmists is exercised in committing themselves to God as the executor of justice. They were willing to leave the vindication of their cause and vengeance upon their enemies in the hands of Him to whom vengeance belongs, Deut. xxxii. 35; Rom. xii. 19. They firmly believed and confidently predicted the final triumph of God's eternal justice against the wicked.

(*f*) *Divine Inspiration.*—The psalms were written by men who at the time were inspired by the Holy Spirit (2 Pet. i. 21), and He has a perfect right to denounce sin and pronounce judgment upon the sinner. Therefore to speak disparagingly of these Scriptures is sheer presumption and calls for the severest reprobation.

(*g*) *Dispensational Truth.*—In the psalms are Spirit-taught prayers fully consonant, as we have seen, with the *period* to which they belong, though not suited to the present Christian dispensation. Here is the real key to the understanding of such Scriptures. Contrast, for example, Elijah's prayer (2 Kings i. 9–14) with a similar desire of the Lord's disciples, Luke ix. 54–56. In the former case, God set His seal upon the prayer, terrible as it was, for the fire came, but in the latter the disciples met with sharp rebuke as being out of sympathy with the mind and purpose of God in the new dispensation. It is now a day of grace, not of judgment. As followers of Christ in His humiliation, Christians cannot curse but bless, Rom. xii. 14; 1 Cor. iv. 12. The Christian path is to do well and, if need be, suffer for it and take it patiently as Christ did. Only prophetically could He be associated with desires and demands for righteous judgment which will have their true place when God's time has come. Christians have a heavenly calling, giving them a place with Christ out of the world (Jno. xvii. 14) whereas Israel's is an earthly calling connected with earthly government, hence they await God's intervention in judgment for their national deliverance. When that day draws near, with the Church already "caught up" out of the world, the faithful Jewish remnant of that time comes into view. Suffering frightful persecution God's people will take upon their lips with the greatest propriety, and according to the purpose of God, the language of these psalms which call for vengeance upon their relentless enemies. These will be gentile nations which have apostatized from God and His Christ, as well as the unrepentant part of their own nation, cf. Rev. vi. 9–10; xi. 18, etc.

Thus the whole secret of these so-called "imprecatory psalms" lies in an accurate distinction between the divine dispensations. Properly understood, every part of the Holy Scriptures falls into its true allotted place and contains a message for the faithful of all ages.

With particular regard to Ps. cix. see notes *in loco*.

APPENDIX V

PROSPERITY AND ADVERSITY FROM THE OLD TESTAMENT VIEWPOINT

In reading the Psalms, especially xxxvii., lxxii. and similar ones, we must ever bear in mind that we have Old Testament truth, not the fuller revelation of the New Testament. Material prosperity was regarded by the godly Israelite as the token of Jehovah's pleasure and vice versa. When, therefore, he saw outstanding instances of the wicked prospering and the righteous suffering adversity, he was greatly perplexed and his faith sorely tried. Very wisely, however, the troubled saint cast himself upon Jehovah, of whose justice and faithfulness he was fully assured, and he sought to wait patiently for Jehovah's time to vindicate His character and support the cause of the righteous. Moreover, it was believed that the law of retribution and recompense could be traced in the destinies of the family if not of the individual, a view constantly borne out by instances in the historical records. The dying-out of a person's posterity was considered a punishment of extreme severity and no better than extinction, see Appendix IV (e). As to the individual, the "cutting off" of the wicked does not imply that he has *no* future whatever, in a word, annihilation. It simply means that he is removed from this earthly scene, where his presence is the cause of so much misery, to await in Sheol the final judgment. Prophetically, all is made clear by our Lord's own teaching in Matt. xiii. 40–43 and xxv. 31–46.

APPENDIX VI

GENUINENESS OF THE PSALM TITLES

Despite the dicta of many critics, there are strong reasons for believing the psalm titles to be trustworthy. The following points are worthy of consideration:—

(1) *Scriptural Analogy*.—See particularly the Prayer of Habakkuk iii. 1, and cf. Isa. xxxviii. 9; and David's elegy "The Bow," *i.e.* a song about one who was expert with the bow, 2 Sam. i. 18 with 22.

(2) *Oriental Custom*.—The practice of prefixing titles to poems is common among Eastern nations.

(3) *Great Antiquity*.—These titles are present in most of the MSS. and in fragments of Aquila, Symmachus and Theodotion.

(4) *General Obscurity*.—The unintelligibility and apparent lack of connection of so many of these titles with their respective psalms, and the desire to assign a late date to the Psalter, led destructive critics to discard them in most cases, if not altogether. Their inclusion in the ancient versions, although incomprehensible

even to the LXX translators in the beginning of the second century B.C. affords, on the contrary, a powerful argument against forgery.

(5) *Significant Omissions.*—Titles are wanting in psalms where conjecture could most easily have been made, *e.g.* in Books IV and V. Note that the enigmatic style of title is exclusively confined to psalms composed by David or by his singers.

(6) *Recent Research.*—To crown all, Dr. Thirtle's valuable critical researches into this very question (see Introduction) have confirmed beyond reasonable doubt their authenticity. According to his conclusions the titles have not only become intelligible, but in most cases are seen to be beautifully appropriate and often throw considerable light upon the contents of the psalms to which they really belong.

Note.—Many objections by critics are dealt with in the "Studies," see, for instance, the attribution of certain psalms to Jeremiah, Ps. xxxi. 13, note.

APPENDIX VII

THE OLD TESTAMENT SACRIFICES

Modernist critics seek to show from Ps. xl. and elsewhere that the practice of offering material sacrifices, particularly those involving the shedding of blood, is divinely repudiated. It is interesting to find that many orthodox Jews now take up a similar attitude. Ps. l. 14 clearly proves the critics wrong. God could not condemn that which He Himself had ordained, but Israel attached primary importance to what was only secondary. God reproves not the act but the attitude. Sacrifices were never intended as a substitute for true worship and a holy walk.

Ritual observance without responsive obedience was not only valueless but hypocritical. It was disobedience that made the sacrifice necessary. The principle announced in 1 Sam. xv. 22 is therefore confirmed, çf. Isa. i. 11 ff.; Micah. vi. 6 ff.; Pss. xl. 6, li., lxix., also xv. and xxiv. The ordained sacrifices "were divinely appointed cheques which God honoured in view of the all-sufficient efficacy of the one great Sacrifice to come, Christ and the Cross;" see Rom. iii. 25-26. Ceremonial observances were all meant to be "object lessons to teach a world in its childhood great spiritual truths."

Gross material notions of sacrifice were, and still are, common among heathen peoples, and Israel, alas, absorbed these ideas from their neighbours. The shadows have now given place to the substance (Col. ii. 17), the types to the antitype. Christ has fulfilled the Law, perfectly glorifying God in it. Believers in this present age enjoy all the fullness of divine grace, brought to them by the person and work of their Lord and Saviour. The Levitical economy was typical and temporary, the sacrifice of the Cross was actual and eternal, all-sufficient for all peoples in all ages; cf. Heb. vii. 27; ix. 12; x. 10; 1 Jno. ii. 2; also 1 Pet. iii. 18.

APPENDIX VIII

THE "MORAL DIFFICULTY" OF ASSERTIONS OF PERSONAL INTEGRITY AND INNOCENCE

These do not indicate, as declared by many critics, "a spirit of self-righteousness and self-satisfaction such as the Pharisees exhibited in our Lord's day," for side by side with these statements will be found the fullest recognition of personal sinfulness and utter dependence upon God for preservation from sin and its consequences. There is no claim to moral perfection. The utterances are often no more than protestations that the writer is not guilty of special charges brought against him by his enemies. Compare Job's answers to his friends. In the historical records, David frequently rebuts specific accusations and declares his innocence. Sometimes the expressions are general professions of sincerity of purpose and single-hearted devotion to God. Compare Paul's assertions of conscious rectitude, Acts xx. 26 ff.; xxiii. 1. On the other hand, here again we have evidence of inspiration by the Spirit of God in that such passages in their prophetic outlook may be applied with the greatest propriety to the perfect Son of God, "Who knew no sin, neither was guile found in His mouth."

APPENDIX IX

EPHRAIM AND JUDAH

The mention of Ephraim in Ps. lxxviii. calls for special notice, as it is one of the alleged "difficulties" dwelt upon by destructive critics of the Bible. A reference to Genesis will show that while sovereignty was invested in Judah, the birthright involving headship was forfeited by Reuben (1 Chron. v. 1-2) and given to Joseph, whose two sons were numbered among the sons of Jacob (Gen. xlviii. 5). The double portion thereby became Joseph's. The birthright was inherited by Ephraim the younger son (Gen. xlviii.) and in the nation's subsequent history we find the tribe claiming the right of leadership and taking prominent part in national enterprises. The claim gained support from two facts, namely, that Joshua the former great national leader was an Ephraimite and that Shiloh, the site of the tabernacle and therefore centre of national worship, was an Ephraimite city.

Following the national failure, and particularly that of the priesthood recorded in the early chapters of 1 Sam., the firstborn's primacy is set aside and God's sovereign choice falls upon Judah in the person of David and in Zion as the seat of the earthly kingdom. The divine purpose so clearly declared in earlier Scriptures (Gen. xlix. 1-10; Jdg. i. 1-2; Ps. lx. 7) is thus seen in historical development, culminating in the fulfilment of Isa. xi. 10-13 in Messiah's glorious reign. This our present psalm clearly indicates. Ephraim with its companion tribes did not submit to David's kingly authority until seven years after he began to reign over Judah, 2 Sam. ii.-iii. Signs of rivalry and envy between Ephraim and Judah (Isa. xi. 13) became increasingly evident during the reigns of Saul, David and Solomon. There was also a tendency to reckon the two tribes and the ten tribes apart. Moreover, we see a readiness on the part of the latter to join rebellious movements (2 Sam. xv.-xx.), which reaches the culminating point in the break-away under Jeroboam after Rehoboam's accession to the throne. In the prophets, the northern kingdom of Israel is sometimes referred to as the house of Joseph or simply as Ephraim, the name of the leading tribe representing the whole. Here then, we find the clue to the psalmist's solemn warning, for Ephraim became leaders also in the apostasy from Jehovah.

APPENDIX X

HEBREW TERMS FOR "MAN"

1. ADAM is man in his humanity; contrasts with deity; a general term but suggesting his lowly origin, *i.e.* from "red earth."

2. ISH is man in his dignity; an honourable appellation; a distinctive term; often signifies "husband."

3. ENOSH is man in his frailty; points to inherent weakness and mortality; sometimes suggestive of worthlessness.

4. GEBER is man in his virility; a strong man; one who possesses physical courage; a hero.

APPENDIX XI

THE SYNONYMS OF PSALM CXIX.

Almost every verse in this psalm contains a title for the word of God under one or other of the synonyms given below. These exhibit various shades of meaning and are not uniformly translated in the English versions. A Young's concordance or Strong's or, better still, Wigram's should be consulted for the occurrences of each. Here is a worthwhile study. Other passages where the words appear should be noted, especially in the Book of Psalms and in the Book of Proverbs.

(1) TORAH occurs twenty-five times, always in the singular, and is translated LAW. It is derived from a Hebrew verb meaning "to put out, to show; then, to teach, to instruct." The word expresses the sum of the divine teaching and embodies the whole duty of man. In scope it is wider than the law given at Sinai. *The Law regarded as the codified instructions of Jehovah's will.*

(2) DABAR occurs twenty-four times (thrice in the plural) and is translated

WORD. The cognate verb means "to set forth in speech." Dabar is an inclusive term and often stands for the Scriptures in general. *The Law regarded as the communicating medium of Jehovah's will.*

(3) IMRAH occurs nineteen times in the singular and means a SAYING. It is from a verb signifying "to bring forth to light, hence to say." Imrah points to the words by which a revelation is imparted, a particular utterance, and elsewhere is usually followed by the words actually used. In the present psalm it often has the force of "promise." *The Law regarded as the uttered expressions of Jehovah's will.*

(4) MITZVAH occurs twenty-two times including nine times in the plural. It means COMMANDMENT, an order issued with all due authority, a constitutional command. *The Law regarded as the imperative requirement of Jehovah's will.*

(5) CHUKKIM occurs twenty-two times in the plural. The word is derived from a Hebrew verb signifying "to engrave, to inscribe, hence, to decree." It is generally translated STATUTES. Chukkim points to enactments set down in writing. *The Law regarded as the permanent record of Jehovah's will.*

(6) PIKKUDIM occurs in the plural twenty-one times and is usually translated PRECEPTS. It is from a Hebrew verb meaning "to place in trust, or to take oversight," and refers to definite injunctions resulting from the work of superintendence. *The Law regarded as the solemn charge of Jehovah's will.*

(7) MISHPAT appears twenty-three times, four times in the plural. It is derived from a verb which signifies "to set upright, hence, to judge." Mishpat may be translated JUDGMENT, indicating a judicial ruling which constitutes a precedent, especially in matters of doubt or perplexity, an established rule. Sometimes the word has the force of providential or judicial acts, the carrying out of the decison, legal sanctions. In verse 132 it is used in the sense of "custom." *The Law regarded as the judicial decisions of Jehovah's will.*

(8) EDAH occurring twenty-three times, including nine times in the plural, means TESTIMONY. *The Law regarded as a constant witness to Jehovah's will.*

(9) DEREK is used thirteen times, including five times in the plural. Only three times, however, does it appear synonymous with the above, but four times it is associated with a true synonym. It means WAY. *The Law regarded as the appointed pathway of Jehovah's will.*

To the above nine words the Massorah adds another, making the number correspond to the ten commandments. This is

(10) TZEDEK which with cognate forms occurs fifteen times. It means RIGHTEOUSNESS and is derived from a verb signifying "to be straight, right, hence just." In most of the occurrences it is descriptive or characteristic and not synonymous with any of the nine words, except possibly in verse 142. The first line of verse 121 virtually means, "I have kept Thy law," and in this sense may be viewed as synonymous.

Some commentators suggest EMUNAH—FAITHFULNESS as a tenth word. It appears five times in the psalm but does not seem to be a true synonym. It is descriptive in verse 86, and in verse 90 is associated by parallelism with "Thy word" in the preceding verse.

One or two expositors give ORACH—PATH which also occurs five times, but only once (verse 15) as a possible synonym. Its significance is important in Pss. xvi. 11; xxv. 4, 10; xxvii. 11 and xliv. 18. It frequently appears in the Book of Proverbs.

APPENDIX XII

MUSICAL INSTRUMENTS MENTIONED IN THE PSALTER

1. TRUMPET. Heb. *shophar*; occurs xlvii. 5; lxxxi. 3; xcviii. 6 (cornet); cl. 3. This was originally a curved ram's horn (Josh. vi. 4), but in later times seems to have been a metal instrument of similar shape. It was blown by the priests (Neh xii. 35-41). It is better rendered "horn."

2. TRUMPET. Heb. *chatsotserah*, xcviii. 6. This was a long, straight metal trumpet usually of silver (Num. x. 2), and is often mentioned elsewhere in the Scriptures.

3. PSALTERY. Heb. *nebel*; occurs xxxiii. 2; lvii 8; lxxi. 22; lxxxi. 2; xcii. 3; cviii. 2; cxliv. 9; cl. 3; elsewhere in Scripture sometimes rendered "viol." The "nebel" usually had but one string but occasionally more (xxxiii. 2; cxliv. 9) and was the prototype of the modern violin. Like the harp it was played by the Levites (Neh. xii. 27).

4. HARP. Heb. *kinnor*. This instrument is first mentioned in Gen. iv. 21. It had many strings and apparently became the national instrument of the Jews. Its association only with times of joy and gladness is implied in cxxxvii. 2. From David's time it was connected particularly with the worship of Jehovah. This king, as a shepherd lad, became a skilful harper, an unusual accomplishment for such as he, because the shepherd's instrument is generally a flute or pipe. Thus his fame, even in the court of Saul, is accounted for (1 Sam. xvi. 16-23). "Kinnor" occurs in Pss. xxxiii. 2; xliii. 4; xlix. 4; lvii. 8; lxxi. 22; lxxxi. 2; xcii. 3; xcviii. 5; cviii. 2; cxxxvii. 2; cxlvii. 7; cxlix. 3; cl. 3.

5. TEN-STRINGED INSTRUMENT. Heb. *asor*. This is distinguished from the psaltery in xcii. 3, and is better rendered "decachord," a musical instrument known in ancient times.

6. STRINGED INSTRUMENTS. Heb. *minnim*, only occurs at cl. 4. It is a general term to which we have no further clue than that suggested by the name.

7. PIPE. Heb. *ugab*, found in the Psalter only at cl. 4. It is mentioned with the harp in Gen. iv. 21 and is better rendered "pipes," for it consisted of a set of reeds of different length over which the player passed his mouth. It is the well-known "Pan's pipe" (Gk. syrinx). The A.V. translates the Hebrew word as "organ." The "ugab" must not be confused with the "pipe" (Heb. *chalil*) which consisted of a single or a double reed played like a modern oboe. This instrument was, and still is, favoured by shepherds as it is easily made and easily played, 1 Kings i. 40. Only the cognate verb is found in the Psalms, see lxxxvii. 7, R.V.m.

8. TIMBREL or TABRET. Heb. *toph*; occurs lxxxi. 2; cxlix. 3; cl. 4. This is the oriental hand drum of various sizes and shapes. The smaller ones are chiefly played by females, cf. lxviii. 25; 1 Sam. xviii. 6; Exod. xv. 20. It is often associated with the dance (Heb. *machol*, xxx. 11; cxlix. 3; cl. 4). It must be remembered that in Eastern Countries men and women never danced together.

9. CYMBALS. Heb. *tseltselim*; in the Psalms appears only in cl. 5 (twice). Schor maintains that this points to the tambourine, the true cymbals being represented in Scripture by an entirely different word (Heb. *metsiltayim*). The latter does not occur in the Psalms but is mentioned elsewhere. "Tseltselim" is from a verb meaning to make a rustling, rumbling noise as of a swarm of locusts on the wing. These instruments of percussion were used on all festive occasions, see 1 Sam. vi. 5 (cymbals). In cl. the words "loud" and "high sounding" also seem to be inexact translations. As to the former the Heb. *teruah* mean "shout" or "shouting" and points to the shout of joy or of jubilee, or of challenge and victory in battle. It is found variously translated, xxvii. 6; xxxiii. 3; xlvii. 5; lxxxix. 15. Regarding the latter the Heb. *shema* means "hearing" or "report" and is found connected with the conveyance of important tidings. It occurs in the Psalter only at cl. 5, but see *e.g.* Deut. ii. 25. The use of these words is highly significant when the prophetic import of Psalm cl. is considered.